THE STATE IN INDIA

The State in India
Past and Present

edited by

Masaaki Kimura and Akio Tanabe

OXFORD
UNIVERSITY PRESS

OXFORD
UNIVERSITY PRESS

YMCA Library Building, Jai Singh Road, New Delhi 110 001

Oxford University Press is a department of the University of Oxford.
It furthers the University's objective of excellence in research,
scholarship, and education by publishing worldwide in

Oxford New York

Auckland Cape Town Dar es Salaam Hong Kong Karachi Kuala Lumpur
Madrid Melbourne Mexico City Nairobi New Delhi Shanghai Taipei Toronto

With offices in

Argentina Austria Brazil Chile Czech Republic France Greece Guatemala
Hungary Italy Japan Poland Portugal Singapore South Korea Switzerland
Thailand Turkey Ukraine Vietnam

Oxford is a registered trademark of Oxford University Press
in the UK and in certain other countries

Published in India
By Oxford University Press, New Delhi

First published 2006

ISBN-13: 978-0-19-567277-0
ISBN-10: 0-19-567277-1

Typeset in Naurang (Times New Roman) in 10/12
by Excellent Laser Typesetters, Pitampura, Delhi 110 034
Printed in India at Ram Printograph, Delhi 110 051
Published by Manzar Khan, Oxford University Press
YMCA Library Building, Jai Singh Road, New Delhi 110 001

Contents

Preface

The main theme of this volume is to rethink the past and the present of the state in India taking into consideration the predicament of the state system and the global order in the post-Cold War period. The form and role that the state should assume in the current complex political situation should be carefully reconsidered. By discussing the state in India in the context of its own history and society, this book attempts to go beyond the criticisms of the Indian state in view of the ideal type of state based on Eurocentric models. It also seeks to understand the existing difficulties of the Indian state, bearing in mind both the particular socio-political characteristics of India and the universal problematic of the state posed by the contemporary dynamics of the global order.

This book is a product of an international workshop on 'The State in India: Past and Present' held in Kyoto from 2 to 5 December 1999. The workshop was funded by the Japanese Ministry of Education as part of the Center of Excellence Project entitled 'The Making of Regions: Formation, Transformations and New Formations in Asia and Africa'. In addition to the authors represented in this volume, Toshiaki Ohji, Takeshi Fujii, Sunil Khilnani, Yogendra Yadav, and Takako Hirose also presented papers at the workshop. Gen'ichi Yamazaki did not present a paper at the workshop, but agreed to contribute one for this volume in response to our request. The workshop was full of lively discussions and insightful comments. We would like to thank all those who presented papers and everyone else who joined us in the four days of intense and exciting academic exchange. We would also like to express our gratitude to the members of staff at the Center of Southeast Asian Studies and the Graduate School of Asian and African Area Studies at Kyoto University for supporting the project.

The workshop and the publication of this volume were planned and organized jointly by Masaaki Kimura and Akio Tanabe. Kimura took the initiative of defining the overall framework of the workshop, pointing out the various issues around which discussions would be based. However, since Kimura became the Dean of the Faculty of Law at Kyoto University from April 2001, he has been unable to spend much time on this particular project. Although we had planned to write the 'Introduction' together, unfortunately it was no longer possible. Therefore, the 'Introduction' was written by Tanabe who has tried to extend the framework defined by Kimura, weaving in the various implications from the multiplicity of arguments given by each paper in the volume and reflecting the essence of the presentations and discussions that took place at the workshop.

Lastly, we would like to thank the editors at Oxford University Press, New Delhi, without whose support the publication of this volume would not have been possible.

MASAAKI KIMURA and AKIO TANABE
October 2005

Contributors

DIRKS, NICHOLAS B., Vice President of the Arts and Sciences and Franz Boas Professor of History and Anthropology, Columbia University.

KIMURA, MASAAKI, Professor, Graduate School of Law, Kyoto University.

KOTANI, HIROYUKI, Professor (Emeritus), Faculty of Humanities and Social Sciences, Tokyo Metropolitan University.

KULKE, HERMANN, Professor (Emeritus) of Asian History, Kiel University.

MIZUSHIMA, TSUKASA, Professor, Faculty of Letters, Tokyo University.

NANDY, ASHIS, Senior Fellow, Centre for the Study of Developing Societies.

SUBRAHMANYAM, SANJAY, Professor, Department of History, University of California at Los Angeles.

TANABE, AKIO, Associate Professor, Institute for Research in Humanities, Kyoto University.

TANAKA, MASAKAZU, Professor, Institute for Research in Humanities, Kyoto University.

VAN DER VEER, PETER, University Professor, Utrecht University.

YAMAZAKI, GEN'ICHI, Professor (Emeritus), Faculty of Letters, Kokugakuin University.

ZUBERI, MATIN, Professor (Emeritus), Jawaharlal Nehru University.

Introduction

Akio Tanabe

THE STATE IN THE POST-COLD WAR PREDICAMENT

Since the end of the Cold War, a tremendous change has taken place in the world order. Communism has lost its ideological appeal and neo-liberalism has come to dominate the political scenario. At the same time, however, religious nationalism, ethno-nationalism, and various kinds of so-called fundamentalism as well as other kinds of claims for political and social entitlements by ethnic, religious, regional, linguistic, gender-sexuality, and caste groups and communities have emerged vigorously and come to pose serious challenges in many parts of the world. This situation suggests that the modern state system, earlier sustained under the 'balance-of-power' structure of the Cold War, has now been shaken from its foundation. Hitherto latent political and social forces have begun to surface. India is no exception in this sense. Not only have new problems emerged in this region, but various old problems also seem to have reappeared with a new vigour. Such moves are forcing us to reconsider presuppositions regarding what the state is and ought to be.

There is now a plethora of groups and communities—religious, ethnic, linguistic, caste, etc.—which demand legitimate rights of participation, autonomy, and resource distribution from the state in India.[1] The basic question seems to be, 'Who has what entitlement and agency in which sphere?' Like in many other areas of the contemporary world, Indian state and society now seem to be going through a process of redefinition of entitlements and agencies of different peoples, in which many groups and communities are attempting to maximize their legitimate presence in the socio-political sphere. In the democratic set-up of a nation-state, the question of entitlement and agency is directly related to the question of representation: 'Who are to represent and be represented in the Indian nation-state?' There are now increasing demands and violence that surround questions of who legitimately represent the nation and who have legitimate claims on the state.[2] This question of 'who?' is the essence of what is called identity politics in India today. In this cultural–political process of redefinition of public entitlements, agency, and representation of groups and communities, the nature and function of the Indian state are under serious intellectual and political contestation.[3]

Incidents of violence in modern India after the Cold War—especially the caste upheaval regarding application of the Mandal report in 1990, the communal clashes in the Ayodhya case in 1992, and most recently the massacre in Gujarat in 2001—seem to have cast doubts among observant global citizens about not only the maturity of democracy in India but also its very possibility. Are divisions along caste and religious lines so deeply rooted in Indian culture that it is not possible to overcome them unless Indianness is negated altogether? Our answer should be a definite 'No' to such a facile essentialist and colonialist understanding. If we contextualized these incidents in the global process of redefinition of entitlements, agency, and representation under the post-Cold War predicament, they would be seen as violent eruptions of the pain and difficulties which such a redefinition process unfortunately and inevitably incurs. It should be clear that the outbreaks of violence are not due to any Indianness. Nevertheless, if we are to understand the particular nature of cultural–political processes in India in which these brutal incidents took place, it is also necessary to understand the specific characteristics of Indian state and society. The kind of identity politics that is emerging in the current situation can only be understood if we take into account the nature of the relationships between the state and society in the history and culture of India.

In this volume, we focus on the state because it is a space where contemporary problems can be found in a condensed form. The focus will be on the nature of the state in India in the past and present. By considering the state, we hope to recognize the roots of contemporary problems in India and the surrounding world.[4]

THE QUESTION OF SOVEREIGNTY AND LEGITIMACY: ON 'CRISIS' OF THE INDIAN STATE

One of the questions in the emerging global order lies in defining the function of the state, that is to say, the extent to which the state would maintain its sovereignty. The modern international state system, allegedly established by the Westphalia Treaty (1648) in Europe, presupposed that the state was the main source of security for the people and the only legitimate player in international politics. Thus the state was given a privileged position as the sovereign agent in international as well as domestic politics. However, it is precisely the state's sovereignty that is now under question. Is the state supposed to command monopoly over the total and monolithic sovereignty? Are independent sovereign states the only legitimate players in international politics? Or should limitations be placed on their sovereignty and cessions made to supra-national and sub-national communities and groups? These are fundamental questions the answers to which will largely decide the nature and form of future democracy and global order.

The problem of the state, at the level of the regime, can be captured as a crisis of 'legitimacy'.[5] The legitimacy of a democratic regime rests in effective representation. There now appears to be growing discontent over the lack of proper representation among various groups and communities in India.

The growing discontent and demands are related to the ironic fact that post-colonial India succeeded in establishing the 'state at the core of India's society'.[6] The state 'infiltrate(d) the everyday lives of Indians, claiming itself responsible for everything they could desire'.[7] Thus although the state has succeeded in establishing itself as responsible for people's welfare, it has not, in reality, been able to provide many people with basic needs for survival and dignity. Under this failure of governance, it is natural that there are active political demands and discontent towards the state through which people aspire to fulfil their desires and basic needs.[8]

In other words, it is because the state has monopolized the function of legitimate redistribution of resources that the question of representation and entitlements in state politics has become a crucial issue in modern post-colonial India.[9] Distribution of resources in pre-colonial India, however, as we will touch upon later, was mainly managed by the social system of rights rather than by the state. Thus monopoly of the function of distribution of resources by the state, people's discontent over the present set-up, and active demands over representation and entitlements in state politics stem from the modern transformations in the form and function of the state. So, in order to reconsider what is required of the state and society today, we must locate the present form and function of the Indian state in the context of a longer history.

Although the people's expectations towards the state have increased, the working of the Indian state does not seem to match the responsibility it has increasingly taken on itself. This has led to the situation where there is a 'growing crisis of governability'[10] and 'crisis of political institutions'[11] in India. With the growing concentration of responsibility and power of the state, instead of the development of governability, unfortunately there has been a rise of everyday malfunctions and corruptions that have become a part of the built-in system of the post-colonial Indian state.[12] As Bishnu Mohapatra points out, 'It is not inappropriate to say that the "crisis" of institutions and the erosion of norms and values in India have indeed become "routine" and "every-day"'.[13] In this situation, there is now serious reconsideration of the role and function of the state in India.

THE PLACE OF THE STATE IN INDIAN HISTORY

One of the crucial questions related to the predicament of the contemporary Indian state is how to understand the position of the state in Indian history. This question is important since a historical understanding of the Indian state would greatly influence the evaluation of the contemporary situation. The issue here is whether we should see the present kind of state exercising influence on society as a continual development from the pre-colonial Indian state or as a new introduction by British colonial rule.

It is commonly perceived that the state in pre-colonial traditional India occupied a marginal place. Most influentially professed by Dumont,[14] this view of India holds that the domain of power is encompassed by, and therefore hierarchically inferior to, the religious domain which defines status in caste society. Thus, according to this view, 'a crucial feature of traditional Indian society was its ability to marginalise the political order'.[15] Here, instead of the state controlling society, the regulative norm of society is seen to check the state's power.[16] As a consequence, the Indian state is considered to lack the 'developmental potential of pre-modern European states'.[17] Thus, Khilnani says, 'Unlike the history of Europe, that of pre-colonial India shows no upward curve in the responsibilities and capacities of the state'.[18]

If we hold this kind of view on the traditional Indian state, we will have to assume an unbridgeable gap in the history of India between the weak and marginalized traditional state on the one hand, and the modern state with its coercive power and systemized administration on the other. As a corollary, Khilnani says that 'the state as a sovereign agency...did not exist' in the pre-colonial period and that 'foreign rulers brought with them to India a concept of the state'.[19] Kaviraj goes as far as stating that under colonialism, there was 'a process of state-formation in the entirely literal sense of the term: i.e. the complex of institutional mechanisms that we call the "state" was in fact "formed", literally brought into existence'.[20]

There is no doubt that a radical change took place in the concept and structure of power under colonialism. However, we are of the opinion that the kind of historical understanding which assumes a complete break between the pre-colonial and the modern Indian state cannot be maintained. There have been vigorous ethnohistorical and anthropological criticisms on Dumont's understanding of the traditional Indian state by 'neo-Hocartians' such as Dirks, Raheja, and Quigley who stress the importance of the workings of the state for the social order, especially caste.[21] The problem is not only about revising the understanding of 'traditional' India. The question of continuity and change of the Indian state over history is important for the evaluation of the contemporary Indian state as it is related to how we comprehend the derivation of the contemporary Indian state. If we suppose that the state was formed only under colonialism, we will have to admit that the legitimacy and idea of the present Indian state came from the West. The problem is that this kind of view would necessarily place the Western state, or at least its ideas, as the model to be imitated by non-Western colonized countries. Under such assumptions, the 'crisis' of the Indian state will only be assessed in terms of how India failed to imitate the model correctly. This will strip Indians of their agency in creating their own nation-state.[22] However, if we view the present 'crisis' of the Indian state as part of the historical process of redefinition of its structure in relation to the particular nature of Indian society, our understanding of the Indian state will be contextualized in its own history of structural development over a longer span of time. What we aim to do in this volume is precisely such contextualization of understanding of the Indian state in the past and present.

THE BIRTH OF THE STATE IN INDIA AND ITS DEVELOPMENT IN RELATION TO SOCIETY

It is a recognized fact that the term 'state' is very difficult to define or conceptualize.[23] When we attempt to dissect the state from society, it becomes impossible to find a clear boundary separating the two. However, if it is impossible to answer the essentialist question of what the state is at a theoretical level, it is all the more important to see what the state has been in its relation to society in history.

The first section in this volume, 'Formation and Concept of the State', attempts to discover the characteristics of state formation and concept of the state in India. Special attention will be paid to questions on the nature of the state in relation to society as regards the organization and legitimacy of power.

The first essay in Section I by Gen'ichi Yamazaki deals with the process of state formation in ancient north India in the period of the Sixteen *Mahājanapadas* (sixth–fifth centuries BC). This is an interesting intermediate period between the period of preceding tribal kingdoms (*janapada*) and the eventual hegemony of the Magadha.[24] There were different types of states competing in this period. Yamazaki presents an interesting comparison of the different types of states in this period showing the patterns of relationships between the state and society.

Yamazaki tells us that the Gaṇa-Saṅga system of the 'tribal republic' represents the state before kingship. The state was collectively ruled by the heads of households. In this kind of polity, there is no clear division between the state and society. The structure of the state overlapped with that of social power in the community. Regarding early 'tribal kingship', Yamazaki explains that it was born in the upper Ganga valley where Brahmanical culture had developed with Vedic literature, rituals, and varṇa social system since the later Vedic period (c. 1000–600 BC). However, there was hardly any development of kingship in the later period.

These states of tribal republic and tribal kingship lost their independence one after another with the development of the Magadha kingdom of the lower Ganga valley. Yamazaki describes the successful development of 'autocratic kingship' of Magadha by not only referring to the availability of rich natural resources in the region but by also pointing out that this region was relatively free from the varṇa social system and Brahmanical tradition as it was located in the eastern frontier of the Aryan world. The king was able to make efforts to increase the strength and efficiency of the state without the constraints of tribal bonds and varṇa system. Yamazaki's clear explanation enables us to see that it was from the Magadha kingdom onwards that the state began to have its own agency beyond the social system. As Romila Thapar points out, it is when the sovereignty of the state becomes independent of the power structure and cultural norms in society that we can see the true development of the state.[25]

However, this does not mean that a simplistic distinction can be drawn between the state and society. Through Yamazaki's analysis, we can deduce that the state had to be free from social constraints in order to develop its strength, but also depended on society for provision of resources. Also, the state had to present itself as the protector of social norms in order to legitimize its sovereign power over society. Such nuanced relationships between the state and society remain an important topic of discussion throughout this volume.

THE MULTIPLE LAYERS AND AGENTS OF THE INDIAN STATE: INTEGRATION THROUGH COMPETITION

The second article by Kulke presents a lucid and comprehensive account of state formation in early medieval India with an analysis of their genesis and historiographical contexts. Kulke re-examines his concept of 'integrative model' mainly vis-à-vis theories of feudalism represented by R.S. Sharma and the segmentary state proposed by B. Stein.[26] He critically evaluates the contributions and future possibilities of his integrative model. The importance of the integrative model is that it sheds light on the aspect of integration in the process of state formation rather than on the aspects of fragmentation and segmentation which theories of Indian feudalism and the segmentary state tended to stress.[27]

Kulke reintroduces his processual model of state formation where there was integral development from 'tribal/Hindu chieftaincy' which consisted of a small nuclear area, to the 'early kingdom' which extended its political authority to the hinterland and had a 'circle of tributary neighbours', to the 'imperial regional kingdom' which possessed plural major nuclear areas and respective tributary neighbours. An important point is that although local dynasties ceased to exist in the core areas, 'local autonomous corporate institutions...continued to exist within and autonomous tributary kingdoms outside these enlarged imperial core areas'. Many of these institutions—temples, pilgrimage centres, monasteries, etc.—and lesser kingdoms retained their own identity and even enhanced their importance after integration. Thus Kulke's model has attempted to place processes of integration as 'a counterpoint to the processes of fragmentation and segmentation', and not to deny them.

Kulke, however, concedes that the integrative model so far 'has primarily focused on modes of integration from the centre'. He calls for the need to pay more attention to the processes of competition and contestation from the periphery involved in the integration process.[28] He also contends that we should look at how state ideologies and legitimation are constantly redefined in continuous processes of competition and negotiation. Kulke in the end proposes the phrase 'integration through competition' through which he hopes to concede 'a stronger participation and a more active role to the many local and subregional institutions, without, however, deconstructing the royal centre'. His newly paraphrased 'integration through competition' is definitely a step forward in the model of state formation allowing more space to the various agents in the periphery and from below in the overall process of integration.

Kulke's contribution to the understanding of state formation in India is particularly important as it contains the potential of explaining the mechanism of state integration with the simultaneous existence of autonomous spheres and agents within. One of the important characteristics of the traditional Indian state is that the sovereignty of the state was never monolithic but rather 'layered and shared'.[29] Multiple layers of polities are known to have existed within the state.[30] Moreover, there were other important autonomous spheres and agents within the Indian state, such as temples, religious sects, caste communities, markets, and banking networks.

It may be said that characteristics of the pre-colonial Indian state are based on the fact that it reflected and coordinated the balance of interests and values of different groups, communities, and polities. At the same time, the state could render itself as representing the universal and higher values that transcended the differences and thus appear as the central point of unity and integration of these multiplicities. With the legitimacy of the universal value it represented, the state could command authority over social groups and lesser polities. But since the machinery of governance was so dependent on the social groups and lesser polities, the state's strength could not derive from being a monolithic sovereign entity. Its power came about instead by offering an integral sphere of coordination, competition, and contestation between different groups, communities, and polities. In turn, these groups and communities in society could live together as their contestations and clashes were arbitrated by the state as the unifying centre around which they were connected and coordinated. In Bayly's words which Kulke quotes, 'Further model (on Indian state formation) might stress that the state was neither centralised nor decentralised, but something which depended on its ability to arbitrate between contending local groups, tribes, classes, etc., i.e. its strength was not so much an essential feature but a reflection of the nature of society it was trying to govern'.[31] Kulke's model of 'integration through competition' points towards creating such a model of state formation.

THE STATE AND SOCIETY IN INDIA

If the feature of the Indian state lay in its 'reflection of the nature of society it was trying to govern', the questions we must ask as a corollary are what was the nature of Indian society and how was it reflected in the state's structure? The third article by Kimura attempts to answer these questions.

Kimura suggests that it is the socio-political powers at the village level which condition the structures of larger level politics and the state. He compares the Indian case to the Japanese, pointing out the differences in their internal structures. He points out that the pre-war Japanese political system of the 'family-state' was rooted in similar power relations in the Japanese village community, where the relationships of 'patriarchal governance-cum-protection' and 'filial obedience' between landlords and tenants were given importance. Kimura goes on to argue that, unlike the case of Japan, the Indian village structure is characterized by a system of division of labour called the '*jajmani* system' in the previous literature which did not rest on personal relationships but on exchange of protection, payment, and services fixed by custom. By jajmani system, Kimura does not mean dyadic patron–client relationships but the impersonal relationships based on land or rights inherent in the land. He suggests that this kind of 'impersonal' arrangement of rights enabled the Indian village community to retain its integrity despite caste divisions. The importance of such 'rights-based' structure of the Indian local community is also pointed out by Kotani (*vatan* system), Mizushima (*mirasi* system), and Tanabe (system of entitlements) in this volume. In our understanding, it was one of the most important aspects of Indian medieval society that had a large influence also on the structure of the Indian state.

Kimura points out that it was precisely this kind of impersonal system of rights in the Indian social structure that led to the segmented character of the Indian state.[32] The lack of contractual relationships and the waning of personal allegiance of the inferior towards the superior is an extension of the impersonal relationships in the Indian village community. In such social context, land granted to the inferior is easily transformed into independent rights and share.[33] The segmented structure of the Indian state where semi-independent political powers overlap is thus a result of the political culture of impersonal arrangement of rights in India.

He further points out that in comparison to Japan, contemporary India faces difficulties in maintenance of governability, just as the segmented character of the Indian state allowed subordinate groups a large degree of independence without binding ties to the superior body. The segmentary character of the state and society meant that a Nehruvian, socialist, state-run policy of economic development was doomed to fail. However, on the other hand, Kimura suggests, there are possibilities of dynamic socio-economic development if India rebuilds her political authority, since in today's age of globalization, the autonomy of subordinate groups is an asset for cultivating close relationships with transnational or international organizations.

Kimura's article explains the nature of the Indian state in reference to the features of Indian society characterized by impersonal arrangements of rights and segmentary structure. This kind of sociological explanation, however, must be contextualized in a specific time and place to test its validity. In Section II of this volume, we go on to look at the forms of the state in particular regional and historical contexts and see how they transformed over history especially during early modern and colonial periods.

SOCIAL SYSTEM, IDEOLOGY, AND THE STATE IN MEDIEVAL INDIA

Section II of this volume, 'Forms and Process of the State', deals with the forms and process of transformation of the Indian state from medieval to early modern and colonial periods. Changing characteristics of the Indian state through history in relation to society and economics are taken up.

First, let us again consider the point raised by Kimura regarding the 'rights-based' Indian social system and its influence on the form of the state. There have been attempts to describe and give a name to 'yet some unspecified "medieval Indian social formation"'[34] or the 'medieval Indian system'.[35] Pioneered by Fukazawa's seminal work on reconsideration of the system of division of labour in pre-colonial Indian society,[36] Kotani, Mizushima, and Tanabe point to the existence of similar social systems prevalent in pre-colonial India. There was a set of patrimonial rights—variously called vatan, *miras*, etc.—that involved claims upon shares of local products, certain socio-political roles, and ritual privileges and duties.[37] Now the question is what position and role the state had in relation to such rights-based society.

The first article of Section II by Kotani looks at the relationship between society and the state in medieval Deccan. He pays attention to the predominant ideology of *doṣa* (sin)–*prāyaścitta* (penance), and considers what kind of role the state played in relation to such ideology. It should not be misunderstood that Kotani is suggesting another set of oppositional values to explain Indian society in a structuralist manner. Rather, the point of his argument is that there was a clear public code of proper behaviour and its violation resulted in the 'sin' of the individual and related parties that had to be rectified through 'penance'. The public code of proper behaviour was defined according to one's position in the social order, at the core of which was the caste and the vatan system. The sin–penance ideology played an important part in sustaining the state order and social stability. The material basis of this ideology, Kotani argues, was the '*doṣa* (crime)–*daṇḍa* (punishment) relationship' as physical power of compulsion was implemented by the state (*sarkārdaṇḍa*) and communal control was applied by the local society through caste penalty (*jātidaṇḍa*).

Thus, according to Kotani's argument, the ideology of sin–penance functioned to legitimize the power structure which, in turn, worked to maintain the social order through crime–punishment relationships. In this way, both the state and the local society drew on the same 'sin–penance ideology' for the maintenance of stability and order; and they did so fairly independently of each other through their respective and mutually complementary functionaries. It is interesting that not only social power but also the state commanded control over the social order. Although the state seems rather dependent on the social order for its overall stability, it also had distinct authority beyond social power to maintain order through coercive power.

Mizushima's article on south India in the eighteenth and nineteenth centuries also argues that the system based on patrimonial rights, which he calls the 'mirasi system', was at the core of the socio-political structure. In this system, all levels of participants from the village functionaries to the state performed their respective duties in lieu of shares in the production. The state was an important and essential part of this system in the late pre-colonial period. Mizushima suggests that the mirasi system was the grammar in the social architecture, built upon the main central pillar of the local society supported by other main pillars of the state, large *poligar*s (military groups), and influential temples.

There are some nuanced differences between Kotani and Mizushima in the way the state is placed in relation to the vatan and mirasi systems respectively. In Kotani's formulation, the vatan system is seen basically as a social system in which the state interferes as another authority. In Mizushima's framework, however, the state is seen not as being outside but as constituting an essential part of the mirasi system. The question we must ask here is whether the system of patrimonial rights was the overall system in which both the state and society were embedded or the state had a distinct authority and existence independent of the social system. The reality seems to be that there is truth in both aspects. The state certainly had its duty and share in the system of patrimonial rights. In the arena of the system of rights, the state and other players competed against each other to enhance their own shares, as Mizushima argues.[38] At the same time, it is also true the state had its distinct existence, role, and authority beyond society as Kòtani suggests. Although the state had a role to play in the system of rights, what made the state 'the state' was not its role in this social system. As the article by Yamazaki clearly shows, the state exists as the state when it transcends the bonds of social relations. It is necessary to further investigate what position and role the state had in relation to the social system of patrimonial rights in medieval India.[39]

THE EARLY MODERN STATE, COMMERCE, AND VALUES

Tanabe's article in this volume takes up the question of the relationship between the social system of rights—which he calls 'the system of entitlements'—and the state of Khurda in eighteenth-century Orissa. He introduces the concept of the 'sacrificer state and sacrificial community' to describe the relationship between the Khurda kingdom and the local community. He argues that the system of entitlements in the local community took shape as the sacrificial organization as the duties prescribed by the system were performed as sacrifice. However, the sacrificial organization in the local community was ideologically made incomplete without the symbolic presence of the king who had established his authority as the sacrificer. It was the king then who legitimized each entitlement and functioned as the symbolic centre of the system of rights though he stood outside and beyond the local community. Tanabe suggests that the formation of 'sacrificer state and sacrificial community' may be related to the early modern development of the state when 'administrative technologies of surveillance, numeration, calculation and recording' penetrated into the system of entitlements. Each entitlement was calculated and recorded in cowry numbers and tax was taken by the state from there. Numeration of resources in the locality led to linking local communities to a larger sphere of market and trade. At the same time, there was 'ritualization and divinization of the king' in Khurda kingdom as the king represented Lord Jagannath, the 'real ruler of Orissa', on earth. It was the divine king as the central sacrificer who enabled each individual entitlement holder to 'transform the performance of duty according to his place under the system of entitlements as service to the divine'.

Tanabe's article indicates the prospect of widening the scope of research on the state and locating it in relation to administrative, social, commercial, and religious aspects. In future research, it is necessary to further historically contextualize the process of state formation and transformation of the relationship between the state and society in a wider perspective. In particular, we have to pay attention to the early modern development of administrative technology, social transformations, trans-local and transcontinental commercial activities, and *bhakti* religious movements in order to understand the eighteenth-century Indian state.

The vibrant development of marketing and financial systems in India from the sixteenth to eighteenth centuries has been recognized by scholars since the 1980s, mainly due to the initiative of Chris Bayly's influential work, *Rulers, Townsmen and Bazaars*.[40] This insight has undermined the imperialist understanding of the eighteenth century as an age of decline. There have been ample researches—by Perlin, Stein, and Washbrook to name but a few—of revision of eighteenth-century India from this point of view.[41] However, the early modern transformation of India in the eighteenth century was not restricted to the economic sphere and we must develop a more holistic understanding of the period.[42]

Mizushima in this volume deals with social transformation in south India in the late pre-colonial period and considers its effects on the form of the state. In this period, the mirasi system began to collapse as *mirasidar*s emerged as village lords and attempted to control the distribution of shares previously managed by the system of patrimonial rights. This led to the balance of power between the mirasidars and the state shifting to the favour of the former. Mizushima argues that this deconstructive change in the mirasi system can be seen as the most important factor leading to political instability in eighteenth-century India. Mizushima's perspective on late pre-colonial transformation in relation to market economy, social system, and the state gives an important insight into the dynamics of eighteenth century.

Regarding the relationship between the state and market economy, previous explanations tended to be formulated in a simple cause and effect manner. As Subrahmanyam's article in this volume neatly summarizes, previous accounts took two routes. In the 'forced commercialization' hypothesis, expounded by Eric Wolf for example, the state tax forced commercialization in society.[43] In the 'commercialization of state power' hypothesis, most famously espoused by Chris Bayly, the development of market economy made the king 'the biggest accountant and grocer of the realm'.[44] Although these two routes are to be highly regarded, Subrahmanyam proposes a third way in which he attempts to reconsider the process of 'state-formation' by taking into account the relationship between the market and its rationality, as well as other principles in the society 'such as honour, warrior status, and the capacity to gamble' which played significant roles in political and ethical organizing of society. Subrahamanyam's attention on values and ethics of the early modern state shares perspectives with Tanabe[45] and Bayly.[46] This viewpoint is of particular interest since eighteenth-century Indian statecraft has often been seen as a world of *realpolitik* and calculations.[47]

Subrahmanyam's article approaches the issue by focusing on historical materials regarding a mid-eighteenth century conflict in coastal northern Andhra called the 'Bobbili War'. He points out the significant presence of a commercialized and monetary economy. But this did not mean, he argues, there was a straightforward parallel development in the political field. The economy is not determined by politics and politics is not just a product of developments in the economic sphere. He illustrates the complexities in the 'language of politics' where prices and values coexisted in a twisted manner in late pre-colonial India, pointing out how the historical materials presented offer various hermeneutics according to the 'epistemological framework within which they are located'. Subrahamanyam successfully describes, through his vivid illustrations, the complexity of the situation where the moral economy of values of loyalty and honour and the political economy of power and money intersected.

Understanding eighteenth-century India is of particular importance since it is the period when we witness early modern transformations of the country prior to the advent of modernity under colonialism. It is necessary to trace the routes of early modern developments carefully in order to assess the effects of colonialism on state formation in India.

COLONIALISM, SOCIETY, AND NATION

Tanabe in this volume points out that one of the most important aspects of the transformations of the Indian state and society under colonialism was the separation between the rational and the religious. In pre-colonial Orissa, there was an inseparable development of the religious and the rational which the divine king mediated. This coexistence of the religious and the rational finds a parallel in south India described by Subrahmanyam where there was a twisted connection between values and prices. During colonial rule, however, there was a 'significant disjunction between the rational and the religious, the former being represented by the colonial state and the latter by the colonized society' according to Tanabe. The complex relationship between the rational and the religious under colonialism will be taken up again later in relation to van der Veer's argument.

Tanabe points out the twin aspects of continuity and change in the transformative process under colonialism. From the viewpoint of continuity, the development of colonial administration was an extension of the pre-existing growth in the administrative technologies of the state as well as the banking and trade networks. From the viewpoint of disjunction, there was a separation of the 'rational state' and 'religious-ritual society', where 'village, caste and kingship' came under the latter, while a centralized colonial government, army, and court were introduced to lead India 'towards rationalization and civilization according to the universal principle of modernity'. This led to a particular 'reorganized continuation' of the decontextualized and reified elements of certain aspects of religion, caste, and kingship that took on new meanings and functions in the field of cultural politics of identity formation.

If we follow Tanabe's argument, there was certainly a development in the capacities of the state in pre-colonial India *pace* Khilnani. In fact, it seems that the colonial government was able to extend its vast network of administration down to the local level precisely because of this pre-colonial development of government. It appears that there was more continuity of development in governmental administrative technology and expansion than generally recognized. On the other hand, it is also important to note that there came to be an unprecedented harsh-wedged separation between the state and society under colonialism. In this sense, Khilnani and Kaviraj have a point regarding the birth of the state in 1857 that had coercive control and surveillance over society.

Thus, under colonialism, there was an emergence of a strong state which distinguished itself sharply from society. The separation of the state from society did not mean, however, that society was left as it was. The introduction of a new system of law and administration as well as penetration of colonial economy into the locality meant that there was a major transformation of Indian society especially in the latter half of the nineteenth century.[48]

At the level of local society, there was complete destruction of the system of patrimonial rights under colonialism. People of wealth and power—such as mirasidars in south India—who had accumulated patrimonial rights through purchase in the eighteenth century, declined in their influence as the legal claim on the land product was now transferred to landownership. Mizushima's article in this volume argues that the position of mirasidars waned in the late nineteenth century as they lost their economic power, though their status as village lords was acknowledged and institutionalized by the colonial administration. *Pattadar*s, whose ownership of land was recognized through registration, took over the central role in villages as landholders and a wider section of the society was able to join this category. There had been a process of transferring the basic sphere of social entity from the local society to the village in the late pre-colonial period. Further, the basic sphere was passed over from the village to the land lot by the colonial administration before this shift was completed. Pattadars, the products of colonial rule, were just holders of land lots and were unrelated to the local society and the village. Thus in colonial society, Mizushima says, the Indian villager had neither local society nor village to depend on to stand against the state.

By the latter half of the nineteenth century, people could no longer rely on a concrete system or site in the local society or village as a basis for their identity and existence. The system of patrimonial rights was fragmented into individual proprietary rights. In this situation, Indian people attempted to reformulate their identity on various other bases such as religion, caste, language, and civilization. These different routes of identity formation led to the formation of various trends in Indian nationalism. Meanwhile, the colonial state started to extend its surveillance onto Indian 'culture' largely by categorizing, objectifying, and essentializing caste and religious communities in Indian society. This project of colonial power of knowledge gave a powerful twist to the way Indians imagined their nation as we see in Dirks' article in this volume.

Colonial state in the latter half of the nineteenth century set up a vast project of surveying and recording customs, beliefs, and characteristics of the peoples and communities of Indian society in the form of census and ethnographic investigation. As Kaviraj says, this was 'an attempt to grasp cognitively this alien society and bring it under intellectual control'.[49] Dirks in this volume highlights this kind of characteristics of knowledge and power of the colonial state in the late nineteenth and early twentieth centuries. By introducing the term 'ethnographic state', he points out that anthropology rather than history became the 'principal colonial modality of knowledge and rule' for the colonial state. He argues that the colonial state had to find different kinds of strategies for imperial rule after the 1857 rebellions. Land tax and mercantile trade—which characterized the colonial state in first half of the nineteenth century as an 'extractive' state—had disturbed the 'circuits of political and economic vitality' of the eighteenth century. Although they remained as important sources of revenue even in the latter half of the nineteenth century, from this period onwards, the state adopted new kinds of 'policies of indirect rule' and 'non-interference' in which colonial anthropology played a crucial role. Dirks says that the 1857 rebellions led the British to distinguish communities in India as either loyal or disloyal to the colonial state. Under such a regime, colonial knowledge of Indian peoples and cultures came to be employed in order to evaluate matters of loyalty and not revenue. Paradoxically, 'the policy of non-interference thus necessitated a new commitment to colonial knowledge about the subjects of its rule'.

Further, Dirks points out that the 'ethnographic state' was a cause of long-lasting communal and national problems since it categorized Indian people into different communities according to caste and religion and then enumerated and characterized them as distinct categories. Dirks argues that this kind of colonial epistemology of the ethnographic state went on to dominate post-colonial India 'long after its contradictions unleashed the historical inevitability of partition'. It functioned to legitimize the nationalism of figures such as V.S. Savarkar and also gave scope for 'extreme nationalist ethnographic imaginaries' which continue to have tragic consequences in South Asia even today.

THE SECULAR STATE AND RELIGIOUS SOCIETY: DISJUNCTION AND INTERSECTION

In Section III, 'Ideas and Problematics of the State', we have four articles which discuss the position and role of the Indian state relating to contemporary issues.

Van der Veer's article focuses on the issue of secularity of the state. He takes up what he calls the 'central feature of the idea of secular modernity', namely the 'separation of church and state' in the context of the colonial encounter between India and Britain. By giving examples from this historical relationship, he points out the mutual interdependence between the secular and the religious, and its importance in the emergence of a public sphere. According to van der Veer, 'the separation of Church and State... indicated a shift in the location of religion in society from being part of the state to being part of a newly emerging public sphere'. The secularity of the state is required not to create a secular society but to ensure diverse religious activities in the public sphere. He argues that 'it is not so much that religion cannot be allowed to enter the public sphere in order to let the modern nation-state exist, but that religion creates the public sphere and in doing so is transformed and moulded in a national form'. Vigorous activities of Christian missionaries in India led to detaching the state from patronizing native religious institutions, thus secularizing the state. This also resulted in the creation of a public sphere where religious movements produced modern forms of Hinduism which defined themselves in opposition to the colonizing state. Van der Veer thus convincingly tells us how religion is crucial for the creation of a public sphere in opposition to secularist understanding of the public sphere most famously espoused by Habermas.[50]

He also points out the common misunderstanding regarding 'opposition between religious intolerance and secular liberty', since 'rise of the nation-state and the related emergence of a public sphere makes new, modern forms of freedom and unfreedom, tolerance and intolerance possible'. Van der Veer explains the complexity by pointing out that it was the missionary societies which demanded secularity of the state and freedom of religious opinion, but it was also they who embraced the notion of evolutionary progress which legitimated the colonial project. He further points out that Hindu movements resisted the colonial project for freedom, but also created a Hinduism containing communal tendencies.

The characteristics of secular state and religious society—each attempting to extend its own sphere of influence—continue to be found in today's post-colonial period. We can see a concrete example of the intricacy of the relationship between secular state and religious public sphere from the account of south Indian temples given by Tanaka in this volume.

Tanaka's article on the politics surrounding south Indian Hindu temples analyses and draws out implications of the controversies involved in lawsuits between temples and the local government. He deals in detail with the case of the Nataraja temple of Chidambaram and says that there apparently exists a realm of 'pure religion' which is 'realized outside the influence of politics'. This is in spite of the fact that the state government often tries to interfere in temple affairs by arguing for the necessity of state intervention in the form of 'law and order' due to chaos and corruption in the temple's financial situation brought about by power politics among the local leaders. In this scheme, the state government sees itself as the king, the maintainer of righteous law (dharma).

However, Tanaka goes on to say that this kind of intervention fails to gain support from the general public as 'politicians and the bureaucrats are not accepted as the keepers of dharma or as faithful devotees (*bhakta*)'. Moreover, if we consider what is happening carefully, there is a 'nationalization of temples or the centralization of temple management' in actuality. That is to say, outwardly there is the principle of separating politics and religion, but in reality, the process of politicization meant that religious spheres came under political control, as the government sought to gain popularity and votes by resorting to all sorts of tactics. The judiciary tends to support the temple's opinions and does not allow state interventions. However, as Tanaka notes, this judgement by the court comes from an interpretation of modern law and not the principle of dharma or devotion. Significantly, the temple's response to government intervention by instigating lawsuits has in fact led to a situation where it is 'caught up in the web of the judiciary system', which is after all a part of the state system, and this leads to the temple's increasing secularization.

Thus Tanaka's article clearly illustrates the complexity of the interrelationship between the secularity of the state and the religiosity of an institution in the public sphere (the temple), as expressed by van der

Veer. As the temple attempts to maintain its sphere of 'pure religion', it takes up the principle of secularism to keep the state away from interfering in the religious sphere. Tanaka takes the argument further to say that the temple is bound to use the law court for realizing its demand on secularity of the state. By doing so, the temple is led to define its positionality not in terms of a religious framework but in a modern, legal discourse and paves the way for its own self-fashioned secularization.

Here we can see how the relationship between 'the rational state and religious society' under colonialism was not a simple dichotomous separation but an intricate, interdependent, and negotiated process of mutual definition in complex historical dynamism.[51] Dirks demonstrates the process from the state's point of view and how the epistemological framework of the ethnographic state contributed to the production of religious identities in Indian society and further to the rise of communalism. Van der Veer's account shows us how the development of a public sphere in India involved religious movements which tried to identify themselves against the colonial state. In the process of construction of 'self' in opposition to 'others', some of the modern forms of Hinduism that were created by this politics of identity formation took an increasingly communal turn. We also discover in Tanaka's article how a religious institution attempts to defend its 'pure religiosity' by referring to the supposed secularity of the state, and ends up becoming more secularized in terms of its organization by depending on modern legal processes for protecting its religiosity.

In more general terms, it can be said that in this process of mutual definition of the secular state and religious society in colonial and post-colonial India, the state has come to position itself as representing the general will beyond social divisions. Furthermore, the state has attempted to hold power of knowledge and more actual coercion over society based upon this legitimacy.[52] Meanwhile, many societies (including para-communities)[53] and institutions in the public sphere have tried to make religion the basis of their identity, which the modern state cannot take over due to the principle of secularity, and secure their autonomous sphere outside the state. In this process, however, the religious societies and para-communities are becoming increasingly like modern organizations or political groups demanding more representation and entitlements in the name of their particular religious identities. This brings us back again to the question of democracy and representation in Indian politics.

DEMOCRACY AND REPRESENTATION IN POST-COLONIAL INDIA

The paradox of Indian democracy is pointed out succinctly by Kaviraj as follows: 'The paradox... is that if Indian politics becomes genuinely democratic in the sense of coming into line with what the majority of ordinary Indian would consider reasonable, it will become less democratic in the sense of conforming to the principles of a secular, democratic state acceptable to the early nationalist elite'.[54] Kaviraj is probably right about the difficulty of reconciliation between the Nehruvian ideal of state politics and what the majority of ordinary Indians would find reasonable. The religious character of Indian society is apparently at odds with the 'secular' idea of the state.

However, first, we should not mistake the non-secular characteristic of Indian society as something that belongs to its pre-modern 'traditional' character. As we have seen, a complicated disjunction between the secular state and religious society developed in the modern, especially colonial, history of India. In other words, it is not so much that the traditional characteristics of Indian society do not allow the realization of a modern secular state. Rather, it is the plight of modern Indian society that it was formed in opposition to the rationalist state in colonial and post-colonial history amongst the complexity of power relationships between state hegemony and pursuit for liberty. For the state to remain secular and non-interfering, society had to prove its religiosity. It was only after the 'majority' religious group felt that they could use the state to their advantage that some people started to question the secular character of the state and demand that the state accepted religious principles.

If this is so, second, we may go on to argue that it is necessary to question and deconstruct the presupposed antagonistic dichotomy between secular state and religious society. It seems to me that the ongoing discussion over the issue of 'secularism' in India is still caught in the colonial division of 'the secular state' and 'religious society'. There is said to be a 'great divide' among Indian intellectuals over whether they would like to promote secular rationality of the modern state or religious communitarian values of the indigenous society.[55] Such a divide persists partly because there is a tendency to dichotomize secularity and religion and look for an answer in either of the two that would direct both the state and society in a monolithic manner. However, in fact, there will be no contradiction if we set our aim on upholding a democracy that promotes a space for socio-political negotiation where multiple sections of people with diverse values can interact openly and freely. The state should be supportive of such public spheres, including religious ones, without trying to take over the social function of negotiation and interaction. In this line of thought, the principle of secularism in the sense of non-interference and neutrality of the state in religious spheres—and not in the sense of 'hyper-rationality'[56] of negating religious values—seems beneficial and necessary not only for protecting public interests from certain religious ideology but also for protecting religious values in society from the arbitrary interference from the state. Surely, an unmediated reflection of a majoritarian socio-religious value on the state would be detrimental to healthy development of an open society where religious values can prosper in free interaction.

Then, there seems no reason why there cannot develop a balance between secularism of the state and religious values of the society. What complicates the matter, however, is that there is no agreement but rather a huge gap in the understanding among Indian intellectuals about the desired balance between the state and society and which of the two should take the leading role in socio-political changes. Nandy's article in this volume describes the situation as follows echoing the 'great divide' mentioned above: 'This is a country where the intellectual culture and traditions of political analysis can be divided into two parts. One comprises those who think that the state is a major instrument of social and political change and must be given primacy in social life; the other comprises those who think that, for civil society to thrive, the state must be contained and redefined'. Nandy himself definitely belongs to the latter group, while Zuberi's article in this volume seems closer to views held by the former.

Nandy in this volume argues that the modern nation-state has been a difficult instrument of democracy in non-Western countries including India and discusses the Indian ambivalence towards the state in the last thirty years. In order to analyse and clarify where the distortion of the present Indian state lies, he takes up three images of the Indian state that have dominated the last 150 years of Indian politics. They are 'the state as a protector' of society from oppressors and outsiders, 'the state as a modernizer or liberator' of society from tradition to the modern world, and 'the state as an arbiter' where social relationships can be renegotiated. He says that currently the first two images have cornered the image of the state as an arbiter and, as a result, its pure political aspect is overruling the possibility of the state as a space for cultural self-renewal through open renegotiation of social relationships. The state as protector and liberator takes the prerogative in the 'pursuit of social justice, human rights and cultural survival' which would in fact be better facilitated by open politics of social participation. The actual realization of such values has become more difficult for the state in the present condition. Moreover, the breakdown of the image of 'state-as-an-arbiter' has led to a situation in which the state neither protects nor liberates. Access for the citizen to the state and its major institutions decreases as new hierarchies are established that are designated by modern institutions, including the bureaucracy, technocracy, security establishment, and community development. Despite all this, Nandy maintains, or rather hopes, that certain aspects of the image of 'state-as-an-arbiter' have retained the ability to underwrite an open polity as well as a new relationship between Indian traditions and open politics. He also points out that although the Indian state may have grown stronger, it has become less legitimate as an arbiter, protector, and liberator. As a result, legitimacy of the political order is often sought in a field outside the political system such as science, technology, sports, culture, and art. Nandy in the end calls us to seriously reconsider a more attenuated role of the state in order for civil society to thrive and create new forms of political imagination.

The gulf between those who place primacy on the state as an agent for socio-political development and those who would rather have the state's role limited in order for society to develop *sui generis*, seems to be wider than can be filled in a short discussion here. However, it may be pointed out that the form and role of the state can only be decided in a democratic process of interaction between the state and society. If this is so, the question is not whether it is the state or society which should have primacy, but what is the proper way of democratic representation so that both state and society can build up a mutually supportive relationship rather than that of competition for wider sphere of agency. Ways must be insured for public opinion to be freely formed in society and represented democratically in state politics. In contemporary India, the process of democratization in terms of increasing popular participation in politics seems to be an ongoing process. In this process, the political system is bound to go through further transformation and it would not be without reactions and frictions. Polemics aside, we cannot but pray with Nandy that this process of democratization may bring about an open polity that would establish new links between Indian social values and system of political democracy, formulating a space of renegotiation of socio-political relations towards a better state and society acceptable for Indian people.

NATION-STATE IN THE TWENTY-FIRST CENTURY

The last article in this volume by Zuberi looks at the history of independent India and assesses its achievements. In Zuberi's evaluation, contrary to what Khilnani and Kaviraj say, the colonial Indian state lacked the capacity to reorganize or develop Indian society and is fundamentally pre-modern.[57] In his reckoning, the 'formation of a modern democratic state... represents a major, perhaps *the* major, Indian achievement' in the post-colonial period. As we have discussed, if healthy development of a nation can only be achieved when there is a link between society and the state through a proper route of democratic representation, Zuberi is definitely right about the colonial state being incapable of developing society and the creation of a democratic regime in independent India marking a major breakthrough.[58]

Zuberi's concern lies in how the Indian state can maintain its autonomous agency in international politics. He says that the present international order 'seeks to build a durable structure of inequality and peace enforced by the powerful'. So the established powers resist the entry of new aspirants to equality. The nuclear club is the most exclusive in the contemporary world, and its members have created an 'imposed order' of the 'Nuclear Non-Proliferation Regime' made up of domination of five nuclear powers. According to Zuberi, discriminatory political moves that forcibly attempted to exclude new members from the club pushed India into exercising the nuclear option. This was necessary as 'the Indian State's ability to provide security and to conduct an independent foreign policy is dependent on the degree of self-reliance in defence'.

Zuberi predicts that 'international order of the first decades of the twenty-first century is likely to be marked by American attempts to maintain a preponderance of power at the global level while establishing balances of power in various regions of the world'. In this context, he suggests that it is the 'aspirations of autonomy' of India as a state that will continue to govern its future moves. He credits India for managing to 'cope with diverse international and domestic pressures in a democratic framework'. He cites India's success in the fields of science and technology and also in the recent resilient economy. Nevertheless, he anticipates that the present 'reconstitution of society' will be a long-drawn process with tensions and occasional turbulences. He suggests that the primary instrument for managing this process will be the state and the state resources will be 'heavily stretched'. In the end, however, he is hopeful that 'economic prosperity and diplomatic leverage is propelling India towards the role of an "actor" rather than that of a "subject" in the evolving international order'.

Zuberi thus sees the nation-state as continuing to be a primary player in the world order and national politics of the twenty-first century. In the emergent new global order, the nation-state will probably find it more necessary to concede parts of its sovereignty to the supra-national and sub-national levels, giving up the monolithic unity of state sovereignty. In this process, however, there is no doubt that the nation-state will continue to be the most important apparatus of democracy through which people will represent and exercise their will, even in the decision of limiting and conceding state sovereignty. Moreover, the necessary 'reconstitution of society' pointed out by Zuberi—that is, the same agenda as 'renegotiation of social relations' mentioned by Nandy—can only be achieved if there is a democratic society supported by a democratic state. To what extent the state will participate in this reconstitution process and what role it will play will have to be decided in the very process of democratic representation of people's will. There is little consensus regarding the ideal image of the state among concerned scholars; nevertheless both Nandy and Zuberi seem to agree on the point that we have to expect further socio-political transformations with the development of democratization and that it is necessary to seriously consider what role the state can play thereof.

CONCLUSION

The contemporary volatile process of redefinition of entitlements and representations of diverse groups and communities, mentioned at the beginning of this chapter, is taking place as a necessary reconstitution of socio-political relationships since the process of democratization involves increasingly more agents in the arena of political participation. The form of the state, which the widening democracy of India will decide, would probably be different from what western political philosophers have prescribed. The forms of modernity and democracy which India will decide for its own future remain to be seen.[59]

In order for this reconstituting process to take place with minimum tension and violence, it is the state's duty to facilitate the renegotiation and restructuring of socio-political relationships of diverse groups and communities by providing democratic routes for enunciation and dialogue of voices. In this sense, the state continues to play an important role in ensuring healthy socio-political development. The state and society, rather than opposing and competing for spheres of power and hegemony, should find ways to be mutually supportive. But this is much more easily said than done considering the colonial and post-colonial history of India. Coordination of the relationship between 'powers as they are legally constituted in the domain of the state' and 'powers as they are actually exercised and negotiated in the local societies' is still a 'central problem of Indian politics'.[60]

As we have seen, the viability of the state in India throughout history—arguably including the colonial period—rested in its ability to arbitrate and coordinate the powers and entitlements of diverse groups and communities.[61] The state has been instrumental in providing a common arena of negotiation between various values and interests. Socio-political integration was achieved not by imposing an order but through competition and negotiation in which the state itself took part.

The redistribution of resources and allotment of entitlements were managed in a system of patrimonial rights at the social level in medieval India and the state functioned to assist in maintaining its order. The contemporary Indian state, on the contrary, has largely monopolized the function of redistribution of resources. This is one of the reasons why the state is the target of political demands by so many groups and para-communities. The concentration of power of redistribution in the hands of the state has also brought about corruption. Social demands for access to state resources have led to over-politicization of socio-religious relations. It seems mandatory then that the state recovers its ability to arbitrate socio-political relationships so that production and distribution of resources can be managed in a manner acceptable to the emerging Indian democratic values.

For the state to play this role, it should not identify itself with a particular value or interest in society. The secularity of the state is necessary so that it will not be partial to any religious or non-religious creed. However, this does not mean that the kind of dichotomous division between the secular state and religious society developed through the colonial period must continue. Rather, it remains one of the most important agendas in post-colonial India to overcome such a dichotomy. A key to a viable relationship between the state and society seems to lie in mutual respect for socio-religious values and secularity of the state. We hope this volume helps us to see the relationships between the state and society and those between secularity and religiosity in India in a better historical and cultural perspective, rather than presupposing their antagonistic contradiction.

Needless to say, India will occupy one of the most crucial and critical positions in the world order in the twenty-first century. An understanding of the past and present of the Indian state is important for discerning present problems as well as looking into future possibilities. Moreover, the Indian state's experience in dealing with its multicultural and heterogeneous condition might provide us with some hints for achieving a better future in a globalized world.

NOTES

1. Freitag talks of the process of 'the redefinition of Indian civil social space and who will be allowed to participate publicly inside that discursive space' (Sandria B. Freitag, 'Contesting in Public: Colonial Legacies and Contemporary Communalism', in David Ludden [ed.], 1996, *Making India Hindu: Religions, Community, and the Politics of Democracy in India,* New Delhi: Oxford University Press, p. 232). There is indeed such a process of redefinition of public entitlements going on. However, it is also necessary to consider larger conditions for viable civil society. Alongside the issue of participatory rights in civil society, the actual issue in contemporary India seems to be to ensure proper governance from the state through the working of the 'political society' and to form viable political and social ethics through the working of 'moral society'. See Partha Chatterjee, 1998, 'Community in the East', *Economic and Political Weekly,* No. 33, pp. 277–82, and *idem*, 2000, 'Two Poets and Death: On Civil and Political Society in the Non-Christian World', in Timothy Mitchell (ed.), *Questions of Modernity,* Minneapolis & London: University of Minnesota Press, pp. 35–48, on the concept of 'political society'. See Akio Tanabe, 2002, 'Moral Society, Political Society and Civil Society in Post-colonial India: A View from Orissan Locality', *Journal of the Japanese Association for South Asian Studies*, No. 14, pp. 40–67, on the discussion of 'civil society', 'political society', and 'moral society'.

2. There has been an increase of tension and conflicts as there has been the promulgation of democratic ideas and institutions into the non-elite, subaltern population who place increasing and multiplying demands on the government and do not conform to the behavioural patterns of supposed 'secular' and 'rational' civil society. Cf. A. Kohli, 1990, *Democracy and Discontent: India's Growing Crisis of Governability*, Cambridge: Cambridge University Press. This leads us to reconsider the nature of the relationship between subaltern-empowering 'democracy' and urban–elite centred 'civil

society'. They may not be as mutually supporting in post-colonial societies as one might want to think. Cf. Chatterjee, 2000, *op. cit.*, pp. 35–48.

3. See, for example, Sugata Bose and Ayesha Jalal (eds), 1998, *Nationalism, Democracy and Development: State and Politics in India,* New Delhi: Oxford University Press, and quoted literature thereof to know the basic contents of the debates.

4. One of the central questions regarding the emerging global order lies in the future of 'nation-states'. Will the nation-state become obsolete in the global modernity of 'diasporic public spheres' that characterize the 'post-national formation' as Appadurai says, or will it continue to be the main frame of reference as regards the problem of democracy and proper governance 'within nation' as Partha Chatterjee argues? See Arjun Appadurai, 1996, *Modernity at Large: Cultural Dimensions of Globalization,* Minneapolis: University of Minnesota Press, and Partha Chatterjee, 1998, 'Beyond the Nation? Or Within?', *Social Text,* Vol. 16, No. 3, pp. 57–69.

5. See J. Linz Juan, 1978, *The Breakdown of Democratic Regimes: Crisis, Breakdown, and Reequilibration*, Baltimore: Johns Hopkins University Press, and Sumantra Bose, 1998, '"Hindu Nationalism" and the Crisis of the Indian State: A Theoretical Perspective', in Sugata Bose and Ayesha Jalal (eds), *op. cit.*, p. 108.

6. Sunil Khilnani, 1999, *The Idea of India* (with a new introduction), New Delhi: Penguin Books (original edn. 1997), p. 41.

7. Ibid., p. 41.

8. Partha Chatterjee ingeniously takes up the concept of 'political society' in order to capture the space of political activities that mediates between the 'population' and the state in post-colonial democracies (Chatterjee, 2000, *op. cit.*, pp. 35–48).

9. Kohli points out, 'The spread of competitive politics in a setting in which the state has disproportionate control over societal resources provides the broad context for overpoliticization' (Kohli, 1990, *op. cit.*, p. 401).

10. Kohli, 1990, *op. cit.*

11. Sudipta Kaviraj, 1984, 'On the Crisis of Political Institutions in India', *Contributions to Indian Sociology* (n.s.), Vol. 18, No. 2, pp. 223–43. See also Nandy's and Zuberi's articles in this volume.

12. Cf. Akhil Gupta, 1995, 'Blurred Boundaries: The Discourse of Corruption, the Culture of Politics, and the Imagined State', *American Ethnologist,* Vol. 22, No. 2, pp. 375–402; Chris J. Fuller and Véronique Bénéï (eds), 2000, *The Everyday State and Society in Modern India,* New Delhi: Social Science Press; Jonathan P. Parry, 2000, 'The "Crisis of Corruption" and "The Idea of India": A Worms-Eye View', in Italo Pardo (ed.), *Morals of Legitimacy: Between Agency and System,* Oxford: Berghan Books, pp. 27–55. Shiv Visvanathan and Harsh Sethi (eds), 1998, *Foul Play: Chronicles of Corruption*, New Delhi: Banyan Books; Tanabe, 2002, *op. cit.* Also see Nandy's article in this volume.

13. Bishnu N. Mohapatra, 1997, 'The Problem', *Seminar*, No. 456, p. 12.

14. Louis Dumont, 1980, *Homo Hierarchicus,* Chicago: Chicago University Press.

15. Kaviraj, 1984, *op. cit.*, p. 232.

16. Thus, 'Everyday caste practice disciplined social conduct without frequent direct recourse to the power of the state; the holders of political authority were themselves governed by the rules of caste order and barred by its regulations from exercising legislative power over the productive arrangements of society' (Sudipta Kaviraj, 2000, 'Modernity and Politics in India', *Daedalus*, Vol. 129, No. 1, p. 141).

17. Burton Stein, 1998, *A History of India*, Oxford: Blackwell, p. 19. Stein here criticizes such a view on the Indian state.

18. Khilnani, 1999, *op. cit.*, p. 20.

19. Ibid., 1999, *op. cit.*, pp. 20, 21.

20. Kaviraj, 2000, *op. cit.*, p. 143.

21. Nicholas Dirks, 1987, *The Hollow Crown: Ethnohistory of an Indian Little Kingdom*, Cambridge: Cambridge University Press; Gloria Goodwin Raheja, 1988, *The Poison in the Gift: Ritual, Prestation and the Dominant Caste in a North Indian Village*, Chicago: University of Chicago Press; Declan Quigley, 1993, *The Interpretation of Caste*, Oxford: Clarendon Press.

22. Cf. Mohapatra, 1997, *op. cit.*, p. 12; Chris A. Bayly, 1998, *Origins of Nationality in South Asia: Patriotism and Ethical Government in the Making of Modern India*, New Delhi: Oxford University Press, p. 3; Partha Chatterjee, 1993, *The Nation and its Fragments: Colonial and Postcolonial Histories,* Princeton Studies in Culture/Power/History, Princeton: Princeton University Press, p. 5. These criticisms go against the kind of view held by Anderson who sees Asian and African nationalisms as having been derived from Europe and America and leaves no room for the creative agency and imagination of Asian and African nationalism; Benedict Anderson, 1991, *Imagined Communities: Reflections on the Origin and Spread of Nationalism*, revised edition, New York: Verso.

23. Philip Abrams, 1988, 'Notes on the Difficulty of Studying the State (1977)', *Journal of Historical Sociology*, Vol. 1, No. 1, pp. 58–89; Timothy Mitchell, 1991, 'The Limits of the State: Beyond Statist Approaches and Their Critics', *American Political Science Review*, Vol. 85, No. 1, pp. 77–96.

24. Kulke and Rothermund explain as follows: 'Early state formation in India usually proceeded in three phases. In the Gangetic region, the first phase of this process was characterised by the transition of the small seminomadic tribes (*jana*) of the period of Aryan migration to a large number of tribal principalities of a definite area (*janapada*). During the second phase in a period of competition, 16 major *mahajanapada*s emerged in the late seventh and early sixth centuries BC. The third or imperial phase was reached when one of these *mahajanapada*s (in this case Magadha) established its hegemony over the others'. (Hermann Kulke and Dietmar Rothermund, 1991, *A History of India*, New Delhi: Manohar, p. 57.)

25. Romila Thapar, 1984, *From Lineage to State: Social Formations in the Mid-first Millennium B.C. in the Ganga Valley*, Bombay: Oxford University Press.

26. R.S. Sharma, 1983, *Material Culture and Social Formations in Ancient India*, Delhi: Macmillan India; Burton Stein, 1980, *Peasant, State and Society in Medieval South India,* New Delhi and New York: Oxford University Press; see also N. Karashima, 2001, *History and Society in South India: The Cholas to Vijayanagar Comprising South Indian History and Society, Towards a New Formation*, New Delhi: Oxford University Press and *idem*, 2002, *A Concordance of Nayakas: The Vijayanagar Inscriptions in South India*, New Delhi: Oxford University Press for detailed epigraphical studies that scrutinize political relationships in medieval south Indian states. Karashima's work corroborates some aspects of the feudal model and criticizes Stein's segmentary model, at the same time paying attention to the politically integral aspects of the state.

27. See Hermann Kulke 'Introduction', in Kulke (ed.), 1995, *The State in India 1000–1700,* New Delhi: Oxford University Press for an overview of the studies on the medieval state in India.

28. In the same vein, Chattopadhyaya says as follows: '(T)he structure of early medieval polity was a logical development from the territorially limited state society of the early historical period to a gradual but far greater penetration of the state society into local agrarian and peripheral levels, generating continuous fissions at such levels. The feudatory and other intermediary strata in the early medieval structures of polity...may thus be seen in terms of an "integrative polity", with potential sources of tension built into the structures' (Brajadulal Chattopadhyaya, 1995 (1983), 'Political Processes and the Structure of Polity in Early Medieval India', in Hermann Kulke (ed.), 1995, *The State in India 1000–1700*, *op. cit*., p. 231).

29. See Sugata Bose and Ayesha Jalal, 1998, *Modern South Asia: History, Culture and Political Economy*, London and New York: Routledge, p. 243 for the idea of 'a political and state system based on layered and shared sovereignties'.

30. See Richard G. Fox, 1971, *Kin, Clan, Raja, and Rule: State-hinterland Relations in Preindustrial India*, Berkeley: University of California Press. Kaviraj summarizes the situation as follows: 'Political power is often distributed between several layers of legitimate authority stretching from the village or locality at the micro level, through regional kingdoms, to immense empires like the ones set up by the Mauryas or the Mughals' (Kaviraj, 2000, *op. cit.*, p. 142).

31. Personal communication from Bayly to Kulke (Hermann Kulke 'Introduction', in Kulke [ed.], 1995, *op. cit.*, p. 47).

32. Stein, 1980, *op. cit.*

33. Dirks says that the land was granted not as 'fief' but as 'gift' (Dirks, 1987, *op. cit.*).

34. Burton Stein, 1985, 'Politics, Peasants and the Deconstruction of Feudalism in Medieval India', in Terence J. Byres and Harbans Mukhia (eds),

'Feudalism and Non-European Societies', Special Issue of *Journal of Peasant Studies*, Vol. 12, Nos 2–3, p. 83; cf. Kulke, 1995, *op. cit.*, p. 16.

35. Irfan Habib, 1985, 'Classifying Pre-Colonial India', in Byres and Mukhia (eds), *op. cit.*, p. 49; cf. Kulke, 1995, *op. cit.*, p. 16.

36. Hiroshi Fukazawa (in Japanese), 1972, *Indo Shakai Keizaishi Kenkyu* (*Researches on the Socio-economic History of India*), Tokyo: Toyokeizaishin-posha; *idem*, 1982, 'Agrarian Relations and Land Revenue: The Medieval Deccan and Maharashtra', in T. Raychaudhuri and I. Habib (eds), *The Cambridge Economic History of India 1, c. 1200–c. 1750*, New Delhi: Orient Longman and Cambridge University Press, pp. 249– 60; *idem*, 1991, *The Medieval Deccan: Peasants, Social Systems and States: Sixteenth to Eighteenth Centuries*, New Delhi: Oxford University Press.

37. See Hiroyuki Kotani, 1996, 'The Vatan-System in the Sixteenth-Eighteenth Century Deccan: Towards a New Concept of Indian Feudalism', in D.N. Jha (ed.), *Society and Ideology in India: Essays in Honour of Professor R.S. Sharma*, Delhi: Munshiram Manoharlal Publishers, pp. 249–68; *idem*, 2002, *Western India in Historical Transition,* New Delhi: Manohar; Tsukasa Mizushima, 1996, 'The Mirasi System and Local Society in Pre-Colonial South India', in P. Robb *et al.* (eds), *Local Agrarian Societies in Colonial India: Japanese Perspectives*, London: Curzon Press, pp. 77–145; Akio Tanabe, forthcoming, 'The System of Entitlements in Eighteenth-century Khurda, Orissa: Reconsideration of "Caste" and "Jajmani system" in Pre-colonial India', *South Asia*, Vol. 28, No. 3.

38. Mizushima, 1996, *op. cit.*

39. In this connection, it would be useful to add the aspect of the development of medieval social system to Kulke's processual model and consider what effect it had on the process of state formation.

40. Chris Bayly, 1992, *Rulers, Townsmen and Bazaars: North Indian Society in the Age of British Expansion, 1770–1870* (Indian edition), New Delhi: Oxford University Press (original 1983).

41. See for example, Burton Stein, 1989, 'Eighteenth Century India: Another View', *Studies in History,* Vol. 5, No. 1 (n.s.), pp. 1–26, *idem*, 1985, 'State Formation and Economy Reconsidered', *Modern Asian Studies*, Vol. 14, No. 3, pp. 387–413; David A. Washbrook, 1988, 'Progress and Problems: South Asian Economic and Social History c. 1720–1860', *Modern Asian Studies,* Vol. 22, No. 1, pp. 57–96; *idem*, 1990, 'South Asia, the World System and World Capitalism', *The Journal of Asian Studies,* Vol. 29, No. 3, pp. 479–508; Frank Perlin, 1983, 'Proto-industrialisation and Pre-colonial South Asia', *Past and Present*, Vol. 98, pp. 30–95; *idem*, 1985, 'State Formation Reconsidered. Part Two', *Modern Asian Studies,* Vol. 19, No. 3, pp. 415–80; *idem*, 1993, *'The Invisible City': Monetary, Administrative and Popular Infrastructures in Asia and Europe 1500–1900,* Aldershot: Variorum; Chris Bayly, 1988, *Indian Society and the Making of the British Empire*, Cambridge and New York: Cambridge University Press; *idem*, 1990, 'Beating the Boundaries: South Asian History,

c. 1700–1850', in Sugata Bose (ed.), *South Asia and World Capitalism,* New Delhi: Oxford University Press, pp. 27–39; *idem*, 1993, 'Pre-colonial Indian Merchants and Rationality', in M. Hasan and N. Gupta (eds), *India's Colonial Encounter: Essays in Memory of Eric Stokes*, New Delhi: Manohar, pp. 3–24. It should be noted that there are considerable variations in the argument of 'revisionists'. For criticisms against the 'revisionist' group, see for example M. Athar Ali, 1986, 'Recent Theories of Eighteenth Century India', *Indian Historical Review,* Vol. 13, Nos 1/2; Chatterjee, 1993, *op. cit.*, especially the second chapter; Kum Kum Chatterjee, 1996, *Merchants, Politics and Society in Early Modern India: Bihar 1733–1820,* Leiden: E.J. Brill; Sushil Chaudhury, 1995, *From Prosperity to Decline: Eighteenth Century Bengal*, New Delhi: Manohar.

42. In Chris A. Bayly's later book (1998), *Origins of Nationality in South Asia: Patriotism and Ethical Government in the Making of Modern India*, New Delhi: Oxford University Press, he takes into account the aspect of values and ethics of the early modern development of state formation.

43. Eric R. Wolf, 1982, *Europe and the People without History*, Berkeley: University of California Press.

44. Bayly, 1983, *op. cit.*

45. Tanabe in this volume and Tanabe, 2002, *op. cit.*

46. Bayly, 1998, *op. cit.*

47. See André Wink, 1986, *Land and Sovereignty in India: Agrarian Society and Politics under the Eighteenth-century Maratha Svarajya,* Cambridge: Cambridge University Press.

48. The 'revisionists' such as Washbrook, Stein, and Bayly point to the basic continuity of the social structure from the eighteenth century till the early nineteenth century. See note 40 above.

49. Kaviraj calls this endeavour 'an enormous discursive project' of the colonial state (Sudipta Kaviraj, 2000, 'Modernity and Politics in India', *Daedalus*, Vol. 129, No. 1, p. 144).

50. Jürgen Habermas, 1989, *The Structural Transformation of the Public Sphere: An Inquiry into a Category of Bourgeois Society*, translated by Thomas Burger, Cambridge, Mass: MIT Press.

51. Sugata Bose points out that 'colonial modernity was a complex and concrete phenomenon; its reasons of state were deeply enmeshed with the communities of religion'. He calls for 'a dynamic and historicized conception of religion that might enable us to consider how the place of the "religious" in Indian public and political life changed in the course of India's colonial history' (Sugata Bose, 1998, 'Nation, Reason and Religion: India's Independence in International Perspective', *Economic and Political Weekly,* August, pp. 2091–2).

52. Washbrook points out that 'British ruling elite ideas about the nature of representation' held that 'members of civil society could only represent specific and sectional interests since it was axiomatic that societal integration

took place only through the state and thus the state executive alone could represent the "whole" society.... It was, and remains, a crucial strategy of this kind of state, to preserve its authority, that civil society be seen as "naturally" divided' (David Washbrook, 1998, 'The Rhetoric of Democracy and Development in Late Colonial India', in Sugata Bose and Ayesha Jalal [eds], *op. cit.*, p. 40).

53. By 'para-communities', I am referring to the modern reorganized communities that are decontextualized from networks of kinship and territoriality. They usually have a characterizing essence—caste, religion, culture—by which they define their community membership.

54. Sudipta Kaviraj, 1991, 'On State, Society and Discourse in India', in J. Manor (ed.), *Rethinking Third World Politics*, London: Longman, p. 93.

55. See Pranab Bardhan, 1998, 'The State against Society: The Great Divide in Indian Social Science Discourse', in Sugata Bose and Ayesha Jalal (eds), *op. cit.* Bardhan names Ashis Nandy, Partha Chatterjee, and T.N. Madan as 'anarcho-communitarians'. There have been criticisms on them by André Beteille, van der Veer, Sugata Bose and Ayesha Jalal, and Amartya Sen among others. See A. Nandy, 1992, 'The Politics of Secularism and the Recovery of Religious Tolerance', in V. Das (ed.), *Mirrors of Violence: Communities, Riots and Survivors in South Asia*, New Delhi: Oxford University Press, pp. 69–93; Partha Chatterjee, 1994, 'Secularism and Tolerance', *Economic and Political Weekly*, 28, 29 (9 July), pp. 1768–77; T.N. Madan, 1987, 'Secularism in Its Place', *The Journal of Asian Studies*, Vol. 46, No. 4, pp. 747–59; *idem*, 1997, *Modern Myths, Locked Minds: Secularism and Fundamentalism in India*, New Delhi: Oxford University Press; A. Beteille, 1994, 'Secularism and Intellectuals', *Economic and Political Weekly*, Vol. 24, No. 5 (5 March), pp. 559–66; van der Veer, 1994, *Religious Nationalism: Hindus and Muslims in India*, Berkeley and Los Angeles: University of California Press, esp. p. 197; Sugata Bose and Ayesha Jalal (eds), 1998, *Modern South Asia: History, Culture, Political Economy*, New Delhi: Oxford University Press; *idem*, 1998, *Nationalism, Democracy and Development*, *op. cit.*, esp. 'Introduction'; Amartya Sen, 1998, 'Secularism and its Discontents', in Rajeev Bhargava (ed.), *Secularism and its Critics*, New Delhi: Oxford University Press.

56. Dipesh Chakrabarty, 1995, 'Radical Histories and the Question of Enlightenment Rationalism', *Economic and Political Weekly,* April, pp. 751–9.

57. It is true that the centralized colonial state apparatus was largely inherited by the post-colonial state. It poses a lasting colonial legacy on the nature of post-colonial India. See Ayesha Jalal, 1995, *Democracy and Authoritarianism in South Asia: A Comparative and Historical Perspective*, Cambridge: Cambridge University Press, on this point. It should be added, however, that there was also a major transformation in the meaning and legitimacy of these state apparatuses under independent India.

58. Although Ludden is correct when he says, 'By 1900, institutional foundations of the state information apparatus and the surrounding constellations of public debate and expertise that sustain India's development regime today were in place' (David Ludden, 1992, 'India's Development Regime', in Nicholas Dirks [ed.], *Colonialism and Culture,* Ann Arbor: University of Michigan Press, p. 261), these instruments of development lacked the legitimacy and orientation of democratic national development. Cf. Sugata Bose, 1997, 'Instruments and Idioms of Colonial and National Development', in Frederick Cooper and Randall Packard (eds), *International Development and the Social Sciences: Essays on the History and Politics of Knowledge*, Berkeley: University of California Press, pp. 45–63.

59. On 'forms of modernity', see Akio Tanabe and Yumiko Tokita-Tanabe, 2003, 'Introduction: Gender and Modernity in Asia and the Pacific', in Y. Hayami, A. Tanabe, and Y. Tokita-Tanabe (eds), *Gender and Modernity: Perspectives from Asia and the Pacific*, Kyoto and Melbourne: Kyoto University Press and Trans Pacific Press, pp. 1–16. On effects of globalization on the world order, see P. N. Abinales, N. Ishikawa and A. Tanabe (eds), 2005, *Dislocating Nation-States: Globalization in Asia and Africa*, Kyoto and Melbourne: Kyoto University Press and Trans Pacific Press.

60. Partha Chatterjee, 1997, 'The Political Process: Resistance', in Partha Chatterjee (ed.), *State and Politics in India*, New Delhi: Oxford University Press, p. 438.

61. Sugata Bose says, 'What got marginalized in 1947 were conceptions of a state of union forged from below that reflected and presided over the balance and harmony of free regional peoples and religious communities' (Sugata Bose, 1997, *op. cit*., p. 52). It is necessary that we attempt to shed more light on such a form and idea of the state in Indian history.

SECTION I

Formation and Concept of the State

CHAPTER 1

State and Kingship in the Period of the Sixteen *Mahājanapada*s in Ancient North India

Gen'ichi Yamazaki

INTRODUCTION

In ancient India, there was a theory that the state, kingdom (*rājya*), is constituted of seven elements (*sapta-prakṛtayaḥ*) or seven limbs (*sapta-aṅgāni*). According to the Manu-smṛti (IX, 294) edited around the first/second century AD, the seven elements are:

1. King (*svāmin*)
2. Minister (*amātya*)
3. City (*pura*)
4. Domain/territory (*rāṣṭra*)
5. Treasury (*kośa*)
6. Army (*daṇḍa*)
7. Ally (*suhṛd, mitra*)

Out of these, 2 refers to the system of government (bureaucratic organization) with the ministers at the apex, 3 to cities and citizens, 4 to territory and provincial inhabitants, 5 to financial affairs in general, 6 to military power, and 7 to international relations centred on a particular state.

The Manu-smṛti goes on to explain that each one of the seven elements has its own particular characteristic and can be the most important factor in its respective purposes. However, from the point of view of being the cause of a great disaster, the preceding element surpasses the succeeding element (IX, 295–7). That is to say, the state as an organic system exists by its essential elements, which correspond to each part of the body, functioning independently; and within this system the king is seen as the most important element that integrates the other six and determines the state's destiny.

Also, in the Arthaśāstra, the political treatise said to have been written around 300 BC by Kauṭilya who was the prime minister at the Mauryan court (edited as its present form in third to fourth century AD), it is explained that a state is composed of seven elements (VI, 1, 1). However, the order of the third and fourth elements is reversed from that given in the Manu-smṛti, and the third element is said to be the province (janapada) and the fourth element the fortified city (*durga*). According to this treatise, the king is seen also as the centre of seven elements, and it is stated that the other elements and even the rise and fall of the kingdom depend on the king (VI, 1, 15–18). For instance, if the king is diligent, the other elements will follow in the same manner; but on the other hand if he is inattentive, the various elements will also turn towards negligence (VIII, 1, 16–18). Therefore, of the calamities that are brought about by the seven elements, those that originate from the king are the most serious (VIII, 1). This central position of the king is expressed by the short phrase, 'the king is [the basis of] the kingdom' (*rājā rājyam*) (VIII, 2, 1).

This paper deals with state and kingship in the time of the Sixteen *Mahājanapadas* which was the formation period of the state equipped with these seven elements. Before coming to the main arguments, let me give a brief introduction to the period concerned and the research material.[1] When Gautama Buddha founded Buddhism (sixth–fifth centuries BC), there were states having the generic name of 'Sixteen Great States (Mahājanapadas)' in north India which competed with each other. Eventually, four powerful mahājanapadas, namely Kosala, Magadha, Vatsa, and Avanti, gained supremacy, and finally Magadha established a unified empire. This unification process is similar to what China underwent at around the same period, where there was a historical development from the age of rival warlords in the Spring and Autumn period to the seven powerful states in the Warring States period and further to the unification of the whole country by the Qin dynasty.

'Janapada' in the term 'Mahājanapada' means 'the foothold of tribes (jana)' and is a term which was employed to refer to the tribal state in the later Vedic period (*c.* 1000–600 BC). Most of the names of the 'states' at that time and the sixteen 'great states' in the period that followed originated from tribal names.

There are some discrepancies regarding the composition of the Sixteen Mahājanapadas. The Southern Buddhist canon (Pāli canon) mentions the following states:[2] Aṅga, Magadha, Kāsi (Kāśi), Kosala (Kośala), Vajji (Vṛji), Ceti (Cedi), Malla, Vaṅga, Kuru, Pañcāla, Vaccha (Vaṃsa, Vatsa), Sūrasena (Śūrasena), Assaka (Aśmaka), Avanti, Gandhāra, and Kamboja.

There were some states among those that were called 'Mahājanapada' that could not actually be called states for they lacked sufficient territory and organization of government. Besides, the number 'sixteen' was probably used for the sake of convenience, and the concept of 'Sixteen Mahājanapadas' seems to have been established after Buddha's time. In spite of these ambiguities, there is no doubt that most of the states listed were influential powers during the period of the establishment of Buddhism. In this paper, I deal with the following three types of states out of these Mahājanapadas: (1) the state of Magadha which developed a powerful autocratic kingship and was fully equipped with the seven elements, (2) the states of the Licchavis and the Mallas which lacked the king as the centre of the seven elements and maintained the tribal system, and (3) the states of the Kurus and the Pañcālas, which were unable to go beyond the limitations of the tribal system in spite of having developed kingship very early. The order of appearance of these three types of states is (2), (3), (1). However, I would first like to deal with the state of Magadha.

It is a well-known fact that ancient Indians did not leave behind literature that could be termed as 'history'. Though inscriptions are important sources for research on ancient India, the earliest are those of King Aśoka during the Mauryan dynasty (third century BC). Therefore, the writing of the history of the period of the Sixteen Mahājanapadas which precedes Aśoka must rely mainly on religious literature of Buddhism, Jainism, and Brahmanism (Hinduism). The Buddhist canon frequently referred to in this paper was edited two to three hundred years after Buddha's death (that is to say, after the period of the Sixteen Mahājanapadas) hence its value as a source for historical research is low. However, it is also true that such religious literature does give historical facts to some extent (sometimes it gives considerable amount of historical facts), and researchers of ancient India have been writing history based on this assumption. This paper is also based on the same assumption.

THE FORMATION OF THE KINGDOM OF MAGADHA

The first records mentioning the name Magadha are the later Vedic works, the Atharva-veda and the Yajur-veda.[3] Therefore, it can be assumed that by the middle of the later Vedic period, probably around 800 BC, the Aryan immigrants (people speaking the Aryan group of languages; the racial purity had been lost to a great extent due to intermixing with the indigenous population) had followed two paths, one via the Himalayan foothills and another along the River Ganga, and spread to the land of Magadha in the middle and lower Ganga valley. The Aryan migration to Magadha took place at a considerable pace, and eventually this region became the greatest centre of activity surpassing all other western Aryan states. This development was probably due to the fact that this region was the largest producer of iron ore. Moreover, it had vast and fertile lands that were ideal for agriculture, was blessed with forests and their products, and the Ganga and its tributaries provided it with means of transport. The immigrant Aryans lived without being bound by the conservative teachings of Brahmanism and the various rules of the varṇa social system in these frontier regions. They lived together with the indigenous people and brought about their Aryanization. The inhabitants of Magadha were criticized and despised by the Brahmins of the upper Ganga valley for the disorder of the status system, but on the other hand, it can be said that they were full of dynamic vitality as a mixed race.

There are many legends regarding the origin of the kingdom of Magadha. In one of them, it is said that when the great Kuru king Vasu divided his territory among his five sons, the eldest son Bṛhadratha established the Bārhadratha dynasty in the land of Magadha. This dynasty set up its capital at Rājagṛha (Girivraja) and became very powerful during King Jarāsandha's time. However, the king died by fighting with Bhīma, a younger brother of the five Pāṇḍavas (the main characters of the Mahābhārata) who was sent by his eldest brother Yudhiṣṭhira. Jarāsandha's son Sahadeva died in the great war fought at Kurukṣetra. According to Purāṇa legend, the Bārhadratha dynasty survived over a long period after this war, and was later replaced by the dynasty established by Śiśunāga (Śaiśunāga dynasty). The fifth king of this new dynasty, which continued for ten generations, was Bimbisāra, the sixth was Ajātaśatru, and the son or the grandson of the latter was the eighth king Udayin who moved the capital to Pāṭaliputra (Kusumapura).[4]

On the other hand, the Buddhists recount a very different lineage of Magadha kings from that of kings given by the Brahmanical literature. Out of these, according to the list of various kings given in the Dīpavaṃsa (III, 52–61; V, 97–9) and the Mahāvaṃsa (II, 25–31; IV, 1–7) of the

Theravāda sect of Sri Lanka, Bimbisāra is said to have been king before Śiśunāga, as opposed to the list given in the aforementioned Purāṇa literature. His son is said to be Ajātaśatru, Ajātaśatru's son is said to be Udayabhadda (Udayin), and Śiśunāga is said to be the minister who conquered their dynasty and established a new one. There is no absolute evidence to determine which account is true, but the Theravāda Buddhist account is more credible from the point of view of reliability of sources, and many historians discuss the history of Magadha based on this account.

In the history of the kingdom of Magadha, Bimbisāra is the first king whose political achievements are relatively well mentioned. According to the Dīpavaṃsa and the Mahāvaṃsa, this king was five years younger than Buddha, ascended to the throne succeeding his father Bodhisa at the age of fifteen and reigned for fifty-two years. The period of his reign cannot be determined at this stage since the controversy regarding the year of Buddha's nirvāṇa has not been resolved.[5] However, according to the Theravāda tradition, which says that the years of birth and death of Buddha are around 566 BC and 486 BC, respectively, it would be around 546–494 BC.

If we survey the development of Magadha from the point of view of the seventh element (international relations), Bimbisāra first annexed the neighbouring kingdom of Aṅga in the east, which had been prospering through trade near the mouth of the Ganga, and strengthened his position in international relations by skilful manipulation of marriage alliances. According to legend, when Bimbisāra married the daughter of King Mahākosala of the powerful neighbouring state of Kosala in the west, he gained a village of the Kāsi kingdom, which had been annexed by Kosala, as her cosmetics fee. He also married a bride from the neighbouring Licchavis (or Videhas) who had been extending their influence in the north. Moreover, he maintained friendly relationships with the kings of powerful states far away, such as the king of Gandhāra whose capital was Takṣaśilā in north-west India and the king of Avanti whose capital was Ujjayini in west India. However, he spent his last years in misfortune and died in confinement in the hands of his ambitious son Ajātaśatru.

Magadha further developed during the era of the next king Ajātaśatru. He aimed to conquer the state of the Licchavis (and also the Vṛji confederacy which was led by this tribe) and that of Kosala, and was successful in annexing these two states after a long period of war. According to Theravāda Buddhist tradition, Ajātaśatru was killed by his son Udayabhadda (Udayin) after thirty-two years in power (c. 494–462 BC). As we have seen above, according to the Purāṇa literature, during the reign of this new king, the capital of Magadha was moved from Rājagṛha, which was famous as an impregnable fort, to Pāṭaliputra, which was located on the bank of Ganga and was a strategic place from the point of view of transportation. This move was essential for the state of Magadha which continued to develop towards building an empire. Later, Magadha succeeded in dominating over the entire Ganga valley under the Nanda dynasty which rose in the middle of fourth century BC. Kings of this Nanda dynasty exercised enormous power while expanding the territory, but their coercive measures incurred ill feelings, and after a short period of rule, the throne was usurped by Candragupta, the founder of the Mauryan empire.

KINGSHIP IN MAGADHA

Here, taking Magadha as an example, I would like to consider the question of the 'king' which is listed as the first of the seven elements.

When we compare kingship in Magadha and kingship in states that preceded it, the most important difference is that kings, represented by Bimbisāra and Ajātaśatru, acted as 'individuals' who had completely broken away from tribal bonds. They did not face tribal restrictions when they exercised their powers. Moreover, in the land of Magadha, which was relatively free from the constraints of the varṇa social system, it was possible in some cases for those who were not born as kshatriya to climb to the king's position through their abilities. A good example is the case of Mahāpadma (middle of fourth century BC) who founded the Nanda dynasty with his wealth and power in spite of being despised as one with a lowly birth.

Where then did the Magadha kings seek legitimacy for their rule and how did they express it? In the Aryan states of tribal kingship, which emerged in the upper Ganga valley, the kshatriya successor to the throne was consecrated through Vedic rituals starting with the enthronement ceremony (*rājasūya*), and his divinity and the legitimacy of his rule were acknowledged. That is to say, he became the heir to the kingship granted by God with the support of Brahmin priests. The strengthening of kingship through these rituals would be seen in Kāsi and Kosala in the middle Ganga valley, though there were differences in degree. The kings who ruled over Magadha, which was located in the eastern frontier of the Aryan culture area, also called themselves kshatriya and performed rituals such as the coronation with *abhiṣeka* (water-sprinkling). However, these became formalities and the king's divinity acquired through such rituals almost lost its previous importance. In a later period, King Aśoka of the Mauryan dynasty did not emphasize his divinity in the inscriptions, and went no further than employing the title Devānampiya (loved by the gods) for self-reference.

The Magadha kings emphasized administrative and military abilities as the bases of their legitimacy rather than the divinity got through the traditional rituals of Brahmins. In other words, they emphasized the fact that they had the ability to protect the people and maintain social order. They used coronations, audiences, ordinances, inspections, and marching of troops in order to stress the fact that they had succeeded to the throne from their fathers, or had been crowned after conquering an incapable king, and the fact that they had a powerful army that could carry out their aims. Furthermore, they gave huge donations to Brahmins and unorthodox religions such as Buddhism in order to widely demonstrate their pious faith. Donations to Brahmins were often made in the form of donation of villages (rights to collect taxes) and land (proprietary and management rights). This was accompanied by the expectation that the Brahmins would fulfil their roles as intellectual elites in the administration and maintenance of social order.

Kings who appear in the Buddhist canons may be said to reflect such an image of the Magadha kings.[6] According to the canons, the king was placed in the centre of the state and the rise and fall of the state depended on the ability of the individual king. As for the people, they counted on the ability of the king as the 'giver of good fortune'. Some Buddhist canons express the great importance of the king's role in the following ways.[7] 'If the king rules the state properly, there will be timely rain, crops will be abundant, people will live long and be beautiful, there will be no lawsuits, and there will be no need for courthouses. If the king rules unlawfully, the opposite situations will arise and the people will suffer endless fear and misfortune.'

Furthermore, the following words reflect the strength of the kingship in its developmental stage.[8] 'The king conquers the earth by violence and controls all the territory up to the sea. But he is not satisfied with owning just this side of the sea and seeks to gain the other side also.'

The Buddhists feared the unlimited exercise of power of a king with such character and created the following kind of legend regarding the origin of kingship.[9] In ancient times, human beings were slaves of their desires and fought amongst themselves. The world fell into chaos. So the people came together, selected a person who excelled in appearance and ability, and decided to have their lives and wealth protected by him on the condition of handing him over a certain amount of the harvest as tax. In this way, the first king named Mahāsammata (the Great Selected) was born with rights over jurisdiction and exercise of military power. Hence the king's duty is the protection of the people and maintenance of social order. A king who does not do this duty properly is fated to be ousted by the people.

In the Buddhist canon, the correct administration by the king is called 'administration according to dharma'. Dharma is one of the basic concepts in Indian thought which means justice, truth, duty, and is also used to refer to 'Buddha's teachings'. Dharma that should be followed by a king is the duty of the king mentioned above. Buddhists call the ideal king, who rules over the world on earth according to dharma, '*cakravartin* (king who turns the wheel of justice)'. The concept of king's dharma (*rājadharma*) is discussed in more detail in the orthodox Brahmanical texts of later ages.

ORGANIZATION OF GOVERNMENT AND ECONOMIC BASIS

Let us now deal with the second (organization of government) and sixth (army) elements out of the seven.

In tribal states, members of the tribe mainly supported the chief or king in administrative and military affairs. As opposed to this, a group of 'individuals' who were dissociated from their tribes supported kings of Magadha such as Bimbisāra and Ajātaśatru. They became the king's vassals as their abilities were recognized. Among the influential men who served Bimbisāra or Ajātaśatru, there were the Brahmin chief minister Vassakāra (Varṣakāra) and the doctor Jīvaka, who both belonged to tribes or varṇa different from the king's. The same was probably true for the minister Sunidha, and the chief treasurer who was the father of Kumbhaghosaka. Bandhula who served King Prasenajit of Kosala and his nephew Dīgha-Kārāyaṇa were talented generals hailing from the neighbouring state of the Mallas.

At the uppermost rank of the organization of government was a group of high officials whose generic title was amātya (*amacca*) or *mahāmātra* (*mahāmatta*). They were called by titles according to their office, such as minister of law (*vinicchaya-amacca*), minister of general affairs (*sabbatthaka-mahāmatta*), minister of finance (*gaṇaka-mahāmatta*), and the chamberlain (*upacāraka-mahāmatta*). It seems that influential persons among the ministers became members of the council of king's advisers (*pariṣad*). Below the ministers were middle-level officials who were in charge of finances and administration, and at the bottom were lower-level officials who did work such as collecting taxes in the cities and villages. The army consisted of four forces (*caturaṅga*), namely elephants, chariots, cavalry, and infantry, led by the general (*senāpati*). The king often appointed soldiers irrespective of their place of birth and position in the varṇa social system in order to maintain a strong army. In the Jātaka there is a story of archers complaining when they came to know that an archer from a distant country was appointed by the king with a high salary (Jātaka No. 80) and a story of a man excelling in martial arts who goes to see a king to apply for position (Jātaka No. 181). These are anecdotes in the Buddhist canon, but it can be said that they give an account of a certain aspect of the kingdom at that time. In Jain literature, it is said that King Ajātaśatru of Magadha used new weapons of mass destruction such as great catapult and mace-attached chariot in the war against the Licchavis.[10] The drastic use of such new tactics was no doubt possible in Magadha because it was free from old traditions.

Regarding the third (city), fourth (territory or province), and fifth (treasury) elements, it can be said in a few words that the kingdom, with the king at the apex, was sustained by the various taxes paid by the inhabitants of the cities and villages. Rājagṛha, the capital of Magadha, was a centre of commercial activities. There, the propertied citizens generically called *gṛhapati* (*gahapati*), influential persons among them called *sārthavāha* (*satthavāha*, traders), and the citizens' representative called *śreṣṭhin* (*seṭṭhi*) took part in almost unrestricted economic activities as 'individuals', free from restrictions of tribes and varṇa social system.[11] Out of these people, there were many who rejected Brahmanical thought, which looked down upon trade, and embraced new religions such as Buddhism, which rightly valued their economic activities. Buddha and Jina (the founder of Jainism) used to carry out their ascetic practices and religious propagation by accepting support from these traders in cities where there was freedom of thought and action. The urban traders established a kind of guild organization called *śreṇi* (*seṇi*) and *pūga* and often worked in collaboration. Artisans, such as jewellers, ivory craftsmen, weavers, carpenters, and leather-workers, also organized similar groups. The strengthening of kingship in Magadha was a response to the expectations of the urban traders who were expanding their activities beyond the boundaries of tribal systems and territorial borders, and of the craftsmen who supported the traders' activities by production, and also of the new religious organizations which were in the process of expansion.

The autocratic kingship of Magadha also responded to the expectations of the local people by preventing the threat of enemy invasion and bringing about order and stability in the local society.

In the middle and lower Ganga valley during this period, the cultivation of forest areas was in progress. Sometimes there were even state-level projects for creating settlements.[12] There were many people who had left the ties of tribes and varṇa among those who participated in the cultivation. A new order was established in the villages newly formed by such people that replaced the tribal social order (based on blood relations) found in the old type of villages. This was an organization centred on the influential class, known generically by the same name as the urban wealthy person, gṛhapati, and their representative was in charge of the maintenance of village order as the village head (*grāmika/gāmika*). The development of Magadha was mainly sustained by the productive activities of these new villages situated on fertile lands. In the Buddhist canon, there is a story about King Bimbisāra bringing together 80,000 village heads in his kingdom,[13] and another about the tax-collector who measured paddy fields using a rope (Jātaka No. 276). The historical value of these anecdotes are less, but it can be said that they provide historical evidence of the fact that the king used to rule over the villages through village heads and collect taxes through a considerably well organized tax collection system. The establishment of territorial borders became more important for the state than ever before. This was because the strength or weakness of the state was determined by the number of villages within its territory. The account in the Buddhist canon regarding war between Magadha and Kosala over the acquisition of one village in the ruined kingdom of Kāsi symbolically illustrates this situation.

TRIBAL STATES (*GAṆA-SAṄGHA* STATES)

There were two states among the Sixteen Mahājanapadas that adopted the tribal form of government. One, the state of Vṛjis, was the alliance of various tribes such as the Videhas and Vṛjis, centring on the Licchavis. The other was the state of the Mallas. There was no man of power corresponding to a 'king' in either of these states and there existed collective government by influential members of the ruling tribe. This kind of state was referred to as *gaṇa* or *saṅgha*, which meant 'community' and 'group'. European and Indian historians have referred to this Gaṇa-Saṅgha state as a republic or oligarchy. As a form of government, this kind of state is placed at a stage before the formation of kingship, but it also contains elements which can be seen as the beginning of the birth of kingship.[14] Neither the Licchavis (often confused with the Vṛjis) nor the Mallas appear in the literature of the early Vedic period. There is a dispute among scholars about whether they were Aryan tribes who migrated from west while maintaining the tribal form of organization, or indigenous non-Aryan peoples. In a legend of origin, it is said that they belonged to the royal line of the Aryan Ikṣvākus, but I think that it would be more appropriate to consider them as Aryanized indigenous peoples due to the same reasons as in the case of the Śākyas, which I will go on to discuss below.

The Licchavis

The capital of the state of this tribe was Vaiśālī, a city on the northern bank of the Ganga, where government was carried out by 7707 influential persons who referred to themselves as rājā (Jātaka Nos 149, 301). Rājā is a term which means 'king', but in this case it can be seen as referring to the kshatriya status that was in charge of political and military affairs. The Licchavis, who were the indigenous people of this region, had probably adopted the status order of the varṇa social system promoted by orthodox Brahmins and called themselves rājā (kshatriya) in the process of Aryanization. The number 7707 was used for convenience and may be interpreted as referring to 'a large number'. In other words, the heads of households of the Licchavis who had the title of rājā ruled collectively in this Gaṇa-Saṅgha state. For a member of the Licchavis to gain the status of rājā, he had to perform *abhiṣeka* (water-sprinkling ceremony) in a special pond (Jātaka No. 465). In the Northern Buddhist canon, Mahāvastu (I, 254–71), there is a passage describing the diplomatic contact between the state of the Licchavis and the state of Magadha facing each other with the river Ganga between them. There it is said that the former was represented by the inhabitants of the city of Vaiśālī (many rājās) and the latter by the king of Magadha.

The centre of political, economic, and cultural activities of the Licchavis was the meeting place called *santhāgāra*. The rājās gathered there regularly, discussed state politics, competed in martial arts, and invited and received the teachings of religious guides such as Buddha. The proceedings of the meetings were carried out according to set procedures by elected representatives. The fact that these procedures were very well organized can be seen in the rules of the Buddhist order laid down in the Vainaya Piṭaka, which were presumably influenced by them. For instance, we can see such influence in the arrangements regarding convocation, qualification of membership, proceedings, principle of unanimity, mediation or decision by majority as the second best, and so on. Moreover, in the annotative literature of later periods, it is mentioned of the judicial system of the Licchavis that seven stages of trials were required before the sentence was decided for a suspected thief. It is difficult to imagine that such a complicated procedure was actually followed in practice, but it tells us something about the nature of the Gaṇa-Saṅgha state.[15]

The Mallas

There is very little material that gives an account of the Mallas who adopted the Gaṇa-Saṅgha system. According to the Buddhist canon, the santhāgāra was also the centre of all the activities of this tribe. In those days, the Mallas were divided into two groups based in the two towns of Pāvā and Kuśinagara (Kusināra). It is said that Buddha was invited by the Pāvā Mallas as the first person to use the new santhāgāra.[16] When Buddha decided to enter nirvāṇa in Kuśinagara, he sent his disciple Ānanda to the Mallas residing there. At that time, they were in the middle of a meeting in the meeting place, but when they heard the news, they suspended their meeting and all went to bid farewell to Buddha taking their family members along. Ānanda went to the santhāgāra of Kuśinagara again after Buddha's nirvāṇa. It is said that they suspended their discussion when they heard the news and began to prepare for the funeral.[17]

The Characteristics of Gaṇa-Saṅgha State

The meetings of the Licchavis and the Mallas were probably presided over by persons chosen from particularly influential families of rājās. For instance, it was the most influential rājā who passed the sentence in the final seventh stage of the judicial system among the Licchavis mentioned above. However, he was no more than the representative of his fellows and his authority was not the same as 'kingship'. It is said that persons called *uparājā* (probably rājā's eldest son), senāpati (general), and *bhāṇḍāgārika* (official in charge of administration of property) lived in same numbers as the rājās in the city of Vaiśālī (Jātaka No. 149). However, it is unlikely that each rājā had retainers with such titles. It is reasonable to interpret this account as pointing to a certain degree of stratification within the tribe. It is also said that in Buddha's funeral, eight chiefs (*pramukha/pamukha/pāmokkha*) of the Mallas carried the body and four chiefs tried to light the funeral pyre.[18] In this, we can also find evidence of a certain degree of stratification.

Gaṇa-Saṅgha states vigorously resisted invasion from neighbouring kingdoms. It is said that Buddha took the example of the Vṛjis (the Licchavis) and gave the following seven reasons to explain the strength of this kind of state:[19]

(1) They hold meetings often and many people gather together.
(2) They act in cooperation with each other.
(3) They do not break traditional laws and do not establish new laws aimlessly.
(4) They respect the elders and listen to their words.
(5) They do not force or act violently against their women.
(6) They worship the tumulus or shrines (*caitya/cetiya*) both inside and outside the cities and never let the offerings be exhausted.
(7) They welcome and protect those who have completed their spiritual practices (*arahant*).

In order to weaken this powerful Gaṇa-Saṅgha state, it was necessary to destroy the tribe's solidarity from the inside. It is said that Ajātaśatru of Magadha fought against the Licchavis as he aimed to gain ground in the northern bank of the Ganga. When he failed in achieving his aim, he changed his strategy to disturbing the internal affairs through conspiracy. This was successful and he destroyed the powerful enemy. The strategy involved bringing about a split between the rājās by pointing out the unequal distribution of wealth and so on.[20] The desire for private property among the inhabitants of Vaiśālī made the continuation of the Gaṇa-Saṅgha system impossible. This stage was supposed to lead to the formation of kingship, but in the case of the Licchavis, this formation was prevented due to annexation by Magadha which had developed a powerful kingship.

The Licchavis continued to maintain their tribal organization and remained as a local power. According to the Arthaśāstra (XI, 1, 5), this tribe, along with the Vṛjis and the Mallas, was known as 'those who live calling themselves rājā (kṣatriya) (*rājaśabdopajīvin*)'. In the Manusmṛti (X, 22), they are referred to as 'inferior kshatriya (*vrātya-kṣatriya*)' just as the Mallas are.

The Śākyas

Although the Śākyas do not belong to the Sixteen Mahājanapadas, I would like to discuss this tribe into which Buddha was born. This tribe called itself kshatriya and lived in the hilly regions at the foot of the Himalayas in the present-day border area between India and Nepal. According to the story of origin given in the Buddhist canon, their ancestry can be traced back as far as the first king of the human race, Mahāsammata. It is also said that the four princes of the famous house of Ikṣvāku (Okkāka) of the Aryan solar race (*Sūryavaṃśa*), moved to the Himalayan foothills after being expelled from their country, married their half-sisters and founded the basis of later prosperity.[21] However, some scholars of history throw doubt on these Buddhist legends which say that the Śākyas were a distinguished Aryan tribe. I also think that the Śākyas were rather an influential indigenous agricultural tribe who had assimilated Aryan culture and called themselves kshatriyas. The reasons for this can be given as follows:

(1) The name of this tribe cannot be found in the early Vedic literature.
(2) There were Brahmins living inside the territory but people did not place importance on the Brahmanical rituals and maintained their indigenous beliefs, such as tree worship and caitya (tumulus or shrine) worship.
(3) They were critical of the privileged position of Brahmins in the status system.
(4) They enthusiastically accepted non-Brahmanical religions such as Buddhism.

These reasons also apply to the neighbouring Koliyas as well as the Licchavis and the Mallas mentioned above.

According to Buddhist legends of later ages, Śuddhodana, the father of Buddha (Gautama Siddhārtha), was the king of the Śākyas, and Gautama had spent his days living in splendour as the prince and heir to the throne. However, according to the early Buddhist canons, the situation was quite different. The Śākyas adopted the Gaṇa-Saṅgha form of government whose members called themselves rājā (kshatriya) and discussed matters regarding domestic affairs and diplomacy with each other in the santhāgāra.[22] They probably did not have sufficient organization to become a state and were dependent on the powerful neighbouring state of Kosala in the south-west. The influential persons among the Śākyas lived in the small city of Kapilavastu and the general members probably lived scattered in their respective villages.

There is an incident which gives an insight into the organization of the Śākyas. This was a dispute over the use of the water from the river Rohiṇī with the neighbouring Koliyas. The news regarding the dispute, which began as a fight between the subordinate labourers (*karmakaras*) of both tribes, reached the rājās after having been reported to the notables (amātyas) of the Śākyas. The rājās then decided to make war and began to prepare for battle (Jātaka No. 536). There are also accounts which say that the Śākyas were led by one or a few influential rājās. For instance, Śuddhodana, the father of Gautama, and Bhaddiya who was called the king of the Śākyas (Śākyarājā) and is said to have behaved like a king before his renunciation.[23] If this is the case, the government of the Śākyas was at a stage just before tribal kingship. Needless to say, the authority of neither could be called 'royal'. Emergency situations, such as the dispute over water with the Koliyas and the diplomatic problem with the kingdom of Kosala, were dealt with by Śākya rājās as a group and there is no appearance of a rājā invested with leadership corresponding to that of a king.

STATES UNDER TRIBAL KINGSHIP

The States of the Kurus and the Pañcālas

The name of the Kurus appears for the first time in the later Vedic literature. However, it seems that the origin of this tribe can be traced back to an influential Aryan tribe in the early Vedic period. Scholars consider that tribes such as the Bharatas and the Pūrus of the early Vedic period were united to form the powerful Kuru tribe in the later Vedic period.[24] According to legend, they strengthened the kingship and grew to be a powerful force in the upper Ganga valley in the days of a chief named Kuru. The central city was Hastināpura, and Indraprastha (around present-day Delhi) on the banks of the river Yamunā was the sub-centre. The famous Mahābhārata war originated from an internal dispute between two groups of princes, the Kauravas and the Pāṇḍavas, over territory. After this great war, the royal line of the Kurus continued to flourish with Hastināpura as the capital and bore the great king Parikṣit, and his son Janamejaya who performed great Brahmanical sacrifices such as *aśvamedha* (horse sacrifice). In this period, the upper Ganga valley, which included the dwelling place of the Kurus, was the centre of Brahmanical culture. The later Vedic literature was compiled, Vedic rituals were developed, and the varṇa social system with the Brahmin at the apex was established on this land. It is also in this region at this period that various rituals were developed for strengthening kingship. This region was really the birthplace of early kingship in ancient India.

It is said that the royal line of Kurus (Paurava dynasty in the Purāṇa literature) moved the capital to Kauśāmbī 300 km downstream because the previous capital Hastināpura was damaged by flooding of the Ganga during the period of King Nicakṣu. Since then, the royal line continued on this land in the middle Ganga valley and by Buddha's time Kauśāmbī was the capital of the powerful state of Vatsa. After the transfer of the capital, the state named Kuru still existed in the upper Ganga valley and was counted as one of the Sixteen Mahājanapadas. However, it seems that it did not develop beyond a small kingdom and its history is hardly known.

In the south-east of the state of the Kurus was the state of the Pañcālas.[25] The name of the Pañcālas who were the dominant tribe of this kingdom appears in the later Vedic literature just as the name of the Kurus does. Since '*pañca*' means 'five', legends exist from the olden times pointing to the origin of this state as a union of five tribes or five clans related to influential tribes in the early Vedic period. The state of the Pañcālas was divided from its early stage into north Pañcāla with the capital Ahicchatrā and south Pañcāla with the capital Kāmpilya. Moreover, the Kurus and the Pañcālas seem to have been closely related and are often found in the literature in a combined form as 'Kuru-Pañcāla'. The Pañcālas, like the Kurus, adopted kingship in its early stages. According to legend, King Śoṇa-Sātrāsāha who performed the aśvamedha, King Durmukha who is known as a conqueror, and King Pravāhaṇa-Jaivali, the great philosopher, appeared one after another. However, in reality, as in the case of the Kurus, kingship did not develop sufficiently and though it is counted as one of the Sixteen Mahājanapadas in Buddha's time, it did not reveal any prominent activities.

Stagnation in Kingship and the State

It is notable that later on there was hardly any development of kingship and the state in the upper Ganga valley, the birthplace of kingship.

According to the Buddhist canons, there were kings in the states of the Kurus and the Pañcālas during the time of Buddha, but as I have discussed above, their powers were weak and their activities were not remarkable. And both states were conquered by the Nanda dynasty of Magadha in the middle of the fourth century BC. The reason why the Purāṇa literature criticizes the Nandas as 'annihilating all kṣatriyas'[26] is probably because it deplored the way in which this dynasty of *Śūdra* origin strengthened its kingship and destroyed the states in the upper Ganga valley which had been maintaining the tradition of kshatriya dynasties.

In the Arthaśāstra (XI, 1, 5), which gives an account of the political situation during the early period of Mauryan dynasty to some extent, the Kurus and the Pañcālas are included in the list of 'those who live calling themselves rājā (kṣatriya)' along with the Licchavis and the Mallas mentioned above. It seems that after they lost their independence, kshatriyas of this region adopted the Gaṇa-Saṅgha system of government. The Manu-smṛti (VII, 193) recommends using warriors (kshatriyas) from the Kuru-Pañcāla region as the vanguard in battle. In other words, in the Kuru-Pañcāla region in the upper Ganga valley, those of kshatriya status maintained political and military roles over a long period but there was no development of kingship and state.

Why then was there no further development of kingship in the upper Ganga valley? The answer to this question can be found by comparing this region with the middle and lower Ganga valley where mighty kingdoms were formed.

As I have already mentioned, the lower Ganga valley where Magadha flourished was a newly developing area blessed with rich natural resources. Moreover, it was located in the eastern frontier of the Aryan world and was relatively free from the status order of the varṇa social system and Brahmanical tradition. In the cities, traders accumulated wealth through economic activities without prejudice of the varṇa social system, and the king made efforts to increase his power almost ignoring the constraints of the tribal tradition and the varṇa social system. What is more, new philosophies, starting with Buddhism and Jainism, were born one after another denying orthodox Brahmanical thought.

As opposed to this, in the upper Ganga valley, orthodox Brahmanical thought remained influential and conservative societies existed which strongly maintained the tradition of the varṇa social system. The strengthening of kingship beyond limits was prevented by Brahmins who emphasized their superiority in the status order. Moreover, a marked development of kingship was also prevented by kshatriyas who tried to protect their exclusive status in political and military affairs while maintaining the tribal tradition. 'Those who live calling themselves rājā' in the Arthaśāstra probably belonged to this conservative military class. Furthermore, the development of trade in the cities was suppressed by the concept of varṇa status which discriminated against traders and their activities. As a natural result of all these factors, there was no development of a kingdom beyond a particular region. States there maintained the old kind of tribal kingship and were destined to be conquered by the new eastern kingdom of Magadha.

SUMMARY

In this paper, I took up five states from the Sixteen Mahājanapadas and analysed the relationship between their forms of government and kingship. The five states I discussed were Magadha which developed an autocratic kingship, the states of the Licchavis and the Mallas which were at a stage before kingship formation, and the states of the Kurus and the Pañcālas which remained at the stage of tribal kingship. It is not possible to add comments regarding the other eleven states due to lack of space. However, as a conclusion, it can be said that kingship in these states may be seen in terms of their place in a continuum between the autocratic monarchy of Magadha on the one end and the Gaṇa-Saṅgha system of the Licchavis and the Mallas on the other. In Figure 1.1, I have tried to show the approximate positions of each state in their stage of development of kingship, keeping in mind that there are differences in the dates of their rise and fall. However, these states did not all necessarily proceed towards strengthening kingship (going upwards according to the diagram), and sometimes showed tendencies of becoming tribal republics (going downwards according to the diagram). And, as I have repeatedly said, these states lost their independence one after another with the development of the kingdom of Magadha and finally they all merged into the territory of the Mauryan empire. I have also shown this process on the diagram with straight lines and arrows.

ADDITIONAL WORDS: LATER DEVELOPMENTS

After the collapse of the Mauryan empire at the beginning of the second century BC, many indigenous forces gained power in various parts of north India. These indigenous powers maintained their power while

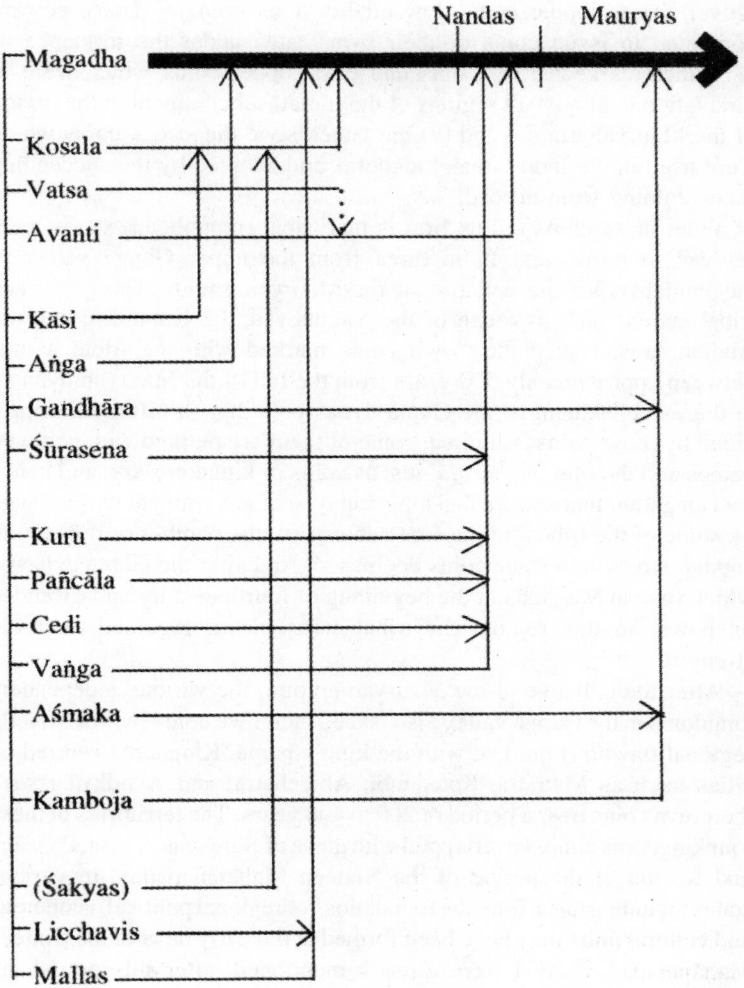

FIG. 1.1: From Sixteen States to the Mauryan Empire

having all kinds of relationships, namely independence, subordination, opposition, and alliance with various races who came from Central Asia and dominated north-west and central India (Indo-Greeks, Śakas, Pahlavas, Kuṣāṇas, etc.). The history of these indigenous powers can be seen not from documents but mainly from the coins they issued (silver coins, copper coins, low quality alloy coins).[27] These powers competed to issue coins of their own states under the influence of (1) punch-marked silver coins and cast copper coins which were in circulation in almost all regions of the Indian subcontinent in the period of the Mauryan empire and (2) the Greek style die-struck coins which were used in the Indo-Greek kingdoms and adopted by the succeeding races coming from abroad.

What these coins tell us first is that tribal (republican) states were revived in north-west India (area from the upper Ganga valley to the Punjab) after the collapse of the Mauryan empire. Over fourteen tribal states, such as those of the Yaudheyas, the Kuṇindas, and the Audumbaras, issued their own coins marked with the tribal names between approximately 500 years from the fall of the Mauryan dynasty to the establishment of the Gupta dynasty. Although information provided by these coins is limited, some of them are marked with personal names and the title '*mahārājā*' just as coins of kingdoms are, and hence we can gather that some tribal kingship type of government was adopted by some of the tribes. In the first century AD, the number of tribes with enough strength to issue coins decreased. And after the Gupta dynasty, which rose in Magadha at the beginning of fourth century and extended its power to this region, the tribal states never regained their old strength.

After the collapse of the Mauryan empire, the various independent kingdoms in the Ganga valley also issued their own coins (with distinctly regional flavours) marked with the king's name. Kingdoms centred on cities such as Mathurā, Kauśāmbī, Ahicchatrā, and Ayodhyā issued their own coins over a period of 200 to 400 years. The territories of these four kingdoms almost overlapped with those of Śūrasena, Vatsa, Pañcāla, and Kosala of the period of the Sixteen Mahājanapadas. In various states including these four, the foundations of regional political, economic, and cultural units may have been formed at the early days of the Sixteen Mahājanapadas. As I have already mentioned, after this period, all states were conquered by Magadha and came under its domination. However, even during the period of unification of north India under the Nanda and the Maurya dynasties, the particular characteristics of each region were maintained along with the common characteristics found in all regions of north India. In the period of disunity after the collapse of the empire, each region rose again as a political, economic, and cultural unit. The manifestation and latency of regional characteristics were to be repeated in the period after the Gupta dynasty.

NOTES

1. Regarding the Sixteen Mahājanapadas, see H. Raychaudhuri, 1972, *Political History of Ancient India*, 7th edn, Calcutta: University of Calcutta, pp. 85–210; Hajime Nakamura, 1997, *History of India 1* (Collected Works of Hajime Nakamura, definitive edn, 5), in Japanese, Tokyo: Shunjusha, pp. 261–517. For the history of development of state and kingship in ancient India, see R.S. Sharma, 1968, *Aspects of Political Ideas and Institutions in Ancient India*, 2nd revised edn, Delhi: Motilal Banarsidass; R. Thapar, 1984, *From Lineage to State: Social Formations in the Mid-First Millennium B.C. in the Ganga Valley*, Bombay: Oxfod University Press (Japanese translation by G. Yamazaki and A. Narusawa, Tokyo: Hosei University Press, 1986); K. Roy, 1994, *The Emergence of Monarchy in North India, Eighth to Fourth Centuries BC*, New Delhi: Oxford University Press.

2. Aṅguttara-Nikāya (PTS ed.), Vol. I, p. 212.

3. Regarding the state of Magadha, see B.P. Sinha (ed.), 1974, *The Comprehensive History of Bihar*, Vol. 1, Part 1, Patna: Kashiprasad Jayaswal Research Institute, pp. 299–419; H. Raychaudhuri, *op. cit.*, pp. 166–210; H. Nakamura, *op. cit.*, pp. 388–413. For names of kings and persons given in the Buddhist canons mentioned in this paper, see G.P. Malalasekera, 1960, *Dictionary of Pāli Proper Names*, 2 Vols, London: Luzac.

4. F.E. Pargiter, 1962, *The Purāṇa Text of the Dynasties of the Kali Age*, 2nd edn, Varanasi: Chowkhamba Sanskrit Series Office, pp. 20–2, 68–9.

5. For the date of Buddha's nirvāṇa, see H. Bechert (ed.), 1991–7, *The Dating of the Historical Buddha*, 3 parts, Göttingen: Vandenhoeck & Ruprecht; G. Yamazaki, 1995, 'The Lists of the Patriarchs in the Northern and Southern Legends', ibid., Part 1, pp. 313–32; H. Bechert (ed.), 1995, *When Did the Buddha Live? The Controversy on the Dating of the Historical Buddha*, Delhi: Sri Satguru Publications; A.K. Narain (ed.), 2003, *The Date of the Historical Śākyamuni Buddha*, Delhi: B.R. Publishing Corporation.

6. G. Yamazaki, 1994, *Kingship and Religion in Ancient India—Kings and Brahmans* (in Japanese), Tokyo: Tosui Shobo, pp. 87–104, 195–219.

7. Aṅguttara-Nikāya II, pp. 74–6. Jātaka Nos 77, 151, 194, 276, 334, 520.

8. Thera-Gāthā, v. 777.

9. Aggañña-Suttanta. Dīgha-Nikāya (PTS ed.), III, pp. 84–93; Mahāvastu, Senart (ed.), Luzac, I, pp. 338–48.

10. A.L. Basham, 1951, *History and Doctrines of the Ājīvikas, a Vanished Indian Religion*, London: Luzac, pp. 69–70.

11. For an account of cities and urban life at the time, see G. Yamazaki, 1987, *Society in Ancient India—Social Structure and Middle and Low Classes* (in Japanese), Tokyo: Tosui Shobo, pp. 155–209.

12. For an account of villages and rural life at the time, see ibid., pp. 211–67.

13. Vinaya-Piṭaka (PTS ed.), I, p. 179.

14. For an account of tribal republic system, see B.C. Law, 1922, *Kshatriya Clans in Buddhist India*, reprinted, Delhi: Indian Bibliographic Bureau, 1987; J.P. Sharma, 1968, *Republics in Ancient India, c. 1500 BC–500 BC*, Leiden: E.J. Brill; H.N. Jha, 1970, *The Licchavis of Vaiśālī*, Varanasi: Chowkhamba Sanskrit Series Office.

15. B.C. Law, *op. cit.*, pp. 120–1; H.N. Jha, *op. cit.*, pp. 84–5.

16. Saṅgīti-Suttanta. Dīgha-Nikāya III, pp. 207–9.

17. Mahā-Parinibbāna-Suttanta. Dīgha-Nikāya II, pp. 147–8, 158–9.

18. Ibid., pp. 159–64.

19. Ibid., pp. 73–6.

20. B.C. Law, *op. cit.*, pp. 130–6. The Arthaśāstra devotes the whole of the eleventh book on the question of *Saṅgha* (tribal powers) and the tactics how the king should deal with these kinds of powers (Arthaśāstra XI, 1, 1–56).

21. Ambaṭṭha-Sutta. Dīgha-Nikāya I, pp. 92–3.

22. Ibid., p. 91. Jātaka No. 465.

23. Vinaya-Piṭaka II, pp. 181–4. Jātaka No. 10.

24. Regarding the Kuru state, see H. Raychaudhuri, *op. cit.*, pp. 11–43, 63–4, 120–1.

25. Regarding the Pañcāla state, see ibid., pp. 64–8, 121–3; K.M. Shrimali, 1983, *History of Pañcāla, to c. AD 550*, 2 Vols, New Delhi: Munshiram Manoharlal, pp. 1–54.

26. F.E. Pargiter, *op. cit.*, pp. 26, 69.

27. Regarding the coins of this period, see M.K. Sharan, 1972, *Tribal Coins, A Study*, New Delhi: Abhinav Publications; K.K. Dasgupta, 1974, *A Tribal History of Ancient India, A Numismatic Approach,* Calcutta: Nababharat Publishers; B. Lahiri, 1974, *Indigenous States of Northern India, c. 200 BC to 300 AD*, Calcutta: University of Calcutta; S.R. Goyal, 1994, *Indigenous Coins of Early India*, Jodhpur: Kusumanjali Prakashan; G. Yamazaki, 1994, 'On the Tribal Coins of Ancient India' (in Japanese), *Kokugakuin Daigaku Kiyo* (Kokugakuin University Review), Vol. 34, pp. 1–24; *idem*, 1999, 'Coins of Indigenous Kingdoms of Northern India in the Post-Mauryan Age' (in Japanese), ibid., Vol. 37, pp. 37–59.

CHAPTER 2

The Integrative Model of State Formation in Early Medieval India

Some Historiographic Remarks[1]

Hermann Kulke

In the Introduction to *The State in India 1000–1700*[2] I had tried to analyse various theories and debates on the pre-modern state in India by identifying five basic models. According to their dates of origin, these models were the colonial and Marxian twin models of oriental despotism and Asiatic mode of production, which were followed and countered by the unitary or imperial state model of Indian national historiography. Although this model 'still dominates the literature',[3] at least as far as the number of publications in India is concerned, its 'hegemony' over the sometimes rather heated debates on the nature of the Indian state has been contested during the last decades by three new models. The lead was taken in the early 1960s by R.S. Sharma's Indian feudalism model, followed in the late 1970s by B. Stein's and S. Blake's models of the segmentary and the patrimonial-bureaucratic state.[4] Through the introduction of these three models, the debate on the Indian state reached a new scientific historiographical level. Even though they raised several issues of crucial importance for the understanding of the Indian history for the first time, such as, 'urban decay' or the economic and political role of land donations to religious institutions, their major disadvantage was the application of the idea of a full-fledged early Indian state to the analysis of the early medieval or medieval Indian state. Sanjay Subrahmanyam therefore rightly complained about 'the dependence of the historiography of received models', especially from Europe and to a lesser extent from Africa.[5] Nevertheless there can be no doubt that it was mainly through these two 'received models' from Europe and Africa of feudalism and the segmentary state that the existence of diachronic structural changes of state formation on the one hand and synchronic or spatial differentiation of state performance on the other hand were fully realized. Both theories, despite the heated debates between their main protagonists, R.S. Sharma and B. Stein,[6] brought to a virtual end the concepts of a '(historically) unchanging India' and of '(spatially) unitary states' in pre-modern India, although the vast majority of Indian PhD theses on early medieval India still seem to follow the national parameters of unchanging greatness of unitary regional statehood.

Since the mid-1980s, however, a paradigmatic change emerged from the studies of a number of scholars who, although influenced by, and partly even involved in the ongoing debate on Indian feudalism and the segmentary state, are reluctant to subscribe to any of the above theories. A major emphasis of their works is the study of processes of state formation rather than the state as a given entity in early medieval India. Their contributions were therefore classed as a 'non-aligned' group of conceptual studies.[7]

Important issues of these studies were social formations and local and sub-regional pre-state and tribal origins of early medieval state formation. In the context of early historic north India, R.S. Sharma's and R. Thapar's contributions on material development, social formations, and the early state in the first millennium BC had already prepared the ground for these studies.[8] Central India followed suit with the studies of S. Seneviratne, A. Parasher-Sen, and B.D. Chattopadhyaya.[9] The study of the tribal context of early medieval and medieval state formation in eastern and central India had been initiated several decades ago by S. Sinha's famous paper on Rajputization in central India which was followed more recently by the edition of an impressive anthology of papers on 'Tribal Polities and State Systems'.[10] N. Dirks' seminal ethnohistoric studies on the Little Kingdom in South India initiated an important paradigmatic change as they shift the focus of historical research from the centre to the much neglected periphery of late medieval and early modern regional kingdoms.[11] Dirks was followed by G. Berkemer, B. Schnepel, and A. Tanabe who modified, extended, and thus established Dirks' Little Kingdom concept as another seminal conceptual tool for the analysis of state formation at the Hindu-tribal frontier of eastern India.[12]

Another focus of these 'non-aligned' studies is the analysis of political processes and structural changes within regional states. Whereas the theories of the segmentary and the patrimonial-bureaucratic states and of Indian feudalism allocate their respective states to very different positions on a continuum of governance formation, they are reluctant to concede structural changes in the historical development of their 'model states'. Well-known examples of the difficulties faced by adherents of a specific theory were B. Stein's vacillating attempts to define Vijayanagara either as a segmentary or as a proto-patrimonial-bureaucratic state and the rather unsuccessful attempts of proponents of Indian feudalism to explain through their own model the fading away of feudalism in India in the thirteenth century.[13] For the study of 'Political Processes and Structure of Polity in Early Medieval India', B.D. Chattopadhyaya's Presidential Address to the Indian History Congress held at Burdwan in December 1983 was a major breakthrough.[14] As meanwhile it has become a key paper and will be referred to in some more detail below, suffice it here to mention that it emphasized various political processes as major features of regional state formation and thus reintroduced the political realm into a debate which had been dominated largely by socio-economic issues. The analysis of political development and structural change was particularly impressive in the case of the Chola state which, ironically, had also formed the very base of B. Stein's segmentary state theory. Y. Subbarayalu's and J. Heitzman's careful analyses enable us to form a differentiated picture of the Chola state, both in its diachronic historical development and its synchronic or spatial dimension.[15] Heitzman shows a remarkable increase of local penetration through royal orders under the 'imperial Cholas and a greater concentration of tax-collecting power of superior central agencies as well as a decline of the importance of cesses collected and officially controlled by village authorities' in the eleventh century. But, on the other hand, he also stresses 'the rapid decrease in the penetration of all aspects of royal influence with increasing distance from the centre of the polity. Even within the outer reaches of Cholamandalam, the core area of an extended polity, the kings were more likely to strike deals with local leadership than to implement a centralized administrative apparatus'. Heitzman thus emphasizes against B. Stein the dynamics of vertical extension of the central state apparatus in the core area whereas he follows Stein's analysis of the territorial structure of the Chola state with its central, intermediate, and peripheral zones and their decreasing degree of 'royal presence'.

Subbarayalu contradicts the existence of these 'three inferential zones' and criticizes in this context the results of G.W. Spencer's and K.R. Hall's joint study which seems to confirm Stein's 'zones'.[16] His analysis of the Chola state is, to my mind, paradigmatic for the 'non-aligned' attempts to analyse structural dynamics of extension and contraction of early medieval regional states and therefore may be quoted at some length:

> We may summarise the growth of the Cōḷa state as follows. In the first century of its existence the Cōḷa state was a small kingdom claiming sovereign rights over a restricted territory. At this time wars were waged mainly to get tribute from vanquished rulers. No outside territory was annexed to the central area in the real sense. Locality bodies and groups enjoyed their traditional power without much governmental interference. With the close of the 10th century and with the accession of Rājarāja I the situation changed to a great extent. Clear attempts at centralisation of the political power were made by Rājarāja I and his immediate successors. Territorial reorganisation (creation of *vaḷanāḍu* and *maṇḍalam*), elaboration of the bureaucracy, land survey and new revenue settlements, government control of temples and *brahmadeyas*, mobilisation of a big standing army both for external aggression and for maintenance of internal order were some of the ways and means to achieve centralisation. This centralisation worked under three generations of able monarchs until the close of the 11th century. The same centralising trend could not continue in the 12th and 13th centuries due to socio-economic changes which led to the development of a feudal structure. [...] Centrifugal tendencies appeared in form of dispersed armies commanded by various locality chiefs and in the form of multiplicity of tax-collecting authorities. With a decrease in revenue flows from most parts of the empire, the governmental apparatus, the bureaucracy as well as the army, became diminished in size and importance. This phenomenon paved the way gradually for the decline and demise of the Cōḷa state.[17]

In his Heidelberg PhD thesis of 1986, S.K. Panda followed Subbarayalu's approach and came to rather similar conclusions in his study on the eastern Gangas of Orissa.[18] Particularly impressive is his concluding chapter 'From Kingdom to Empire' which depicts the incipient administrative development of Ganga rule during its 'pre'- and 'proto-imperial' phases, the temporary extension of the central state apparatus in the extended core area during the 'imperial phase', and its contraction during, the 'Twilight of the Empire'.

In this context of vertical and horizontal extension of royal authority, may I be permitted to introduce my own thoughts on state formation in early medieval India with a few rather personal remarks on their genesis and historiographical contexts? Trained as a student of 'classical' German Indology, I also read a bit of Marx and a lot of Max Weber in my minor subject of political science; in fact Weber's sociology of domination ('Soziologie der Herrschaft') was the major theme of my examinations in this subject. When a few years later in 1970, I was lucky to come to Orissa as a member of the former Orissa Research Project, my picture of the Indian state, I am afraid, was rather Indological as it has been well depicted quite recently by H. Scharfe.[19] But at the same time, Weber's 'Soziologie der Herrschaft' loomed large in my mind, particularly his deliberations on patrimonialism and the many devices a patrimonial ruler had to use in the process of extending his political authority beyond his patriarchal household. These seemingly contradicting perceptions of pre-modern statehood entered a very fruitful synthesis in my trying to understand the historical processes in early medieval and medieval Orissa. The most fascinating discovery in these days was the continuous existence of 'post-tribal' chieftaincies and small kingdoms throughout the history of Orissa rather than the certainly equally impressive rise of the Gajapati kingdom since the twelfth century which, of course, was the main concern of conventional historiography.

In this situation, three papers of B. Stein, R.S. Sharma, and G.W. Spencer proved to be of great heuristic value to my understanding of Orissa's early history. Luckily, Stein had just published his paper on the agrarian system of south India[20] in which for the first time he introduced his concept of nuclear areas (*nāḍu* and *periyanāḍu)* which he regarded as the 'central element' of the political system of south India until the thirteenth century. Sharma, too, in a paper on land system in medieval Orissa which he added as an appendix to his *Indian Feudalism*[21] speaks of congeries of territorial units under tribal chiefs. It was of particular relevance for my studies that, whereas in his Indian feudalism theory Sharma regards land grants and their Brahmin donees as major agents of 'feudal fragmentation' of the early medieval state of India, in his paper on Orissa he stresses their 'positive' effects on the process of state formation in the hinterland of coastal Orissa: 'The significance of land grants to brāhmaṇas is not difficult to appreciate. The grantees brought new knowledge which improved cultivation and inculcated in the aborigines a sense of loyalty to the established order upheld by the rulers, who could therefore dispense with the services of extra staff for maintaining law and order'. Spencer's seminal paper on Tanjore,[22] too, had just been published. It was another eye-opener during these days as it emphasized for the first time the political function of a great temple complex in an early medieval Indian kingdom,[23] a subject which soon became one of the central themes of the Orissa Research Project and its study of Puri and its Jagannath cult. For late medieval history of Orissa, particularly during Mughal rule, and for the processes of local state formation in tribal regions of eastern India, S. Sinha's above-mentioned paper on Rajputization was of equal importance.

On the basis of epigraphical studies and strongly influenced by these papers and by Weber's evolutionary paradigm of patrimonial state[24] formation, I wrote in the late 1970s a few papers on early state formation and social change ('Kshatriyazation') in the Hindu-tribal frontier region and on royal temple policy and the structure of medieval kingdoms.[25] Their major theme was the variety of modes of 'ritual policy' as a means of political integration and vertical and horizontal legitimization.[26] In the following years I began to systemize and extend these ideas in the broader context of early medieval Indian history. In the paper 'Fragmentation and Segmentation versus Integration?' I emphasized 'integration as a major factor of medieval Hindu kingdoms'[27] against the theories of Indian feudalism and the segmentary state. The inherent integrative element of medieval Hindu kingdoms was exemplified mainly by a stepwise territorial integration of Orissa's nuclear areas of incipient local state formation into the regional kingdom of the Gajapatis and by parallel processes of religious and ideological integration of local and sub-regional deities. In early 1983, at a conference at Heidelberg, I went a step further and outlined a model of regional state formation which attempts to correlate three successive stages of political development with three spatial spheres of concentric state formation.[28] This German paper is rather unknown so may I be permitted to quote at some length from its English summary:

> The three spatial parameters are (1) a nuclear area in the centre (usually a fertile riverine area), (2) its fringes or peripheral zones (usually mountainous or jungle areas) and (3) beyond them neighbouring core areas (usually also located in fertile areas). The variants of the time factor are determined by the historical process of a stepwise expansion of political authority radiating from the nuclear area into the peripheral zones and the neighbouring areas. The major political and structural differences between these three stages of state formation may be summarized as follows:
>
> The pristine *tribal/Hindu chieftaincy* consisted of a rather small nuclear area which had only limited relations with its peripheral zones.

Under the *early kingdom* the political authority expanded from the nuclear area into its hinterland. Some of the formerly independent neighbours became tributary chiefs or 'kings' (*sāmanta*). A major characteristic of the early kingdoms was their surrounding 'circle of tributary neighbours' (*sāmanta-cakra*) who remained outside the central administration and enjoyed a high degree of autonomy.

The *imperial regional kingdom* originated from a forcible unification of at least two major nuclear areas and their respective samanta-cakras. Within this considerably enlarged core area of the imperial kingdom, autonomous local dynasties usually ceased to exist. Some of the former feudatory or samanta states were transformed into provinces under centrally appointed governors. Local autonomous corporate institutions, however, continued to exist within and autonomous tributary kingdoms outside these enlarged imperial core areas. The cultural integration within these large core areas has to be regarded as the major heritage of the regional kingdoms. Some of them became the forerunners of the 'state regions' of contemporary India.

At a conference in Canberra in early 1984, I applied the concept of these three stages of early medieval state formation and its distinction of the 'Early and the Imperial Kingdom' to South-east Asia, too.[29] These terms were then used again in the translated and slightly revised version of the Heidelberg paper 'The Early and the Imperial Kingdom: A Processural Model of the Integrative State Formation in Early Medieval India', published in 1995 in *The State in India*.[30]

In the meantime, B.D. Chattopadhyaya had come up with a series of papers on various subjects like 'Irrigation in Early Medieval Rajasthan', 'Origin of Rajputs', and 'Trade and Urban Centres in Early Medieval North India'.[31] A major emphasis of these papers is the analysis of multiple local processes of socio-political changes which influenced and in some cases even may have caused trans-local state formation in post-Gupta and early medieval north India. Among the processes he depicts political expansion through agrarian extension, irrigation, peasantization, and 'castification' of tribes, the rise of local markets to urban centres with trans-local networks, the proliferation and spread of ruling lineages, etc. Although Chattopadhyaya cites various examples of superior ('royal') and external initiatives (such as, irrigation works and foreign traders), the evidence he produces leaves no doubt about the prevailing existence of 'local agency' till the late tenth century when state administration gained stronger influence on local affairs.

In 1983, Chattopadhyaya delivered his already mentioned Presidential Address of the Ancient India Section at the Indian History Congress at Burdwan. From its title, it is evident that he extended his studies on local and regional political processes to the pan-Indian level and its theoretical debates on early medieval state formation. He criticizes the 'construct of Indian feudalism' as a 'rather one-track argument, wholly centred around a particular value attached to the evidence of the land grants for the emergence of the [feudal] structure in pre-Gupta and Gupta times'. The model of the segmentary state, on the other hand, defines 'ritual sovereignty rather than political sovereignty as the major integrative factor', an attempt which Chattopadhyaya regards as a 'fine example of study of the State *sans* politics', an idea untenable in the context of supra-local polity. He instead suggests the study of political integration in the contexts of contemporary economic, social, and religious processes and mentions particularly agrarian extension, caste formation ('the horizontal spread of the dominant ideology of social order'), and the integration of local cults and sacred centres into a supra-local structure. 'Applied to the study of the political process, these parallels would suggest consideration of three levels: presence of established norms and nuclei of State society, horizontal spread of State society implying transformation of pre-State polities into State polities, and integration of local polities into structures that transcended the bounds of local polities' (p. 10). Chattopadhyaya therefore points out that 'the genesis of the specific features of early medieval polity cannot be satisfactorily comprehended either by isolating a single unit and analysing the relationship of its segments in ritual terms or by the notion of decentralised [feudal] polity in which bases of power are created from above through individual or institutional agents.... [Instead] the structure of early medieval polity was a logical development from territorially limited State society of the earlier historical period to a gradual but far greater penetration of State society into local agrarian and peripheral levels'. He concludes that state formation 'may thus be seen in terms of "integrative polity"'.[32]

In a more recent critical argumentation with the concept of feudalism, Chattopadhyaya concluded: 'In any case what this construct [of Indian feudalism] has bypassed almost totally, in failing to understand their implications for a study of the period 400–1200, are two major processes which characterize Indian history in general: (1) transformation of pre-state society, through what is generally called the process of state formation, and (2) transformation of tribe into peasant and through this transformation, the positioning of its segments in the hierarchy of caste system, within the framework of varna ideology.'[33]

Moreover, in his Introduction to *The Making of Early Medieval India*, a selection of his articles, he also points out that 'the making of early medieval India... may have to be seen in terms of the scale of certain fundamental movements within the regional and local levels'.[34] In this context he refers again to the above-mentioned two processes of expansion of state society through peasantization of tribes and caste formation but adds as a third process 'cult appropriation and integration' (p. 16). However, he also emphasizes that 'cult assimilation does not necessarily imply a harmonious syncretism, but it does also imply the formation of a structure which combines heterogeneous beliefs and rituals into a whole while making (or transforming) specific elements dominant' (p. 30). And he concludes his 'Introduction' again with the statement that 'the most dominant pattern [of early medieval India] seems to be the shaping of regional societies... [which] was essentially a movement from within' (p. 34f).

To my own surprise, and I guess to B.D. Chattopadhyaya's, too, the integrative approach to state formation meanwhile seems to have found some acceptance as an alternative model. To my knowledge, B.P. Sahu of Delhi University in 1988 was the first to take it up in an analysis of historiographic trends in recent studies of early medieval Orissan history.[35] After summarizing these studies, he categorized them into three 'broad types' which follow either the Indian feudalism model of R.S. Sharma or the 'paradigm of integration advocated by Kulke' whereas a third group consists of 'exercises in pure and simple dynastic history [...] with no distinctive imagination, method or aim'. Sahu is of the opinion that the 'integration model', addressed to the problem of state formation in early medieval/medieval Orissa, adds a new dimension to historiography, and he substantiates his statement mainly by referring to various aspects of ritual policy and their distinct modes of integration. But he also points out that social and economic integration are mentioned, 'but passingly and not elaborated sufficiently'. In the context of Orissan history, S.K. Panda too included the concept of 'concentric integration' into his historiographic delineations. After referring to the unitary model and the models of Indian feudalism and the segmentary state, he mentions as a fourth category 'the recently advanced three-stage model of "concentric integration" in which a continuous process of integration leads to the foundation of trans-local (or sub-regional) early kingdoms and culminates finally in the establishment of imperial regional states of medieval India'.[36] More recently, B. Schnepel in his study on the 'Jungle Kings' of Jeypore in

Orissa elaborates on the integrative model. According to this model, state formation represented a kind of Kosambian 'feudalism from below' rather than 'the degeneration and fragmentation of a formerly larger empire into a number of smaller segments, as envisaged in conventional images of the feudal state.... The state in Orissa and elsewhere on the subcontinent did not only *consist* of little kingdoms but also *developed* from little kingdoms'.[37] As another major advantage of this state model, Schnepel regards the new interpretations of several important phenomena, such as, of land grants to Brahmins and the role of the *samanta*s in peripheral zones as agents of integration rather than fragmentation or segmentation.[38]

In his 1994 Presidential Address to the Andhra History Congress, K.M. Shrimali discussed the 'integrative model' in the broader context of recent Indian historiography.[39] After a short reference to R.S. Sharma's 'construct of Indian feudalism' which, according to Shrimali, dominated post-Independence historical writing in India, he introduced the integrative model as an alternative paradigm: 'Broadly speaking, the feudal construct has given rise to two alternative paradigms which tend to underline the segmentary or integrative aspects of the early medieval polity. While the former has been worked out in greater detail in the context of peninsular India, the latter has so far received larger attention in the context of Rajasthan and Orissa.' Shrimali is of the opinion that 'amongst the notable exponents of the integrative polity apart from Kulke, *B.D. Chattopadhyaya deserves special attention*' (emphasis added). He elaborates on Chattopadhyaya's theses, mainly on the basis of the latter's 1983 Presidential Address in the same line as has already been done above. In 1996, T.K. Venkatasubramanian, too, in his Presidential Address to the Indian History Congress at Chennai discusses in some detail the 'processural model of integrative state formation'.[40] In fact, he chooses it as the only state model in the introduction of his chapter 'Towards State' and refers in this context also to Chattopadhyaya's concept of 'State Society'.

Recently two PhD theses from Hyderabad University and Jawaharlal Nehru University (JNU) referred extensively to various aspects of the 'integrative model'. Tejaswini Yarlagadda underlines in the context of her studies on early medieval western Deccan the importance of Chattopadhyaya's concept of the emergence and spread of ruling lineage groups as a major integrative factor on supra-local state formation.[41] In her JNU thesis on the Puri temple, Yaaminey Mubayi is of the opinion that 'the model of the vertical and horizontal integration of ritual and political institutions in Orissa is fundamental to any study of the temple and the state in Orissa'.[42]

A succinct exposition of Chattopadhyaya's 'influential formulations about early medieval' came from Burton Stein. At a conference in Munich in summer 1992, he elaborated particularly on Chattopadhyaya's 'notion of "constituent state" and what he takes to be constitutive'. In this context he emphasizes particularly Chattopadhyaya's 'idea of something he calls "state society". The dispersing agency of the state society conceptions were Brahmans: cult leaders, ritual cognoscenti, and priestly custodians of the numerous sacred centres that had begun to exist after the fourth century AD. ... Whatever state society is taken to mean, Chattopadhyaya has not in mind simply smaller scale unitary polities, empires in miniature, but rather systems cognate with feudal ones. He differentiates himself carefully from upholders of "Indian feudalism", displaying similarities with formulations of "fragmentary" polities by Kulke, and "segmentary" conceptions by me in the sense that in all three salience is given to the formations and structural importance of communities—localized and integrated systems of social, cultural, economic, and political relations and institutions. Communities are seen in something of balanced relations with states. Sometimes, as in the case of the Rajputs and the Orissan kinglets discussed by Chattopadhyaya and Kulke, states emerge directly from previous clan/communal formations; and sometimes, as in the case of the Cholas about whom I wrote, imperial-like states emerged from localized chiefdoms and endure without eliminating that same stratum of their provenance'.[43]

There are, however, several more critical remarks on the integrative model. As regards my own elaborations, B.D. Chattopadhyaya was certainly right when he remarked in his Presidential Address that although he speaks of integration on the regional level he generally avoids 'discussing the political mechanisms of integration'.[44] B.P. Sahu, too, points out that 'the actual process and political mechanism involved in the stepwise integration of marginal areas with the core/nuclear pockets remains somewhat untouched'[45] and that the modes of social and economic integration are not sufficiently elaborated.

The major critique comes mainly from the 'upholders' of Indian feudalism at Delhi University. In his above-mentioned Presidential Address, Shrimali criticizes Chattopadhyaya for speaking of a 'samanta system rather than feudal polity' and for viewing 'this system as an instrument of political integration and a counterpoint to the decentralized polity of the feudal.'[46] Moreover he complains about vagueness in the definition of Chattopadhyaya's terms 'state society' and 'lineage domain' and wonders whether the plea for an integrative polity is actually a step in the direction of segmentary state. And he concludes with the unexpected question: 'Aren't the so-called alternative paradigms of "segmentary state" and "integrative polity" merely extensions of semantic differences rather than connoting any substantiative departure from the "feudal model"'?[47] D.N. Jha however seems to be rather reluctant to reduce this controversy to mere 'semantic differences'. On the one hand, he is of the generous opinion that 'the responses of Stein, Kulke and Chattopadhyaya to the feudal state model, it would appear, have at least one point in common: They all perceive early medieval period as one of parcellized sovereignty and this brings them quite close to the idea of a feudal state'. But, on the other hand, he comes to the rather doctrinal conclusion that 'paradigms like segmentary state and integrative polity, which do not lay adequate emphasis on the economic changes leading to the rise of new social classes and to the new bases of political power, may masquerade as alternatives to the feudal construct but, in reality, are in no position to replace it'.[48] And he even presumes to state that 'the model enunciated by Chattopadhyaya and Kulke ignores the economic basis of the political integration of modes of power in the samanta structure and presents a fine example of state *sans* economics. If Stein, Kulke and Chattopadhyaya would join hands, the state would disappear like a Cheshire cat!'[49]

V.M. Jha, too, refers in the context of 'the controversy over political feudalism in Indian historiography' to the 'integrative polity' and the 'processural model'. In his opinion, their interpretation of the samanta hierarchy as an integrative rather than a feudal polity lacks the explanation 'how the absence of the contract made the overlord-feudatory relation in early medieval India qualitatively different from that in medieval Western Europe'.[50] This is indeed a relevant question. But, to my mind, the ball is in his court, as he has to explain whether feudalism *sans* contract still can be regarded as *political feudalism*. Moreover, according to V.M. Jha, the processural model, 'the second criticism' of the concept of Indian feudalism, 'conflates the structure of a polity with its genesis'. Indeed, this is exactly what the processural model tries to do: to explain the structure through its genesis and not vice versa.

D.N. Jha may be right when he complains that it has not been adequately appreciated that 'Indian Marxist historiography, opposed to the British view of Indian past, has used the European model of feudalism to explain social change in India from the middle of the first millennium'.[51] However, if this is true in the case of feudalism, there should be no harm in using or developing other models for the same purpose, no matter whether they lead to different or even contradictory results. To postulate change in early medieval India is not the monopoly of the concept of feudalism. Moreover, socio-economic and political–ideological processes in early medieval India may have led to feudal-like patterns, for example, the 'samanta-system' or Bhakti religion. But they need not to have developed into full-fledged modes of production. The integrative model is not engaged in the shaping of a new totalizing construct even though B. Stein may have been right when he wrote: 'Chattopadhyaya concerns... reflect his laudable intention to launch upon or to participate in the construction of a generalized model of polity during India's medieval era'.[52]

The integrative or processural model of state formation focuses on processes of change and not on dramatic breaks in explaining the transition from early historical to early medieval and from the latter to the medieval. Its explanations are based on change coming from within local and regional societies and internal processes, deriving from a network of trans-local linkages. It focuses on the importance of regions outside the north Indian plains in 'the making of early medieval India' and concedes the local and sub-regional levels their due share. It locates the domain of ideology and legitimization in the arena of continuous competition and negotiation which has constantly to be redefined.[53]

There remains, as a last point, Y. Mubayi's important argument that my integrative model is 'overlaid with a sense of the dominance of royal authority as an integrative agency'. For her own studies Mubayi therefore came to the conclusion that 'my [Mubayi's] account on the temple-state relationship, while acknowledging many aspects of Kulke's integrative model, seeks to redefine relationship of power as possessing a certain ambiguity and portraying a great deal of ambivalence'.[54] In this context, a few remarks on integration may be necessary. To regard integration as a paradigm of state formation is certainly not completely new. Exponents of the segmentary and the feudal state models, too, reclaim, certainly not entirely without justification, integration as an aspect of their concepts.[55] But to my understanding the major thrust of their concepts is to prove the persistence of segmentary units *despite* integrative processes, respectively of fragmentation *because* of the systematic failure of the feudal structure of early medieval kingdoms. The model of integrative state formation, at the level of theory, interprets processes of integration as a counterpoint to the processes of fragmentation and segmentation.

But integration is not free of ambiguity. Chattopadhyaya is right when he points out that 'identifying [...] societal processes and underlining them as the mechanism of integration do not mean taking an epicentric position'.[56] In my opinion, integration nevertheless has to be distinguished from osmotic processes of mutual penetration. It has the connotation of being integrated into another—usually larger—entity from which the process of integration normally originates.[57] But, at the same time, integration is not tantamount to an appropriation of the identity and agency of the 'integrated object'.[58] Tondaimandalam, for instance, was temporarily integrated into the extended core area of the 'Imperial Cholas' but never lost its own identity. Chidambaram's Nataraja cult, too, was not appropriated by Chola Rajaraja I but integrated into the royal cult of Tanjavur, an act which certainly enhanced the identity and importance of Chidambaram and its priests.[59] Particularly in the case of 'tribal deities at princely courts', royal authority often acted as an integrative agency which raised the status of local cults, their priests, and devotees. Orissa seems to be particularly rich in these matters as revealed exemplarily by the goddesses Ramachandi and Bhattarika. Ramachandi, a former local tribal goddess, rose to the status of a tutelary deity of the small 'fort chieftaincy' in the Khurda state. But during certain rituals 'the power of the indigenous goddess dominates, and the king, the chief and other villagers must recognize the goddess' power in the tribal shaman's body, and act as subordinated devotees of her'.[60] Bhattarika, the 'Great Mother' (*baḍa ambā*) and tutelary deity of the nearby former princely state of Baramba is another excellent example of these relations and various levels of integration. At her place of origin, in a typical late medieval temple at a beautiful spot on the Mahanadi, non-Brahmanical *mali* priests perform the puja of her un-iconical stone image. In the palace of Baramba, her rituals are performed to a Durga image by the *rajpurohita* who also takes over the puja during the (rare) visits of the raja to the temple of Bhattarika.[61] Her integration was achieved at three interconnected levels: at the subregional level as tutelary deity of the small feudatory state of Baramba, at the regional level through her worship of one of the powerful 'Seven Mother Goddesses' (*saptamāṭrikā*s) of Orissa, and at the pan-Indian level through the mythological account that her stone 'image' was pierced by the holy arrow shot by the divine hero Paraśurama from the other side of the Mahanadi. Equally fascinating 'ethnohistorical aspects of politico-ritual life' are known from south Orissan jungle kingdoms.[62]

There is a wide spectrum of important and relevant themes for further studies on cultural and social institutions and their different modes of integration in the context of regional state formation. The great *tirtha*s as places of regional and trans-regional pilgrimage with their priestly groups, *matha*s and influential *mahants* and sectarian leaders were perhaps the most important arenas of integration through competition, negotiation, and even contestation between various social and religious groups and, of course, royal 'agents' too. In this regard the importance of those temple cities may have been greatest which were 'centres out there', beyond the dynastic realm of direct royal influence. A. Appadurai and R.A. Palat produced excellent studies on social conflicts, sectarian leaders, and royal penetration in south Indian temple cities during the Vijayanagara period.[63] Adherents of the segmentary state concept are certainly right to 'appropriate' these studies and their results as a proof of the socio-religious capacity of local institutions. But I do not see any problem in 'contesting' their claims and quoting these studies also as examples of (albeit not always successful) royal attempts to gain influence on, or even a hold over, the redistributive patronage system of key institutions of these tirthas.

The politically most persistently competitive institution of the central royal power was, of course, feudatory or samanta chiefs. In the 'conventional model' of the unitary state, they played only an insignificant role, usually as loyal 'vassals' of their royal overlords. For supporters of the Indian feudalism school, they were the unavoidable products of the process of 'feudal fragmentation' of central authority. In the segmentary state concept, they represented the autonomous segmentary local or trans-local political holders of the 'actual political control' over their own nuclear area. The above-mentioned studies of N. Dirks, G. Berkemer, B. Schnepel, and A. Tanabe, too, confirmed the importance of the 'little kings' as an intrinsic constituent institution of the early medieval Indian state. But these 'ethnohistoric' studies emphasize more strongly the ambivalence of dominance and subordination in the sphere of trans-local authority, as well as the participation in, or even competition and imitation of, regional symbols of authority and sacred manifestations. The integrative model so far has primarily focused on modes of integration which originated from the centre or at least strengthened the central position. But the recent studies on the 'little kings' in the intermediate zone or on 'jungle kings' in the periphery clearly demonstrated that we have to concede more space to them and their various modes of competition and negotiation in the concepts of state formation. In this context Y. Mubayi's intention to 'redefine relationships of power as possessing a certain ambiguity and portraying a great deal of ambivalence'[64] is to be welcomed. But the outcome of such a rethinking may be less an *ambivalence* than a centre–periphery *balance* which, however, continuously had to be reconfirmed.

Historical writing like local chronicles and temple *mahatmya*s were yet another institution of negotiating and consolidating local authority. Previous studies focused on their historical and literary meaning and only rarely were they used as sources for the study of religious processes (for example, Hinduization) or of royal legitimization. But even in these cases, the studies were undertaken primarily from the central or dominant point of view. Local versions of the texts, provided that they were taken into consideration at all, were usually just mentioned as local deviations. But in his ethnohistoric studies on the Jeypore raj in Koraput, Schnepel has shown that the intrinsic value of local genealogies lies exactly in these deviations from the great tradition of Gajapati kingship of central Orissa and in the localization of its royal symbols of sacred and temporal authority. The foundation of the Jeypore dynasty, for instance, is based on a story derived from the famous Kanchi Kaberi legend of pan-Orissan fame about the great Gajapati king Purushottamadeva and his conquest of Kanchipuram with the help of Lord Jagannath.[65] The Jeypore tradition praises its first raja for having stolen the famous Durga *murti*, the future tutelary deity of his dynasty, from Purushottama when he allegedly passed through Jeypore on his way back from Kanchipuram. Another example is the 'Royal Genealogy' of Ranpur in central Orissa. It portrays the quest of Ranpur to establish its claim as the oldest raj in central Orissa through extensive 'quotations' from (and localization of) the literary resources of the dominant religious and royal symbols of Puri and of the successor Gajapatis of nearby Khurda. But Ranpur's striving was competition rather than contestation as its own status depended to a large extent on participation in the weak but superior authority of the Khurda rajas.[66] This authority however was flatly contested by the rajas of Parlakhimedi in south Orissa through the historiographical construct of their descent from the imperial Suryavamsha Gajapatis of the fifteenth century.[67] Puri's famous chronicle of the Madala Panji traces Khurda's origin only to a collateral descent from a rather unimportant successor of the Suryavamsha Gajapatis in the early sixteenth century.

All these 'historiographical claims' may not be exactly historical, at least not for ordinary historians. But they transmit processes of competition and contestation of the dominant ideology of a region as an important source of regional integration.

The four institutions, *devatā*s, tīrthas, sāmantas, and *vaṃśāvali*s (and others may be added) paradigmatically illustrate a mode of regional integration that may be paraphrased as 'integration through competition'. This opens a new dimension of research as it leaves more space for various agencies and their different modes of participation and negotiation within a cultural system of mutually accepted values of the sacred and the profane order. It concedes stronger participation and a more active role to the many local and sub-regional institutions, without, however, deconstructing the royal centre. There are, of course, a number of other aspects of the 'integrative model' which require further research, such as, in-depth studies of various processes of economic integration.[68]

NOTES

1. I am thankful to Prof. B.P. Sahu for his comments on an earlier version of this paper.

2. H. Kulke, 1995, 'Introduction: The Study of the State in Pre-modern India', in *idem.* (ed.), *The State in India 1000–1700*, New Delhi: Oxford University Press, pp. 1–47.

3. General Editors' Preface to the *State in India*, p. VIII.

4. R.S. Sharma, 1957, 'Origin of Feudalism in India (c. AD 400–650)', *Journal of the Economic and Social History of the Orient*, Vol. 1, pp. 297–328 (Sharma's earliest paper on Indian feudalism); *idem*, 1965, *Indian Feudalism, c. 300–1200*, Calcutta: University of Calcutta Press; B. Stein, 1977, 'The Segmentary State in South Indian History', in R.G. Fox (ed.), *Realm and Region in Traditional India*, New Delhi: Vikas, pp. 175–213; *idem*, 1980, *Peasant, State and Society in Medieval India*, New Delhi: Oxford University Press; S.P. Blake, 1979, 'The Patrimonial-Bureaucratic Empire of the Mughals', *Journal of Asian Studies*, Vol. 39, pp. 77–94.

5. S. Subrahmanyam, 1986, 'Aspects of State Formation in South India and Southeast Asia', *Indian Economic and Social History Review*, Vol. 23, p. 375.

6. R.S. Sharma, 1989/90, 'The Segmentary State and the Indian Experience', *Indian Historical Review*, Vol. 16, pp. 81–110; B. Stein, 1990, 'The Segmentary State: Interim Reflections', *Puruṣārtha*, Vol. 13, pp. 217–38 (Repr. in Kulke 1995, pp. 134–61).

7. In a paper written in 1981 and finally published in summer 1984 ('Fragmentation and Segmentation versus Integration? Reflections on the Concepts

of Indian Feudalism and the Segmentary State in Indian History', *Studies in History* 4 (1982), pp. 237–64, finally published in summer 1984), I stated that at present there exist at least three different structural models of early medieval Indian kingdoms, viz. the conventional [unitary] model and the models of Indian feudalism and the segmentary state. Blake's paper had been published a year ago but remained a matter of Mughal history till 1985 when B. Stein temporarily introduced its Weberian concept into his Vijayanagara studies (see n. 13). The 'non-aligned' group obviously had not yet existed in the early 1980s, at least not to my knowledge.

8. R.S. Sharma, 1981, *Material Culture and Social Formations in Ancient India*, Delhi: Macmillan; R. Thapar, 1980, 'State Formation in Early India', *International Social Science Journal*, Vol. 32, No. 4, pp. 655–69; *idem*, 1984, *From Lineage to State: Social Formations in Mid-First Millennium* BC *in the Ganges Valley*, Bombay: Oxford University Press.

9. S. Seneviratne, 1981, 'Kalinga and Andhra: The Process of Secondary State Formation in Early India', in H.J.M. Claessen and P. Skalnik (eds), *The Study of the State*, The Hague: Mouton, pp. 317–38; A. Parasher-Sen, 1993, 'Culture and Civilisation. The Beginnings', in *idem* (ed.), *Social and Economic History of Early Deccan: Some Interpretations*, New Delhi: Manohar, pp. 66–114; B.D. Chattopadhyaya, 1987, 'Transition into the Early Historical Phase in the Deccan', in B.M. Pande and B.D. Chattopadhyaya (eds), *Archaeology and History: Essays in Honour of A. Ghosh*, Delhi: Agam Kala Prakashan, pp. 727–32.

10. S. Sinha, 1962, 'State Formation and Rajput Myth in Tribal Central India', *Man in India*, Vol. 42, pp. 35–80; *idem* (ed.), 1987, *Tribal Polities and State Systems in Pre-colonial Eastern and North Eastern India*, Calcutta: K.P. Bagchi.

11. N. Dirks, 1982, 'The Past of a Pāḷaiyakārar: The Ethnohistory of a South Indian Little King', *Journal of Asian Studies*, Vol. 41, pp. 655–83; *idem*, 1987, *The Hollow Crown: Ethnohistory of an Indian Kingdom*, Cambridge: Cambridge University Press.

12. G. Berkemer, 1993, *Little Kingdoms in Kalinga: Ideologie, Legitimation und Politik Regionaler Eliten*, Wiesbaden: Franz Steiner Verlag; G. Berkemer and M. Frenz (eds), 2003, *Sharing Sovereignty: The Little Kingdom in South Asia*, Berlin: Schwarzber Verlag; B. Schnepel, 1997, *Die Dschungelkönige. Ethnohistorische Aspekte von Politik und Ritual in Orissa*, Stuttgart: Franz Steiner Verlag; *idem*, 2002, *The Jungle Kings: Ethnohistorical Aspects of Politics and Ritual in Orissa*, New Delhi: Manohar, A. Tanabe (this volume), 'Early Modernity and Colonial Transformation: Rethinking the Role of the King in the 18th and 19th centuries'.

13. B. Stein, 1985, 'Vijayanagara and the Transition to Patrimonial Systems', in A. Dallapiccola (ed.), *Vijayanagara: City and Empire*, Stuttgart: Franz Steiner Verlag, Vol. I, pp. 73–85; *idem*, 1989, *Vijayanagara* (The New Cambridge History of India I, 2), Cambridge: Cambridge University Press.

N. Dirks, too, complains that Stein's model does not facilitate a detailed analysis of changes or variations in the Indian state (N. Dirks, *The Hollow Crown*, p. 404).

14. B.D. Chattopadhyaya, 1983, 'Political Processes and Structure of Polity in Early Medieval India: Problems of Perspective', Indian History Congress, Presidential Address, Ancient India Section, 47th session, Burdwan (repr. in Kulke, 1995, pp. 195–232).

15. Y. Subbarayalu, 1984, 'The Cōḷa State', *Studies in History*, Vol. 4, pp. 265–306; J. Heitzman, 1987, 'State Formation in South India, 850–1280', *The Indian Economic and Social History Review*, Vol. 24, pp. 35–61 (repr. in Kulke 1995, pp. 162–94).

16. G.W. Spencer and K.R. Hall, 1974, 'Towards Ritual, an Analysis of Dynastic Hinterlands: The Imperial Cholas of the 11th Century South India', *Asian Profiles*, Vol. 2, pp. 51–62.

17. Y. Subbarayalu, *op. cit.*, p. 304f.

18. S.K. Panda, 1986, *Herrschaft und Verwaltung im östlichen Indien unter den späten Gangas* (ca. 1038–1434), Stuttgart: Franz Steiner Verlag; rev. and transl., *The State and the Statecraft in Medieval Orissa under the Later Eastern Gangas* (AD 1038–1434), Calcutta: K.P. Bagchi, 1995.

19. H. Scharfe, 1989, *The State in Indian Tradition*, Leiden: E.J. Brill.

20. B. Stein, 1969, 'Integration of the Agrarian System in South India', in R.E. Frykenberg (ed.), *Land Control and Social Structure in Indian History*, Madison: University of Wisconsin Press, pp. 175–213.

21. R.S. Sharma, 1960, 'Land System in Medieval Orissa (c. AD 750–1200)', in *Proceedings of the Indian History Congress*, 23th session, Aligarh, Part I, pp. 89–96; republished in *Indian Feudalism: c.300–1200*, Calcutta: University of Calcutta Press, 1965, pp. 274–86. In her Heidelberg PhD thesis, 1985, Swapna Bhattacharya, too, emphasizes the 'decisive role of Brahmins in the processes of integration and centralization' under the Palas. *Landschenkungen und staatliche Entwicklung im frühmittelalterlichen Bengalen (5. bis 13. Jahrhundert n. Chr.)*, (Land Donations and State Formation in Early Medieval Bengal, 5th to 13th Centuries), Wiesbaden: Franz Steiner Verlag, p. 82.

22. G.W. Spencer, 1969, 'Religious Networks and Royal Influence in Eleventh Century South India', *Journal of the Economic and Social History of the Orient*, Vol. 12, pp. 42–56.

23. The major emphasis of B. Stein's unpublished Chicago PhD thesis of 1958, 'The Tirupati Temple: An Economic Study of a Medieval South Indian Temple', and of his early papers was 'The Economic Function of a South Indian Temple' as his first (1959–60), important paper in *Journal of Asian Studies*, Vol. 19, pp. 163–76 is entitled; see also *idem*, 1961, 'The State, the Temple and Agricultural Development: A Study of Medieval South India', *Economic and Political Weekly*, Vol. 13, pp. 179–89.

24. J. Rösel, 1986, 'Max Weber and the Patrimonial State', in D. Kantowsky

(ed.), *Recent Research on Max Weber's Studies of Hinduism*, München: Weltforum Verlag, pp. 117–52.

25. H. Kulke, 1976, 'Kshatriyazation and Social Change: A Study in Orissa Setting', in S.D. Pillai (ed.), *Aspects of Changing India: Studies in Honour of Prof. S.G. Ghurye*, Bombay: Popular Prakashan, pp. 398–409; *idem*, 1977, 'State Formation and Royal Legitimation in Late Ancient Orissa', in M.N. Das (ed.), *Sidelights on the History and Culture of Orissa*, Cuttack: Vidyapuri, pp. 104–21; *idem*, 1978, 'Royal Temple Policy and the Structure of Medieval Kingdoms', in A. Eschmann, H. Kulke, and G.C. Tripathi (eds), *The Cult of Jagannath and the Regional Tradition of Orissa*, Delhi: Manohar, pp. 125–38. In this context I would like to thank again my colleagues of the former Orissa Research Project, especially the late Anncharlott Eschmann and G.C. Tripathi, the co-editors of its final report, and J. Rösel and G. Pfeffer for their comments during our numberless discussions during those days.

26. In 1977, a grant was awarded to me by the Social Science Research Council and the American Council of Learned Societies for similar studies in East Java. Its results were presented by a paper 'Early State Formation and Ritual Policy in East Java' at the Eighth Conference of the International Association of Historians of Asia at Kuala Lumpur in 1980.

27. H. Kulke, *op. cit.* (see note 7), p. 260.

28. H. Kulke, 1985, 'Die frühmittelalterlichen Regionalreiche: Ihre Struktur und Rolle im Prozeß staatlicher Entwicklung in Indien'(Early Medieval Regional States: Their Structure and Role in the Process of State Formation in India), in H. Kulke and D. Rothermund (eds), *Regionale Tradition in Südasien*, Wiesbaden: Franz Steiner Verlag, pp. 77–114.

29. H. Kulke, 1986, 'The Early and the Imperial Kingdom in Southeast Asian History', in D.G. Marr and A.C. Miller (eds), *Southeast Asia in the 9th to 14th Centuries*, Singapore, Institute of Southeast Asian Studies, pp. 1–22 (repr. in H. Kulke, 1993, *Kings and Cults: State Formation and Legitimation in India and Southeast Asia*, New Delhi: Manohar, pp. 264–93).

30. H. Kulke, 1995, 'The Early and the Imperial Kingdom: A Processural Model of Integrative State Formation in Early Medieval India', in *idem*, *The State in India 1000–1700*, New Delhi: Oxford University Press, pp. 253–62.

31. B.D. Chattopadhyaya, 1973, 'Irrigation in Early Medieval Rajasthan', *Journal of the Economic and Social History of the Orient*, Vol. 16, pp. 298–316; *idem*, 1974, 'Trade and Urban Centres in Early Medieval North India', *Indian Historical Review*, Vol. 1, pp. 203–19; *idem.*, 1976, 'Origin of Rajputs: The Political, Economic and Social Processes in Early Medieval Rajasthan', *Indian Historical Review*, Vol. 3, pp. 59–82.

32. B.D. Chattopadhyaya, *op. cit.* (note 14), p. 19. In this context, he also referred to my then still unpublished paper 'Fragmentation and Segmentation versus Integration?'

33. B.D. Chattopadhyaya, 1995, 'State and Economy in North India: Fourth Century to Twelfth Century', in V.R. Thapar (ed.), *Recent Perspectives of Early*

Indian History, Bombay: Popular Prakashan, p. 331. The article was written several years earlier.

34. B.D. Chattopadhyaya, 1994, *The Making of Early Medieval India*, New Delhi: Oxford University Press, p. 17. See also B.P. Sahu's review of the book in *Indian Historical Review*, Vol. 18 (1996), pp. 137–40.

35. B.P. Sahu, 1988, 'Early Medieval Orissa: Recent Historiographic Trends', in *Proceedings of the Indian History Congress*, Dharwad session, pp. 160–7.

36. S.K. Panda, 1995 (note 18), p. 116.

37. B. Schnepel, 2001, 'Kings and Rebel Kings: Rituals of Incorporation and Dissent in South Orissa', in H. Kulke and B. Schnepel (eds), *Jagannath Revisited: Studying Society, Religion and the State in Orissa*, Delhi: Manohar, p. 289f (italics by B. Schnepel).

38. B. Schnepel, *The Jungle Kings*, pp. 77–80.

39. K.M. Shrimali, 1994, *Reflections on Recent Perceptions of Early Medieval India*. Presidential Address. Section IV Historiography, Andhra Pradesh History Congress, XVIII session, Tenali, p. 2; K.M. Shrimali's Appendix (1992) to Chapter 24(A) on 'Political Organisation of Northern India', in *A Comprehensive History of India*, Vol. IV, ed. by R.S. Sharma and K.M. Shrimali, New Delhi: People's Publishing House, p. 739 contains a similar statement.

40. T.K. Venkatsubramanian, 1996, *Chiefdom to State: Reflections on Kaveri Delta Social Formations*, Presidential Address, Ancient India Section, Indian History Congress, 75th session, Chennai.

41. T. Yarlagadda, 1998, *Rural Settlements and Social Stratification in South Western Deccan 1000–1200*, Hyderabad: University of Hyderabad.

42. Y. Mubayi's, PhD thesis of the year 1999 was recently published under the title *Altar of Power. The Temple and the State in the Land of Jagannath*, New Delhi: Manohar, 2005, p. 31.

43. B. Stein, 1997, 'Communities, States, and "Classical" India', in B. Kölver (ed.), *Recht, Staat und Verwaltung im klassischen Indien* (The State, the Law, and Administration in Classical India), München: R. Oldenbourg, pp. 15–26.

44. B.D. Chattopadhyaya, 1995, (note 14), p. 231, note 119.

45. B.P. Sahu, *op. cit.*, (note 35) p. 163.

46. K.M. Shrimali, 1994, (note 39), p. 6.

47. K.M. Shrimali, *op. cit.*, p. 4.

48. D.N. Jha, 2000, 'Editor's Introduction', in *idem* (ed.), *The Feudal Order: State, Society and Ideology in Early Medieval India*, New Delhi: Manohar, p. 24.

49. D.N. Jha, *op. cit.*, p. 53, note 144. Jha will be glad to know that we had the chance to 'join hands' with B. Stein during the above-mentioned conference in Munich in 1992. But I can assure him that the state—or to put it more correctly, the numerous states—in early medieval India were very much present during our talks.

50. V.M. Jha, 2000, 'Feudal Elements in the Caulukya State: An Attempt at Relocation', in D.N. Jha, *op. cit.*, pp. 211–47 (240).

51. *Op. cit.*, p. 11. By calling B. Stein in this context an 'avowedly neo-colonialist historian', Jha puts himself in a rather awkward position as every-body will agree who knows Stein's personal biography.

52. B. Stein, *op. cit.*, p. 145 (see note 6).

53. I am grateful to Dr B.P. Sahu for his succinct summary of these matters in a personal communication.

54. Y. Mubayi, *op. cit.*, (note 42), p. 31.

55. K.M. Shrimali, 1994, (note 39), p. 5: 'We have remarked elsewhere that integration [...] can be explained in terms of land grants which formed the crucial element in the feudal structure. In as much as local landlords or chieftains derived their fiscal and administrative power from the king, paid tribute and performed military and administrative obligations towards him, they worked for integration'. B. Stein, in a personal communication commented on my 'Fragmentation and Segmentation versus Integration' paper: 'I contend that the segmentary state formulation is precisely about integration, *given* segmentation. It is not one or the other, but the interaction of essentially segmentary and integrating forces in the societies [...]. Thus I consider your title mistakes the case: it is not segmentation *versus* integration, but segmentation *and* integration.' Quoted in H. Kulke, *op. cit.*, (note 7), p. 263, postscript.

56. B.D. Chattopadhyaya, *op. cit.*, 1994, 'Introduction', p. 16.

57. A. Tanabe seems to be of the same opinion as he speaks of 'incorpo-ration' instead of 'integration', 'Indigenous Power, Hierarchy and Dominance: State Formation in Orissa, India', in H.J.M. Claessen and J.G. Oosten (eds), *Ideology and the Formation of Early States*, Leiden: E.J. Brill, 1996, pp. 205–19.

58. In this context I have some reservation against Chattopadhyaya's use of the term 'appropriation' in his above quoted third major process ('cult appropriation and integration'), although I agree that 'cult assimilation does not necessarily imply a harmonious syncretism', Chattopadhyaya, *op. cit.*, (note 56), (p. 30).

59. H. Kulke, 1993, 'Functional Interpretation of a South Indian Māhātmya: The Legend of Hiraṇyavarman and the Life of the Cōḷa King Kulottuṅga I', in *idem*, *Kings and Cults: State Formation and Legitimation in India and Southeast Asia*, Delhi: Manohar, pp. 192–207; Y. Ogura, 1999, 'The Changing Concept of Kingship in the Cōḷa Period: Royal Temple Constructions, c. AD 850–1279', in N. Karashima (ed.), *Kingship in Indian History*, New Delhi: Manohar, pp. 119–41; K. Veluthat 1993, *Political Structure of Early Medieval South India*, Delhi: Orient Longman, also speaks of 'the importance of the temples of Tanjavur and Gaṅgaikoṇḍacōḷapuram in the cultural device of political integration of the Cōḷa empire' (p. 252).

60. A. Tanabe, *op. cit.* (note 57), p. 215.

61. H. Kulke, 1993, 'Tribal Deities at Princely Courts: The Feudatory Rajas

of Central Orissa and the Tutelary Deities (*iṣṭadevatās*)', in H. Kulke, (note 59), pp. 114–36.

62. B. Schnepel, 1995, 'Durga and the King: Ethnohistorical Aspects of Politico-Ritual Life in a South Orissan Jungle Kingdom', *Journal of the Royal Anthropological Institute*, Vol. 1, pp. 145–66; *idem*, 1996, 'The Hindu King's Authority Reconsidered: Durgā-Pūjā and Dasarā in a South Orissan Jungle Kingdom', in A. Boholm (ed.), *Political Ritual*, Göteborg: Institute for Advanced Studies in Social Anthropology, Gothenburg University, pp. 126–57.

63. A. Appadurai, 1977, 'Kings, Sects and Temples in South India, 1350–1700', in B. Stein (ed.), *South Indian Temples*, Delhi: Vikas, pp. 47–73; R.A. Palat, 1986, 'Popular Revolts and the State in Medieval South India: A Study of the Vijayanagara Empire', *Bijdragen tot de Taal-, Land-en Volkenkunde*, Vol. 142, pp. 128–44.

64. Y. Mubayi, *op. cit.*, (note 42), p. 31.

65. G.N. Dash, 1978, 'Jagannātha and Oriya Nationalism', in A. Eschmann, H. Kulke, and G.C. Tripathi (eds), *The Cult of Jagannath and the Regional Tradition of Orissa*, Delhi: Manohar, pp. 359–74; B. Mohapatra, 1996, 'Ways of Belonging: The Kanchi Kaveri Legend and the Construction of an Oriya Identity', *Studies in History*, Vol. 12, pp. 187–217.

66. H. Kulke, 2004, 'The Making of a Local Chronicle: The Ranapur Rajavamsa Itihasa', in A. Malinar *et al.* (eds), *Text and Context in the History, Literature, and Religion of Orissa*, New Delhi: Manohar, pp. 43–66.

67. G. Berkemer, *op. cit.*, (note 12), pp. 308ff and 342; see also his 'The Chronicle of a Little Kingdom: Some Reflections on the Tekkali-tālūkā Jamīṃdārla Vaṃśāvali', in B. Kölver, *op. cit.*, (see note 43), pp. 65–96.

68. A rewarding example of advancing our understanding of these processes is B.D. Chattopadhyaya, 1990, *Aspects of Rural Settlements and Rural Society in Early Medieval India*, Calcutta: K.P. Bagchi.

CHAPTER 3

The Social Background of State Formation in India

Masaaki Kimura

The structure of a state is influenced by the configuration of powers in the village community. This theme has been one of the main topics in Japanese political science. In analysing the pre-war ultra-nationalist state system, Masao Maruyama emphasizes agrarianism as a significant element in its ideology. According to Maruyama, the ultra-nationalist state aimed to reconstruct Japanese society, which was being threatened by the onslaught of industrialism, by revitalizing the traditional Japanese system that was still being maintained in the village. In this manner, pre-war ultra-nationalism signified a continuation of the development of the state system in the sense of the 'family-state', which found its ideal, albeit in an embryonic shape, in the traditional Japanese village. Therefore ultra-nationalism was the culmination of Japan's political development following the Meiji reformation and was an exemplification of Japanese political culture, which was deeply rooted in the traditional Japanese village. In other words, the highly autocratic regime of the pre-war Japanese political system was the outgrowth of similar power relations in the Japanese village community, where there was an intricate nexus of patriarchal governance-cum-protection and filial obedience between landlords and tenants. The form of social and political consciousness cultivated in these social milieus exerted a strong influence on human behaviour outside the village.

Indeed, people who were accustomed to giving filial obedience towards landlords in the village, tended to behave similarly towards their superiors outside the village. For instance, their attitude towards district leaders, presidents of companies, and municipal or national administrators was deferential. And this kind of deferential attitude was to become crystallized into the personal cult of the Emperor, who was regarded as the patriarch of the whole Japanese people.

The basic characteristic of the Japanese State structure is that it is always considered as an extension of the family; more concretely as a nation of families composed of the Imperial House as the main family and of the people as the branch family. This is not merely an analogy as in the organic theory of the State, but is considered as having a substantial meaning. It is maintained, not as an abstract idea but as an actual historical fact, that the Japanese nation preserves unaltered its ancient social structure based on blood relationship. It is true that the idea of a nation of families, and the idea (derived from it) of the conformity of the two virtues of loyalty and filial piety, had been the official ideology of the absolute State since the Meiji era, and are not the monopoly of the fascist movement.[1]

As Maruyama maintains in the above, the peculiar character of the Japanese family system was at the root of Japanese political culture. Due to its flexibility, both the ruler and the ruled were able to be regarded as members of the same family group, and their relationship was given the possibility of being regulated by a family ethos. In other words, given that the Japanese family could include non-kinship members, it could become the basic principle for regulating extensive areas of human life. This kind of situation could be found clearly in everyday life in the traditional Japanese village. In this connection, the analysis of traditional village life in Japan by Kizaemon Aruga is highly suggestive. According to Aruga, in a traditional Japanese village, both landlords and tenants were often regarded as members of the same family. Tenants were obliged to worship the same ancestor god as the landlord and were regulated by the corresponding ethical principles. Of course, some of the tenants were members or descendants of branch families of the landlords. However, other tenants who originally had no kinship relations with the landlords were liable to be included among the family members in due course when they served the landlord continuously and diligently. Therefore the landlord's estate comprised a fairly large household (*dōzoku*) that contained both kinship and non-kinship members. It was natural for all of the tenants to offer social and economic service to the landlord. Besides providing extra labour during the busy season for farming, the tenants were obliged to call on the landlord to offer various kinds of assistance on the occasion of marriages, births, and funerals in the landlord's family. Similarly, on certain auspicious days such as the New Year's celebration and the village festival, they were to pay a courtesy call on the landlord. In return for these exertions, the tenants were entitled to various kinds of protection and provisions, the range of which was wide enough to include small gifts and financial assistance at their own marriages, births, and funerals in addition to the small huts that they lived in and the small plot of land that they acquired ownership of in due course. In this sense their mutual relationship was very close and intimate, though not always a harmonious one because of the tension inherent in their mutually unequal relationship. Moreover, when this kind of relationship was inherited generation after generation, their ties became highly consolidated ones.[2]

The post-war land reform and subsequent modernization led to the relaxation and eventual collapse of the traditional village structure, so that the contemporary Japanese state is different from the pre-war family state. Nevertheless, similar relationships have been reproduced in various organizations outside the village, and still determine the basic social institutions in contemporary Japan. So-called Japanese management is an outgrowth of exactly the same social relationship. Moreover, if the prognosis of the contemporary Japanese political system by Karl van Wolferen is correct, we can detect the same function in contemporary Japan as a whole. According to Wolferen, Japan is composed of various semi-autonomous groups with a high level of cohesion, all of them coordinated with each other and integrated, albeit loosely at times, into the entire political system.[3] Of course, without the erstwhile omnipotent authority of the Emperor, the state in contemporary Japan is destined to withdraw into the background and delegate some of its functions to the private sector. Nevertheless, Japanese society is a highly integrated one, and the contemporary Japanese state is, basically, a corporate state that coordinates, manipulates, and controls various subordinate groups through formal as well as informal means.

II

The structure of the village community in India is entirely different from that in Japan. In India, the village community is more autonomous and autarchic than in Japan. However, this village community is composed of mutually exclusive caste groups. It is therefore impossible to cultivate a mutually cordial relationship between landlord and tenant, let alone to integrate them into the same family, if they belong to different caste groups. At the same time, even though almost all of what people need is produced in the community and the village is entirely independent from the outside world as well, the village community is far from being a common moral community.

In this sense, it is pertinent to analyse more closely the internal structure of the Indian village community. As a reflection of its autonomous character, the Indian village contains various artisans and service people who provide menial services to the villagers with a strict form of division of labour established between these people and the peasants or landlords. In this sense, the division of labour, the *jajmani* system, is the backbone of the village community. Moreover, there are some protective elements inherent in this system. First, the amount of service as well as the payment of artisans and service people is fixed by custom. Therefore, as long as they perform their prescribed service, they are entitled to emolument in the form of grain, the amount of which is fixed according to custom. Second, they can expect some direct assistance in the case of drought or famine.

> Some are tailors, some potters, some grain parchers, some oil pressers, and many are personal servants and farm hands. Their lot is to supply the wants of their farmer patrons. If the patrons are satisfied with them, they are content. They accept whatever each day brings, leaving plans and responsibilities for the morrow in the hands of their patrons.... They know that as long as there is grain in the storehouses of their patrons they will not starve. They may go further into debt, but debt is a familiar associate. Only if the patron is ill unto death, or if a series of calamities threatens his storehouse, is there real anxiety.[4]

Thus write William and Charlotte Wiser on a village in Uttar Pradesh in north India. Of course, no one can deny the existence of inequality between patron (*jajman*) and client (*kamin*) and the exploitative elements between them. However, since there are some protective elements inherent in the relationship, this jajmani system can be regarded as the indispensable institution for the common village people to survive in the harsh environments of India. It is precisely because of this system that common village people can maintain their minimal living standards. In the case of their being in debt, the interest beyond double the principal is usually cancelled. However, if we were to infer from this behaviour a cordial relationship between these patrons and clients, it would be highly misleading, for such protective activities are not based on a personal foundation between these two parties. Similarly, protection does not always signify an affectionate relation between them.

In this connection, it is necessary to go still deeper into the internal structure of the jajmani system. One of the main reasons for the protection afforded to artisans and service people is the strength of their caste organization. When landlords or peasants violate the traditional rights of artisans and service people, the latter attempt to resist the violation by withholding their services on the basis of their caste organization, which extends beyond their own village. Being boycotted by people both in and outside the village, it is not uncommon for the landlords or peasants to find themselves without the service of the artisans or service people whose rights have been violated. In this sense, the caste organization functions as a trade union for artisans and service people and contributes a great deal to the protection of their prescriptive rights.

However, if we look more carefully at the internal structure of the jajmani system, we can also detect a mechanism that induces patrons to extend protection to their clients in spite of the absence of a personal or affectionate relationship between them. In this connection, the analysis of Henry Orenstein is very suggestive. According to Orenstein, the jajmani system entails patron–clientele relationships which connect the patron and client not directly but via land, that is, indirectly. As he elucidates in the case of rope-makers, leather-workers, and potters in a village in Poona district during the 1950s, the client's emolument is not decided by personal negotiation, but embedded in the land of the patron, the amount of which is fixed by custom. Therefore, the landholder who holds the land is liable to pay a specified amount in the form of grain so long as he holds the land and receives service from the artisans or service people who have a share in that land. On the other hand, artisans and service people are entitled to emoluments as long as they live in the village and provide the prescribed services.

> The right to serve landowners on a given part of the village was allocated, not the right to serve particular landowners. Some landlords owned land in different parts of the village, hence they gave *bālutā* and took service from two or more *bālutedārs*. If a man lost his land, he lost the services of the *bālutedārs* who worked on that land; and if he bought land in another part of the village, he paid *bālutā* to the man who served that part. Landlords often owned the same plots for many generations, so family-to-family ties were sometimes formed.... [But] the family-to-family bond was not an attribute of the system. It was a situational phenomenon, like the friendship groups formed on the basis of neighborhood.[5]

In other words, this patron–client relationship functions regardless of the shape of their personal relationship. They exchange protection and services even if they do not know each other personally or even if they are on unfriendly terms. Moreover, this impersonal aspect of the system becomes clearer when we recognize that artisans and service people can sell their right or 'share' to other persons without the permit of their patrons.

In this respect, the village community in the pre-modern period is not different from that which Orenstein describes. According to Hiroshi Fukazawa, in eighteenth-century Maharashtra, this jajmani system was integrated into the village community more closely. For instance, when the number of artisans or service people became double that required earlier they were to be constrained to reduce their services to half of their previous amount, instead of dividing their customers. This was mainly to avoid a chasm in the village community and maintain its integrity. Moreover, in some villages, all the products of the village were first assembled in one place and then distributed to all the villagers according to the ascertained rights or shares which each of the villagers enjoyed. In this sense, it is not an exaggeration to maintain that the artisans and service people were employed not by individual patrons, but by the village as a whole. Nevertheless, the artisans or service people were allowed to sell their right to serve or shares to other persons without the permit of their patrons.[6] In other words, even during this period when the integrity of village community was paramount, the mutual relationship of the villagers did not rest on a personal basis but on land or the shares ingrained in it. Similarly, the village community was far from constituting one moral community, in spite of its autonomous and autarchic character.

All in all, the internal structure of the Indian village community is entirely different from that of the Japanese. Morally speaking, the Indian village is a plural society, even if the villagers are interconnected more closely by an elaborate system of the division of labour. Therefore, although in India the patron is obliged to assist the client in the case of an emergency, it is not because of his personal affection or sympathy towards the client but his own consciousness of prestige. His behaviour might be regarded as highly selfish or degrading if he does not assist his client in such circumstances. Similarly, it might satisfy his sense of prestige to calculate the expense of his dependents (kamin) at a more expensive rate than the market price.[7] Moreover, if the village community in India has been able to maintain its integrity in spite of the existence of mutually exclusive caste groups, it is precisely because of this kind of impersonal arrangement amongst the villagers.

III

Such impersonal relationships are highly significant for understanding Indian society and politics. For example, they are one of the reasons why the Indian village community has been able to maintain its prototype in spite of recurrent land transfer which has occurred since the commencement of British Raj. If the human relations in the village had had a personal character, the change of landownership would have destroyed the prototypical structure by severing the age-old personal connections among the villagers and transformed the village qualitatively, as some British officers feared.

Further to this, as in Japan, the human relationships cultivated in the village have exerted a tremendous influence outside the village and have created the peculiar type of social, political, and state structure in India. For example, their influence is to be detected in the inefficiency and confusion of the estate management of landlords in India. According to Thomas Metcalf, who undertook intensive research on landlords of nineteenth-century north India, some of the estate management organizations of big landlords were highly sophisticated. Emulating the public administration of the British Raj, the landlords tried to establish bureaucratic or semi-bureaucratic estate management organizations and appointed experienced revenue officers as well as their personal friends to important posts. Nevertheless, when these agents succeeded in gaining footholds in the estate's service, they tended to put their feet down and attempt to make their rights hereditary. Similarly, in cases where the land agents were paid with a lease in perpetuity over land instead of cash, the land came to be regarded as the exclusive share of the grantee, and the grantee tended to become independent from the landlord and withhold faithful service towards him.

> The top estate employees were paid partly in cash and partly by the award of *dawami patta*s (permanent leases) of estate villages.... But such permanent leases by no means always secured the loyal service of the recipient. While the dawami patta tied its holder to the estate, at the same time it encouraged him to flaunt his independence of the raja. Swami Sewak Singh, or so Pratab Bahadur complained, neglected his duties as diwan once he had obtained his dawami patta, and even insolently refused to receive the raja when the latter visited his village during the course of an estate tour.[8]

Thus writes Metcalf regarding one case of the estate management of a *taluqdar*. In order to hold this kind of abuse and usurpation in check, the landlords contrived an elaborate system. After the model of the

British Raj, they sometimes recruited spies from the lower caste groups in order to watch the misdeeds of the land agents. However, as is apparent from the above, since this kind of checking system did not function properly even in the close circle of the landlords, it is hardly surprising that the estate management in the remote areas was sometimes in complete disarray. In these remote areas it was quite common that the land agents became independent of the landlords and sold and mortgaged their rights without the permit of the landlords. Moreover, when this kind of sub-infeudation happened still further down, the estate management system became highly complicated and numerous intermediary rights in the land emerged between the landlord and the cultivators.

> The all-important task of revenue management was administered through a pyramidal structure of tribute-collecting rights, at the apex of which stood the *zamindar*. Below the big *zamindar*s and *Raja*s existed a much more numerous class of high-caste smaller gentry, holding *taluqs*, service grants and rent-free lands, who enjoyed a proprietary right of collecting revenues of a defined territory, a right which, like that of their overlord, was freely inherited, alienated and sold. From *zamindari* at the top (*sadr*) a chain of revenue-collecting rights went down in the interior (*mufassal*) to the village level, where the system was confronted by the village heads—a class of superior *raiyat*s—who controlled the revenue of the village and paid it to the lowest grade of revenue collector.[9]

The relationship between landlords and their agents in India, like that between landlords and tenants, is thus entirely different from that in Japan. In Japan, the agents of landlords were regarded as family members or stewards of the landlord and were expected to swear faithful allegiance. On the other hand, in India the original personal relationship between the landlord and his agents was destined to be eclipsed in due course and be replaced by an impersonal relationship based on the land or the rights inherent in the land. The agents became independent of the landlord as their emolument was transformed from rights in the land granted by the landlord in return for service into their own personal holding. In addition, when the agents disposed of their share on their own account, the entire system of estate management suffered from various kinds of confusion, and land tenure as a whole became highly complicated. In this sense, it is not an exaggeration to point out, in line with P.J. Musgrave, the incompetence of the big landlords in terms of collecting rent as well as controlling their own estates. According to Musgrave, the estate of the big landlord was far from 'a tightly organized and closely structured social fact'[10] as various intermediary strata gained entrenched rights all over the estate.

IV

Turning from rural structure to the sphere of state structure, one can detect the same peculiarities. As has often been maintained, Japan experienced a period of feudalism, but this feudalism was qualitatively different from that of western Europe. In western Europe, the relationship between the lord and the vassal was regulated by a contract, which was reciprocal. In Japan, however, the vassal was regarded as a son or a family member of the lord and therefore his obligation was unilateral. In other words, in western Europe the vassal was obliged to be loyal to the lord on condition that the lord fulfilled his obligations inscribed in the feudal contract, while in Japan the vassal was destined to be loyal unconditionally.

In India, in spite of the recurrent categorization of the state system as Asiatic despotism, various kinds of plural or decentralized state systems emerged, but these state systems were different from those of western Europe and Japan. Dealing with the medieval stage of India after the Mauryan empire, R.S. Sharma outlines the decentralized political system of this period. According to Sharma, the decline of commerce after the ancient period caused the centralized bureaucratic organization of the Mauryan empire to disintegrate and forced the political overlords to take recourse to the granting of land to solicit the political allegiance of their subordinates. This is precisely what happened in western Europe after the decline of the Roman empire and the decay of the Mediterranean commercial world. However, when we look at the internal political structure of this system more carefully, some qualitative differences surface. This is mainly because the political allegiance or obligation of the subordinates was very ambiguous and insecure. In return for military and administrative service, the political overlords or kings granted land to their own kinsmen as well as to officers who had no kinship relationships with them. However, in India their services were, according to Sharma, not always explicitly codified by contract as in western Europe, so that the relationship between the 'lord' and the 'vassal' was destined to become a precarious one in due course.

'Curiously enough none of the secular grants clearly states the obligations of the beneficiaries, which are laid down only by the

Lekhapaddhati. Therefore for the country as a whole there did not exist any legal norm to which the parties could appeal in case of dispute or violation of engagements entered between the two.'[11]

Thus writes Sharma with regard to western India in the twelfth and thirteenth centuries. In *Lekhapaddhati*, it was stipulated that in some cases the beneficiary was obliged to furnish a hundred foot soldiers and twenty cavalry for the service of the headquarters of the overlord.[12] However since this kind of stipulation was exceptional, the whole of the political structure was bound to become highly precarious. It is therefore no wonder that these plural state systems suffered from both internal and external strife.

Moreover in these systems it was common that the grantee himself granted a part of his rights to his subordinates, even without the permit of his overlord. According to Sharma, this kind of sub-infeudation originated in the granting of land to Brahmins and temples, which was done lavishly, reflecting the revival of Brahmanism in the post-Mauryan period. In some cases it was explicitly stipulated that royal officers were not to cause any disturbance in the enjoyment of the grant of a village by the grantees or the getting of such a grant by others.[13] However, in the case of secular grants, when the 'vassal' would grant land out of his own assignments to temples and Brahmins or farm out his granted right to merchants and their associates for revenue collection even without the permit of the overlord, the political foundation of the state was likely to be undermined and the process of disintegration was bound to be carried on further. Moreover when a similar process proceeded downward and took place at the lower level of the power structure, the whole political system was destined to face a very critical situation.[14]

Of course, sub-infeudation was also prevalent in west European feudalism, but always with the permit of the overlords. In India, on the other hand, because of the precarious character of the 'feudal' relationship, sub-infeudation proceeded at each level without the permit of the overlord. In this sense, although the notion of fidelity as a religious or moral duty was propagated among the vassals in various didactic texts, it did not have such a great effect on them. And the causes of the precarious character of this kind of 'feudal' relationship can be reduced to various social factors. As Henry S. Maine maintains, the contractual system presupposes the relaxation or disintegration of primordial kinship groups such as clan and tribe, which tend to integrate the members by 'instinct' and thereby make them instinctively indifferent or hostile towards others.[15] It was therefore highly difficult to cultivate a faithful and stable relationship if the lords and vassals belonged to different castes. However, even if they belonged to the same caste, it was hardly possible to establish a stable relationship between them. This is mainly because there were inevitable contradictions between the feudal relationship and the one cultivated amongst caste groups. In the case of the latter, all members of the same caste group were regarded as basically equal and their leader was regarded as *primus inter pares*. On the other hand, the relationship between the lords and vassals was essentially an unequal one and therefore contained something repugnant for the ordinary caste members.

> Sri Maharaja and ourselves are of one stock, all Rahtores. He is our head, we his servants.... His forefathers have reigned for generations; our forefathers were their ministers and advisers, and whatever was performed was by the collective wisdom of the council of our chiefs. Before the face of his ancestors, our own ancestors have slain and been slain; and in performing services to the kings, they made the state of Jodpoor what it is.... [But] when our services are acceptable, then is he our lord; when not, we are again his brothers and kindred, claimants and laying claim to the land.[16]

Thus wrote the Rajputs in Marwar to the Political Agent of the British government at the beginning of the nineteenth century, when their land was confiscated and even their lives were threatened by the chief. In this statement, we can discern the basic contradiction between the feudal system and the caste system along with the concomitant instability inherent in a political system based on the caste system.

In connection with this, the concept of 'segmentary state', which Burton Stein used to characterize the medieval south Indian state structure, is very suggestive. According to Stein, though the medieval south Indian political system was plural, it cannot be characterized as feudal because there was generally no explicitly formulated contractual relationship between the king and the subordinates, such contractual relationship constituting an integral part of a feudal system.[17] In contrast, the 'segmentary state' was composed of political entities with a similar kind of structure, which overlapped one another but were not mutually interconnected by any solid political allegiance, let alone contract.

For example, under the reign of Vijayanagara, which was more centralized and martially oriented than its predecessor, the Chola dynasty, there were many semi-autonomous local political chiefs called *nayaka*. They were composed of various kinds of people who originated as colonizers of the wasteland, local chieftains with long-held indigenous power bases from the time of Chola and beyond, and the descendants of the political servants of the Vijayanagara kings, who expected political and military support from all of them in case of emergency. However, these kinds of obligations were not written down in a contract or consolidated into any of the conventions. In other words, the Vijayanagara state, though centralized, was nonetheless still a loosely constructed political system, this looseness being one of the basic reasons for its political instability. In this kingdom, personal allegiance, even if it was strong at the incipient stage, was bound to wane in due course. Similarly, following this kind of transformation, any granted land was destined to become the personal 'share' of the grantee, and military or civil service associated with the land grant was destined to be omitted.

> These Telugu warriors were not, however, to remain simply agents of the Vijayanagara kings; they could not because there was no political framework through which an agency of this sort was capable of being sustained. Telugu *nayaka*s quickly became locality figures in their own rights.... And, what is of great importance, this intermediary role was not a usurpation, an illegitimate appropriation of authority. Neither Telugu nor Tamil chiefs were completely, nor even primarily, agents or officials of the Vijayanagara state.[18]

Of course, it was a usurpation to proclaim formal independence, which would incur punitive action against the claimant. However, if the political allegiance of these subordinates was not consolidated into either contract or convention, the political system of the Viyayanagara kingdom was necessarily rather fragile, in spite of its apparent martial character and centralization. Under these circumstances, the military forts were crucial until the sixteenth and seventeenth centuries for maintaining the regal authority. They were situated in strategically important areas and manned by Brahmins, who were expected to be more loyal as well as more easily manipulated because of their rivalry with other castes.[19] Similarly, religious authority played a crucial role in consolidating the entire kingdom by supplementing the lack of political authority. It was precisely for this purpose that the king gifted land both to temples and some prominent religious leaders.[20] However, when the nayakas themselves made a similar kind of religious donation to individual Brahmins as well as to temples, it exemplified the same fragile structure at the local levels as well.

All in all, Burton Stein's concept of the 'segmentary state' is of utmost importance for our understanding of the social background of state formation in India. The unstable relationship between the superior and the inferior, especially the waning of the personal allegiance of the inferior towards the superior, is precisely an outgrowth of the impersonal relationship which was cultivated in the village community. Mediated by this kind of relationship, the land granted by the king to the nayaka was bound to become independent from the king and be transformed into the nayaka's own share in due course. And these aspects become more conspicuous when we look at the process of granting land more carefully.

In this connection, the analysis of Nicholas Dirks is very suggestive. Analysing the minor kingdom in Madurai in the eighteenth and nineteenth centuries, Dirks emphasizes that in this kingdom, the land was granted not as a 'fief', which would entail the obligation of faithful military service, but as a 'gift' for the remuneration of military service which had already been performed. Therefore the king was obliged to promise to grant other land as well as other privileges when he expected further military service from someone who had already received some land from him. In this sense, this political system is qualitatively different from the feudalism of western Europe. According to Dirks, 'In Europe lands were held by vassals on the condition of service. In south India, however, service was offered first, with the hope/expectation that gifts (of land, title, emblems, honors, privileges, etc.) would follow, in turn leading to new opportunities to offer service.'[21]

This was mainly because political allegiance in this little kingdom was very precarious. Having been granted land and other privileges, the grantee became conscious of his own political power and prestige, and felt independent from the overlord. For instance, the great nayakas of this little kingdom, which became independent from Vijayanagara in the seventeenth century, originated from the royal family of the Vijayanagara dynasty. These nayakas were usurpers of the former kingdoms. However, since a similar process was continuously proceeding in the political system, the political situation in this kingdom itself was bound to become very fluid. Indeed conspiracies and revolts were endemic within this kind of political system. In order to curb these tendencies, the king was obliged to give more gifts through enlarging his political resources.

> The necessary response of any superordinate lord or king to the logic of political relation is to keep escalating his command over the symbolic and material capital of his rule, simultaneously getting and giving more. The gift as a mode of statecraft compelled the king to engage in expansive and incorporative

> activity. Plunder and warfare were far better suited to this political modality than revenue 'systems' and bureaucratic rule. Little kingdoms, themselves often perched on precarious agrarian bases and therefore dependent on a political economy that could usually generate wealth by plunder more readily than production, were well suited to this kind of activities.... Expansion, incorporation, plunder, battle and gifts all made the state inherently dynamic.[22]

As shown above, the Indian state system was a complicated one. It was composed of various kinds of intermediary political entities whose political allegiance was highly precarious. In other words, each Indian state was just like a layer cake, which comprised several strata of intermediary political entities, overlapping one another but without a strong bond connecting them. Of course, besides the aforementioned, there are other factors which determined the nature of state system in India. For instance, Burton Stein emphasizes the ecological integrity of a local area, called *nadu*, which was constructed in an alluvial field. According to Stein, it is precisely this nadu that constituted the material or economic foundation of a nayaka's political and military power.[23] Further to this, one also cannot neglect the influence of the caste system because of its tenacious social impact. Once any caste group became firmly rooted in society, it was almost impossible to uproot it, so that it tended to form a cohesive local power.

In this respect, the political reality of 'Asiatic despotism' is no exception. For example, in the Maratha empire the local chieftains, called *watandar*s, with their own fortifications were widespread on the Decan plateau and comprised the real political infrastructure of this centralized empire. It was the local knowledge of these watandars and their own retinue that sustained revenue administration at the grass roots as well as the military strength of this empire.[24] However, it was these same political forces that posed serious problems by constantly seeking a chance to revolt by hatching conspiracies with other chieftains. Therefore, the internal structure of this Asiatic despotism is far removed from the image of a monolithic empire dominated by one omnipotent emperor. On the contrary, being contaminated by recurrent internal strife, the political structure was very fluid. It contained the inherent tendency to expand its territory in order to find the resources to satisfy the aspirations and greed of the subordinates. However, if the internal structure of these local chieftains itself was also full of internal cleavages as a result of the above-mentioned mechanism, it was not difficult to dominate them by manipulating the internal difference. 'Divide and Rule' was thus the political expedient to deal with these local chieftains. The same situation was discernible, though to a lesser extent, at the roots of the Mughal empire.

V

As the foregoing has shown, political and state structure is conditioned by the configuration of social and political powers in the village community. The segmentary state in India, composed of semi-independent political powers overlapping one another, was exactly an outgrowth of the impersonal relationships cultivated in the Indian village community. With the waning of personal allegiance, the rights in land that had been granted were transformed into a personalized 'share', the fruit of which would in due course be enjoyed by the holder irrespective of whether he fulfilled the expected service. This was influenced by the impersonal relationship formed in the jajmani system in the Indian village community. Similarly, the granting of land as a gift for past service reflects the precarious nature of personal allegiance. In this sense, the situation in India was entirely different from that in Japan, where personal relationship had been predominant both in and outside the village community.

A similar interconnection is discernible in other countries as well. For example, in Russia and China, which have both been regarded as the homelands of despotism, it is no accident that village life has been highly fluid and anarchical. Without the institution of primogeniture, it is hardly possible for a family to maintain a predominant position in a village when its land is liable to be divided at each succession. Moreover, without an integrative institution such as the jajmani system, this fluid or anarchical situation has been destined to become more conspicuous. In other words, compared with the Indian village, the village in Russia and China has been more egalitarian while being anarchical as well. And this anarchical situation has functioned as the catalyst for despotic regimes in these countries,[25] for despotism and anarchy constitute exactly opposite sides of the same coin. It is precisely the anarchical tendency at the grass roots that has cultivated the need for despotic power. The more anarchical the tendency in society, the more necessary it is for an oppressive power to curb it.

In western Europe, because of the prevalence of primogeniture, village society was more stable. Moreover, village life itself was dominated by contractual relationships. In this respect, Alan Macfarlane's analysis of English society is very suggestive. According to Macfarlane, from as early as the thirteenth century, contractual relationships penetrated deep into the society and dominated every aspect of the everyday life of the common people. For instance, when parents lived together with their son and his wife, it was not uncommon to regulate minute aspects of their daily life and write down their agreement in the form of a contract. In this sense, the transformation from 'status' to 'contract' had already taken place in England long before the advent of the modern age.[26] Furthermore, representative elements were also inherent in village life itself. In one of the royal domains of the late medieval period of England, most of the wealthy peasants in the village were recruited into the political and judicial system of the manor and were obliged to play indispensable roles on behalf of the rest of the villagers. It was their duty to sit in turn as jurors in the manorial court, which dealt with a wide range of local problems regarding law and order, maintenance of transportation, regulation of the prices and quality of local products, protection of common land, and so on. Similarly, the wealthiest peasants were recruited (first by appointment, then by election) into the administration as manorial bailiffs.[27] In this sense, contractual relationships in western Europe have been inherent in society for a long time and the representative system is rooted deeply in such a social context.

In Japan, as I mentioned at the beginning of this paper, the social and political system as a whole has retained a peculiar character. In spite of the rapid economic development of the last fifty years, so-called Japanese management is predominant in Japan. Similarly, the contemporary Japanese state still has all-encompassing capabilities and has built up a symbiotic relationship between the state and society.

> Many pressure groups will start by going directly to the officials whose cooperation they need for their original purposes. Relatively weak regional industrial and trade associations have used the bureaucracy 'to help them strengthen their organisational foundations through government legislation legalising their status and providing for compulsory membership'. Pressure groups, established to promote specific agricultural or other economic interests, will find open doors at the ministries that must deal with those interests. If a group appears large and potentially powerful enough, it will be actively courted by the officials. In return for having its wishes taken into account it provides detailed information about conditions, personalities and important events in its locality. It thus becomes part of the 'radar' whereby the bureaucrats effectively steer the System as a whole.[28]

In this passage by K. Wolferen, one can gauge the all-embracing character of the Japanese state with its heritage of the family-state prior to World War II. And this symbiotic relationship between the state and society is one of the essential reasons for the successful economic development of Japan up until the 1980s. In contemporary India, however, pressure groups are more independent and assertive, so that the political system as a whole is bound to face a very critical situation. This is mainly because the subordinate groups in India have enjoyed more independence without any connections that bind them to the superior body, as is displayed in a segmentary state. Consequently, in contemporary India, the maintenance of governability is most problematic. Here it is not necessary to delve deeply into the topic. It will suffice to say that the emergence of Hindu revivalism is the symptom of the undermining of political authority in contemporary India. As Rajni Kothari, among others, maintains,[29] this revivalism signifies nothing more than the erosion of political institutions, especially the party system. In other words, religion functions as the alternative expedient for canalizing the political will of the people.

However, if India succeeds in rebuilding political authority, there will be a chance to achieve more dynamic economic and social development. In the age of globalization, the independence and assertiveness of subordinate groups is a necessary precondition for cultivating close relationships with international organizations such as multinational companies and NGOs. In the present circumstances, neo-mercantilism as typified by Japanese industrial policy for the last few decades is not feasible. It is even disadvantageous, as is shown by the present problems of severing the cosy relationship between the public and private sectors which Japan is now striving to solve in order to reactivate the economy. Meanwhile, in India, the Nehruvian 'socialist' economic development policy was doomed to fail in its goal. Due to the inherent weakness caused by the segmentary character of the society as a whole, the state in India did not have enough capabilities to carry out a state-run economic development policy successfully.[30] Yet in an age of globalization, this erstwhile disadvantage has the possibility of transforming itself into an asset. In order to substantiate this possibility, it is of utmost importance to reconstruct the political system in India with due regard to the peculiar character of the state.

NOTES

1. Masao Maruyama, 1963, *Thought and Behaviour in Modern Japanese Politics*, London: Oxford University Press, p. 36.

2. Kizaemon Aruga, 1966, *Nihonkazokuseido to Kosakuseido* (Family System and Tenancy in Japan), Tokyo: Miraisha, pp. 34–255. The name of the family is different if the person has no kinship relation with the landlord or is not adopted into the landlord's family. Therefore, *dōzoku* comprises people with many different family names.

3. Karel van Wolferen, 1989, *The Enigma of Japanese Power: People and Politics in a Stateless Nation*, London: Macmillan.

4. William H. Wiser and Charlotte Viall Wiser, 1969, *Behind Mud Walls 1930–1960*, Berkeley: University of California Press, p. 32.

5. Henry Orenstein, 1965, *Gaon: Conflict and Cohesion in an Indian Village*, Princeton, New Jersey: Princeton University Press, p. 216.

6. Hiroshi Fukazawa, 1972, *Indo Shakaikeizaishi Kenkyū* (Studies on Social and Economic History of India), Tokyo: Tōyōkeizai Shinpōsha, pp. 260–348.

7. Henry Orenstein, 1962, 'Exploitation and Function in the Interpretation of Jajmani', *Southwestern Journal of Anthropology,* Vol. 18, pp. 302–16.

8. Thomas R. Metcalf, 1979, *Land, Landlords, and the British Raj: Northern India in the Nineteenth Century*, Berkeley: University of California Press, p. 261.

9. Rajat and Ratna Ray, 1975, 'Zamindars and Jotedars: A Study of Rural Politics in Bengal', *Modern Asian Studies,* Vol. 9, No. 1, p. 83.

10. P.J. Musgrave, 1972, 'Landlords and Lords of Land: Estate Management and Social Control in Uttar Pradesh 1860–1920', *Modern Asian Studies*, Vol. 6, No. 3, p. 272.

11. Ram Sharan Sharma, 1965, *Indian Feudalism: c. 300–1200*, Calcutta: University of Calcutta Press, p. 199.

12. Ibid., p. 20.

13. Ibid., p. 92.

14. Ibid., p. 156ff.

15. Henry Sumner Maine, 1906, *Ancient Law: Its Connection with the Early History of Society and its Relation to Modern Ideas*, 10th edn, London: John Murray, pp. 373–4.

16. James Tod, 1914, *Annals and Antiquities of Rajast'han*, Vol. 1, popular edition, London: George Routledge & Sons, pp. 159–60.

17. Burton Stein, 1980, *Peasant, State and Society in Medieval India*, New Delhi: Oxford University Press, pp. 374–6.

18. Ibid., pp. 408–10.

19. Ibid., pp. 403–4.

20. Ibid., pp. 412–14, with regard to Stein's recent conceptualization of the segmentary state, see Burton Stein, 1995, 'The Segmentary State: Interim Reflections', in Hermann Kulke (ed.), *The State in India 1000–1700*, New Delhi: Oxford University Press, pp. 134–61.

21. Nicholas Dirks, 1987, *The Hollow Crown: Ethnohistory of an Indian Kingdom*, Cambridge: Cambridge University Press, p. 44.

22. Ibid., p. 48.

23. Stein, *op. cit.*, pp. 270–5.

24. André Wink, 1986, *Land and Sovereignty in India: Agrarian Society and Politics under the Eighteenth-century Maratha Svarājya*, Cambridge: Cambridge University Press, pp. 183–205.

25. Richard Pipes, 1990, *The Russian Revolution 1899–1919*, London: Collins Harvill, pp. 92–100; Tadashi Fukutake, 1951, 'Chūgokuno Nōson to Nihonno Nōson (The Village in China and the Village in Japan)', in *Chūgoku Nōsonshakaino Kōzō* (The Rural Structure in China), Tokyo: Yūhikaku, Appendix pp. 8–18.

26. Alan Macfarlane, 1978, *The Origins of English Individualism*, Oxford: Basil Blackwell, pp. 141–4.

27. Marjorie Keniston McIntosh, 1986, *Autonomy and Community: The Royal Manor of Harvering, 1200–1500*, Cambridge: Cambridge University Press, pp. 201–15.

28. Wolferen, *op. cit.*, p. 57.

29. Rajni Kothari, 1988, *State against Democracy: In Search of Humane Governance*, New Delhi: Ajanta Publications, pp. 244–6.

30. Masaaki Kimura, 1996, 'The Role of the State in Industrial Development: The Case of Japan and India', *Man and Development*, Vol. VIII, No. 2, pp. 1–7.

SECTION II

Forms and Process of the State

CHAPTER 4

Doṣa (Sin)–*Prāyaścitta* (Penance)

The Predominating Ideology in the Medieval Deccan

Hiroyuki Kotani

INTRODUCTION

Two dichotomous concepts of purity–impurity (*śuddha–aśuddha*, assumed to be Brahmanical ideology)[1] and auspiciousness–inauspiciousness (*maṅgala–amaṅgala*, assumed to be kingship's ideology)[2] have often been emphasized as the pivotal ideologies functioning in Indian culture throughout history, regardless of whether these two are considered to have been incompatible with each other or permutable depending on circumstances. So far as my empirical studies on the state and local society in the medieval Deccan indicate, however, the predominating ideology in the medieval Deccan seems to have been rather the *doṣa* (sin in medieval Marathi)–*prāyaścitta* (penance) ideology than the purity–impurity ideology finding expression in the pollution–purification rituals, let alone the auspiciousness–inauspiciousness ideology that was merely implied in the state ritual of *śānti* performed through the medium of Brahmins.

The concept of sin, however, was so closely related to the concept of pollution in Indian culture that difficult problems arise when we try to analyse them into two distinct categories. The difficulty in handling sin and pollution is caused mainly by the fact that both of them were required to be purified, if they should be removed. That the very same word of *śuddhi* (purification) has been applied to both sin and pollution, tends to obscure the distinction between sin and pollution. The difference in the socio-cultural context of sin and pollution, however, can be seen in the difference of the method of purification. In the case of sin, various purification ceremonies collectively known as prāyaścitta had to be performed to remove from the sinner his sin. On the contrary, pollution caused by, for example, the physical contact (*sparśa*) with an untouchable, was commonly held to be purified by ablution (*snāna*). What it means is that in spite of the very same word of śuddhi being applied both to sin and pollution, these two concepts had essentially different origins and functions.[3]

Compared with the ideas of sin and pollution prescribed in classical law books such as the Manu-smṛti, a very salient feature of medieval ideas of sin and pollution seems to have been the predominance of the idea of sin over that of pollution. In other words, the sin–penance ideology weighed much more heavily than the pollution–purification ideology in maintaining order and stability. Thus, the development of sin–penance ideology in history constitutes one of the crucial themes for the study of medieval India.

In medieval India, as was the case with ancient India, the one and same act which was prescribed as a crime to be punished by the state as well as the local society, was, at the same time, a sin required to be purified or removed by the ceremony of prāyaścitta. In other words, the actual or material act constituting a crime was regarded, at the same time, as an ideological act constituting a sin. Thus, the sin-penance concept functioned as the ideological cover of crime–punishment relationship sustained by the physical power of compulsion exercised by the state as well as the communal control exerted by the local society.

This essay aims to clarify the medieval concept of sin–penance which played the pivotal role in ideologically helping maintain state order and societal stability with special reference to the medieval Deccan. I will mainly draw on medieval Marathi documents pertaining to the seventeenth–eighteenth-century Maratha kingdom (AD 1674–1818), as it is difficult to find informative documents of earlier periods in this regard.

SAṂSARGA DOṢA

Of various doṣas in the medieval Deccan, the most interesting and important in the historical context of the development of sin–penance ideology is *saṃsarga doṣa* that was assumed to accrue from association or intercourse with one who was excommunicated by reason of committing a crime or violating a community rule.

The idea of saṃsarga appeared first in classical law books of India. The Manu-smṛti, for example, enumerates the following five 'mortal sins' (*mahāpātaka*): killing a Brāhmaṇa, drinking *surā*, stealing the gold (of a Brāhmaṇa), entering the bed of a guru's wife, and associating (saṃsarga) with such (offenders).[4] The last category of mahāpātaka, that is, association with grave criminals of four former categories, thus, constitutes the principal case of the sin of saṃsarga in the Manu-smṛti. However, association with every sort of criminal excommunicated from society by reason of his crime or violation of communal rules also was regarded as the sin of saṃsarga. Those excommunicated were designated as *patita* and association with patitas in general incurred the sin of saṃsarga on the associator.[5]

In the case of the Manu-smṛti, however, the idea of saṃsarga with the discriminated, such as the Chandala (*cāṇḍāla*), had not yet developed to a high degree with only such an obscure provision as follows: 'A *Brāhmaṇa* who unintentionally approaches a woman of *cāṇḍāla* or very low class, who eats (the food of such persons) and accepts (present from them) becomes a *patita*;...'[6]

The idea of saṃsarga seems to have developed considerably in medieval law books. P.V. Kane points out the following in this regard:[7]

> In spite of this medieval writers gradually extended the scope of *saṁsarga* in a spirit of exclusiveness and over-emphasis on ideas of ceremonial purity. For example, the *Smṛtyarthasāra* (p. 112) remarks that he who associates with the person that associates with a *mahāpātakin* has to undergo half the expiation that the first associator has to undergo. But that work does not go beyond this. The *Mitākṣarā* (on *Yājñavalkya* III. 261) appears to hold that the associator even though he does not become *patita* is liable to undergo expiation and that even the 4th and 5th associators in a series are liable to undergo expiation though it is lesser and lesser.... *Āpastamba-smṛti* (III. 1–32) states: 'If a *cāṇḍāla* stays in the house of any one of the four castes without being known, the latter on coming to know of the fact should undergo expiation, which is *Candrāyana* or *Parāka* for a member of the first three *varṇa*s and *Prājāpatya* for a *śūdra*. Those who partook of cooked food in that man's house should undergo *Kṛcchra*; one should prescribe one-half of *Kṛcchra* for those who took cooked food in the house of 2nd associator and for those who partook of cooked food in the house of these last, one-fourth of *Kṛcchra* is prescribed. So besides the original associator, three more in succession were held to be liable for *prāyaścitta*.

Thus, in medieval law books, the sin of saṃsarga is assumed to be transmittable to one who associated with the original associator, and further from the second associator down to the third and fourth associators with diminishing degree of sinfulness. It seems to mean that the idea of saṃsarga had developed to a high degree in medieval India, though it is not certain whether or not this idea of transmission of the sin of saṃsarga reflects the reality in early medieval India.

Upon this preliminary survey of the idea of saṃsarga in classical and medieval law books, it is now turn to examine the case of saṃsarga doṣa in the Maratha kingdom. There were various cases of saṃsarga doṣa appearing in medieval Marathi documents.

In one case, a Brahmin, Mahadev Bhat Joshi, of the village Kadjalganv, Sevganv district, appealed to the Hozur (Persian word implicating the king; but in the eighteenth-century Maratha kingdom, Hozur indicated the Peshva as the de facto king) as follows:

> My wife killed one of our Brahmin relatives, Vitthal Joshi. Therefore I myself and all of my relatives were excommunicated. My wife executed her wicked act without informing me. Hozur, please do all of us a favour of sanctioning us to undergo *prāyaścitta* in accordance with our *doṣa*.

In response to this appeal, an order was issued to all of the Brahmins of the *kasbe* Sevganv to perform the ceremony of prāyaścitta on Mahadev Bhat Joshi and his relatives in accordance with the nature of their saṃsarga doṣa.[8] In this case, saṃsarga doṣa resulted to the husband and relatives from social association with the criminal wife. Social association thus included not only cohabitation with the criminal but also remote familial relationship. The doṣa of the murderer was assumed to be transmitted to the family members and relatives through saṃsarga. Thus, the husband and relatives had to undergo prāyaścitta, if they should be readmitted to their caste.

In another case, Nibaji Kulkarni of the village Shahrtakli, Nevasa district, was accused of having committed saṃsarga doṣa by contracting a matrimonial relation with a Brahmin of the Paithan party, that is, a group of Brahmins excommunicated by reason of their performance of prāyaścitta on the Brahmin who had been taken a prisoner by the Afghans in the battle of Panipat in 1761 and forcibly converted to Islam, but returned home after ten-years' detention. The following order was issued by the Peshva government in this regard:[9]

> Send the aforementioned Kulkarni with his family to Paithan and make them undergo *prāyaścitta* of *saṃsarga doṣa*, with Chimaji Naik Bhakare as a witness. If he would not undergo *prāyaścitta* to be purified, confiscate his Kulkarni *vatan* (patrimony; see Note 14 below) of the aforementioned village, and pass the proceeds of the said vatan to the government account, while sending his person to the government office.

In this case, saṃsarga doṣa was caused by association (matrimonial relation) with the man who had been excommunicated by the order of Peshva, resembling somewhat the sin of saṃsarga with a patita in classical law books.

Another case of saṃsarga doṣa with a criminal concerned the female slave who committed the crime (sin) of prohibited association. Ranoji Dhumal, the Patil of the village Sonke, Vai province, purchased a female slave (*baṭīka*) who had subsequently served in his home for four years. Thereafter it turned out that this female slave had practised *annavyavahāra* (commensal relation) with a woman convert to Islam (*bāṭgī musalmān*, literally meaning a 'polluted Muslim woman'). Thus, the Patil was ordered to undergo prāyaścitta to purify his saṃsarga doṣa which accrued from having lived together in the same house with this female slave who had violated the commensal rule.[10]

Thus, saṃsarga doṣa with criminals (sinners) occurred very often from various causes in the medieval Deccan. This means that there were in the medieval Deccan many men and women who were obliged to undergo prāyaścitta to remove doṣa transmitted to them from a criminal (sinner) through saṃsarga of various sorts. This made prāyaścitta more and more necessary and important.

Further, the idea of saṃsarga doṣa with the discriminated developed considerably more in the medieval Deccan than as prescribed in classical law books such as the Manu-smṛti. Many cases of this sort appear in medieval Marathi documents.

In one such case, Bajirao Moreshvar and his family had stayed in the home of Anandrao Gopal for four months, at which time it turned out that a maidservant (or a female slave, *kuṇbīṇa*) of Bajirao Moreshvar was a woman of the Chambhar caste. Thus, members of both families were assumed to have unknowingly committed saṃsarga doṣa with an untouchable woman through having been living in the same house, so that they had to undergo prāyaścitta. In this case, prāyaścitta had to be performed to the house and land on which the house stood as well to purify the house and land from saṃsarga doṣa with the untouchable woman.[11] Yet in another case of the same sort, a female slave (baṭīka) of Baraji Mahadev, the Mamledar of the Shivner district, by caste a Prabhu, proved to have committed adultery with a man of *antyaja* (the untouchable), as a result of which family members of the Mamledar had to undergo '*prāyaścitta* of *saṃsarga* with an adulteress who had sexual intercourse with a lowly man' (*nīca-abhigata-yoṣit-saṃsarga-prāyaścitta*).[12]

Thus, in the medieval Deccan, the idea of saṃsarga doṣa with the untouchable developed considerably. The social reality which brought about this development must have included, first, the development of untouchability in medieval India in general and, second, strengthening of the norm-oriented nature of society or norm-consciousness in the medieval Deccan where even physical contact (sparśa) with the untouchable was accused rather in the context of doṣa (crime, sin) of association (saṃsarga) with a prohibited person than in the context of pollution caused by untouchability, as will be discussed in the next section.

In the above-mentioned cases, all of the persons accused of committing saṃsarga doṣa, appealed to the Hozur (Peshva) for sanction to undergo prāyaścitta to be purified, in response to which the Hozur sanctioned it taking *rājadaṇḍa*. What it means is that in the case of the Maratha kingdom, the sin–penance ideology was the state ideology embodied in kingship for the purpose of putting ideological cover over the state punishment (daṇḍa) to be inflicted on the criminal.

However, this function of sanctioning prāyaścitta was not the monopoly of the Hozur. In many cases, the Dharmadhikari (a hereditary officer of dharma) of sacred places exercised the same authority as the Hozur's in the local society perfectly independently of the Hozur or the state. The procedure of sanctioning prāyaścitta by the Dharmadhikari was as follows: (1) the person accused of committing any crime (sin) should submit '*doṣa patra*' (the statement of sin) to the Dharmadhikari stating his sin and ask him to prescribe the adequate ceremony of prāyaścitta, and (2) the Dharmadhikari should prescribe and actually perform the ceremony of prāyaścitta and thereafter issue '*śuddhi patra*' (the certificate of purification). In one such case, the Joshi and Kulkarni of the village Pokhali, Parner district, submitted 'doṣa patra' to the Dharmadhikari of Nasik in the northern Deccan stating that he and his family had committed saṃsarga doṣa with a 'woman of Chandala, the skinners (*carmakī cāṇḍāḷī*)', so they were required to be purified by the adequate ceremony of prāyaścitta. Prāyaścitta prescribed by Brahmins of the sacred place being duly performed, the Dharmadhikari issued 'śuddhi patra' certifying that they have now become fit for the commensal row (*paṅktipāvana*) of the caste.[13] This case indicates that the sin–penance ideology exercised through Dharmadhikari was the ideology of local society by which *jātidaṇḍa* (caste penalty commonly in the form of excommunication) to be inflicted on the offender of caste rules was ideologically covered.[14]

Thus, the Maratha kingdom as well as the local society under it relied upon this same sin–penance ideology, though quite independently with each other through respective functionaries.

SPARŚA: SIN OR POLLUTION?

Sparśa (physical contact) with a certain kind of man and woman was assumed to cause pollution to the contactee. The Manu-smṛti prescribes the following in this regard:

> When he has touched a *cāṇḍāla*, a menstruating woman, a *patita*, a woman within 10 days after childbirth, a corpse or one who has touched them, he becomes pure by bathing.[15]

Thus, in the Manu-smṛti, pollution caused by the physical contact (sparśa) with criminals like patitas and the discriminated such as the Chandala is prescribed to be purified by ablution (snāna). In other words, the physical contact with such men and women is not to constitute a sin required to be purified by prāyaścitta in the case of the Manu-smṛti.

The circumstances, however, were considerably different in the case of the medieval Deccan, where physical contact with the untouchable was rather assumed to be a doṣa (sin) which must have been removed through performance of prāyaścitta than the act which would cause pollution to the contactee. The very interesting and important case in this regard is a rape case committed against an untouchable woman in which doṣa (sin) of rape and pollution caused by physical contact (sparśa) with an untouchable woman seems to be intermingled.

In one such case, Gangaji Jagthap, the Deshmukh of the Sasvad district, and six other men (three Kunbis, one Mali, one Sali, and one Muslim) were accused of having committed rape against a girl of the Mahar caste, though it proved later to have been a false accusation. The very delicate point pertaining to this case is whether the act of rape should be accused as doṣa (sin, crime) or should be blamed for pollution caused by the physical contact (sparśa) with an untouchable girl through the act of rape. That the Deshmukh and other men (except the Muslim man perhaps) who were assumed to have committed rape were ordered by the Peshva government to undergo prāyaścitta after going on a pilgrimage to Varanasi and Rameshvar (Rameshvaram) rather than to be purified by ablution,[16] denotes that the act of rape against an untouchable woman was regarded as doṣa in the medieval Deccan. In other words, the act of rape had to be accused as doṣa, as it constituted violation of the law of the state (the Maratha kingdom) which would have endangered the state order. This act being accused as doṣa, saṃsarga doṣa accrued not only to the relatives of accused persons but also to inhabitants of the kasbe Sasvad as well as the kasbe itself. Thus, the relatives of accused persons were ordered to undergo prāyaścitta after being tonsured and observing three day of fasting. Inhabitants of the kasbe Sasvad were obliged to observe a one-day fast for the sake of prāyaścitta. Further, the ceremony of prāyaścitta had to be performed on the kasbe Sasvad itself to purify the town from saṃsarga doṣa with the criminals.[17]

Thus, of the two blamable aspects of rape, that is, doṣa and sparśa, the graver one for the state (the Maratha kingdom) seems to have been the aspect of doṣa as a reflection of the predominance of the idea of doṣa over that of pollution (purity) in the state ideology.

This was the case with the local society as well in the medieval Deccan. It can be attested by a case pertaining to a barber. One day, a barber residing in Nasik was asked to cut hair by an unknown guest while awaiting customers on the Godavari river. The barber did not ask his caste and the guest too did not intimate it. When the barber began to cut hair, one of the members of the same barber caste came along and accused him of touching the head of a Budhalkar (an untouchable caste of skinners). Thus, having committed the physical contact (sparśa) with an untouchable through unknowingly cutting his hair, he was excluded from the commensal relation of his caste. The embarrassed barber submitted doṣa patra (the statement of sin) to the Dharmadhikari of Nasik and asked him to prescribe a suitable ceremony of prāyaścitta to purify him.[18] In this case also, the physical contact (sparśa) with the untouchable was accused rather as doṣa against the rule of the local society (caste community) than as the act that would cause pollution.

These two cases indicate that physical contact with the untouchable had to be accused as a crime of violating the law of the state in the former case and the rule of local society in the latter case. It is noteworthy that the problem of pollution through the physical contact with the untouchable did not arise in both of these cases. What it means is that discrimination against the untouchable in the medieval Deccan was maintained rather by people's abiding by laws of the state and community rules through the fear of state punishment and social sanction than by the fear of pollution.[19]

SUICIDE: SIN OR POLLUTION?

The other type of case which involves the problem of whether an act constituted sin or pollution, is the suicide case. The Manu-smṛti contains such a provision pertaining to suicide as follows:

> The ceremony of water (*udakakriyā*) shall not be performed on those who have been born in vain (who neglect the prescribed), on those born in consequence of an illegal mixture of *jāti*, on those who are ascetics, and on those who have ruined themselves (who have committed suicide).[20]

This provision follows provisions prescribing the method of purification of pollution such as that caused by the physical contact with a Chandala,[21] so that suicide is deemed as an act which brings about pollution in the case of the Manu-smṛti.

As opposed to this, suicide was doṣa required to be removed by prāyaścitta in the medieval Deccan. The following cases testify this. In one case, Tama, daughter-in-law of a Brahmin, Rangbhat Dekne, was assumed to have committed suicide in the Mutha river on account of some disagreement with her father-in-law. On a night of lunar eclipse in the month of Bhadrapad, she wanted to take her six-year-old son to the river for *sparśasnāna* but her father-in-law dissuaded her from doing so, as the boy was ill at that time. Being offended by this act, she went to the river alone and tried to commit suicide, at which time other female members of the family prevented her and brought her back home. Sometime later, she stole out of the house and went to the river for *mokṣasnāna*. Since then, she vanished and was assumed to have committed suicide, though her dead body could not be found in spite of a six-month search. Upon this, Rangbhat Dekne appealed to the Hozur (Peshva) to sanction the performance of her funeral ceremony to enable the family to celebrate such auspicious ceremonies (*māṃgalya*) as marriage. His appeal was accepted and he was ordered to undergo prāyaścitta, after paying rājadaṇḍa of 100 rupees to the Hozur and *brahmadaṇḍa* to the Brahmins (who prescribed and actually performed prāyaścitta).[22] This case indicates that a suicide victim was deemed as a criminal, to whose family members saṃsarga doṣa was to accrue. Therefore, the father-in-law of Tama, the suicide victim in this case, had to undergo prāyaścitta to be freed from saṃsarga doṣa.

In another case, a mother of two brothers, Hari Jadhav and Ramachandra Jadhav, committed suicide, having been prompted by a quarrel with a female slave (kuṇbīṇa). The two brothers were excommunicated by reason of saṃsarga doṣa with the suicide victim. One year thereafter, they submitted doṣa patra to the Dharmadhikari of Nasik and asked to prescribe a suitable ceremony of prāyaścitta to remove the saṃsarga doṣa from their body. Prāyaścitta being performed accordingly, the two brothers became fit for commensality of their caste (*paṅktipāvana*) and śuddhi patra of this purport was issued by the Dharmadhikari.[23] In this case also, suicide was regarded as a crime (sin) that was to cause saṃsarga doṣa to the family members of the suicide victim.

These two cases show that suicide was assumed as a crime sin by the state (the Maratha kingdom) as well as the local society in the medieval Deccan. That the problem of pollution to be caused by death of family members (*sūtaka*) did not arise in both of these two cases, should not be overlooked, as it also indicates that the idea of doṣa (sin) predominated over the idea of pollution in the medieval Deccan.

Thus, it is clear from these cases of suicide that the same ideology of doṣa–prāyaścitta played the pivotal role in the state apparatus of the Maratha kingdom as well as social organization of the local society in the medieval Deccan. This same sin–penance ideology of the state and local society functioned quite independently but, at the same time, mutually complementarily in maintaining the state order and societal stability.

ŚĀNTI

This same independence and mutual complementarity in ideological functions between the state and the local society can be seen in the rite of śānti (propitiation rite) that is commonly assumed to be the expression of the auspiciousness (maṅgala)– inauspiciousness (amaṅgala) ideology, though the terms maṅgala-amaṅgala hardly appear in medieval Marathi documents.

Śānti is the rite performed by the state as well as in the local society to propitiate when extraordinary natural phenomena occurred. The state ritual of śānti was performed by Brahmins while that of the local society by the untouchables such as the Mahar and Mang. Thus, these two types of śānti must have been essentially different in nature as well as origin.

The following extract shows the procedure of the rite of śānti performed under the government order.

> Khandoji Kondve, the Sarnaik (headman of guards) of the Narayangad fort petitioned the government for sanction to perform the rite of śānti, as a bad star

(*duṣṭagraha*) appeared on the zodiac. Accordingly, a government order was issued to Antaji Kathkar, the Havaldar and the Karkun to make them perform śānti, defraying 10 to 15 rupees for expenses.[24]

The appearance of bad stars, eclipses, comets, and meteors were typical bad omens frequently referred to in the classical literature.[25] On the occasion of a solar eclipse, for example, the Maratha (Peshva) government ordered Brahmins to perform certain rituals and granted *inām* lands to the Brahmins concerned.[26]

An example of more minor bad omens can be seen in the following case. In Pandharpur, lizards touched the image of Vithoba, so the rites of *mahārudra* and śānti had to be performed. For these rites, 1000 Brahmins were gathered in Pandharpur and the government sanctioned an expenditure of 400 rupees to feed those Brahmins.[27] In this case, the physical contact of lizards must have been assumed to be a bad omen.

The state ritual of śānti performed to avert bad omens finding expression in such extraordinary phenomena as an epidemic, a thunderbolt, and an earthquake was called *adbhutaśānti* (*adbhuta* means 'wonder').[28] In one case, an epidemic disease spread in the Visapur fort and affected more than 100 persons with death toll of twenty-five. Therefore the Havaldar of the fort, with the consent of all of the fort personnel, petitioned the government to issue an order that the rite of adbhutaśānti be performed. The government gave assent to it.[29] Another example of adbhutaśānti was the case of thunderbolt. On the *dasarā* day, the flagpole of the Mahuli fort was struck and split by a thunderbolt. Thus, Brahmins were invited to recite the incantation for the planet Saturn (*śanicā japa*) 100,000 times to propitiate. For this rite of śānti, an expenditure of ten rupees in addition to 100 rupees to feed Brahmins thus invited was sanctioned by the government.[30] In the case of an earthquake as well, the rite of śānti was performed. In one such case, the government order was issued to the district official of Kalyan-Bhivandi to summon learned Brahmins and make them perform śānti.[31]

Thus, there is no doubt that the Maratha (Peshva) government used to make Brahmins perform the rite of śānti to avert bad omens which otherwise might have shaken order and stability.

The rite of śānti performed in the local society, however, differed conspicuously from the state ritual of śānti conducted by Brahmins. The salient feature of śānti of the local society was that it was performed to propitiate the anger of devī (goddess of soil), expressed by an epidemic or extraordinary phenomena like an earthquake, with the sacrifice of animals. Due to this characteristic of śānti of the local society, its performers were untouchables such as Mahars and Mangs. Brahmins therefore had no place in this śānti of the local society. The village rite of śānti was more routinely performed in the local society on festive occasions, specifically on the occasion of dasarā. Śānti in this case seems to have been meant for throwing out evil spirits haunting the village outside the village boundary with *peḍhā* (sweetmeats) thrown out of boundary by the Mahar and Mang while walking around the boundary before a buffalo to be sacrificed later for the devī. Thus, the village rite of śānti did not share the state ideology of bad omens or auspiciousness–inauspiciousness.

The relevant portions of a document pertaining to one such case of routine śānti performed in the kasbe Karad read as follows:[32]

1 A Mahar proceeds with a pot [of *peḍhā* (sweetmeat) in hand] and a Mang follows him also with a pot [of peḍhā in hand].

2 A buffalo decorated by turmeric and garland is to be made to walk around the village boundary.

Iraḍa (a head-load of wood?) is held at the head of procession, then the Mahar and Mang with pots of [peḍhā in hand] and then the buffalo walks around the village boundary.

3 A *ratha* (float) made by the Sutar is drawn to the place of the Kumbhar. An idol of Lakṣmī [devī] made by the Kumbhar is put in the ratha and drawn to a temporary *maṇḍapa* behind the Hanuman temple with music. The idol is installed in the maṇḍapa and the ratha is put by the side of the idol.

4 The Mahar worships the buffalo which has come [to the maṇḍapa after walking around the village boundary]. The offering and leaves of betel offered to the idol is to be taken by the Mahar and Mang.

5 The buffalo is taken before the idol and his head is to be cut a certain degree by the Mahar and then to be cut off by the Mang.

6 For three days, the idol is worshipped. All the villagers, old and young, are to bring offerings to the idol.

7 On the fourth day, the idol is to be brought to the village boundary and thrown out of the village.

This document clearly shows that this routine rite of śānti in the local society was a joint activity of the village as a ritual community in which all the villagers played their respective roles with the Mahar and Mang as leading actors.

Thus, the rite of śānti in the local society differed considerably from the state ritual of śānti in nature as well as functionaries. What it means is that the state ideology of bad omens or auspiciousness–inauspiciousness finding expression in the Brahmanical rite of śānti did not permeate down to the local society where the rite of śānti had almost nothing to do with those ideas. In other words, the state and local society conducted the rite of śānti quite independently with respective ideas and functionaries but mutually complementarily with the same intention of maintaining order and stability. This was also the case with the ritual performed on the occasion of an eclipse. In the case of state, Brahmins performed certain rituals, while in the local society people went to a nearby river for ablution, as indicated in the above-cited suicide case of Tama.[33]

This point, however, is in total opposition to what Dirks claims of a south Indian 'little kingdom'. He maintains that the royal gift (kingly grants) to 'village officers, servants, and artisans were concerned with the maintenance of the structure of village ritual' and 'village headmen could not conduct their ritual duties in village festivals without worshipping and prominently displaying the emblems that had been granted by kings'.[34] In the case of the Maratha kingdom as well, the royal gift was bestowed, perhaps once a year, on village headmen (Patils), village scribes (Kulkarnis) and caste headmen (Mhetars). *Śirpāv* (turban) and *pāna* (betel leaf), for example, were to be bestowed on the Patil of the village Bhangaon, Karde district[35] and śirpāv to the Kulkarni of the village Nimbganv, Junnar province.[36] In the case of caste headmen, *taśrīf* (investing with honorary dress) with pāna and/ or *viḍā* was the usual form of the royal gift.[37] These royal gifts of the Maratha kingdom, however, seem to have played no roles in the village rituals such as śānti, since they never appear in the documents pertaining to village rituals as indicated in the afore-cited document on the village rite of śānti. What it means seems to be that the ritual relationship between the state and the local society differed considerably depending on the historical circumstances such as, whether it was a 'little kingdom' or a 'great kingdom'.

CONCLUSION

From the discussion above, it can be concluded that the sin (doṣa)–penance (prāyaścitta) ideology predominated in the medieval Deccan over the ideology of pollution–purification, let alone that of auspiciousness–inauspiciousness. It played the pivotal role of ideologically sustaining the state order as well as societal stability, of which the material basis was the crime (doṣa)–punishment (daṇḍa) relationship with physical power of compulsion exercised by the state (*sarkārdaṇḍa*) and communal control exerted by the local society by means of caste penalty (jātidaṇḍa), respectively. Thus, the state as well as the local society in the medieval Deccan drew on this same sin–penance ideology quite independently through respective functionaries, but mutually complementarily with each other, for maintaining order and stability.

This conclusion implies that the two dichotomous ideas of purity–impurity and auspiciousness–inauspiciousness have been too often overemphasized as playing the central ideological roles in Indian history.[38] These two dichotomous ideas, however, do not seem to have played strong ideological functions, at least in medieval India, as they lacked such a physical basis of compulsion as sarkārdaṇḍa and jātidaṇḍa, as in the case of the sin (doṣa)–penance (prāyaścitta) ideology. The Manu-smṛti is quite categorical in this regard, saying that 'The whole world is kept in order by punishment, for guiltless man is difficult to find; through fear of punishment the whole world yields the enjoyments'.[39] This realism of the Manu-smṛti should always be borne in mind while dealing with ideology, ritual, symbol, and the like.

NOTES

1. Cf. L. Dumont, 1980, *Homo Hierarchicus* [first edn, 1966], revised English edn, New Delhi: Oxford University Press.

2. Cf. R. Inden, 1985, 'Kings and Omens', in J.B. Carman and F.A. Marglin (eds), *Purity and Auspiciousness in Indian Society,* Leiden: E.J. Brill.

3. The concept of pollution itself includes a variety of ideas of different origins and functions. For example, pollution caused by the death of family members and relatives was assumed to die down after the lapse of the prescribed time, during which time, however, the party concerned was obliged to avoid social association with other persons (*Manu-smṛti with the Manubhāṣya of Medhātithi,* ed., Ganganatha Jha, in 2 Vols, V-57–61), while pollution caused by physical contact with the dead body of a stranger had to be purified by ablution (*Manu-smṛti*, ibid., V-84). What it means is that even the concept of death-pollution includes two different ideas of different origins and functions. Thus, the essentialist approach to the concept of pollution, a good example of which is Mary Douglas, saying 'As we know it, dirt is essentially disorder', seems to be destined to fail to grasp the whole range of the concept of pollution (Mary Douglas, 1984, *Purity and Danger: An Analysis of the Concepts of Pollution and Taboo* [first edn, 1966], AKK edition, London and New York: Routledge and Kegan Paul, p. 2).

4. *Manu-smṛti*, ibid., XI–53.

5. *Manu-smṛti*, ibid., XI–180.

6. *Manu-smṛti*, ibid., XI–174. In this paper, I have consulted the English translation of the Manu-smṛti by Bühler (G. Bühler, 1886, *The Laws of Manu*, London: Oxford University Press [The Sacred Books of the East]) as well as the excellent Japanese translation by N. Watase, though the numbers of chapter-verse in the Manu-smṛti referred to in this paper are those of the original text edited by G. Jha.

7. P.V. Kane, 1968–77, *History of Dharmaśāstra*, 5 Vols, Poona: Bhandarkar Oriental Research Institute, second edn, IV 27–8.

8. G.S. Sardesai (ed.), 1930–4, *Selections from the Peshwa Daftar*, 45 Vols, Bombay: Bombay Government Central Press (SPD hereafter), XXXXIII 151.

9. G.C. Vad (ed.), 1905–11, *Selections from the Satara Rajas' and the Peshwas' Diaries*, 9 Vols, Poona and Bombay: Deccan Vernacular Translation Society (SSRPD hereafter), VIII 1133, AD 1785–6.

10. SSRPD I 399. AD 1752–3.

11. SPD XXXXIII 92 AD 1795.

12. SSRPD VIII 1125 AD 1781–2.

13. Bhārat Itihās Saṃśodhak Maṇḍal (ed.), 1934–67, *Aitihāsik Saṃkīrṇa Sāhitya*, 13 Vols, Pune: Bhārat Itihās Saṃśodhak Maṇḍal (ASS hereafter), I 200, AD 1756.

14. This 'autonomous' ritual authority of Dharmadhikari was sustained by the structure of local society which can be conceptualized as the vatan system. In the local society of the medieval Deccan based on the vatan system, all of the full-fledged members of the local society possessed respective vatans (patrimony) such as *deśmukhī* and *deśpāṇḍepaṇa* at the district level, *pāṭīlkī*, *sutālkī*, *mahārkī*, etc. in the village, *śeṭepaṇa* and *mahājankī* in the market place, and *mhetarkī* (vatan of headman) of each caste. The office of Dharmadhikari was also one of these vatans to be hereditarily inherited by particular Brahmin families in sacred places. Thus, the authority of Dharmadhikari in exercising the sin–penance ideology independently of the state was rested on the hereditary right conferred on him by the vatan system. As to the vatan system, see Hiroyuki Kotani, 1996, 'The *Vatan*-system in the Sixteenth-Eighteenth Century Deccan', in D.N. Jha (ed.), *Society and Ideology in India: Essays in Honour of Professor R.S. Sharma*, Delhi: Munshiram Manoharlal, and further on the Dharmadhikari, see Hiroyuki Kotani, 1999, 'Kingship, State and Local Society in the Seventeenth-to-Nineteenth Century Deccan with Special Reference to the Ritual Functions', in N. Karashima (ed.), *Kingship in Indian History*, Delhi: Manohar. This ritual 'autonomy' of the local society in the medieval Deccan is the main theme of my former essay (Kotani, 1999, ibid.).

15. *Manu-smṛti*, ibid., V–84.

16. R.V. Oturkar (ed.), 1950, *Peśve Kālīn Sāmājik va Ārthik Patravyavahār*, Pune: Bhārat Itihās Saṃśodhak Maṇḍal, No. 155.

17. Oturkar, ibid., No. 152, AD 1732.

18. ASS I 193, AD 1795.

19. The so-called untouchables, such as the Mahar and Mang, however, were not merely discriminated beings in the medieval Deccan. They had a somewhat ambivalent existence in the sense, first, that they played an indispensable and leading role in the village ritual of śānti (see the section of śānti in this paper) and, second, that considerable portions of Mahars and Mangs were a sort of hill soldiers posted as *naiks* (hereditary guards) of hill-forts as well as *ṭhāṇa*s (guard-posts) in plains who possessed the *nāikī* vatan (Hiroyuki Kotani, 1997, 'Ati-Śūdra Castes in the Medieval Deccan', in H. Kotani [ed.], *Caste System, Untouchability and the Depressed*, Delhi: Manohar).

20. *Manu-smṛti*, ibid., V–88.

21. *Manu-smṛti*, ibid., V–84.

22. SSRPD VII 592, AD 1765–6.

23. ASS I 203, AD 1806.

24. SSRPD II 319, AD 1747–8.

25. Kane, ibid., V 719–814.

26. SSRPD VII 679, AD 1762–3, SSRPD VII 683, AD 1763–4.

27. SSRPD VIII 1109, AD 1773–4.

28. Cf. Kane, ibid., V 733–4.

29 SSRPD II 326, AD 1753–4.

30. SSRPD II 312, AD 1740–1. Propitiatory rituals for planets seem to be performed often. In one case, the Peshva government defrayed 286 rupees or so for the performance of ritual (*anuṣṭhāna*) to propitiate planets which included incantations (*japa*) of 100,000 times for Saturn, 20,000 times for Jupiter, 20,000 times for Mars, and another 20,000 times for Rahu [SSRPD II 313, AD 1742–3].

31. SSRPD II 325, AD 1751–2.

32. V.K. Rajvade (ed.), 1898–1919, *Marāṭhyāncyā Itihāsācīṃ Sādhaneṃ*, 22 Vols, Poona and Bombay: (MIS hereafter), XXI, 215; cf. Kotani, ibid., 1996: 67–8.

33. Inden refers to the bad omens which were 'destructive of people of the countryside (*jana*), of the royal capital (*nagara*), and also of kings' (R. Inden, 1985, 'Kings and Omens', in J.B. Carman and F.A. Marglin (eds), *Purity and Auspiciousness in Indian Society*, Leiden: E.J. Brill, p. 34), and says as follows:

> The kingdom constituted by the royal capital and the countryside was, in turn, hierarchically related to the king, the overlord of earth and people, their commander and protector. The king, an earthly realization of the Primordial Man (*puruṣa*), the Cosmic Overlord himself, was thought to include within his persona, all of the constituent elements of his kingdom just as the Cosmic Man included the constituent elements of the universe in his (Inden, 1985, ibid: 34).
>
> Yet, because the king includes the people and country of his kingdom within his persona, every portent that appears in his kingdom, no matter who is directly affected, is also a catastrophe for the king. This is why the king,

above all others, was concerned with omens in ancient and medieval India (Inden, 1985: 35).

Though this might have been what was ideologically intended by the kings in medieval India, village people (*jana*) in the medieval Deccan do not seem to have accepted this ideology of kingship as their own, as the village rite of śānti amply indicates.

34. N.B. Dirks, 1987, *The Hollow Crown: Ethnohistory of an Indian Kingdom*, Cambridge: Cambridge University Press, pp. 128, 130.

35. SSRPD I 289, AD 1730–1.

36. SSRPD I 283, AD 1740–1.

37. For a Kumbhar headman's case, see Bhārat Itihās Saṃśodhak Maṇḍal (ed.), 1926–65, *Śiva Caritra Sāhitya*, 13 Vols, Pune: (SCS hereafter). I 34, AD 1650–1; for another Kumbhar headman's case, see I 27, AD 1642; for a Mahar headman's case, see SCS VII 43, AD 1657.

38. It is noteworthy that the popular Marathi terms indicating purity–impurity in the nineteenth and twentieth centuries have been *sovaḷā–ovaḷā*, not śuddha–aśuddha. (See, for example, Baba Padmanji, 1879, *Aruṇodaya*, Mumbai: Bombay Tracts and Book Society, pp. 3–4, 7–8, 45.) Sovaḷā–ovaḷā are the corrupted forms of the Sanskrit terms *sumaṅgala–amaṅgala* (auspicious–inauspicious). How the terms sumaṅgala–amaṅgala have changed their meanings to purity–impurity in Marathi under British colonial rule is an interesting problem yet to be investigated (Kotani 1999: 263–4).

39. *Manu-smṛti*, ibid., VII–22.

CHAPTER 5

The Coin of the Realm

(Un)Making Polities in Late Pre-Colonial South Asia[1]

Sanjay Subrahmanyam

INTRODUCTION

The organizers of this volume having slated me to discuss 'Market and State Formation in Late Pre-Colonial India', I must nevertheless confess to being somewhat reluctant to undertake that task in the two most obvious ways that present themselves. One of these would be to take the familiar route through fiscal structure and taxation, which would lead pretty much ineluctably to a consideration of the so-called 'forced commercialization' hypothesis.[2] Thus, in other words, did the state's tax demands, in cash or in kind, lead to the creation of a limited market in the seventeenth and eighteenth centuries within the aegis of a sort of 'tributary mode of production', to return to the tired terms of Eric Wolf? And was the recalcitrant Indian peasant and artisan then sucked into the market as a consequence of this logic, when he would have been perfectly content in an autarkic moral economy? So runs the first route. The second route, though of more recent vintage than the first, is also a familiar one by now, namely one of the 'commercialization of state power', espoused most famously by C.A. Bayly in order to explain changes in the Mughal successor states of the eighteenth century.[3] Reversing the flow of reasoning in relation to the 'forced commercialization' hypothesis, the links would run here from society to state rather than the other way around. This would take us in turn to such issues as banking networks, revenue farming, and the issue of the articulation between state accounting and the cadastral imagination, and private accounting in the commercial sphere. What was the king then, if not the biggest accountant and grocer of the realm?

Both of the routes sketched above are undoubtedly respectable ones, and have variously been taken by some of the best-known recent historians of late pre-colonial India, such as Irfan Habib, Muzaffar Alam, Frank Perlin, and Stewart Gordon, to name a few. In this essay, I propose however to largely abandon these two routes (though I have myself travelled on them at other times) in favour of a third, rather more risky, alternative venture. My attempt here will be to address the materials around a rather small-scale conflict in coastal Andhra in the mid-eighteenth century, the so-called 'Bobbili War', to see what it tells us about the relationship between the market and its rationality, and other political and ethical organizing principles in that society (such as honour, warrior status, and the capacity to gamble), all of which lead us in the direction roughly of the field of 'state-formation'. This is of particular interest in view of the fact that a number of recent writers (of whom the most extreme is arguably André Wink) have argued that the eighteenth century sees *realpolitik* and cynical calculation as a form of statecraft raised to a height, under the banner of *fitna*.[4] In the world of the Deccan as described by Wink, one rarely fights but everyone still negotiates; and in true Oscar Wildean fashion, these political actors seem to know the price of everything and the value of nothing. To this view, the Bobbili War seems to present a radical counterpoint, as we shall see at length below.

ADVENTURES IN THE 'NORTHERN SIRCARS'

The name 'Bobbili' is said to derive from [*pedda*?] *puli*, 'tiger', and the ethos emblematized by the Bobbili events is well-suited to this etymology. Situated in the northern boundary region of Andhra, in a region consistently defined by texts of the epoch as *manne*, a wild region, beyond the pale of the settled deltaic culture, Bobbili was home to a dynasty of rugged Velama warrior-kings cast in the heroic mould familiar to us from its Telugu Nayaka exemplars from further south.[5] In the 1750s, the most picturesque and beloved of these rulers, Ranga Ravu or Ranga Raya, died in battle with the king of the small northern state of Vijayanagaram, Vijaya Rama Raju, who managed to manipulate the French adventurer Bussy into attacking Bobbili together with his own forces.

A wider picture is critical to any exploration of these events. The Bobbili War took place in 1757, the same year as the celebrated Battle of Plassey, which has naturally received rather more attention from historians than this admittedly obscure engagement in coastal Andhra (in the so-called Northern Circars, north of the Godavari delta). The main protagonists of the conflict were four in number: the rulers (zamindars) of Bobbili and Vizianagaram (Vijayanagaram), the Nizam and his state in Hyderabad, and the French East India Company, which in those years was probably at the height of its political powers and ambitions in South Asia. After desultory attempts in the sixteenth century and the first half of the seventeenth century, it was the French East India Company created in 1664 under the patronage of Jean-Baptiste Colbert, the powerful minister of Louis XIV, that first permitted the French to systematically enter into the trade of the Indian subcontinent. Allied with Asian traders, the French succeeded in the first decade of the reign of Aurangzeb in implanting factories (or *comptoirs*) in Surat, and then at Macchlipatnam on the coast of northern Coromandel. Still later, in the 1670s, they attempted to seize the coastal fortress of São Tomé or Mylapur by force. As yet unsure of the right mix of force and diplomacy to use on the Indian subcontinent, they frequently erred in their calculations. Even so, by 1700, they had managed to establish a clear niche in the trade of eastern India, from their major centre of Pondicherry, that had initially been under the control of the Bijapur Sultanate and the Marathas, and then fell under the aegis of the Mughal empire. Further north, in the area of the Krishna and Godavari deltas, French interests sought a stable centre of operations, in the face of well-entrenched competitors like the Dutch and the English.

Recent work by historians has pointed to the importance of private trading interests in determining the nature of French trade and diplomacy in the first quarter of the eighteenth century.[6] Like the English in the same period (and unlike the Dutch), the French seized upon the idea that the surest way of penetrating the markets of India was by a mix of trade and political activity. They were thus drawn from the 1730s onwards into an involvement in political and military entrepreneurship and adventurism. The first moves in this direction were during the succession crisis at Arcot that followed on the death of Nawwab Sa'adatullah Khan in 1732. Since his successor failed to negotiate appropriately with the Marathas, the 1730s opened up a period of major contest between the Arcot state and the forces of the Peshwa and his auxiliaries, in which the English and the French were gradually able to gain a measure of leverage. As is well known, in the succession struggle that followed on the death of Nawwab Dost 'Ali Khan, the French threw their weight behind the Nawayat candidate Chanda Sahib, and the English chose to support Anwaruddin Khan, who had been nominated by the Mughal court to succeed at Arcot. The English eventually succeeded and the French failed, but during the late 1730s and much of the 1740s, these matters hung in balance.

The political processes of the 1730s were dominated by, and negotiated through, an extraordinary magnate whose role in Deccan politics remains inadequately understood to date. This is the Turani Mughal notable Chin Qilich Khan, better known under the title of Nizam-ul-Mulk Asaf Jah, who founded the Asaf Jahi dynasty at Hyderabad.[7] Mughal sources of the early decades of the eighteenth century make it clear that Nizam-ul-Mulk played a crucial balancing part in the politics of northern India during the reign of the Mughal emperor Muhammad Shah (r. 1719–48). They are naturally less concerned with the Asaf Jahi profile in southern India, even though this happens to be a matter detailed in a number of Deccani texts like the well-known collection of letters by Musavi Khan Ju'rat.[8] It is certain that Asaf Jah had a say in matters of succession at Arcot, and also in the place of the coastal zamindaris in Andhra. Here, as has been shown by John F. Richards and others, the conquest by the Mughals of the region had to be negotiated in an altogether complex fashion.[9] Mughal chronicles point to systematic opposition offered by families of Reddis and Velamas in the region extending from Peddapalli (Nizamapatnam) to Vizianagaram, and this is also confirmed by the Dutch sources of the period. Mughal administrators thus sought to 'pacify' the region in a gradual fashion, and had apparently managed by the 1730s to devise a *modus vivendi* with the zamindars, while using a system of revenue farms that combined fiscal and military functions (*faujdari*s and *shiqdari*s) in the hands of the same intermediaries. Indeed, as Persian documents from the period show, within the erstwhile Sultanate of Golconda, a twofold policy was followed by Asaf Jah and his advisors.[10] The interior, or Telengana, was left to be dominated by powerful local chiefs and magnates, often descendants of the same clans who had controlled the locality under the Qutb Shahi rulers of Golconda.[11] It was in the east, in a set of areas that encompassed Ibrahimpatnam, Devarkonda, and the coastal districts of Srikakulam, Macchlipatnam, and Nizamapatnam, that Nizam-ul-Mulk concentrated his efforts in the late 1720s and 1730s. The three posts of *amin*, *shiqdar*, and *faujdar* were combined in a single person, who was given the duty of collecting the *jama'*, but at the same time allowed to maintain substantial corps of troops from the revenue that he collected. In some instances, it is clearly stated that the collections from the coastal districts were to be remitted to Hyderabad by means of *hundi*s (bills of exchange). The trend seems to be towards consolidation and extension of revenue collection on the one hand, but on the other hand the new structure left the Asaf Jahi state crucially dependent on the efficiency and goodwill of those who held these powerful joint posts. Nor did it mean that the rule of powerful coastal zamindar families came entirely to an end. Rather, being hard-pressed by the exigencies of the reformed administrative and fiscal system, they had to find new means with which to negotiate and defend themselves.

In the preoccupations of coastal Andhra zamindars like those of Rajahmundry, Peddapuram, Pithapuram, and Srikakulam in the 1720s and 1730s, the French must have appeared as no more than minor players. But this situation was to change rapidly. We have already noted that during the 1730s (when Benoît Dumas was governor at Pondicherry), territorial adventurism had begun, particularly in relation to Arcot and its southern neighbour of Tanjavur. This tendency was further consolidated under the governorship of Joseph-François Dupleix, which began in early 1742.

The expansionist policies that Dupleix put in place in the 1740s were based on a mixture of private trade (including that of Dupleix himself and his half-Portuguese wife), military alliance-building, and political entrepreneurship. In order to prosecute these ideas, Dupleix required men who shared at least a part of his vision. One of these was undoubtedly a certain Charles-Joseph Patissier, born in 1720 in Ancienville, a small French village. Patissier took the name of Bussy from his father, an army officer who had served in various European wars of the late seventeenth century. At the age of sixteen, Bussy was sent out to the *île de France* and the *île Bourbon* (at that time French colonies in the Indian Ocean), to participate in the enterprise there as a military ensign. Subsequently, in about 1742 (the very year that Dupleix took over the governorship at Pondicherry after a decade at Chandernagore), Bussy managed to move from the Indian Ocean islands to India itself. There, he spent several years in obscurity, during the time that the English at Madras were at first hard-pressed by the French (to whom they lost Fort St George for some three years, from September 1746), and then gradually reasserted themselves.

In these years, Bussy appears first as a minor subordinate of Dupleix, and his first major action is in the capture of the fortress of Senji (Gingy) in September 1749 for the French Company. He was then sent to participate in the politics of succession at Hyderabad, where matters were in some turmoil after the death of the long-lived Nizam-ul-Mulk Asaf Jah in 1748. Nasir Jang, the first successor to Asaf Jah, was assassinated on 16 December 1750; Muzaffar Jang, the second successor, who was then sent to Hyderabad with French support, was accompanied by none other than Bussy, who at this time had 300 French soldiers and 2000 sepoys. But Muzaffar Jang, who had ceded a number of crucial coastal territories near Macchlipatnam to the French, was then killed in battle on 14 February 1751 by the Afghan faujdars of Savanur, Kadappa, and Karnul.

Salabat Jang, the new *nazim* (or Nizam), was once more backed by Bussy and the French; on 12 April 1751, he and Bussy entered Hyderabad in triumph. The French were flushed with the success of their arms, and at this time, Dupleix even dreamt of sending Bussy to Bengal, to take over the province by defeating Alivardi Khan, but this did not come to pass. In these very months, Bussy wrote to the Financial Controller of the French Company, in a letter of 15 September 1751:

> I am working (...) to free the French of all tolls in the entire dominion of the Mughal emperor. As it is necessary here, more than anywhere else, to bring together trade and war, I am devoting my entire attention to managing the friendship of the lords who rule the places that neighbour our concessions, so that they might favour our commerce.

Bussy now went on to aid Salabat Jang in a succession war against his own older brother Ghazi-ud-Din, who for his part was supported by the Maratha Peshwa, Balaji Baji Rao. This was in winter 1751–2, and in these months, Bussy had a good deal of military success. But the wars and skirmishes were not decisive enough to put paid to the numerous opponents of Salabat Jang. The wars thus continued into late 1752, and by now, Bussy was running out of money and was also not being paid by Salabat Jang, who was himself in somewhat straitened circumstances. By September 1752, Bussy was thus increasingly bitter and angry, and wrote in a well-known letter to Dupleix of 28 November 1752 (which contains most of the elements of Wink's characterization of eighteenth-century fitna):

> The long dealings I have had with the people of this country has taught me to know them; I could hence protest to you that one can never depend on them; treachery and duplicity are natural to them, and we will always be the dupes in our dealings with them. I believe that I have still remarked some vestiges of probity and good faith amongst the Marates, and, if one had to choose, I would rather trust them than the Mogols; but the best of all would be to trust neither the one nor the other, and not to get mixed up in their affairs. These

nations are held back by nothing, they are always ready to sacrifice the most inviolable of engagements to their interests.[12]

Further, by January 1753, Bussy had fallen ill, and he hence went on to Macchlipatnam (which was under French control) to recover. But he soon felt that his successor as French commander was incompetent, and so returned to Hyderabad, threatening Salabat Jang that unless he gave him the four *sarkar*s of Rajahmundry, Eluru, Srikakulam, and Kondapalli, he would make an alliance with the Marathas. Salabat Jang was obliged to give him what he asked for. Bussy then went on to defeat the Maratha commander Raghuji Bhonsle off Hyderabad in April 1754. In this period, at the height of his powers, Bussy—who was scarcely wanting in hubris—had written to Dupleix:

Kings have been placed on the throne by my hands, sustained by my forces, armies have been put to flight, towns taken by assault by a mere handful of my men, peace treaties concluded by my sole mediation, guaranteed, kept and renewed only out of fear of displeasing me, an alliance with me has been sought after by all the powers of the Mughal empire, my friendship has been bought at the price of the riches and the vast domains that the Company possesses (...), the honour of my nation has been taken up to a pinnacle of glory so that it has been preferred to all the others from Europe, and the bounds of the interest of the Company taken beyond its hopes and even its desires.

Paradoxically, at the same time, Bussy took the position in his letters that the French should allow 'Maratha domination to take over from Mughal government in the Deccan'. But Dupleix for his part hesitated to take the plunge in relation to the system of alliances he had envisaged, since he still believed (perhaps with some reason) that the Mughals commanded more prestige than the Marathas, even in the Deccan. But, in turn, Dupleix was recalled to France in 1754 in disgrace, under accusations of extensive private trade, and other misdemeanours, while war with the English was declared once more in Europe in June 1756, and in India from November that year. Bussy now began attacking the English positions in the northern Circars and Orissa, with some success. It is thus sometimes claimed by French imperial historians that the French Company now came to control as much as 600 km of the Andhra coast from Ganjam to Macchlipatnam. This was the time of the Bobbili War, and of operations that went on until about June 1758, when Bussy was recalled to Pondicherry, and the English began to gain the upper hand in the war. They took the crucial fortress of Macchlipatnam in April 1759, and Bussy himself was captured by the English in Vandavashi (near Senji) in January 1760.

To return to the events of 1756–7, however, we must trace Bussy's actions from the time of his triumphant entry into Hyderabad in August 1756 against an alliance of Salabat Jang and some Maratha forces. At this time, writes the nineteenth-century historian G.B. Malleson, Bussy 'felt again, as he had felt before, at Aurungabad in 1753, that he was absolute master of the situation. Again, too, he evinced his unsurpassed tact and judgement, in not insisting too strongly on concessions, which his position as master would have enabled him to enforce'.[13] In fact, Bussy had powerful opponents in the Hyderabad court, men like Muzaffar Beg, Mahmud Khan and above all, a certain Shahnawaz Khan who in 1754 had succeeded Sayyid Lashkar Khan as *diwan*. But, despite their moves against him, Bussy managed to impose himself, partly aided by the aura of invincibility that the campaigns of the preceding decade had conferred upon him, and also doubtless using the mediation of men like Haidar Jang, who served as his own diwan (and whom we shall encounter as a key character below). After remaining in Hyderabad for somewhat under three months (from 26 August to 16 November 1756), he then set out at the head of a force of 500 European and 4000 Indian soldiers in the direction of the coastal districts that had been ceded to the French Company.

The English historian, Colonel G.B. Malleson's account of the campaigns between November 1756 and 25 June 1757, when Bussy's forces took the English factory at Vishakapatnam, is rapid. He writes:

> It is unnecessary to enter into minute details regarding the successful march of Bussy throughout these provinces. His principal object was to reward those who had remained faithful to the French in their hour of difficulty, to punish the chiefs who had evinced disaffection or who had rebelled. Nowhere, except at Bobilee, did he meet with any real opposition. At this place, however—the Rajah of which had a private quarrel with one of Bussy's most trusted feudatories—the resistance was so determined, that the defenders stabbed their wives and children, and then threw themselves on the bayonets of the French, rather than surrender.[14]

The historian of the French Company, and biographer of Bussy and Dupleix, Alfred Martineau, pays somewhat more attention to the episode. He begins by noting the role of the Vizianagaram Raja in the incidents at Rajahmundry in September 1756. Here, the French commander, Duplant de Laval, found himself threatened by a revolt of his Indian soldiery, who were allied both with Ibrahim 'Ali Khan, whom Bussy had made responsible for the revenues of the area around

Srikakulam, and the *qil'adar* of Rajahmundry itself. The situation was resolved in favour of the French, however, on account of the actions of the commandant at Macchlipatnam, M. Moracin, who was considerably aided in this by the Raja of Vizianagaram. When Bussy arrived in the area in December 1756, he was in a situation of considerable political debt to Vizianagaram. French sources claim, at the same time, that Ibrahim 'Ali Khan had struck a secret alliance against Bussy with Ranga Rao of Bobbili, an enemy of Vizianagaram. They thus present matters as if Bussy had no choice but to send a force of 2000 European soldiers and 10,000 Indian sepoys against Bobbili fort, aided besides by a force of 2000 horse and 40,000 men on foot who came from Eluru under the command of Bussy's subordinate, Haidar Jang. This information is supplemented by references to the episode in the diary of Ananda Ranga Pillai, who suggests that the Vizianagaram Raja prevailed on Ibrahim Khan to refrain from entering the combat, while himself arriving to join Bussy at Srikakulam with 2000 horse, 40,000 infantry, 8000 artillerymen, 40 elephants, and extensive supplies. Whether or not we accept these figures, there is little doubt that a substantial force set out against Bobbili, and camped outside the fort.

Bussy and his men then attempted the first attack on the fort, but being unable to make an impression on Ranga Rao's *corps d'élite*, were forced to retreat. At this, the Vizianagaram Raja is reported to have mounted his elephant, and made a second attack, in which straw was thrown into the moat, permitting his men to escalade the walls from one side. Benefiting from this diversion, Bussy now entered the fort from the other side, and the two soon had control of the town. The engagement is said to have cost Bussy eighteen officers and 3200 soldiers, while the Vizianagaram Raja is reported to have lost some 8000–9000 men. The French historian continues:

> As soon as the fort was taken, Bussy advised the Viziam Raja that if anyone were left alive in the town, they would transform themselves into enemies, with whom one would have to deal from that day on. The Viziam Raja hence gave the order to massacre the women and children, and thus about ten thousand were killed, not counting the inhabitants and soldiers, amongst whom was Ranga Rao himself. Private hatreds of which we have little knowledge probably inspired this act of despair. The French flag was at once raised over the town, sweets were distributed to the army, and festivities were ordered.[15]

To this laconic account, in which the motivations and actions of Bussy himself appear under a rather curious light, the historian adds some more details. In the aftermath of the battle, he recounts, Bussy and the Raja had retired to their respective tents, when one of the survivors from Bobbili appeared, claiming to have information concerning a younger brother of Ranga Rao who had been wounded in the battle but had survived. He was thus allowed into the Raja's tent after being searched, but managed nevertheless to kill him with a concealed knife, by stabbing the Raja in the belly. Though the assassin was killed at once, Bussy much regretted the death of the forty-nine-year-old Raja, who had—as it happened—been warned by astrologers that he might die soon. Bussy by way of compensation hence handed over Bobbili fort, as well as its revenues of 200,000 rupees to the Raja's brother, a certain Jagapati Rao.

French accounts, read together with Ananda Ranga Pillai's diary, hence leave us with the impression that this affair much impressed contemporaries, and also suggests that a rather ambiguous reading of Bussy's own comportment was possible in this context.[16] Conversely, the main justification for the action against Bobbili is given in terms of the loyalty of Vizianagaram to the French, who at the time were under considerable threat not so much from the Marathas, but from 'treacherous Moors' within the Hyderabad state itself.

We have so far limited ourselves largely to a reading of French sources, including the letters and despatches of Bussy himself. We can also take the relatively detailed account presented by Robert Orme (1728–1801), the official historian of the English East India Company, writing a mere few years after the events.[17] Orme notes, in his record for the year 1757, that Bussy had in that year used his forces in a rather widespread manner, and that he enjoyed a good deal of independence in his functioning. Thus, writing of Bussy and his army in the Nizam's domains, he notes that from Hyderabad, they went to Bezwada in December 1756, and then 'instead of going to Masulipatam, they struck to the north-east and proceeded by a frequented road, through the province and city of Elore, from whence they arrived on the 19th of December at the city of Ramundrum, situated on the Godaveri'. Orme reports that on Bussy's arrival, the governor of the Srikakulam region, Ibrahim Khan, left to avoid a confrontation; on the other hand, 'the Rajah Vizeramrauze, confident in the proofs he had given of his attachment, met their army accompanied by several other Indian chiefs, with their forces'. The English Company's historian also notes, on this occasion, the existence of a number of local chiefs in the region who claimed to derive from the time when the Gajapati monarchs of Orissa ('a King of Jaggernaut, in Orixa') had ruled over the area. He then goes on to note:

> The first in rank of these Polygars, who all call themselves Rajahs, was Rangarao of Bobilee; the fort of this name stands close to the mountains about 140 miles N.E. of Vizagapatam; the districts are about twenty square miles. There had long been a deadly hatred between this Polygar and Vizeramrauze, whose person, how much soever he feared his power, Rangarao held in the utmost contempt, as of low extraction, and of new note.

Besides, there were problems between Vizianagaram and Bobbili over questions of water management, since the farmers under Bobbili jurisdiction tended to divert water away from his neighbour. Vijaya Rama Raju is thus said to have used 'arguments to persuade Mr Bussy of the necessity of removing this neighbour; and Mr Bussy proposed, that he should quit his hereditary ground of Bobilee, in exchange of other lands of greater extent and value, in another part of the province, but Rangarao treated the proposal as an insult'. Then, a detachment of French soldiers was sent through 'some part of the woods of Bobilee' on an errand, but were attacked en route, and obliged to retreat with several dead and wounded. Using this incident, Vijaya Rama Raju then persuaded Bussy that it was necessary 'to reduce the whole country, and to expel the Polygar and all his family'.

Orme goes on to describe in considerable detail the most formidable of all the fortresses under Bobbili control, which he describes as the 'last refuge' of Ranga Rao and his family. Bussy is said to have marched against this redoubt with 250 horse, and 500 other Europeans, four field-pieces, and some 11,000 'Peons and Sepoys'. The attack then commenced on 24 January 1757, with Bussy and his artillery on the one side, and on the other Ranga Rao 'with all his parentage, 250 men bearing arms, and nearly twice this number of women and children'. However, the attackers had rather limited success during the first wave of attacks, largely because—in Orme's opinion—'the garrison fought with the indignant ferocity of wild beasts, defending their dens and families'. At roughly 2 p.m., he reports, Ranga Rao assembled his 'principal men', and told them it was necessary to 'preserve their wives and children from the violation of Europeans, and the more ignominous authority of Vizeramrauze'. They then proceeded to set fire to all the houses, and to stab 'without remorse, the woman or child, whichsoever attempted to escape the flame and suffocation'. The attack then continued, and Ranga Rao was killed by a musket ball soon after. But even so, none of the defenders agreed to give quarter. Orme's conclusion is sombre in the extreme: 'The slaughter of the conflict being compleated, another much more dreadful presented itself in the area below: the transport of victory lost all its joy: all gazed on one another with silent astonishment and remorse, and the fiercest could not refuse a tear to the deplorable destruction spread before them'.

One survivor was however brought forth: this was the son of Ranga Rao, who was led by an old man to Monsieur Law, who then sent him on to Bussy. Bussy, for his part, refused to enter the fort, and instead offered the surviving infant the position of 'lord of the territory which he had offered the father in exchange for the districts of Bobilee'. But two days later, further incidents followed. It is reported by Orme that, on the third night, four of Ranga Rao's soldiers managed to enter Vijaya Rama Raju's camp, and two of them even got into his tent. He continues:

> Vizeramrauze was extremely corpulent, insomuch that he could scarcely rear himself from his seat without assistance: the two men, restraining their very breath, struck in the same instant with their poniards at his heart; the first groan brought in a sentinel, who fired, but missed; more immediately thronged in, but the murderers, heedless of themselves, cried out, pointing to the body, 'Look here! We are satisfied'. They were instantly shot by the crowd, and mangled after they had fallen; but had stabbed Vizeramrauze in 32 places. Had they failed, the other two remaining in the forest were bound by the same oath to perform the deed, or perish in the attempt.[18]

Bussy and his army, Orme makes it a point to note, then 'hastened to quit this tragic ground', and made their way quickly beyond Ganjam, to the very borders of Orissa.

PRICES AND VALUES

How does one explain an incident like this if one is to believe, with Bussy (and Wink), that all statecraft in eighteenth-century Deccan is a matter of cunning, calculation, and fine-tuned decision-making in the marketplace of politics? What motivated the major actors to behave as they did? And how was the matter perceived by other contemporaries, those who watched from the sidelines, or reflected on the matter in the generation after? By all accounts a gruesome military debacle, the Bobbili war captured the imagination of Telugu singers, poets, and historians from the second half of the eighteenth century on. A considerable body of sources presents competing versions of the story; for our purposes, the advantage of treating the Bobbili war lies in the survival of a complete historiographical sequence in these Telugu sources, from the close reporting and analysis of Peddada Mallesam's *Bobbili-yuddha-katha* (BK) through the reworking of these materials in folk-epic known as *Pedda Bobbili raju katha* (PBR) to a full-blown historical *kavya*, Dittakavi Narayanakavi's *Ranga-raya caritramu* (RRC). Elsewhere, we have examined these texts one by one and attempted to characterize their vision and distinctive features, but that is not the purpose here.

Of all three texts probably closest in time to the events of 1757, Peddada Mallesam's BK was composed in the style of what we tend to call 'oral epic'. The learned editor of the text, Mallampalli Somasekhara Sarma, somewhat hastily classes it as a 'ballad', a category of default in the eyes of an earlier generation of south Indian historians; on the same page, we hear that 'Mallesam borrowed his theme from history and developed it into a classical folk-song-*kavya*'.[19] So much for style; this mode of categorization takes us nowhere. In fact, the text immediately impresses us with its careful attention to detail and its sense of the singularity and facticity of the Bobbili story. Imagine an author, moved by historical feeling, thinking, and experiencing the world in Telugu, living in Bobbili or somewhere near some decades, at most, after the fall. He has a story to tell about dramatic and tragic circumstances that he has heard described from those who may remember them personally; he is also certainly familiar with oral narratives about these events, already circulating in the region. The task he sets himself is to provide a new, perhaps definitive synthesis. He knows the landscape and landmarks of Bobbili, and all the great families; and it is important to him to get it all straight. In addition, he is gifted with a fine appreciation of what we, from a vast distance, might call the 'political system' of late pre-colonial northern Andhra; so he has a good sense of what makes people do some of the things they do. He needs to explain the Bobbili story to himself and to others.

Let us examine in some detail one of the sequences that Mallesam presents us with, in the course of the conflict. Here, Bussy and Vijaya Rama Raja have already begun to make demands on Bobbili, and the Bobbili court for its part has held internal consultations on the nature and gravity of the threat. They come to the conclusion that their own position is quite legitimate and secure, and that they really have nothing to fear. Thus, buoyed up with these reassuring calculations, the Bobbili ruler Ranga Ravu can now send an ambassador to the French. He chooses a certain Damerla Dammaya, also known as Dharma Ravu. But the ambassador is reluctant: the French are ignorant people with no language; how can he speak to them? Ranga Ravu tells him to look first for the interpreter Dubashi Laksmana. Cash, says the king, is no problem: offer to pay the French anything they want; but if anyone asks for a bribe, don't give as much as the stem of a betel leaf. With these business-like instructions (which address both prices and values), Dharma Ravu dresses formally—a red-ochre turban, a pair of *kalamkari* cloths covering his whole body, an emerald-studded sword at his waist—and, together with the fiery Padala Ramudu, pays a visit, on his way out, to the god Gopalasvami at the entrance to the Bobbili fort. But the god seems not to be at home: 'Have you gone off riding on your horse, Gopalasvami? Have you gone away to the mountains? You haven't protected us in even one crisis. If I return safely from meeting the French, I will plate your rock temples with gold and bring round parasols from Cennapatnam [Madras]'. There is no answer from the god. Here is a theme that recurs consistently in the south Indian heroic-historical genres—that of the family deity who mysteriously turns away at the moment of real need.

Dharma Ravu enters the French camp and finds two of the main characters Haidar Jang and Dubashi Lakshmana playing dice—the standard pastime of the epoch, as we know, replete with the suggestion of process unfolding out of the unknown. He offers two bags of money to each of them and pleads with the interpreter: 'Don't cause problems between Bussy and me. It's all up to you. We don't know his language, and he doesn't know ours. We are living in the fort with our women, children, infants, and aged: it isn't right for him to attack'.

On, now, to Bussy, who at first nervously mistakes Dharma Ravu for the Bobbili king. This contretemps resolved, a serious dialogue develops, rich in the nuances of personal and political exigency at this critical moment of transition:

Dharma Ravu: I am not Ranga Ravu, but rather his brother-in-law and minister. I came to discuss the assessment (*jama-bandi*) with you. We want to settle this with you. Bussy (through the interpreter): Until now, who has done the assessment? Dharma Ravu: The Vijayanagaram Raja. Bussy: If the Raja is there, why come to me? Dharma Ravu: We don't see eye to eye with him. He wants to destroy us and rule Bobbili fort himself. Anyway, when the Government (*divanam*) itself is present, why should we bother with the Raja? Bussy: *Divanam* and Raja are the same, not two separate entities. Dharma Ravu: We don't want to have anything to do with the Raja. We have a *farman* directly from the Golconda Nizam himself. Ranga Ravu is just like any Muslim ruler (*turukavanti saradarudu*)—that is why he did not come to see you in Rajamundry. Bussy: Why does he not heed the *divanam*, when the Raja himself has come? Because he did not come to Rajamandry, I was angry and wrote off the rights of Bobbili fort to Anandaraja. Dharma Ravu (getting angry, his left hand on his mustache and his right hand on his sword): If you wrote us off, what do you have for us now? Bussy: We'll give you twelve villages as *jagir* in Palakonda. Live off that *jagir* and serve the Vijayanagaram king. Dharma Ravu: Over our dead bodies! We have the farman from Golconda. What can you do to us without the Nawab's knowledge? The king has 24,000 troops; we have 4000. You stay out of this, let the two sides fight it out alone. Sit on your elephant and watch the fun (*tamasha*) for a few hours. If the Raja wins, give Bobbili fort to him. If we win, give the stone fort of Vijayanagaram to Ranga Ravu. Bussy: The Raja will never agree. Dharma Ravu: Both of us—Bobbili and Vijayanagaram—derive our support (*mettina yadi*)[20] from the *divanam*. We have done no harm to the *divanam*. Adjudicate this dispute impartially. We'll pay the tax we owe as well as a lakh of rupees as a fine to cover your expenses in coming here, and 3000 in honour of Vengala Ravu's [Ranga Rao's brother] marriage. Bussy: If you can persuade the king to settle on these terms, I am agreeable. Dharma Ravu: If the *divanam* is here, why should we deal with the Raja?[21]

It almost works: Bussy directs Haidar Jang to make the assessment. But meanwhile the Raja has intervened with a secret message to Haidar Jang: 'Don't let the negotiations succeed. I will give you 12,000 rupees as *inam*'. The devious Haidar Jang, true to his nature, at once proceeds to insult the Velama messengers: 'Why are you still sitting here? If you give us money as high as the fort itself, we won't leave it alone. We won't go back until dead bodies are stacked as high as the fort'. Dharma Ravu at once realizes that Haidar Jang has been bribed, and says so; the mere mention of the word 'bribe' (*lancamu*) enrages the French, and they throw him out of the audience. In the scrap that breaks out, Dharma Ravu and Padala Ramudu spear the French sentries and kill another 400 white soldiers. On their way back to the fort, they burn seven neighbourhoods (*peta*) outside it.

Dharma Ravu reports to the Bobbili king: the settlement was ruined by a bribe to Haidar Jang; Vijaya Rama Raja is behind it. 'I insulted them so badly they should have killed themselves out of humiliation; a Turk would have done so, but because Bussy is a Frenchman, he just backed off. We cannot buy our way out of this. Get ready for war'.

It is a clear-sighted appraisal. Bussy, as the Velama negotiator notes, is a marginal player in this drama—clearly out of his depth, helpless in the foreign linguistic and conceptual universe of northern Andhra, hence an almost passive spectator at the evolving conflict. Haidar Jang and the interpreter mould matters to their own satisfaction, using Bussy and the French forces to push the Bobbili side into a corner. Deception is the name of the game. All the Bobbili warriors have to oppose it is their ethos of (doomed) heroic pride. The king knows this and accepts it, almost relishing the release implicit in the violent resolution of battle where, in his already archaic world, falsehood and trickery should have no place. Once again, however, disillusion awaits him. The author of our text, for all his sympathy for the dying Velama universe, including above all its active and self-willed elements, takes a hard, realistic look at its brittle, heroic frame.

We may pursue our examination through a brief look at a second text, the RRC of Dittakavi Narayanakavi. Within a generation of the battle, this great historian-poet would set himself the task of retelling the story truthfully and precisely, 'out of a desire to compose a poetic work rich with the flavour of heroic struggle and relating to warriors of my own time' (*idanintana-maha-vira-purusa-paurusa-rasanubandha-bandhuramb' agun' okka prabandhambu raciyimpan gori*, 1.9). Dittakavi's style is lyrical and poignant, to the point of tragedy; but radiating through it are an empiricism and a psychological acuity that energize the entire project he has set himself. We know very little about him, except the central fact of his connection to his patron, the Velama ruler Malraju Ramaraju in Ipuru (or Ippuru) in Vinugonda taluk of present-day Guntur, far to the south of Bobbili. This places Dittakavi in the late eighteenth century.[22] Malraju Ramaraju, whose genealogy is given in detail in the poet's introduction to his work, commissioned the retelling of a story obviously seen as embodying the Velama ethos. The original title of the work, which appears in the colophons to the chapters, must have been *Ranga-raya-kadana-ranga-caritramu*, 'The Story of the Battlefield of Ranga Ravu', but we will refer to it by its modern name, the RRC.[23]

There is a sense throughout this text that the poet knows what he is reporting from sources close to the events, possibly even from contact with (presumably aged) eyewitnesses or other living repositories of first-hand memories. This graphic knowledge, coupled with the attempt to provide a coherent picture of the minds and spirits of the major actors, makes for vivid textures perhaps unique in Telugu historical kavya. Of course, Dittakavi has his own reading of the personalities involved. In his version, the hero of the story, Rangaravu, has become a seasoned, worldly-wise politician, perfectly aware of the probabilities that apply to various courses of action; he is also far from eager to get into a fight. He knows that the true basis behind the unfolding events is greed, a matter of hard cash; and he assumes, wrongly as it turns out, that this motivating economic logic will ultimately save him. Real statecraft (*rajatanambu*), for Rangaravu, lies in finding some means (*upayamu*) to prevent an invasion that is rooted in a bribe (2.73). Bussy cuts a poor figure, often rather passive, but also impulsive and greedy in his own right; it is the hope of squeezing money out of Bobbili that moves him to order the final march to the fort. Most venal is Haidar Jang, bribed by Vijaya Rama Raja with a banker's draft (*sahukaru-tasilim*) which, above all, he wants to cash and run; in the end, his frustration over repeated delays in achieving this noble goal pushes him over the brink, into battle.

Calculations guide Bobbili Ranga Ravu throughout this text. He thinks strategically as well as tactically, and always from the perspective of a self-assured, regal politician or statesman, well aware of the various forces in play at any moment. He is realistic, shrewd, and particularly sensitive to economic motivations. There is a strong normative quality to his thought and action, so strong that we might think of the Bobbili kingship, from its own perspective, as primarily aiming at the preservation of a somewhat precariously balanced political and military order. In this respect, our kavya text stands out as almost anti-heroic in tone and structure: the heroic ethos so prominent in both the BK and the PBR appears here almost as a last resort, when negotiations fail and Bobbili is left with the choice of complete humiliation or a doomed resistance. The Bobbili king, in fact, does all he can to avoid arriving at this impossible choice, which he can see as a menacing and real potential long in advance.

Two quite rational players, Ranga Ravu and Bussy: but between them are the culpable and driven Haidar Jang and Vijaya Rama Raya. The former knows that he has to get the Bobbili warriors out of the fort, at least temporarily, so that Rama Raya can enter—in fulfilment of the terms of the bribe. It almost happens: two successive messengers from Bobbili to the enemy camp, Damerla Dhammanna (Dharma Ravu) and Celikani Venkanna, discuss the possibility that the Bobbili men—or at least the Bobbili king and his retainers—will vacate the fort. The sticking point is Bobbili's refusal to allow Vijaya Rama Raya in; moreover, Bobbili asks for *kaulu*, letters of assurance, in the event of an evacuation. Haidar Jang, masterminding the negotiations, can only insist on full compliance with Rama Raya's terms—this is the only way he can cash his bank draft—but there is a limit to Bobbili's flexibility; they will happily pay anything to make this army go away, but they cannot allow their enemy to enter or to assume the Bobbili throne.

A final embassy from Haidar Jang, in the person of the sympathetic negotiator Hasan 'Ali Khan, fails to break the impasse; there is also the matter, now, of the *naubat* drum that the Bobbili kings have the right to use, but which Haidar Jang violently resents. Hasan 'Ali Khan speaks candidly to the Bobbili king: the real problem lies, he says, with Haidar Jang, who has taken money from Rama Raya; he's like a monkey who has stepped on fire and now can't stop jumping, as if possessed (2.226). Hasan 'Ali Khan quotes the shastras: there are times when suffering has to be borne, as Rama, Yudhisthira, Nala, and Hariscandra did; only 'once in a while' is battle an option (*ẏuddhena kada-cana*, 2.233). If the Bobbili people leave the fort, he himself will bring them back later. But it is too late: Ranga Ravu, angry at last, assumes, in extremis, the full dignity of the insulted Velama hero. 'They invaded us. We cannot leave without suffering ill-fame. Men of courage will never accept the notion that victory or defeat lies in the hands of fate (2.235)'. The ultimate self-affirmation and voluntarism of the south Indian hero of the period, so beautifully stated by the most reluctant warrior of them all, will now shape events to the end.

CONCLUSION

This essay has focused on what may seem at a pan-Indian scale an obscure example (though it was not so in the eighteenth century, and still remains of central importance in Andhra today), but which nevertheless permits one to wander in the bylanes of the history of late pre-colonial state-formation at the level of 'little kingdoms'. What we seem to discern is a landscape of a commercialized economy and a society where money and the values associated with it have made important inroads; it should be repeated, at the risk of provoking boredom, that the old idealistic notion of a natural economy in pre-British India and a happy social equilibrium associated with *Homo hierarchicus* is well and truly untenable. Yet the passage from this form of socio-economic formation to the realm of politics was by no means simple, and one ought not automatically to attribute a hyper-rational field of calculation within which political actors functioned by the middle of the eighteenth century. True, loyalties could at times be bought and sold, but contrary to what the letters of Bussy would have us believe, the discourse of honour did not vest with the French alone. Accommodating these complex and often contradictory strands within the warp and weft of historical analysis is the challenge that faces the historian, especially the one who rejects simple formulaic solutions that have been the staple as much of Dumontians as Hocartians. The 'language of politics' in late pre-colonial India was thus a complex one, and it is hoped that this essay would have helped give the reader a glimpse of this uncomfortable but exhilarating fact.[24]

To conclude, a methodological point. The materials that have been presented here assume different meanings depending on the epistemological framework within which they are located. The intention here has neither been to espouse a rigorously Popperian strategy of the falsification of a thesis, nor has it been the 'micro-historical' approach which presupposes an object of enquiry that is already in fragments. Rather, it has been to argue for a possible hermeneutics through which the moral economy of the actors of this eighteenth-century world could be glimpsed, as an approach to what remains macro-history. For in the final analysis, the market is incomprehensible without an understanding of the rules that circumscribe it, and which are not purely internal to the market itself. Here, the economy was thus not politically determined (as some Brennerian Marxists would have it), but nor was politics merely an outcome of developments in the economic field.

NOTES

1. This paper is the outcome of a research project undertaken jointly with Velcheru Narayana Rao and David Shulman. For a full analysis, see Velcheru Narayana Rao, David Shulman, and Sanjay Subrahmanyam, 2001, *Textures of Time: Writing History in South India, 1600–1800*, New Delhi: Permanent Black.

2. For earlier discussions, see Sanjay Subrahmanyam (ed.), 1994, *Money and the Market in India, 1100–1700*, New Delhi: Oxford University Press; Sanjay Subrahmanyam (ed.), 1990, *Merchants, Markets and the State in Early Modern India*, New Delhi: Oxford University Press.

3. For a summing up, see C.A. Bayly, 1988, *Indian Society and the Making of the British Empire* (The New Cambridge History of India, Vol. II.1), Cambridge: Cambridge University Press.

4. André Wink, 1986, *Land and Sovereignty in India: Agrarian Society and Politics under the Eighteenth-Century Maratha Svarājya*, Cambridge: Cambridge University Press.

5. See discussion in Velcheru Narayana Rao, David Shulman, and Sanjay Subrahmanyam, 1992, *Symbols of Substance: Court and State in Nayaka-period Tamilnadu*, New Delhi: Oxford University Press.

6. Catherine Manning, 1996, *Fortunes à Faire: The French in Asian Trade, 1719–48*, Aldershot: Variorum.

7. One of the most useful studies to date remains P. Setu Madhava Rao,

1963, *Eighteenth-Century Deccan*, Bombay: Popular Prakashan.

8. Rafeeq Fatima, 1975, 'Life and Work of Musavi Khan Jur'at', PhD thesis, Dept. of Persian, Osmania University.

9. J.F. Richards, 1975, *Mughal Administration in Golconda*, Oxford: Clarendon Press.

10. Zahir Uddin Malik, 1975, 'Documents Relating to Pargana Administration in the Deccan under Asaf Jah I', in *Medieval India: A Miscellany*, Volume III, New Delhi: Asia Publishing House, pp. 152–83.

11. Karen Leonard, 1971, 'The Hyderabad Political System and Its Participants', *The Journal of Asian Studies*, Vol. XXX, No. 3, pp. 569–82; J.F. Richards, 1975, *Mughal Administration in Golconda*, Oxford: Clarendon Press.

12. Alfred Martineau, 1935, *Bussy et l'Inde française, 1720–1785*, Paris: Société de l'histoire des colonies françaises, p. 80.

13. G.B. Malleson, 1868, *History of the French in India from the Founding of Pondicherry in 1674 to the Capture of that Place in 1761*, London: Longmans Green & Co, pp. 483–4.

14. Ibid., pp. 486–7.

15. Martineau, *op. cit.*, pp. 222–3.

16. J. Frederick Price and K. Rangachari (eds), 1904–28, *The Private Diary of Ananda Ranga Pillai, Dubash to Joseph François Dupleix, Governor of Pondicherry*, 12 Vols, Madras: Government Press, Vol. X, pp. 333–6, etc.

17. Robert Orme, 1780, *A History of the Military Transactions of the British Nation in Indostan from the Year MDCCXLV*, Vol. II, 3rd edn (reprint, 1990), New Delhi: Today and Tomorrow's Printers, pp. 253–60.

18. Orme, *Transactions*, Vol. II, pp. 259–60.

19. Peddada Mallesam, 1956, *Bobbili yuddha katha* (ed.), Mallampalli Somasekhara Sarma, Madras: Government Oriental Manuscripts Library, p. xiii.

20. That is the house one enters after marriage.

21. Summary of lines 1155–1232.

22. Viresalingam dates the composition of the RRC c. 1790: Kandukuri Viresalingam, *Andhra kavula caritramu* (Rajahmundry, n.p. 1911), 3: 100–17; and see Caganti Sesayya, *Andhra kavi tarangini* (Kapilesvarapuram: Andhra Pracarini, 1971), 14: 202–7. On Narasaravu Peta, one of the three capitals of Malraju Ramaravu (28 miles west of Guntur), see Tumati Donappa, *Andhra samsthanamulu: sahitya posanamu* (Waltair: Andhra Visvakala Parishattu, 1969), pp. 190–6. Dittakavi's son, Dittakavi Ramacandrakavi, was also a poet; he lived in Nandigama in Krishna district and was patronized by Vasireddi Venkatadri Nayudu, the builder of the Amaravati temples.

23. Published in Madras by Ramasvami Sastrulu and Sons, Adisarasvati-mudraksara-sala, 1913.

24. Cf. by way of comparison, Benedict R. O'G. Anderson, 1990, *Language and Power: Exploring Political Cultures in Indonesia*, Ithaca and London: Cornell University Press, especially Chapters 1, 2, and 4.

CHAPTER 6

The *Mirasi* System as Social Grammar

State, Local Society, and Raiyat in Eighteenth–Nineteenth Century South India

Tsukasa Mizushima

Records on late pre-colonial south India reveal a textile of complicated but well-patterned relationships. It was woven from various materials of different colours and lengths and presented a distinctive pattern. Through a succession of changes in the colonial period, however, the textile became unravelled and was rewoven into a different pattern. This paper is an attempt to compare the conspicuous features of these two textiles, one of the late pre-colonial period and the other of the late nineteenth century, by using several sets of village-level records.

The area studied is Ponneri, located to the north of Madras (Chennai) in Tamil Nadu state, India (Fig. 6.1). Supplementary information from other parts of Chingleput, South Arcot, and Tiruchirapalli will be utilized as well.

The main sources are, chronologically, the village accounts compiled by Barnard[1] (*Barnard Report*: 1760s–70s); the revenue accounts prepared by Place[2] (*Place Report*: 1790s); the *Permanent Settlement Records* on zamindari, poligar, and pagoda in 1801; the village-level census of Madras in 1871; and the *Survey and Settlement Registers*[3] of Ponneri (*Settlement Registers*) in 1877. The first three will be analysed for the late pre-colonial period and the last two for the late nineteenth century.

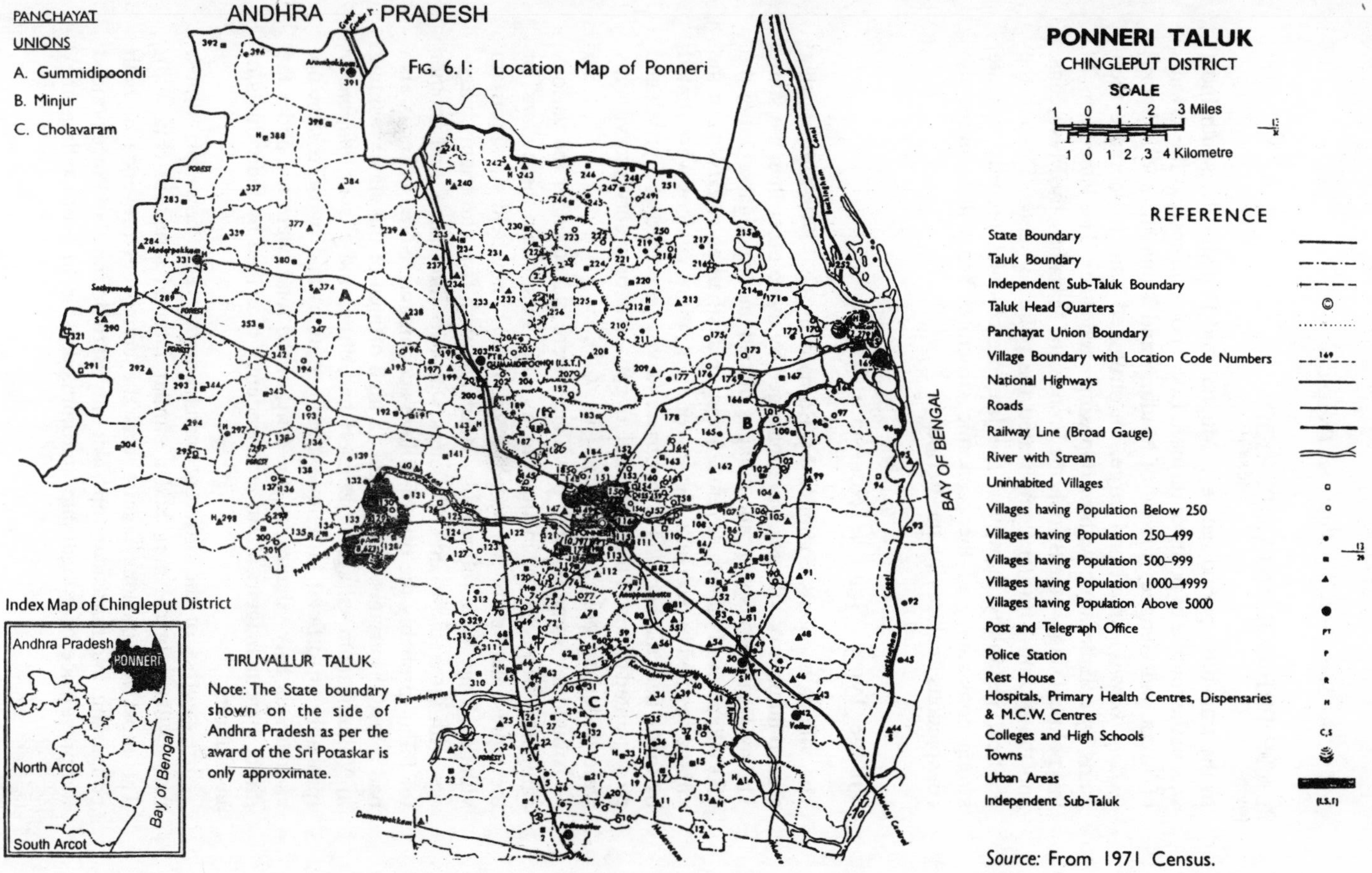
PANCHAYAT UNIONS
A. Gummidipoondi
B. Minjur
C. Cholavaram
ANDHRA PRADESH
PONNERI TALUK
CHINGLEPUT DISTRICT
SCALE
1 0 1 2 3 Miles
1 0 1 2 3 4 Kilometre
REFERENCE
State Boundary
Taluk Boundary
Independent Sub-Taluk Boundary
Taluk Head Quarters
Panchayat Union Boundary
Village Boundary with Location Code Numbers
National Highways
Roads
Railway Line (Broad Gauge)
River with Stream
Uninhabited Villages
Villages having Population Below 250
Villages having Population 250–499
Villages having Population 500–999
Villages having Population 1000–4999
Villages having Population Above 5000
Post and Telegraph Office
Police Station
Rest House
Hospitals, Primary Health Centres, Dispensaries & M.C.W. Centres
Colleges and High Schools
Towns
Urban Areas
Independent Sub-Taluk
BAY OF BENGAL
Index Map of Chingleput District
Andhra Pradesh
PONNERI
North Arcot
South Arcot
Bay of Bengal
TIRUVALLUR TALUK
Note: The State boundary shown on the side of Andhra Pradesh as per the award of the Sri Potaskar is only approximate.
Source: From 1971 Census.
Fig. 6.1: Location Map of Ponneri

LATE PRE-COLONIAL PERIOD

In the transition period between Mughal and British rule, south India was in the middle of political turmoil. Local powers, such as the nawabs of Arcot and Gengee, *nayak*s of Madurai and Tanjavur, and *poligar*s[4] (*palaiyakarans*) small and large, all struggled hard to increase their gains by collaborating with or opposing each other. The latecomers to this political stage—the British, the French, the Marathas, the Mysoreans, and the Nizam—further complicated the political scene. Despite the political instability, however, the late pre-colonial records indicate strong consistency of the economic structure. We will examine the conspicuous features of the period.

Village Types: State vs Non-state

The village accounts compiled by Barnard in the 1770s indicate that a good number of villages were managed by those other than the state. The most numerous were the villages placed under poligars. Out of the 150 villages in Ponneri, seventeen were classified as *mocassah* or the villages owned by poligars. Seven (or eight) more villages were rented by them, and another was a *shrotriam* (a village rented at a privileged rate) granted to one of them. In total, twenty-five (or twenty-six) villages were under the poligars' control (Fig. 6.2).

Around the same number of villages were placed under the various categories of people or institutions as well. First came the *nattar*s[5] or the representatives of the people in the *nadu*. They held six shrotriam villages. They were followed by Brahmins with five shrotriams, pagodas with three shrotriams, Vellalers with two shrotriams, and another for Pillai (probably the title of village accountant). Some officials also had a few shrotriams. A *deshmuk* (a high official of the state) residing in Vellumbacum village in Ponneri had three, and a *stala majumdar* (probably an official in temple administration) had two. To sum up, as many as fifty villages, or one-third of the total, were not under the direct state management but independently managed by individuals or institutions.

Irrespective of the different management types, however, almost every village in the area had a similar internal structure (Fig. 6.3). The most conspicuous feature was the consistent presence of both poligarship and mirasidarship.[6] Not only Barnard but also Place noticed the prevalence of poligarship and mirasidarship in every village they

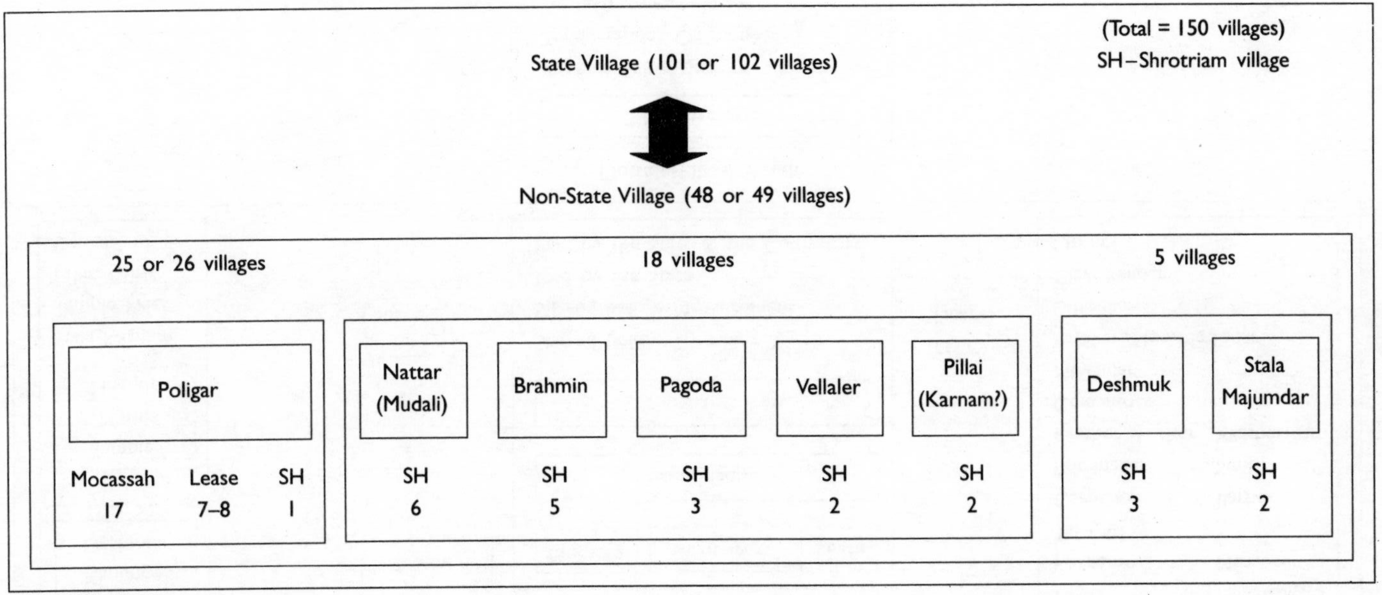

Source: Barnard Report, 1760s–70s.

FIG. 6.2: Village Types in Ponneri

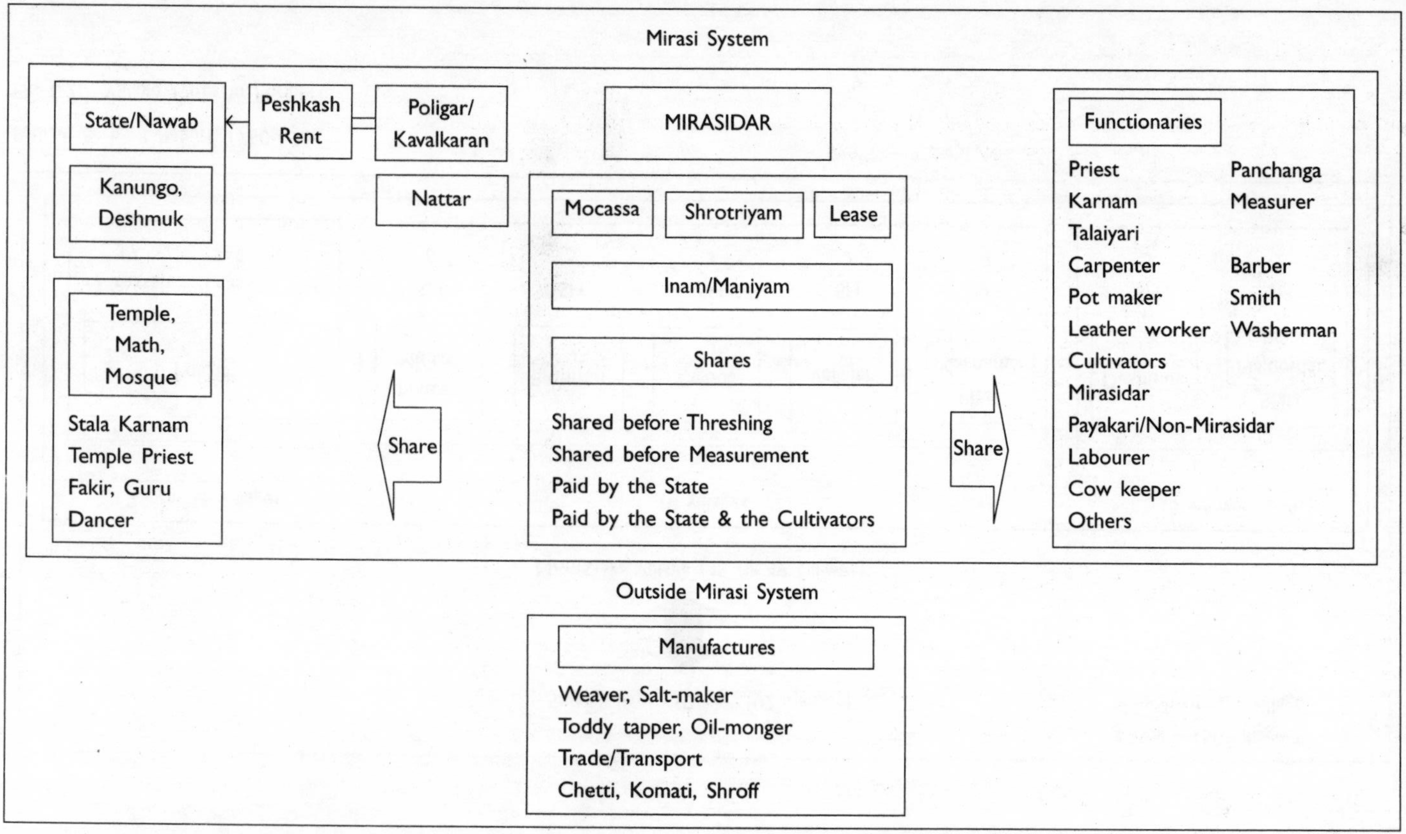

FIG. 6.3: Village Structure in Pre-colonial South India—A Model

surveyed. The identities of poligars and *mirasidar*s with their shares were recorded by them accordingly. As poligars and mirasidars played key roles in the period, we will make an attempt to clarify their position in the society next.

Poligars

First we will take up poligarship by examining Table 6.1. The table indicates the names of the poligars with the number of villages under their jurisdiction. It is clear that a few poligars, like Advy Basavarajah, Advy Vencataputy Rajah, Anoopumbatt Goorvarajah, Coloor Vencatrajah, or Muddycoyel Tappelrajah, held the poligarship in many villages. There were, on the other hand, many poligars with just a village or two under them (see Fig. 6.4).

These figures indicate that the extent of poligars' rights and privileges varied widely, which was also true of other poligars in Chingleput, as indicated in Table 6.2. Whereas several poligars had rights in a large number of villages, a considerable number had rights in only one or two.

The poligars with hundreds of villages under their jurisdiction must have exerted a state-like control over the region through their military followers. Such poligars were truly the professional military and were quite often titled Rajah or Naick. They were the successors of the nayakship in the post-Vijayanagara period. The tiny poligars, on the other hand, though numerically dominant, were a kind of petty policemen who performed their duties in a small locality.

Another striking feature was the entry of agricultural castes into the poligarship. Poligarship of as many as twenty villages was in the hands of Vellalers or the leading agricultural caste (Table 6.1). This finding poses a somewhat different problem, which is related with a new development to be discussed here. These Vellaler poligars, who were the residents of either the villages concerned or neighbouring villages, were found to be mirasidars in their own villages. Their caste background as agriculturists was totally different from the military background of other professional poligars, whose titles were either Naick or Rajah.

These Vellaler poligars took the poligarship in villages located in the central part of Ponneri, as shown in Fig. 6.5. Such spatial concentration in the centre of the locality needs some interpretation. One of the motives for assuming the poligarship was to make economic gain to be expected from the poligarship. It seems, however, that the central part

TABLE 6.1

Poligars and the Number of Villages under their Jurisdiction in Ponneri (*Barnard Report*, 1760s-70s)

Poligar	*No. of Villages*
Advy Basavarajah	8
Advy Basavarajah of Moocasanellaorepollam	1
Advy Basavarajah, Adycavel Goorvappa Naick Moottrian, Adycavel Potty Naick	1
Advy Basavarajah, Adycavel Nayimdasna Naick Mootrian	1
Advy Basavarajah, Adycavel Teagapanaick Mootrian	2
Advy Vencataputyrajah	4
Advy Vencataputyrajah of Tanaperapollam	1
Andiappa Landholder of Coodvanjary*	1
Anoopumbatt Goorvarajah of Gummidipundi	1
Anoopumbatt Goorvarajah of Lutchimeputy Naickpollam	6
Anoopumbutt Goorvarajah	36
Anoopumbutt Goorvarajah of Nallappa Naick Pollem	2
Anoopumbutt Kary Kistamrajah of Vellatoor	2
Auvoor Tuppelrajah	1
Basavarajah	1
Busavarajah of Alimadegechembeliera	1
Caleteappa Naick, Narsuppa Naick of Periapollam	1
Chingleroya Mudali, Reddy Mudali of Chinnacavenum*	1

(*contd*)

Table 6.1: *Contd*

Poligar	*No. of Villages*
Coloor Comaur Vencatrajah	3
Coloor Comaur Vencatrajah, Tookery Agharum Aukulrajah	1
Coloor Vencatrajah	16
Coloor Vencatrajah of Reddypollam	2
Coloor Vencatrajah of Reddypollam In Suttavade District	1
Covray Moottaloo Vengam Naick of Malemoodalambade	3
Culianrajah of Auvoor	3
Davaroyen, Khilen Nelooran, Tooliva Vellaler of Yaresiven*	1
Goorvarajah of Gummidipundi	3
Goorvarajah of Nullapa Naickpollam	2
Karykista Mudali & Gopaul Mudali &Ca.*	1
Karykista Mudali & Gopaul Mudali, Paupa Mudali, Sittapa Mudali, & Ramalinga Mudali*	1
Kistanumrajah of Mulrajapollam	2
Kurian, Tumban, Tooliva Vellaler of Mutteravade*	1
Letchimeputy Naick of Gummidipundi	1
Letchimeputy Naick of Gummidipundipollem	1
Lutchimeputy Naick	1
Mengavel Advy Basavarajah, Adycavel Goorvappa Naick, & Potty Naick	1
Muddycoyel Tappelrajah	3

(contd)

TABLE 6.1: *Contd*

Poligar	*No. of Villages*
Muddycoyel Tappelrajah of Auvoor	3
Nullamootta Mudali & Aroonachela Mudali of Periacavenam*	1
Nynappa, Tooliva Vellaler of Daveranjary*	1
Nynappa, Tooliva Vellaler of Woppalum*	2
Palley Lutchemyputy Naick	1
Reddy Mudali, Chingleraya Mudali, Mootappa Mudali, Coolappa Mudali, Arunachala Mudali of Chinnacavenum*	4
Reddy Mudali, Tooliva Vellaler of Viarungavade*	1
Sadiappa Mudali Landholder of Madras*	1
Tapulrajah of Auvoor	1
Teagappa Naick of Motapollam	1
Vencat Rajah, Vencatram Rajah, & Veerasaumy Rajah of Coloor	1
Vencatachel Naick of Vellyvoil	1
Vencatachel Naick, Chinnatomby Naick, One Residing At [Unreadable], At [Unreadable]	1
Vencatasa Mudali & Candappa Mudali: Tooliva Vellaler of Coommungalum*	4
Vencatrajah	2
Vencatramrajah, Vencatasa Naick, Poligar of a hamlet called Coorkootapu[Unreadable]	1
Vengam Naick of Annama Naick Cooppum	1
NA	5
Total	150

Source: Barnard Report, 1760s–70s.

* Vellaller and other agricultural castes.

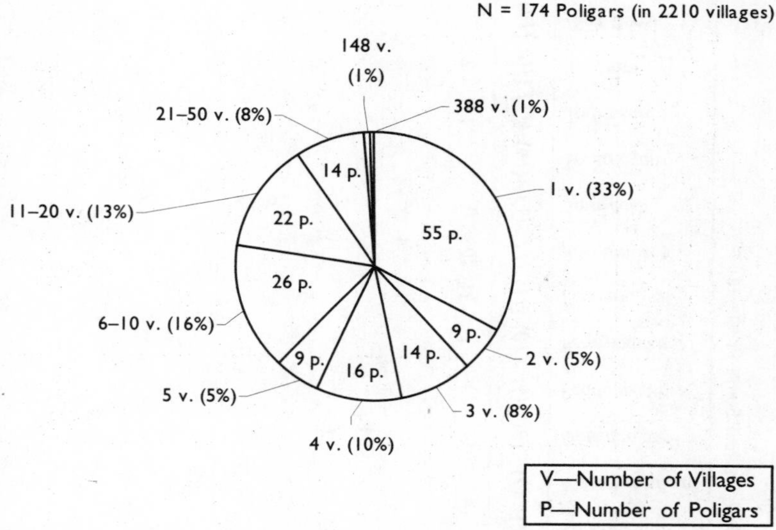

Source: Permanent Settlement Records, Vols. 26, 26a, 26b; Statement of the Privileges of Poligar, in a Letter from Mr Greenway, 30 October, 1801.

FIG. 6.4: Number of Villages where Poligars Collected Fees in Chingleput

was more important than the periphery, not only economically but also politically. These conditions raise the possibility of the emergence of village lords as military leaders. We will come back to this point later.

Mirasidars as Village Lords

Early colonial records widely acknowledged the overlordship of mirasidars. Mirasidars were considered to be the owners of their villages. They were the controllers of production activities as well. The Tamil equivalent of mirasidar is *kaniyatchi-karan*, or a person of inheritance. As they often owned their villages in shares among themselves, they were called *karai-karan* or a person of shares. Mirasi rights were known to be saleable, mortgageable, and inheritable. According to Karashima's study on the sale documents examined by Ellis and Sancarya, many transactions of mirasi rights were observed in the late pre-colonial period. The transactions were between people not only of different villages but also of different castes. Karashima concluded that it was common for mirasi rights to be held by outsiders, and that this

Table 6.2

Number of Villages in Chingleput where Poligars had Some Privileges

Poligar/Paragana	*Carangooly*	*Cavantundlum*	*Chickecotah*	*Chingleput*	*Covelong*	*Kanchipuram*	*Manimungalam*	*Outramalore*	*Peddapollam*	*Perumbaukum*	*Ponneri*	*Poonamallee*	*Salavauk*	*Sautmagan*	*Trepassore*	*Trivatore*	*(Salt Pans)*	*Total*
	(1)	*(2)*	*(3)*	*(4)*	*(5)*	*(6)*	*(7)*	*(8)*	*(9)*	*(10)*	*(11)*	*(12)*	*(13)*	*(14)*	*(15)*	*(16)*	*(17)*	*(18)*
Adevy Vencataputty Rauze									1	1	31	23			13	2		71
Alingeepauk Vengama Rauze									1									1
Ambatoor Pitchal Naick												1						1
Ammyapa Moodely & Namasevoy Moodely								4										4
Ammyapanettoor Vencatachella Naick								2										2
Anapumbut Harekistnama Rauze									9		56			6	3			74
Annamale Naick		2																2
Arimbaloor Gooroovapa Naick													2					2
Arnee Ninapa Naick									5									5
Atteeput Vencatram Naick								1										1
Aulunjary Lingama Naick													2					2
Autoor Condamanaicken & Seddama Naick	2			2														4
Body Naick		8																8

(contd)

Table 6.2: *Contd*

Poligar/Paragana	*(1)*	*(2)*	*(3)*	*(4)*	*(5)*	*(6)*	*(7)*	*(8)*	*(9)*	*(10)*	*(11)*	*(12)*	*(13)*	*(14)*	*(15)*	*(16)*	*(17)*	*(18)*
Boopaty Naick						1												1
Boya Moorty Naick								12										12
Boya Ramassamy Naick				3			4					8			2			17
Bungar Rauze									1									1
Bungaroo Naick & Vencataputty Naick											3			1				4
Calacautoor Verdapa Naick						3												3
Calatoor Condama Naick				8														8
Canaca Rauze & Shashama Rauze														14				14
Cauloor Jatal Naick									5						1			6
Chinnasivendapauda Naick	1												19					20
Chinnoo Naick & Chingama Naick													7					7
Coanama Rauze																3		3
Codumbauk Arnadry Naick																1		1
Codumbauk Aroonachella Naick & Reddyapa Naick												1						
Colatoor Bungar Naick				1														1
Coloor Vencata Rauze									1		30						6	37
Comarasamy Naick													2					2
Comarvady Trimul Naick	1																	1
Comaur Bomma Rauze	20																	20

(contd)

Table 6.2: *Contd*

Poligar/Paragana	(1)	(2)	(3)	(4)	(5)	(6)	(7)	(8)	(9)	(10)	(11)	(12)	(13)	(14)	(15)	(16)	(17)	(18)
Conaty Vengama Naick						1												1
Condama Naick													7					7
Condawar															3			3
Coodoovanjary Moomady Naick				1														1
Coolungacherry Condle Rauze				4														4
Coopa Rauze														2				2
Coopoo Naick								1										1
Coopum Vencatachella Naick						5												5
Cootumbauk Inhabitants														1				1
Cootumbaukum Body Rauze												1		9				10
Coratoor Rama Naick														1				1
Coyembaid Vencatasamy Naick												23				8		31
Cundapa Naick								1										1
Cundloor Verdapa Naick									5									5
Cundrapadoo Vencataaram Rauze									1									1
Cuttacole Peddy Naick formerly but now Potooreddy Condama Naick				41														41
Cutty Cauvil Trimagala Naick		5																5
Delavoy Moommody Naick									15									15

(contd)

TABLE 6.2: *Contd*

Poligar/Paragana	(1)	(2)	(3)	(4)	(5)	(6)	(7)	(8)	(9)	(10)	(11)	(12)	(13)	(14)	(15)	(16)	(17)	(18)
Delavoy Permal Naick															3			3
Doppawar Permall Naick										15					24			39
Eagawar Ramachendra Naick										1								1
Eroolunjary Sawmy Naick						2												2
Goodla Vencatgasamy Naick		15																15
Goommadypoody Lutchemeputty Naick											4							4
Gooroomoorty Naick								3										3
Gooroovapa Naick		1																1
Gooroovapa Naick & Lutchemen Naick		11																11
Hmoorty Naick & Tumboo Naick						1												1
Jemboo Naick						19												19
Kaulyoor Noindama Naick								1										1
Kylasa Naick															1			1
Madoor Veerasamy Rauze											1							1
Madypaukum Ramachendra Naick					2							17				4		23
Manamadara Govinda Naick						1												1
Manelloor Groovapa Naick						6												6
Manimungalum Ramasamy Naick				1			10							1	3			15
Maumundoor Bungar Naick						1												1

(*contd*)

Table 6.2: *Contd*

Poligar/Paragana	*(1)*	*(2)*	*(3)*	*(4)*	*(5)*	*(6)*	*(7)*	*(8)*	*(9)*	*(10)*	*(11)*	*(12)*	*(13)*	*(14)*	*(15)*	*(16)*	*(17)*	*(18)*
Maumundoor Chingle Naick	2																	2
Mohapoor Body Naick														1				1
Mohundry Gungama Naick	34																	34
Moocrumbauk Permal Naick									5						1			6
Mooddoo Moorty Naick								4										4
Moorapa Naick													1					1
Moorty Naick														1				1
Mootial Moosely Naick									5		4	1						10
Motoopolam Tiagapa Naick											7							7
Muddycoyel Teppal Rauze											11							11
Mul Rauze												44		2	9	9		64
Munnar Sidda Naick	4																	4
Murtum Narsimma Naick												6		6				12
Naicoonum Peddy Naick													2					2
Naut Yavalapa Moodely												1						1
Nelvaly Angarapa Naick								1										1
Noindama Naick		10																10
Nueka Vencatarama Naick						45						3			17			65
Nullamoor Peddy Naick	18																	18

(*contd*)

Table 6.2: *Contd*

Poligar/Paragana	*(1)*	*(2)*	*(3)*	*(4)*	*(5)*	*(6)*	*(7)*	*(8)*	*(9)*	*(10)*	*(11)*	*(12)*	*(13)*	*(14)*	*(15)*	*(16)*	*(17)*	*(18)*
Nundrumbauk Gopall Kistnama Naick									10									10
Nungumbauk Sawmy Naick																2		2
Pariatumby Naick		3																3
Paudy Nullama Naick												3						3
Paukum Noindama Naick	40																	40
Paurevaukum Pullees												7						7
Peddapollam Chellapa Naick & Rungapa Naick									15		1				1			17
Peddy Naick																2		2
Peddy Naick & Bolee Naick						2												2
Peddy Naick & Sawmy Naick						78												78
Pedoogoo Permal Naick														2				2
Pennager Shashachella Naick								1										1
Podoovapilla Ninapillah	1																	1
Pootagarum Vencatasamy Naick						2												2
Porponda Chinny Naick	3																	3
Potooreddy Condama Naick				23	24		24											71
Pottary Moommady Naick				1														1
Praliacavary Trimulnaick											2							2
Pullum Vencatachella Naick	37																	37

(contd)

Table 6.2: *Contd*

Poligar/Paragana	*(1)*	*(2)*	*(3)*	*(4)*	*(5)*	*(6)*	*(7)*	*(8)*	*(9)*	*(10)*	*(11)*	*(12)*	*(13)*	*(14)*	*(15)*	*(16)*	*(17)*	*(18)*
Punjetty Mootial Naick									1									1
Puttrawar Yellapa Naick	1																	1
Rama Naick	3																	3
Ramanaick														2				2
Reddyapa Naick																1		1
Reddyapa Naick & Groovapa Naick																1		1
Rettamungalum Vencatachella Naick	2																	2
Royal Naick	179			172	17		18						2					388
Rungapa Naick						1							3					4
Rungapa Naick & Moorty Naick																1		1
Sahil Naick											2	10						12
Salavaty Ramasamy Naick	9							8										17
Sautunjary Chinnoo Naick	3												5					8
Sawmy Naick													2					2
Sawmy Reddy			3															3
Seroovaloor Comboo Naick						1												1
Shadymcoopum Groovapa Naick																3		3
Shashadri Pillah formerly but now Potooreddy Condama Naick	2			18														

(*contd*)

Table 6.2: *Contd*

Poligar/Paragana	*(1)*	*(2)*	*(3)*	*(4)*	*(5)*	*(6)*	*(7)*	*(8)*	*(9)*	*(10)*	*(11)*	*(12)*	*(13)*	*(14)*	*(15)*	*(16)*	*(17)*	*(18)*
Siddama Naick		1																1
Sooria Narrain Rauze											1							1
Soorootel Sawmy Naick						1												1
Streerama Sengama Naick		1		38		3	18			3		18		1	46	20		148
Stumby Soobaroy Pillah														21				21
Tanawar Condama Naick				1			3					17		7				28
Termagula Naick								1										1
Teroovarcaud Angarapa Naick												1						1
Tiagapa Naick												3						3
Timma Rauze														1				1
Timmoo Naick		6																6
Tremul Naick												4						4
Trimul Naick & Sawmy Naick													9					9
Tripanungaud Tumboomoorty Naick	15																	15
Vadamanjiwar Taunapah Naick & Rungapa Naick									5	11		10			57			83
Vaipary Narsemma Naick																3		3
Valayooda Naick																1		1
Vaundravasee Annamala Naick															1			1
Veerabadra Naick & Vencatachella Naick		5																5

(contd)

Table 6.2: *Contd*

Poligar/Paragana	(1)	(2)	(3)	(4)	(5)	(6)	(7)	(8)	(9)	(10)	(11)	(12)	(13)	(14)	(15)	(16)	(17)	(18)
Veeranarrain Vencatachella Naick	2																	2
Veeraragava Naick		1																1
Vellacondama Naick		1																1
Vellaputtoor Permal Naick													1					1
Vellytembauk Cundapa Naick				1														1
Vencata Rauz & Gooroova Rauze									4									4
Vencatachella Naick								3					1					4
Vencataram Naick												2						2
Vencatasamy Naick & Moodoo Naick						8												8
Vencatasen & Pariapyen						3												3
Vendoty Vencatachella Naick						15									11			26
Vendy Siddama Naick								1										1
Vendy Veerasamy Naick	6							11					4					21
Vendy Vencata Naick								6										6
Vendy Vencatachella Naick													2					2
Venty Yellar Naick	6							3					1					10
Verdapa Naick & Shashapa Naick																1		1
Village Inhabitants Cavaly	8																	8
Voragumbauk Mootial Naick																1		1

(contd)

Table 6.2: *Contd*

Poligar/Paragana	*(1)*	(2)	(3)	(4)	(5)	(6)	(7)	(8)	(9)	(10)	(11)	(12)	(13)	(14)	(15)	(16)	(17)	(18)
Vundavassee Permal Naick						2												2
Vypoor Vencatachella Naick				12														12
Woocul Groomoorty Naick						7												7
Woollawoor Conary Naick				2														2
Woollawoor Groovapa Naick	4																	4
Woonjel Treple Naick	18																	18
Wootoocaudoo Chinnama Naick						1												1
Woragadum Peddyapa Naick														1				1
Woratty Narnapa Naick	5																	5
Wottyvauk Paupa Rauze				40	16		2											58
Yechoor Veerapermal Naick	2			13											4			19
Yerrama Naick	18																	18
Total	446	70	3	382	59	209	79	64	89	31	153	204	72	80	200	63	6	2210
Frequency	29	14	1	19	4	24	7	18	17	5	13	22	18	19	18	17	1	

Source: Permanent Settlement Records, Vols 26, 26a, 26b; Statement of the Privileges of Poligar, in a Letter from Mr Greenway, 30 October 1801.

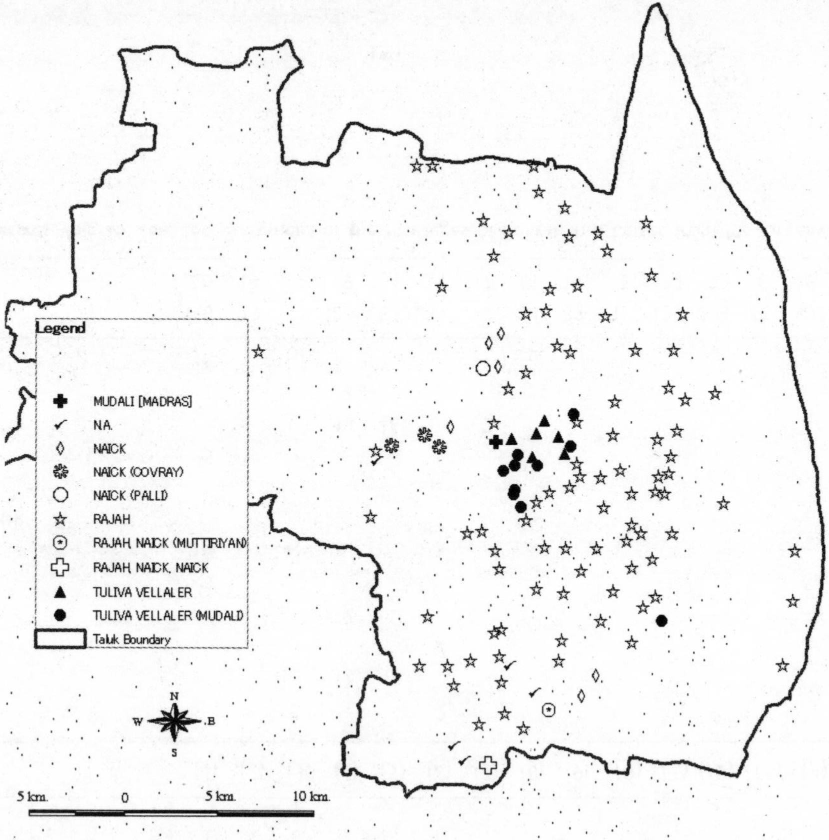

FIG. 6.5: Distribution of Poligarship held by Different Castes in Ponneri

threatened the solidarity of village communities and accelerated their disintegration as well.[7]

Sources currently available give information about the results of such transactions. Table 6.3 indicates the places of residence of mirasidars in the 144 villages recorded in the *Barnard Report*. Out of the 119 villages where the mirasidars' places of residence were known, 107 villages were held either by the resident mirasidars (eighty) or by those in the vicinity (twenty-seven). A further eight villages were held by residents of other villages which, while not neighbouring, were neither very remote. Thus, mirasidarship in most cases was held by the mirasidars living in the proximity.

Further investigation is possible by the *Place Report* of 1797, which lists the mirasidars' personal names with their respective shares. In total, 534 mirasidars' names are recorded in Ponneri, some of them more than once. Assuming that the same personal name signifies the same person, 382 mirasidars can be counted. Of these, 361 mirasidars or 91 per cent held the mirasidarship in just one or two villages (Fig. 6.6). These evidences lead to the conclusion that the mirasidars mostly functioned at the village level.[8]

Mirasidar vs State

Several important exceptions to village-level mirasidarship need to be analysed. The first were the cases of absentee mirasidars. We can find a few villages where the mirasidarship was held by people living in Madras. The second was a case where the mirasidarship was purchased

TABLE 6.3
Mirasidars' Places of Residence in Ponneri
(*Barnard Report*, 1760s–70s)

Place of Residence	*Cases*
Same village	80
Neighbouring village	27
Other villages	8
Madras	3
Arcot? (Nawab)	1
Unknown	25
Total	144

Source: Barnard Report, 1760s–70s.

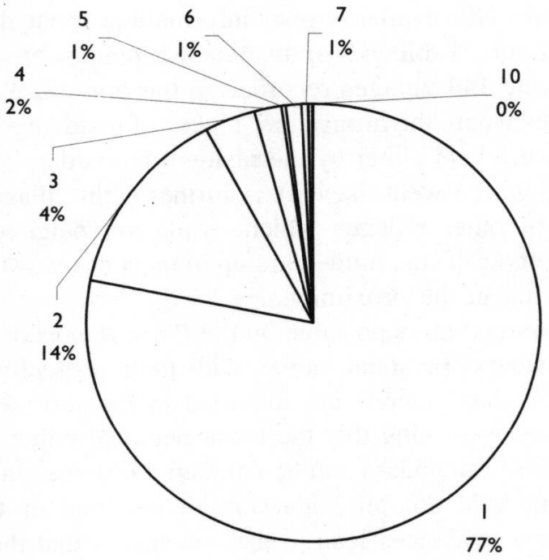

Source: Abstract State of the Number of Meerassee Shares and of Meerassee Holders in the Several Districts of the Jagheer in Fusly 1207 shewing also the Quantity of Meerassee unclaimed & occupied by Pyacarries, *Board's Collections*, 2115 & 2116, Vol. 112, F/4/112, OIOC.

FIG. 6.6: Number of Villages where Mirasidars had Shares in Ponneri (*Place Report*, 1797–8)

by Nawab Mahfuz Khan.[9] These cases indicate first of all that the mirasidarship, to which some privileges were attached, had become an object for investment. The Nawab's case, on the other hand, has far more important implication. It is significant that the Nawab did not usurp mirasidarship by force but had to purchase it. The autonomy of mirasidarship from the state will become a point to be discussed later.

Mirasidar vs Poligar, *Shrotriamdar*

As stated above, poligars and various shrotriamdars took on the management of many villages independently from the state. To clarify the position of mirasidars, it is necessary to investigate the differences among the mirasidars, poligars, and shrotriamdars. The related evidences were as follows. Only two shrotriamdars held mirasidarship.[10]

No poligars held mirasidarship, although many villages were held by poligars either as mocassah, rent, or shrotriam. The caste composition was distinctively different between the poligars on one hand and the shrotriamdars and the mirasidars on the other. Most of the poligars had the titles of either Naick or Rajah, while shrotriamdars and mirasidars were dominantly Mudalis (Vellalers) or Brahmins[11] (Table 6.4 and Fig. 6.7).

The first two pieces of evidence imply that shrotriamdarship was of secondary or supra-village level whereas the mirasidarship was of the primary or village level. Though information about the grants of privileged shrotriam tenure is not available, it is certain that those shrotriamdars like nattars, *pagodas*, deshmuks, or *stala karnam*s (temple accountants) performed some roles to assist the state control in the local society.

The third and the fourth findings, along with the fact that most of the poligars in the area had just one or two villages under their jurisdiction, indicate that the difference between most of the poligars and the mirasidars lay not in the social level but in the social role each played in the local society. While the former took charge of keeping peace and order, the latter controlled the social relations in the village.

Mirasidars and their Power Base

How, then, was the mirasidars' control over their villages possible? Several possibilities can be considered. First could be dominance of their fellow caste members in the villages. This was, however, not necessarily the case so far as the numerical dominance was concerned. The percentage of mirasidars' fellow caste members in each village[12] indicated in Table 6.5 shows that in an appreciable proportion of villages (32 out of 150), the mirasidars were without any fellow caste men.

If numerical strength did not necessarily count at the village level, what was the situation in the supra-local level? In eighteenth-century Chingleput, it was *magan* rather than *parru* or *simai* that was commonly used as a unit larger than a village. Early colonial records used it regularly in referring to the concerned area. A magan, which generally consisted of several or tens of villages,[13] was supposed to be a social entity with some distinctive features. Our task here is, however, to examine the mirasidars' power base in a wider area than a village rather than clarifying these features. We will adopt magan as the unit for analysis.[14]

TABLE 6.4

Number of Mirasidar Castes in the Different Magans in Ponneri (*Place Report*, 1797–8)

Caste/Magan	*Ayanellore*	*Cautoor*	*Chinnapulacavary*	*Cholaverum*	*Coloor*	*Munjore*	*Nayer*	*Ponnary*	*(Shrotriam)*	*(Mocassah)*	*(Dutch Villages)*	*Total*
	(1)	*(2)*	*(3)*	*(4)*	*(5)*	*(6)*	*(7)*	*(8)*	*(9)*	*(10)*	*(11)*	*(12)*
Achari	2				1							3
Aiyangar												
Chetti		2					12		6	1		21
Gurukkal				3								3
Mootan											3	3
Mudali	2	31		5	19	19	18	63	32	4	4	197
Naick		7	3	3		3	2		4	3		25
Ninar										1		1
Pagoda				2								2
Pandaram				1								1
Pillai	2	5					1	1	3			12
Rauze					7		1		2			10

(*contd*)

Table 6.4: *Contd*

Caste Code	(*1*)	(2)	(3)	(4)	(5)	(6)	(7)	(8)	(9)	(*10*)	(*11*)	(*12*)
Reddi		11		4	11	1	3		3	1	4	38
Row				1			2	1	2			6
Shastri									4			4
Unidentified (Agraharum Nuttum)	6											6
Unidentified (Agraharum)	5	22		27	19		8	28	26	12		147
Unidentified (Dutch Village)											19	19
Unidentified (Nuttum)		12	7	1	4	2	2	8				36
Unidentified (n/a)												
Total	17	90	10	47	61	25	49	101	82	22	30	534

Source: Abstract State of the Number of Meerassee Shares and of Meerassee Holders in the Several Districts of the Jagheer in Fusly 1207 shewing also the Quantity of Meerassee unclaimed & occupied by Pyacarries, *Board's Collections*, 2115 & 2116, Vol. 112, F/4/112, OIOC.

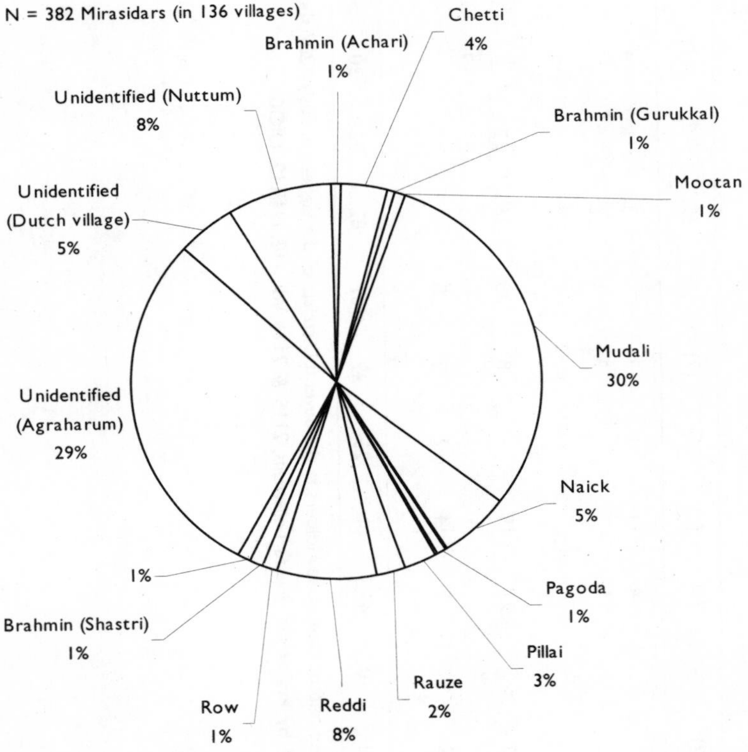

Source: Abstract State of the Number of Meerassee Shares and of Meerassee Holders in the Several Districts of the Jagheer in Fusly 1207 shewing also the Quantity of Meerassee unclaimed & occupied by Pyacarries, *Board's Collections*, 2115 & 2116, Vol. 112, F/4/112, OIOC.

FIG. 6.7: Percentage of Mirasidar Castes in Ponneri (*Place Report*, 1797–8)

Table 6.4 above shows the distribution of mirasidar castes in the respective magans. The caste identification of a considerable number of mirasidars cannot be ascertained, so that the situation in the period is not easy to reconstruct. Even after excluding the unidentified cases, however, it can be concluded that all the magans had at least a few mirasidar castes. Only Ponnary (Ponneri) magan showed an exceptional dominance of Mudalis (Vellalers) among the mirasidars. This dominance could, however, probably be denied if the unidentified cases were

TABLE 6.5

Mirasidars' (Landholders') Fellow Caste Members (*Barnard Report*, 1760s–70s)

1971 Census Code	Village Name	Names of Landholders and Their Shares	Land-holder's Caste (wide)	Land-holder's Caste (narrow)	Total House-holds (calcu-lated)	Land-holders Fellow Caste-Men (wide)	Land-holders Fellow Caste-Men (narrow)
(1)	(2)	(3)	(4)	(5)	(6)	(7)	(8)
PO116A	Tirvapady	Karykista Moodely & Gopaul Moodely, Paupa Moodely, Sittapa Moodely, & Ramalinga Moodely	Vellaler	Tuliva V.	30	0%	0%
PO081E	Vilpacum	Vadama Brahmins	Brahmin	Vadama Br.	6	67%	0%
PO112D	Tudyperumbauk	Vadama Brahmins	Brahmin	Vadama Br.	20	30%	0%
PO184A	Codavoor	Niyogee Brahmins residing at Suttavadoo	Brahmin	Niyogee Br.	15	7%	0%
PO115A	Kistnaporum	Ancient landholders are Palleys from whom the Chettys purchased the landholdership & from whom bought Tuliva Vellalers who are landholders now	Vellaler	Tuliva V.	14	0%	0%
PO098A	Cudapacum	Niyogee Brahmins of Tuttamunjey 30,	Brahmin	Niyogee Br.			
		Purcotah Vellalers of Vallar 2	Vellaler	Purcotah V.	22	5%	0%
PO108A	Colatoor	Vepary Brahmins of Coommungalum	Brahmin	Vepary Br.	24	0%	0%

(*contd*)

TABLE 6.5: *Contd*

(1)	(2)	(3)	(4)	(5)	(6)	(7)	(8)
PO106A	Ariapillaycopum	Purcotah Vellalers	Vellaler	Purcotah V.	11	36%	0%
PO089A	Marattoor	Vistnoo Brahmin landholders. Their residency unknown	Brahmin	Vistnoo Br.	11	0%	0%
PO052A	Tottacaud	Condighetty Vellala of Nuthvoil who mortgaged their village to Nunda Gopauler.	Vellaler	Condighetty V.	28	4%	0%
PO079B	Autriamungalum	Gentoo Brahmins their residence unknown 12	Brahmin	Gentoo Br.	9	0%	0%
PO083D	Davedanum	Solia Vellala of unknown place	Vellaler	Solia V.	25	0%	0%
PO049A	Areyempoil	Condighetty Vellalers of unknown place	Vellaler	Condighetty V.	6	0%	0%
Unidendified	Collapudey	Condighetty Vellalers of Munjoor	Vellaler	Condighetty V.	10	0%	0%
PO182B	Chittarsoor	Ancient landholder. Palley, their residency unknown Purcotah Vellalers or Arsoor, they cultivate this village on 24 Shares	Vellaler	Purcotah V.	38	3%	0%
PO175A	Poorvame	Purcotah Vellalers of Poodechary	Vellaler	Purcotah V.	16	0%	0%
PO167B	Praliumbacum	Gentoo Vellalers	Vellaler	Gentoo V.	22	18%	0%
PO248A	Mangode	Purcotah Vellalers of unknown place	Vellaler	Purcotah V.	8	0%	0%
PO249A	Kearapacum	Purcotah Vellalers of unknown place	Vellaler	Purcotah V.	5	0%	0%
Unidentified	Cooleynauvel	Palleys of Wopesamoodrum	Palli	Palli	18	0%	0%
PO222A	Cungaunmade	Tuliva Vellalers of Wommepade	Vellaler	Tuliva V.	1	100%	0%
PO143K	Tirooparoo	Gentoo Brahmins of Cunasumpacum. Arsoor Vencatachel Modaly purchased part of land & has taken for mortgage the other part of land from Gentoo Brahmin landholders of Tirooparoo	Brahmin (Nattar)	Gentoo Br. (Nattar)	10	0%	0%

(*contd*)

TABLE 6.5: *Contd*

(1)	(2)	(3)	(4)	(5)	(6)	(7)	(8)
PO035A	Mahafoose Cawn Petta	Nabab Mahafoose Cawn	Nawab	Nawab	19	0%	0%
PO037C/ PO213A	Parymullavoil	Gentoo Brahmin. Landholders of unknown place, Another Gentoo Brahmin residing at Garacan. And Rungaputy Pundit Stil Mojumdar residing at Promary, Vengamrajah Niyogee Residing at Aroomunda (who purchased landholdership). [Vepary Brahmin (who purchased Landholdership from ancient Landholder, Gentoo Brahmin), Gentoo Brahmin (who held Daunum or gift of land)]	Brahmin	Gentoo Br. Niyogee Br. Vepary Br.	7	0%	0%
PO041A	Simaporam	Vistnoo Brahmins of Anoopumbut	Brahmin	Vistnoo Br.	17	0%	0%
PO006B	Sirneyem	Vistnoo Brahmins of unknown place	Brahmin	Vistnoo Br.			
		Condighetty Vellaler of Choleporam	Vellaler	Condighetty V.	8	0%	0%
PO028A/ PO200A	Voraycaud	Condighetty Vellalers of Choleveram	Vellaler	Condighetty V.	3	0%	0%
PO025A	Auttoor	Vistanoo Brahmins of unknown place	Brahmin	Vistnoo Br.	11	0%	0%
Unidentified	Tindagariumbutt	Condighetty Vellalers	Vellaler	Condighetty V.	11	0%	0%
PO026A	Cornwoday	Condighetty Vellalers of Choleporam	Vellaler	Condighetty V.	35	3%	0%
PO019A	Marumbull	Gopaliah Vistanoo Brahmin landholder of Girdaporam	Brahmin	Vistnoo Br.	16	0%	0%
PO020A	Coombanoor	Condighetty Vellaler of Aungaud	Vellaler	Condighetty V.	10	0%	0%

(contd)

Table 6.5: *Contd*

(1)	(2)	(3)	(4)	(5)	(6)	(7)	(8)
PO143A/ PO212A	Punapacum	Vistnoo Brahmin	Brahmin	Vistnoo Br.	74	3%	1%
PO022A	Choleporam	Condighetty Vellalers	Vellaler	Condighetty V.	98	5%	3%
PO223C	Woomepade	Tuliva Vellaler	Vellaler	Tuliva V.	31	6%	3%
PO111A	Aulaud	Landholder Brahmins residing in the following villages, Vepary Brahmin at Coommungalam, Vedma Brahmin at Vembauk, Vistnoo, Gentoo Brahmins at Cattaroor	Brahmin Brahmin Brahmin	Vepary Br. Vedma Br. Vistnoo Br. Gentoo Br.	25	4%	4%
PO044A	Ennoor	Landholder. Resides at Poolidavacum & auttypade, Condighetty Vellaler landholder & Cow keeper who purchased landholdership: Condighetty Vellalers 6, Condighetty Vellaler purchased from above landholders. 5, Cow keeper purchased from above landholders.1	Vellaler Cow keeper	Condighetty V. Cow keeper	57	7%	5%
PO016A	Codypullum	Covrays who purchased landholdership	Covrai	Covrai	36	6%	6%
PO213B	Coloor	Purcotah Vellalers	Vellaler	Purcotah V.	154	8%	6%
PO127A	Chelembade	Purcotah Vellalers	Vellaler	Purcotah V.	83	11%	6%
PO211A	Elpacum	Gentoo Brahmins of unknown place 32 fixed.	Brahmin	Gentoo Br.	33	9%	6%
PO090A	Tanapacum	Purcotah Vellalers	Vellaler	Purcotah V.	14	14%	7%
PO143D	Moodalambade	Gentoo Brahmins	Brahmin	Gentoo Br.	129	9%	8%
PO218A	Cooriveporam	Tuliva Vellalers	Vellaler	Tuliva V.	38	11%	8%

(*contd*)

TABLE 6.5: *Contd*

(1)	(2)	(3)	(4)	(5)	(6)	(7)	(8)
PO050C	Minjoor	Condighetty Vellalers	Vellaler	Condighetty V.	112	13%	8%
PO164A	Viarungavade	Reddy Mudali, Tooliva Vellaler of Viarungavade	Vellaler	Tuliva V.	24	13%	8%
PO056E/ PO056C	Vunnypacum	Gentoo Brahmins	Brahmin	Gentoo Br.	69	9%	9%
PO053A	Vellumbacum	Desmook Ram Row	Deshmuk	Deshmuk	11	9%	9%
PO065A	Alunjepacum	Vadamals [Vadama Brahmin]	Brahmin	Vadama Br.	21	38%	10%
PO091C	Voiloor	Gentoo Brahmin of Voiloor 1, Tutavajee Brahmin at	Brahmin	Gentoo Br.	48	10%	10%
		Valloor 1, Niyogee Brahmin at Madras 1,	Brahmin	Niyogee Br.			
		Vistanoo Brahmin at Menjoor 1,	Brahmin	Vistnoo Br.			
		Numby & Siva Brahmin at Madras 1, Conicoply 1	Brahmin	Numby & Siva			
			Kanakapillai	Br. Conicoply			
PO034B	Nauyer	Condighetty Vellalers, Conicoply Ponny Narain Pillay	Vellaler	Condighetty V.	133	11%	11%
			Kanakapillai	Conicoply			
PO107A	Mulooporam	Gentoo Brahmin	Brahmin	Gentoo Br.	9	11%	11%
PO050B	Luchimiporam	Vepary Brahmin of Coommungalum 4 1/2,	Brahmin	Vepary Br.	8	13%	13%
		Vadama Brahmini 4 1/2, Vellaler 1	Brahmin	Vadama Br.			
			Vellaler				
PO021A	Aungaud	Condighetty Vellalers	Vellaler	Condighetty V.	23	17%	13%
PO040B	Madoor	Gentoo Brahmins	Brahmin	Gentoo Br.	97	18%	13%
PO080A	Elevunbutt	Tuliva Vellalers [Angooreddy Moodely]	Vellaler	Tuliva V.	22	23%	14%
PO085A	Cauneyembacum	Tuliva Vellalers	Vellaler	Tuliva V.	48	15%	15%

(*contd*)

TABLE 6.5: *Contd*

(1)	(2)	(3)	(4)	(5)	(6)	(7)	(8)
PO183A	Arsoor	Ancient landholder. Palley. Their residence unknown. Purcotah Vellalers changeable shares 24 fixed.	Vellaler	Purcotah V.	91	46%	15%
PO149A	Periacavenum	Nullamootta Mudali & Aroonachela Mudali of Periacavenam [Tuliva Vellaler]	Vellaler	Tuliva V.	60	22%	17%
PO051A	Naithvoil	Condighetty Vellalers, Nunda Gopauler who bought landholdership	Vellaler	Condighetty V.	83	23%	17%
PO092B	Cautpulley	Purcotah Vellalers 3, Nulvellaler 1	Vellaler	Purcotah V. Nul V.	40	23%	18%
PO115C	Cusba of Ponary	Tuliva Vellaler, head landholders: Karykista Moodely & Gopaul Moodely, Paupa Moodely, Sittapa Moodely, & Ramalinga Moodely	Vellaler	Tuliva V.	81	23%	19%
PO105B	Tirvellavoil	Tuliva Vellalers	Vellaler	Tuliva V.	24	29%	21%
PO186A	Colloor	Covelgar of the village. [Gentoo Brahmin, Vipaury Brahmin, Vistnoo Brahmin?]	Brahmin	Gentoo Br. Vaipary Br.	19	26%	21%
PO227A	Oulidilumbade	Tuliva Vellalers	Vellaler	Tuliva V.	23	22%	22%
PO215A	Annamulacherry	Kalians	Kalian	Kalian	9	22%	22%
PO177A	Vembade	Purcotah Vellalers	Vellaler	Purcotah V.	31	23%	23%
PO031A	Nareconnum	Vadama Brahmins	Brahmin	Vadama Br.	22	23%	23%
PO045B	Poolidarvacum	Condighetty Vellalars 3, Cow keepers bought share 1	Vellaler Cow keeper	Condighetty V. Cow keeper	57	23%	23%

(*contd*)

Table 6.5: *Contd*

(1)	(2)	(3)	(4)	(5)	(6)	(7)	(8)
Unidentified	Nalevaley	Gentoo Brahmins 30, Vistnoo Brahmins 10, Vadma Brahmins 20	Brahmin	Gentoo Br. Vistnoo Br. Vadma Br.	47	28%	23%
PO151A	Coodvanjary	Tuliva Vellalers	Vellaler	Tuliva V.	8	25%	25%
PO224B	Sakenium	Gentoo Brahmins 62, Purcotah Vellalers 2	Brahmin Vellaler	Gentoo Br. Purcotah V.	20	35%	25%
PO184A	Cattavoor	Purcotah Vellaler	Vellaler	Purcotah V.	92	33%	26%
Unidentified	Soalpacum	Vistanoo Brahmin Sreenevasah, Moodookistniah, Ayyaniah	Brahmin	Vistnoo Br.	26	27%	27%
PO208A	Aynellore	Vistnoo Brahmins, ancient shares 60 now fixed 7 1/2.	Brahmin	Vistnoo Br.	40	28%	28%
PO104A	Attamunachary	Gentoo Brahmins	Brahmin	Gentoo Br.	21	29%	29%
PO102A	Somunanjary	Pally	Palli	Palli	36	31%	31%
PO099A	Cattoor	Purcotah Vellalers	Vellaler	Purcotah V.	113	34%	31%
PO115B	Coommungalum	Ancient landholders Palleys, from whom Chittys purchased the landholdership. From the Chittys Tuliva Vellalers purchased. Thus changeable shares 5 fixed.	Vellaler	Tuliva V.	91	34%	33%
PO162C	Perembade	Gentoo Brahmin Appaviar & Poorooshetienaier, Vistnoo Brahmins, Purcotah Vellalers	Brahmin Vellaler	Gentoo Br. Vistnoo Br. Purcotah V.	104	37%	35%
PO210A	Comeranjary	Tuliva Vellalers	Vellaler	Tuliva V.	20	40%	35%
PO242C	Chunambcolum	Pallys	Palli	Palli	150	35%	35%

(*contd*)

TABLE 6.5: *Contd*

(1)	(2)	(3)	(4)	(5)	(6)	(7)	(8)
PO059C	Serpacum	Gentoo Brahmins 40, Tuliva Vellaler 2	Brahmin Vellaler	Gentoo Br. Tuliva V.	12	42%	42%
PO051A	Culpacum	Pally	Palli	Palli	19	42%	42%
PO078A	Aumoor	Gentoo Brahmins 15, Purcotah Vellalers 1	Brahmin Vellaler	Gentoo Br. Purcotah V.	71	31%	45%
PO157A	Chinnacavenum	Tuliva Vellalers	Vellaler	Tuliva V.	108	50%	49%
PO110A	Sevaporam	Tuliva Vellalers	Vellaler	Tuliva V.	2	50%	50%
PO155A	Daveranjary	Tuliva Vellalers	Vellaler	Tuliva V.	2	50%	50%
PO160A	Yaresiven	Nelloran, Andiappan, Cuttan (Tuliva Vellalers)	Vellaler	Tuliva V.	8	88%	50%
PO212A	Punapacum	Gentoo Brahmins ancient share 24 now 1, Purcotah Vellalers ancient share 8 now 1	Brahmin Vellaler	Gentoo Br. Purcotah V.	12	25%	50%
PO122A	Paulvoil	Gentoo Brahmins	Brahmin	Gentoo Br.	4	50%	50%
Unidentified	Agharum	Gentoo Brahmin	Brahmin	Gentoo Br.	4	100%	50%
PO100A	Tuttamunjey	[Niyogee] Brahmins 120, Purcotah Vellalers 8	Brahmin Vellaler	Niyogee Br. Purcotah V.	69	52%	51%
PO243B/ PO243C	Wopesamoodram	Palleys	Palli	Palli	61	52%	52%
PO145A	Cunacumbacum	Gentoo Brahmin, Vistnoo Brahmins, share 30, Rakeapa Modely purchased the landholdership, share 2	Brahmin Vellaler	Gentoo Br. Vistnoo Br. V.	7	43%	57%
PO071A/ PO208D	Tadarsoor	Ancient landholders Pallys who made this village Agraharum to the Brahmins their residence unknown. now purcotah Vellalers changeable share 24 fixed	Vellaler	Purcotah V.	5	60%	60%

(*contd*)

Table 6.5: *Contd*

(1)	(2)	(3)	(4)	(5)	(6)	(7)	(8)
PO055A	Moorchambutt	Gentoo Brahmins	Brahmin	Gentoo Br.	8	63%	63%
PO207A	Andavoil	Tuliva Vellalers	Vellaler	Tuliva V.	15	73%	73%
PO217A	Periavepattoor	Palleys	Palli	Palli	15	80%	80%
PO077A	Vaducaputt	[Vadama] Brahmins 15, Purcotah Vellalers 1	Brahmin Vellaler	Vadama Br. Purcotah V.	7	100%	100%
PO084A	Coommersirlpacum	Solia Vellalers	Vellaler	Solia V.	8	100%	100%
PO101A	Ennakeracherny	Gentoo Brahmins	Brahmin	Gentoo Br.	1	100%	100%
PO076A	Sayenaporam	No data	No data	No data	17	No data	No data
PO081A	Anoopumbutt	Rajahs	Raja	Raja	24	No data	No data
PO113C	Trevengadaporam	Landholders share 4 fixed and they are residing in other 4 different villages: Seavacolenda of Coommungalum 1, Ambelanum of Periacavenum 1, Rakeappen of Oudavoor 1, Puvlumula Modely of Chentadrypetta 1	Unknown	Unidentified + Mudali	0	No data	No data
PO156A	Agharum	Tuliva Vellalers of Chinnacavenum	Vellaler	Tuliva V.	0	No data	No data
PO154A	Coventangel	Tuliva Vellalers of Chinnacavenum	Vellaler	Tuliva V.	0	No data	No data
PO153A	Purkaputt	Tuliva Vellaler [Poligar and head inhabitant Nyneppa, Tuliva Vellaler residing at Woppalom]	Vellaler	Tuliva V.	0	No data	No data
PO161A	Arevakum	Ancient landholder. Tooliva Vellaler who granted their landholdership as gift to Hury Pundit residing at Coommungalum	Brahmin	Br.	0	No data	No data

(*contd*)

TABLE 6.5: *Contd*

(1)	(2)	(3)	(4)	(5)	(6)	(7)	(8)
PO167B	Pullembacum	Landholders residing at Cattavoor	Unknown	Unknown	0	No data	No data
PO148A	Cuncavullyporam	Sadiappa Mudali landholder of Madras	Vellaler	Vellaler	0	No data	No data
PO075A	Perinjary	Tuliva Vellalers residing at Madras	Vellaler	Tuliva V.	0	No data	No data
PO103A	Silladpanjary	Purcotah Vellalers at Tattamunjey	Vellaler	Purcotah V.	0	No data	No data
PO109A	Lingasamoodram	Vistnoo Brahmin of Lingurpatah Yelembade, Vepary Brahmins	Brahmin	Vistnoo Br. Vepary Br.	0	No data	No data
PO086A	Serveloor	Purcotah Vellaler of Nagachary & Xx	Vellaler	Purcotah V.	0	No data	No data
PO151A	Cudamunjary	Purcotah Vellaler of Nagachary, their share I fixed, Landholder Bramans. Their shares unknown	Brahmin Vellaler	Purcotah V.	0	No data	Nc data
PO104A	Sattamungalchary	Purcotah Vellaler of Nagachary	Vellaler	Purcotah V.	0	No data	No data
PO212A	Panapacum	Landholder. Their residence & shares unknown	No data	Unknown	0	No data	No data
PO040B	Mudiyoor	Landholder. Their residence & shares unknown	No data	Unknown	0	No data	No data
PO216A	Chinnavapatoor	Kalian landholders of Annamulacherry	Kalian	Kalian	0	No data	No data
PO040B	Mudiyoor	Condighetty Vellaler of Nauyer	Vellaler	Condighetty V.	0	No data	No data
PO037A	Chinnamullavoil	Covray landholders. of Codepuliom, Covray Cooppe Chitty who purchased landholdership	Covrai	Covrai	0	No data	No data
PO032A	Girdherporam		No data	No data	0	No data	No data
PO033A	Boodoor		No data	No data	0	No data	No data
PO027A	Sodyperembade	Gentoo Brahmins of Comovoday	Brahmin	Gentoo Br.	0	No data	No data
PO030A	Sackenjary	Vadama Brahmins of Nayconnum	Brahmin	Vadama Br.	0	No data	No data
PO143A	Punnepacum	Vistnoo Brahmins of unknown place	Brahmin	Vistnoo Br.	0	No data	No data

(*contd*)

Table 6.5: *Contd*

(1)	(2)	(3)	(4)	(5)	(6)	(7)	(8)
PO002A	Autuntangel		No data	No data	0	No data	No data
PO003A	Vilianellore		No data	No data	0	No data	No data
PO158A	Lingapierpetta	Margasahasuwara Pagoda	Pagoda	Pagoda	27	Pagoda	Pagoda
PO174A	Tirpalvenam	Palaswara Swamy Pagoda	Pagoda	Pagoda	43	Pagoda	Pagoda
PO195D	Coodrayput-tumcandica	Pagoda of Boodary Eswaraswamy of Nauyer	Pagoda	Pagoda	4	Pagoda	Pagoda
PO008A	Padianellore	Teagarajaswamy of Tirvettur	Pagoda	Pagoda	14	Pagoda	Pagoda
PO159A	Mutteravade	Head landholders: Tumban, Kurian, Nynan of Madras	Unknown	Unidentified	7	Unidentified	Unidentified
PO152C	Woppalum	1. Kanamaula Vencaten's share purchased by Andeappean who residing at Coodvary, 1. Raghaviah have one... residing at Chennacavanum, 2. Sooriya Sola & C. residing at Coommungalum	Unknown	Unidentified	8	Unknown	Unknown
PO082A	Pooleycolum	Landholder. Their name & residence unknown	No data	Unknown	11	Unknown	Unknown
Unidendified	Ilvuntangel	Landholder. Their residence & shares unknown	No data	Unknown	21	Unknown	Unknown
PO172A	Pacum	Landholder. Name and place unknown	No data	No data	25	Unknown	Unknown
PO218A	Coryevoil	Landholders residing at Chinnacavanum.	Unknown	Unknown	3	Unknown	Unknown
PO214A	Serlpacum	Landholders of unknown place	Unknown	Unknown	0	Unknown	Unknown
PO163A	Munymoghumiandika	Gentoo Brahmins of Munymoghumeandika	Brahmin	Gentoo Br.	0	Unreadable	Unreadable
PO165A	Asanpoodoor	Niyogee Brahmins residing at Tuttamunja, Gentoo Brahmins whose residence unknown, Purootah Vellaler residing at Madras	Brahmin Brahmin Vellaler	Niyogee Br. Gentoo Br. Purcotah V.	0	Unreadable	Unreadable

(*contd*)

TABLE 6.5: *Contd*

(1)	(2)	(3)	(4)	(5)	(6)	(7)	(8)
PO087B	Veloor	Purcotah Vellalers	Vellaler	Purcotah V.	0	Unreadable	Unreadable
PO087A	Nagachary	Purcotah Vellalers	Vellaler	Purcotah V.	0	Unreadable	Unreadable
PO054D	Nauloor	Vistanoo Brahmins of unknown place share 4	Brahmin	Vistnoo Br.	0	Unreadable	Unreadable
PO209A	Auvoor	Tuliva Vellalers	Vellaler	Tuliva V.	0	Unreadable	Unreadable
PO208E	Vitatandelum	No data	No data	No data	0	Unreadable	Unreadable
PO115E	Vonebacum	Palleys of unknown place	Palli	Palli	0	Unreadable	Unreadable
PO250A/ PO250B	Wooppoonelvoil	Purcotah Vellalers	Vellaler	Purcotah V.	0	Unreadable	Unreadable
PO029A	Soorapade	Condighetty Vellaler landholders. From whom purchased the landholdership by Luchumajee Pundit of Ponary	Brahmin	Br.	0	Unreadable	Unreadable

Note: [Wide] neglects the differences between smaller caste categories, whereas [Narrow] recognizes them.

Source: Barnard Report, 1760s–70s.

clarified.[15] The first possible explanation, that is, the numerical dominance of fellow caste men, is thus ruled out.

Mirasi System as Social Grammar

If the mirasidars' power was not based upon the numerical caste/communal dominance, what mattered instead? How could the individual mirasidars claim their mirasidarship in the village where they often did not have any fellow caste members? The available evidence suggests that the notion of mirasidarship itself was firmly established.

As noted earlier, even the Nawab could not usurp mirasidarship by force but had to purchase it. Such established notion about mirasi rights as observed here was not an isolated case. Actually, eighteenth-century village accounts were none other than accounts of various mirasi rights that covered the entire sphere of local society. Village production was elaborately distributed in shares among the different categories of people and institutions in the local society. Not only the mirasidarship but also the shares allocated to various roles performed by villagers were acknowledged as mirasi rights. Though each village had different rates in share proportions, the notion of mirasi system itself was firm and uniform. The mirasi system was a system that provided everyone in the period with a way of living, wealth, esteem, status, and power. In this sense, it operated as the social grammar for people to express themselves in the society.[16]

If the mirasi system operated in an autonomous way in the period, our next task is to clarify the positions of the state and the local society in relation to the system.

State and the Mirasi System

In what way was the relation between the state and the local society expressed in the mirasi system? The first point to be noted is that the state was never a bystander in relation to the system. According to the *Barnard Report*, the state and the cultivators divided the major share (two-thirds to three-fourths) of the village production at the final stage after several categories of shares were distributed. This process, which was observed in every village, indicates that the state and the cultivator were the major competitors for shares in the mirasi system. As the cultivator belonged to the local society, the relation between the two can be deemed to be the one between the state and the local society. The categories used by Barnard in classifying different shares, such as 'dues paid by circar [state] alone' or 'dues paid half by the cultivator and half by the circar', indicate clearly the fundamental feature of the mirasi system, too.[17]

The power balance between the state and the local society was basically expressed in the different proportional shares. The ever-fluctuating balance between the two in the different ecological/social/political settings was expressed in the elaborately established proportions.

A few points should be considered in this regard. First is the effect of political instability of the period upon the mirasi system. It was often observed in the period that the arrears of revenue were recovered only when the state demanded payment by force.[18] Even so, it seems the notion of the mirasi system was so strong that the proportional shares, including those for the state, never failed to be acknowledged. The survival of the elaborately defined share proportions till the time of the Barnard's survey is the clear evidence of this. Second is the position of those influential religious institutions or big poligars vs state in the mirasi system. As mentioned before, some big poligars controlled hundreds of villages independently. The same could be observed in the case of big temples. The shrotriamdars discussed above managed their villages independently, too. South Indian states might be visualized not as having a pyramidal structure but as constituting one of the pillars in a multi-pillar social architecture.

If the mirasi system could be defined as such, what type of changes could be observed other than the changes in share proportions? What would occur to the system once the power balance between the state and the local society started critically changing? Our next task is to clarify this process.

Mirasidars in Local Society

Structural change in the period in question was occurring in two spheres, one within the mirasi system and the other outside it, and the two were interrelated. In this paper we will take up only the changes occurring within, namely, the process of deconstruction of mirasi system by the mirasidars themselves.[19]

If the mirasi system functioned as the social grammar in the period, in what way could the mirasidars extend their power in their relations, first with the state, second with other mirasidars, and third with others, in the local society? Three possible choices were open. The first was to acquire mirasidarship from other mirasidars. The evidence that the majority of mirasidars had shares in just one or two villages indicates that most of such transactions, if they occurred, were confined in the proximity. The second was to acquire other mirasi-type shares. Their entry into the poligarship in twenty villages as studied above can be counted as such. The third and seemingly most significant was the deconstruction of the mirasi system by the mirasidars themselves. We will examine the last point next.

As stated above, each share recipient was assigned some specific role in the local society. Under the system it was, for instance, possible for a village accountant (*karnam*) to acquire other accountants' posts with the attached shares. On the other hand it was not possible for the accountant to acquire the post and the share of, for instance, the washerman, which was totally unrealistic under the caste system.[20] What the mirasidars attempted instead was to place under their control various shares originally assigned to other people in their villages and to distribute the scooped shares through their own hands. This was exactly what was observed among the village lords in South Arcot in the late pre-colonial period. Table 6.6 is one of the lists detailing the 'unauthorized collection and disbursements by the *monigar* or village headman' submitted by a collector of South Arcot to the Board of Revenue at the initial stage of colonial administration. It reveals that the village headman collected a certain amount and paid from it various types of allowances directly to the functionaries on different occasions.[21] As this type of usurpation and disbursement by village headmen was not the established custom, the collector must have defined it as 'unauthorized'. Some mirasidars in Chingleput headed towards the same direction. They deconstructed the long-established mirasi system to their advantage, which made it possible for some of them to emerge as village lords in the period.

The emergence of mirasidars as village lords swung the power balance between them and the state to their favour. The process had a grave impact upon the relations between the state and the local society, between the mirasidar and the local society, and the mirasi system itself. Political instability in the eighteenth-century India was the combined result of several factors, the most important being the change in the mirasi system.

SOUTH INDIA IN THE LATE NINETEENTH CENTURY

In 1802, the permanent settlement was introduced in Chingleput. Under the settlement Chingleput was divided into sixty zamindari estates,[22]

TABLE 6.6

List of 'Unauthorized' Collections and Disbursements by a Village Headman in Carangooly Village, Bhovangherry District, 1804–5

	P.F.C.
Amount of Unauthorized Collections made by the Gramattan [Village Headman] or Puttah Monigar [Superintendent, Headman]	*110.35.12*
Disbursements therefrom by Putta Monigar or his Order	
By Cash	
[Revenue Administration]	
Paid conicopillah [village writer] Mootien on account of batta [extra allowance]	4.42.15
Paid on account of olahs [palm-leaf] for writing village accounts	0.10.44
Paid to the Mahatidee peon who came to collect money	3.18.22
Paid bribe to Narrain Row Tahsildar [high official] for withholding the collection of false shavie [blighted corn]	29.00.00
Paid Colundavalapilla Zareebdar [surveyor?] for making onto false account of shavie	30.00.00
Paid Notagar [money-changer] from this collection, his allowance fixed by the circar [state] having been embezzled by the Monigar	1.14. 05
Taken by Veerah Reddy Monigar on account of batta	11.22.40
Taken by Veerah Reddy Monigar in ready money	5.14.05
Paid batta for exchanging pagodas deficient in weight	4.24.49
[Security]	
Paid Coollun Taliar [village watchman] his allowance, paid by the circar having been embezzled by the Monigar	1.09.67
Paid Totty [village watchman], his allowance fixed by the circar having been embezzled by the Monigar	2.36.45

(*contd*)

TABLE 6.6: *Contd*

	P.F.C.
Amount of Unauthorized Collections made by the Gramattan [Village Headman] or Puttah Monigar [Superintendent, Headman]	*110.35.12*
Disbursements therefrom by Putta Monigar or his Order	
By Cash	
[Religious Activities]	
Paid the church [Hindu pagoda] on account of daily expenses	5.16.70
Paid Appajiyah on going to Rameswaram [pilgrimage]	1.00.00
[Others, unidentified]	
Paid batta to circar people and charitable purposes	6.05.50
Paid alms to Ramalingyah	1.00.00
Paid sundry charges in the village	2.00.00
Paid Teeroovengadyah on account of his marriage	1.00.00
Total	110.35.12

P-Pagoda, F-Fanam, C-Cash

Source: Letter from the Principal Collector in the Southern Division of Arcot, 15 December 1805, *Board of Revenue Proceedings*, 2 January 1806.

[ ]—Notes by Mizushima.

which were offered for sale at the permanently fixed revenue. Many of the zamindari estates so auctioned, however, soon became bankrupt, and the *raiyatwari* system was introduced into such bankrupt areas from the 1810s. The basic principle of the raiyatwari system was to assume the state as the sole and exclusive landowner, to acknowledge a cultivator as a *raiyat*, and to grant a *patta* (title deed) to the raiyat. The raiyat who obtained a patta was designated as a *pattadar* and could retain the land lot as long as he paid the land assessment to the state. If this principle operated as it was intended, there could be just two claimants to each land lot, that is, the state and the pattadar. It was, however, not the case in many parts of south India, especially in Chingleput.

One of the most conspicuous features of the colonial land administration in Chingleput in the first half of the nineteenth century was the acknowledgement of mirasidars' overlordship besides the state's. This unique treatment, which was established in the course of early revenue administration, especially by Place,[23] took the form of a *dittam* system. Under the dittam system, mirasidars registered annually the land lots under cultivation in their pattas. They allowed other lands to be cultivated by non-mirasidar cultivators called *payikari*. The lands cultivated by the payikaris were registered in one *samudayam* (common) patta in the chief mirasidars' names.[24] The payikaris had to pay the landlord rent called *swatantram* to the mirasidars, acknowledging the latter's overlordship upon these lands (called *pangu* land). The pangu land sometimes covered an entire village area.

The dittam system was, however, abolished in 1856, and a new system was introduced in an attempt to curtail the mirasidars' overlordship. Village lands were now categorized into pangu, *durkhast*, and waste. The pangu lands, which had been jointly held by all the mirasidars in shares, were now redivided among the mirasidars and registered separately in the respective mirasidars' pattas. This separate registering system dealt a serious blow to the unity of the mirasidar body. In addition each mirasidar, now designated as pattadar like any other pattadars of non-mirasidar origin, was to pay the full assessment upon all his holdings whether he cultivated them or not.[25] This compulsory payment of all the assessment upon one's holdings, even those not under cultivation, dealt a similar blow to the mirasidars. It now became economically unwise for a mirasidar to register his entire holdings in his own name in an attempt to exclude non-mirasidars. The second category, durkhast, was the land for which new landholders had not previously paid any share to the mirasidars. This category was newly created to ratify the recently acquired landholding by payikaris despite mirasidars' oppositions. Henceforward these new landholders did not become liable to pay any share to the mirasidars.

Some concessional measures for mirasidars were taken at the same time. The first was the creation of the category of wasteland, for which an applicant was liable to pay shares to the mirasidars. The second was the rule for the land that became relinquished but taken up again under the categories of both pangu and durkhast. The new landholders were to be charged with the fee at the rate of two annas per rupee of assessment, and the fee was to be paid to the mirasi body.

In the mid-nineteenth century, Chingleput thus witnessed a new policy intended to break up the mirasidars' privileged position and to make the landholding structure as simple as the raiyatwari system was originally designed to be. The mirasidars' power was greatly undermined under the new policy, even though they continued having pre-emptive claims over others.

Along with such changes, many relevant measures had been introduced since the beginning of the colonial land administration. Various types of fees and *inam*s (tax-exempted land), upon which many people had been dependent, were selectively requisitioned, so that many had to switch to other course of dependency, like the *jajmani* system.[26] In a word, the old mirasi system was being replaced by the emerging agrarian order based upon land lots.

Our task next is to assess the significance of these changes through the analysis of the land records in the 1870s. The main source to be utilized is the *Settlement Registers* of 1877. The records contain the pattadars' names and other details of every lot. According to the 1871 Census, 153 out of 254 villages in Ponneri were under the raiyatwari tenure, whereas shrotriam and zamindari tenures accounted for forty-seven and fifty-four villages respectively (Fig. 6.8). Those villages under shrotriam and zamindari tenures, which were not directly managed by the government, are excluded from the following study, as detailed land records are currently not available.[27]

Mirasidar

Three classes could be identified under the raiyatwari system in late-nineteenth-century Ponneri. They were mirasidars, pattadars, and the rest. First we will examine the features of mirasidars.

Several salient features could be observed in the 1870s. First was the complex caste composition of the mirasidars in contrast to the

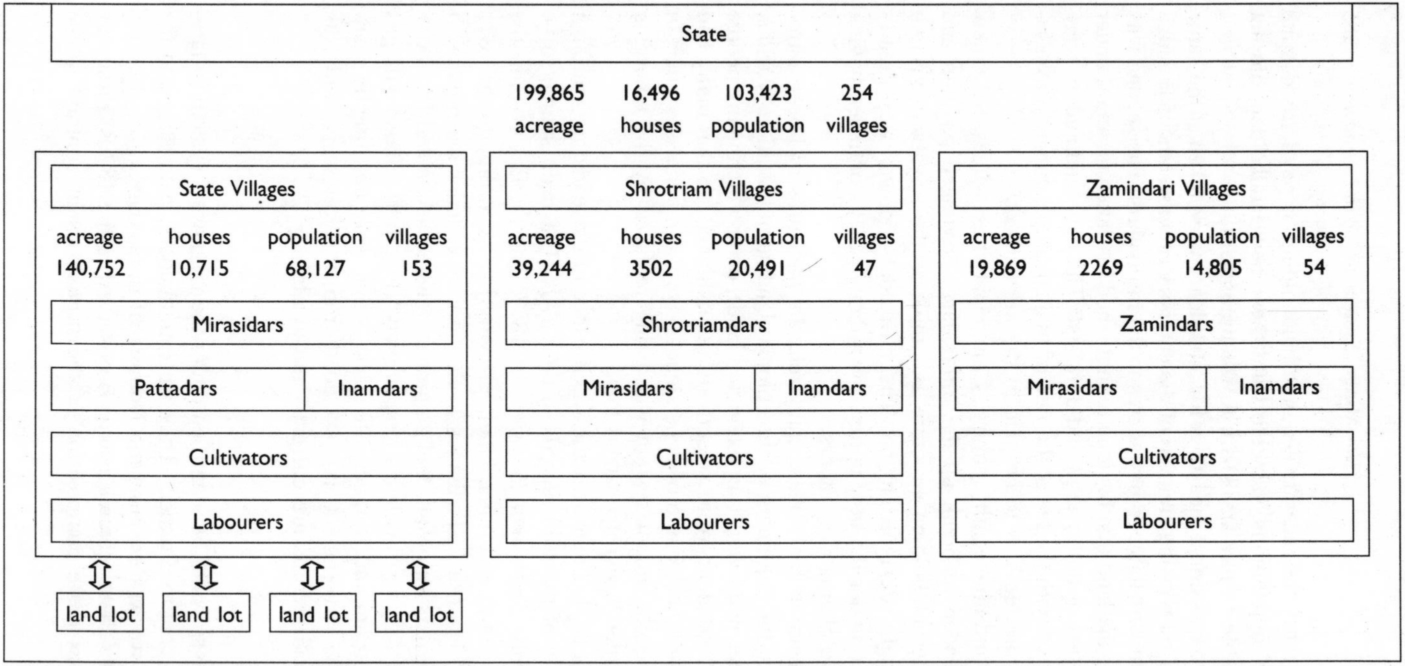

Source: Madras Census 1871 Supplementary Tables. VI h. – A Detailed List of Sub-Divisions of each Hindu Caste as shown in the Schedules received from the several Districts of the Madras Presidency, No. 16 Caste.

FIG. 6.8: Village Structures in Ponneri in the 1870s

simpler composition in the 1770s. The *Barnard Report* of the 1770s, for instance, shows that 115 out of 141 villages had within each village just one mirasidar caste only (Table 6.7). In the *Place Report* of the 1790s, the number of villages with one mirasidar caste numbered eighty-eight out of 130 (Table 6.8). On the other hand, the corresponding figure from the *Settlement Registers* of 1877 was as low as twenty-three villages

TABLE 6.7
Number of Mirasidar Castes in Villages in Ponneri
(*Barnard Report*, 1760s–70s)

No. of Mirasidar Castes	*Cases*
1	115
2	18
NA	3
'Unknown'	5
Total	141

Source: Barnard Report, Ponneri, 1760s–70s.

TABLE 6.8
Number of Mirasidar Castes in Villages in Ponneri (*Place Report*, 1797–8)

8A. Including Unidentified Cases

Number of Mirasidar Castes	*No. of Villages (Total = 130)*
1	88
2	31
3	8
4	3

8B. Excluding Unidentified Cases

Number of Mirasidar Castes	*No. of Villages (Total = 130)*
0	34
1	75
2	19
3	2

Source: Abstract State of the Number of Meerassee Shares and of Meerassee Holders in the Several Districts of the Jagheer in Fusly 1207 shewing also the Quantity of Meerassee unclaimed & occupied by Pyacarries, *Board's Collections*, 2115 & 2116, Vol. 112, F/4/112, OIOC.

TABLE 6.9

Number of Mirasidar Castes in Villages in Ponneri

9A. Including Unidentified Cases

Number of Mirasidar Castes	*No. of Villages*
0 (Non-Mirasi villages & those without information)	39
1	23
2	21
3	18
4	11
5	7
6	7
7	4
8	3
9	2
10	1
11	0
12	1
Total	137

9B. Excluding Unidentified Cases

Number of Mirasidar Castes	*No. of Villages*
0 (Non-Mirasi villages & those without information)	39
1	24
2	23
3	16
4	14
5	9
6	4
7	4
8	2
9	1
10	0
11	1
Total	137

Source: Settlement Registers of 1877.

out of 137 (Table 6.9). The number of villages with more than two mirasidar castes increased from eighteen in the *Barnard Report*, to forty-two in the *Place Report*, and finally to seventy-five in *Settlement Registers* of 1877. There was even a village with twelve different mirasidar castes in the 1870s.[28]

The second noticeable feature was the reduced scale of mirasidarship not only in the number of villages in which they had shares but also in the aggregated mirasi shares. The *Place Report* indicates that most of the mirasidars had shares in just one or two villages.[29] The same feature was also observed in the 1870s. As indicated in Fig. 6.9, 1246 mirasidars or 88 per cent out of the 1412 mirasidars had their shares

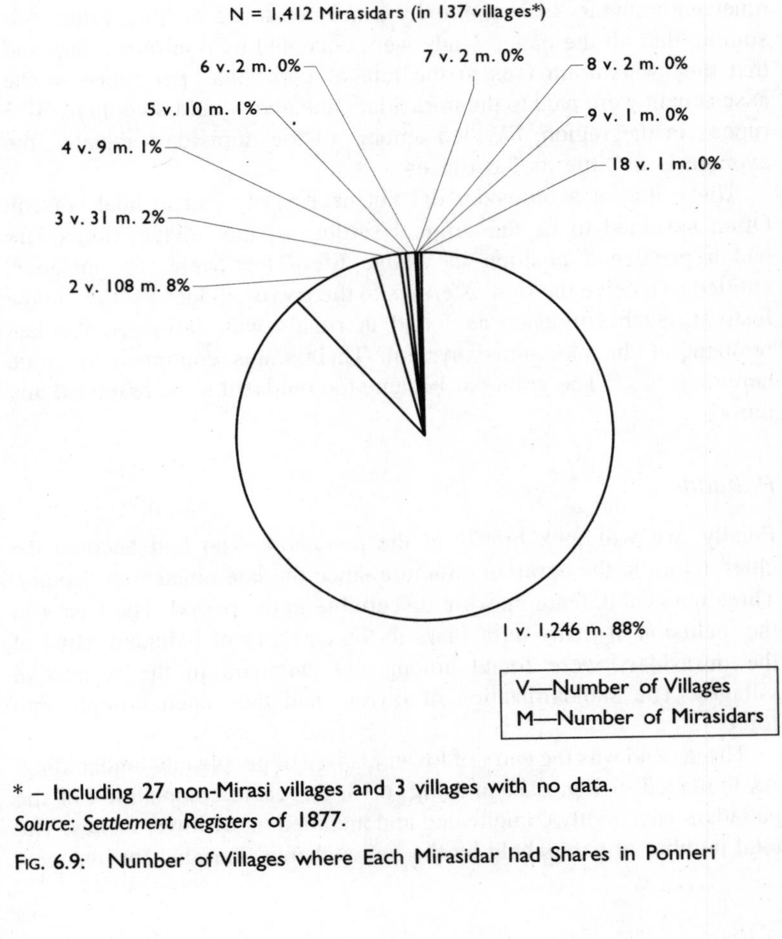

* – Including 27 non-Mirasi villages and 3 villages with no data.
Source: Settlement Registers of 1877.

FIG. 6.9: Number of Villages where Each Mirasidar had Shares in Ponneri

in a single village. Adding those having shares in two villages, the figure becomes 1354 or 96 per cent.

The reduced scale of mirasidarship in the 1870s is obvious from the data on aggregated shares (Fig. 6.10 and Fig. 6.11). According to the *Place Report* in the late 1790s, only one mirasidar (out of 382) had less than one-hundredth of a village share (one village = one share), while 74 per cent of mirasidars had more than one-tenth. On the contrary, as many as 445 mirasidars, or 32 per cent out of the total of 1412 mirasidars, had less than one-hundredth of a village share in the 1870s, and 84 per cent had less than one-tenth. In short, the size of mirasidarship had been greatly diminished by the 1870s.

What, then, was the meaning of having mirasidarship in the late nineteenth century? Economically it seemed to be of little value. Assuming that all the pangu lands were occupied by non-mirasidars and that the swatantram fees at the rate of two annas per rupee of the assessment were paid to the mirasidars, the total would amount to 5083 rupees in the region. Divided among all the mirasidars equally, the average is as little as 3.6 rupees.

The status of a mirasidar did not necessarily end in land control. Often assumed to be the original settlers of the village, mirasidars had a privileged position in village life. They were, for instance, entitled to receive the first offerings to the god or goddess at the village festival. Such eminence as found in rituals was, however, the last remnant of the old mirasi system. Their status continued to erode hereafter, too.[30] The grammar became too outdated to be practised any more.

Pattadar

Finally, we will look briefly at the pattadars, who had become the chief actors in the agrarian structure since the late nineteenth century. Three noticeable features were discernible in the period. The first was the inclusion of many mirasidars in the category of pattadar. Most of the mirasidars were found among the pattadars in the respective villages. The standardization of raiyats had thus been brought into force.

The second was the entry of lower classes of people into landholding. As indicated in Fig. 6.12 and Fig. 6.13, the caste composition of the pattadars was highly complicated and included many lower castes. The total number of pattas held by the 'untouchable' Pariahs, for instance,

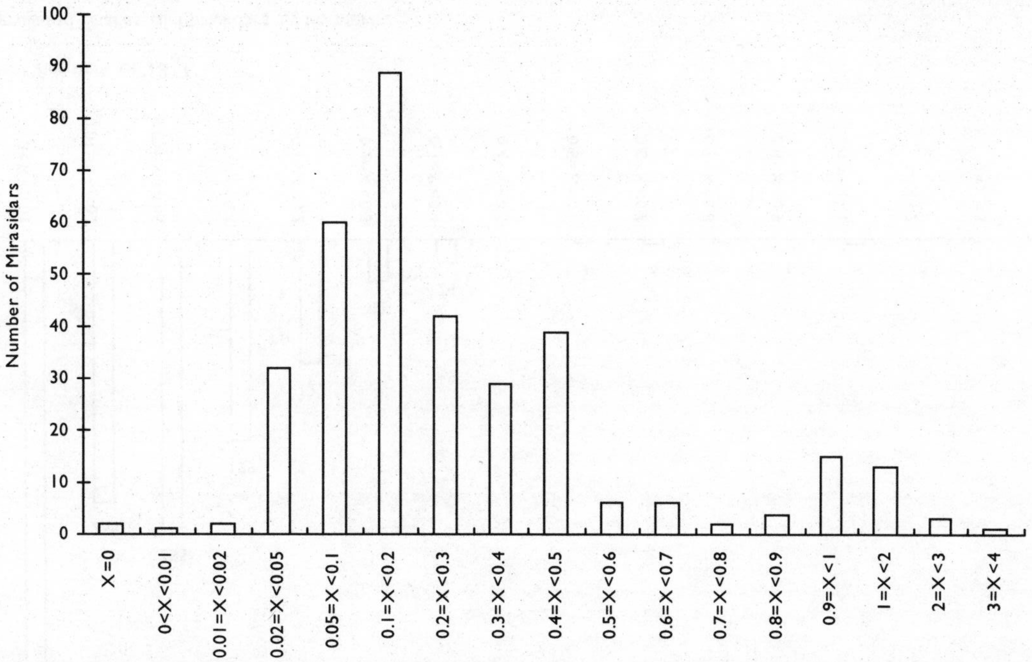

Source: Abstract State of the Number of Meerassee Shares and of Meerassee Holders in the Several Districts of the Jagheer in Fusly 1207 shewing also the Quantity of Meerassee unclaimed & occupied by Pyacarries, *Board's Collections*, 2115 & 2116, Vol.112, F/4/112, OIOC.

FIG. 6.10: Aggregated Shares of Mirasidars in Ponneri (*Place Report*, 1797–8)

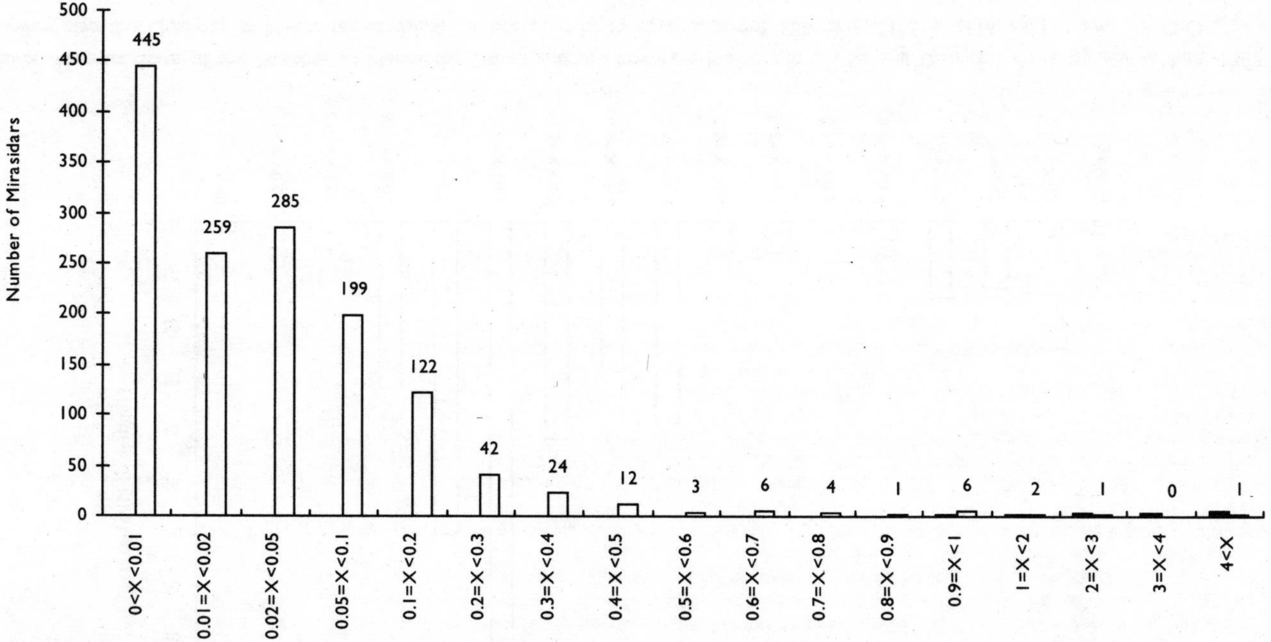

Source: Settlement Registers of 1877.

FIG. 6.11: Aggregated Shares of Mirasidars in Ponneri

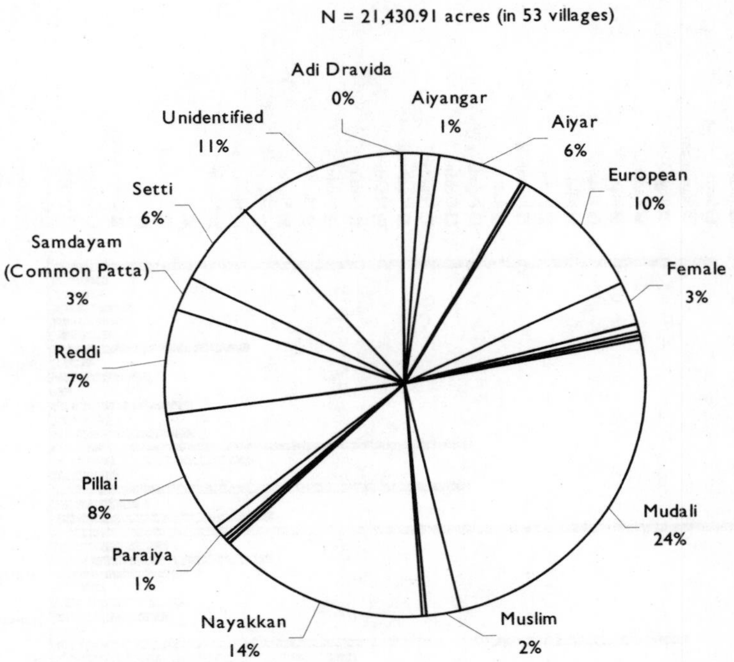

Source: Settlement Registers of 1877.

Fig. 6.12: Percentage of Landholding by Castes in Ponneri

was fifty-eight. They owned a total of 207.08 acres in thirty-two out of the fifty-four villages under study.[31] Such acquisition of landed interests among the lower castes must have had a great impact upon the agrarian structure in the region.

The third was the variance in landholding structure among the villages in the area. Fig. 6.14 indicates the percentages of landholding by the top five landholders in each of the villages in Ponneri. The top five occupied more than 80 per cent of the total patta land[32] in fourteen out of the fifty-four villages, and more than half of the patta land in thirty-three villages. There were, on the other hand, several villages that had many small pattadars. Thus, many villages were monopolized by a few big pattadars, while others were held by many small pattadars. Further investigation is required to clarify the village conditions that produced such differences.

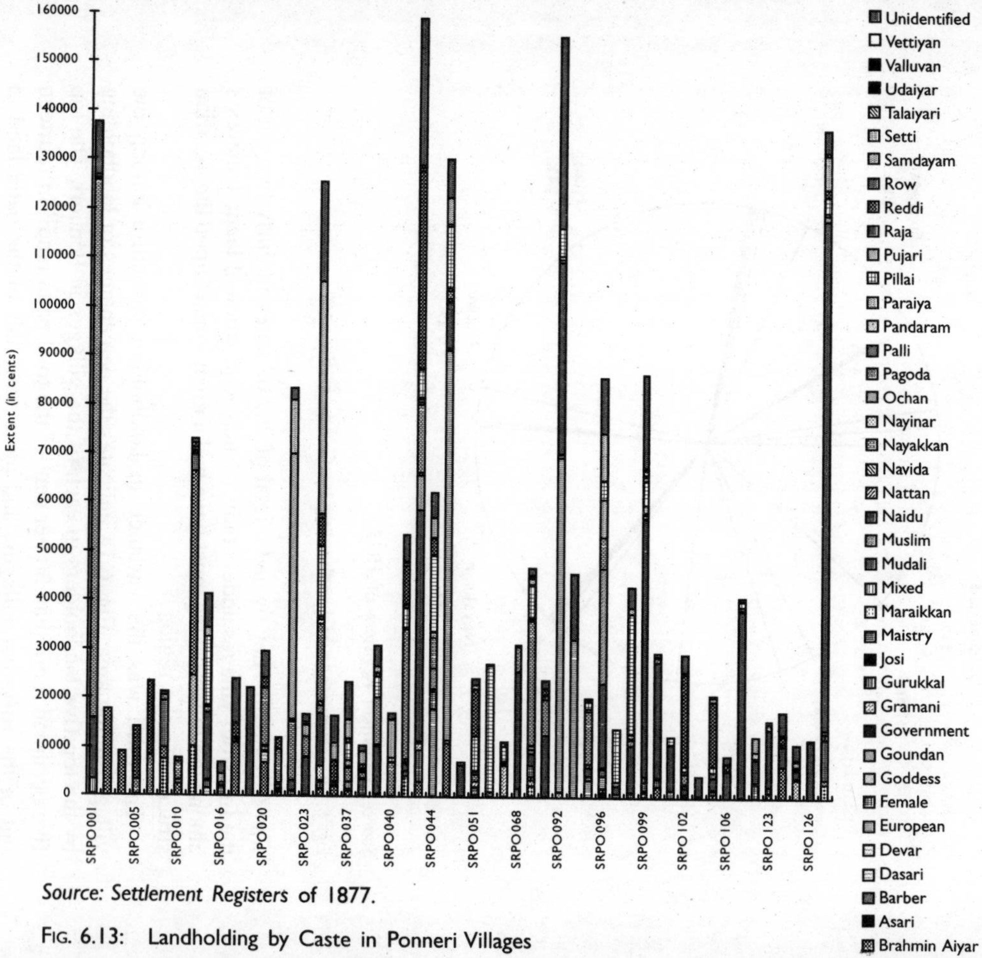

Source: Settlement Registers of 1877.

FIG. 6.13: Landholding by Caste in Ponneri Villages

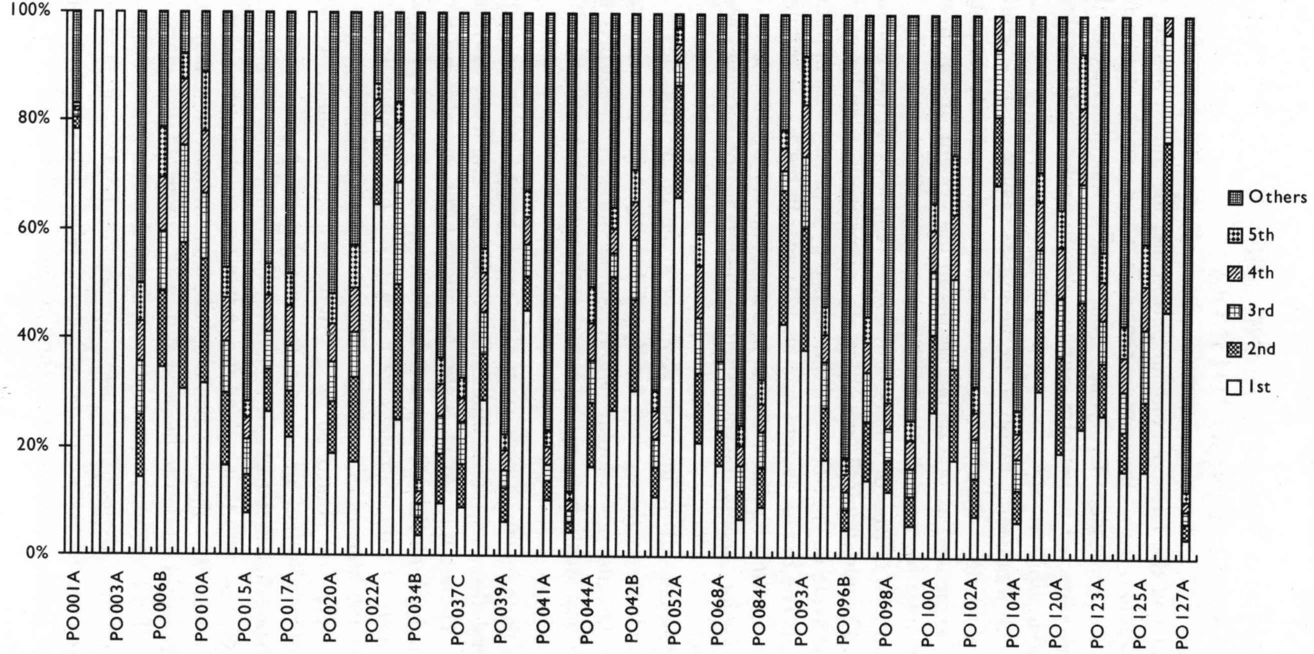

Source: Settlement Registers of 1877.

FIG. 6.14: Percentage of Landholding in Ponneri Villages for Top Five Landholders

CONCLUSION: THE STATE AND THE MIRASI SYSTEM IN SOUTH INDIA

South India in the late pre-colonial period had the mirasi system as social grammar. It was the grammar through which wealth, status, and power were expressed. Everyone, from village functionaries to the state, was expected to perform certain roles in exchange for a share in the production.

The state was deeply involved in the mirasi system as an essential part of it. As long as the system continued, the state could expect stable revenues expressed as one of the shares in the system. It was in the state's interest to maintain the mirasi system.

The same was true of others. Influential temples and big poligars controlling hundreds of villages were also components-cum-beneficiaries of the system. Together with the state, they formed its main pillars (Fig. 6.15). The mirasi system was the grammar in the social architecture built upon these pillars. The main body in its centre was, however, the local society, that is, the sphere where the production activities were carried on.

Changes caused by the emergence of some of the mirasidars as village lords threw the system fatally off balance and caused its collapse in the late pre-colonial period. Some mirasidars usurped the functions previously born by the mirasi system and deconstructed it to their advantage.

In the late nineteenth century or after experiencing the colonial rule for several decades, south India was facing a completely different situation. Though mirasidars' status as village lords was still acknowledged and institutionalized to a certain extent, their economic prospects became insignificant. Pattadars were now given the central role in the village as the holders of land lots. Though a considerable number of villages were still controlled by a few hands at this stage, a wider section of people had already entered into this category.

It is to be noted that the basic sphere of social entity had been shifting from a local society to a village in the late pre-colonial period. What was important was that the basic sphere had already shifted from a village to a land lot before the first shift was completed. Pattadars, the creature of the colonial rule, had nothing to do with either the local society or the village. They were simply the holders of land lots (Fig. 6.16). No local society, no village society—that was the setting where an Indian villager had to start in the colonial society.

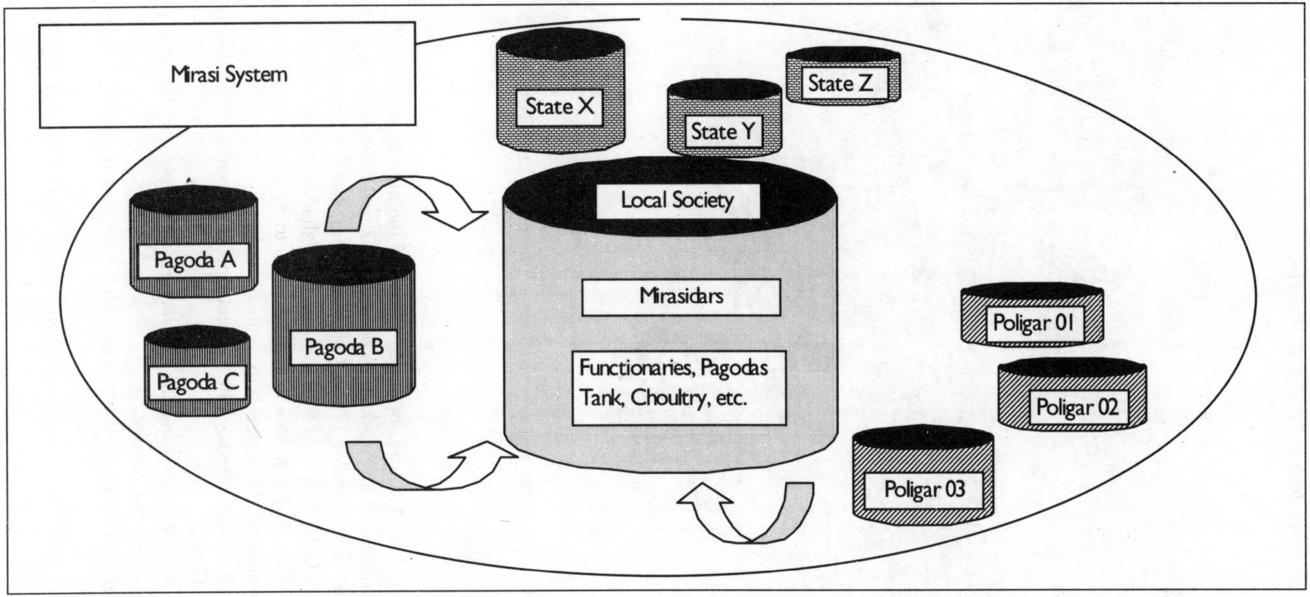

FIG. 6.15: Pre-Colonial South Indian Society—A Model

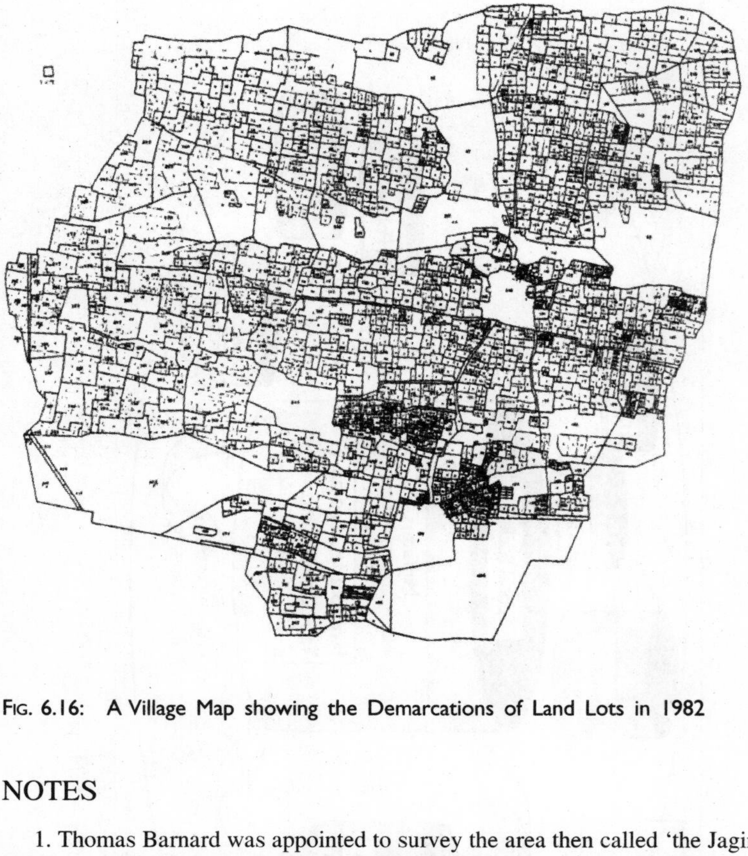

FIG. 6.16: A Village Map showing the Demarcations of Land Lots in 1982

NOTES

1. Thomas Barnard was appointed to survey the area then called 'the Jagir'. Barnard commenced the work in February 1767 and completed it, after many interruptions, in November 1773 (R.H. Phillimore, 1945, *Historical Records of the Survey of Indi*a, *Vol. 1* [*18th Century*], published by order of the Surveyor-General of India, India, p. 88). The Jagir came to be designated as Chingleput at the beginning of the nineteenth century.

2. Place was appointed as the Collector of the Jagir in 1794 and resigned the post in 1799.

3. Land registers showing the particulars of every land lot with relevant information about the village.

4. Poligars were the military who were assigned the role of maintaining security.

5. All the *nattar*s discussed here had a caste title of Mudali. No Brahmins were included.

6. Some proportional shares in the village produce were linked to some roles performed in the local society. These shares as well as roles were considered to be inheritable and transferable, and were called *mirasi*. For instance, a hereditary share allotted to a washerman was a mirasi right of the washerman and the washerman was a mirasidar (mirasi holder). Village officers, service castes, or any others who held such inheritable right could be thus called as mirasidar. On the other hand there was a class of people who asserted a superior overlordship in the village. These people controlled their village and claimed lordship over others in share. When British records used the term 'mirasidar', they referred exclusively to the latter. To distinguish the latter from the former, I will use 'mirasidarship' to refer to the latter in this paper.

7. Noboru Karashima, 1984, 'Mirasidars in the Chingleput Area', in *South Indian History and Society: Studies from Inscriptions*, AD *850–1800*, New Delhi: Oxford University Press, p. 178.

8. We can find some cases of mirasidars having mirasidarship in several villages. Though the same personal name is here assumed to signify the same person, there is an ample possibility of different people having coincidentally the same personal names.

9. Mahfuz Khan was the son of Nawab Dost Ali Khan. He held the nawabship in the years 1740–2. According to the *Barnard Report*, it was purchased from Condighetty Vellalars.

10. In the first case, the nattar, Arsoor Vencatachel Modely [sic.], was the shrotriamdar of the concerned village (Tirooparoo). According to the *Barnard Report*, this nattar bought a part of the village mirasidarship and mortgaged the rest from the mirasidars (Gentoo Brahmins of Tirooparoo). In the second case the deshmuk, Ram Row, was the shrotriamdar of Vellumbacum and bought the village mirasidarship from Jainy [sic.] Vellalers. Both of the transfers had occurred in the recent past.

11. Though many of the cases under the category of 'Unidentified (Agraharum)' can be assumed to be the Brahmin castes, there were many exceptional cases, too.

12. The differences within the major categories of castes, such as Vishnu Brahmin and Siva Brahmin, are neglected here to compare numerical strength.

13. According to the *Place Report*, there were 223 *magan*s of various extents. They included 2241 villages in total (*Place Report*, 1799, para. 320).

14. An attempt to assess the entity of a magan unit was done by the author elsewhere by using the *Barnard Report*. (T. Mizushima, 1986, *Nattar and the Socio-Economic Change in South India in the 18th–19th Centuries*, Institute for the Study of Languages and Cultures in Asia and Africa (ILCAA), Tokyo: Tokyo University of Foreign Studies; *Idem*, 1990, *18–20 seiki minami indo zaichi syakai no kenkyuu*, ILCAA, Tokyo: Tokyo University of Foreign Studies). The unit was found to have lost its entity so far as the Salavakam villages in Chingleput were concerned.

15. See note 11.

16. The competitive powers operating in the period were expressed in the mirasi system. As this point has been discussed elsewhere (T. Mizushima, 1996, 'The Mirasi System and Local Society in Pre-Colonial South India', in P. Robb *et al.* (eds), *Local Agrarian Societies in Colonial India: Japanese Perspectives*, London: Curzon Press, pp. 77–145), suffice it here to say that the two major competitive powers were the state and the local society, and that the power balance between the two was expressed in their respective shares in the mirasi system.

17. T. Mizushima, 1996, *op. cit.*

18. *The Private Diary of Ananda Ranga Pillai* (1736–61) has many references to these cases.

19. The changes occurring outside the mirasi system are partly discussed in T. Mizushima, 1990, *op. cit.*

20. In this sense, the mirasi system was closely related to the caste system. See Hiroyuki Kotani, 1989, *Indo no chuusei shakai—Mura, kaasuto, ryoushu*, Tokyo: Iwanami Shoten.

21. The author has studied the accounts in detail elsewhere (T. Mizushima, 1986, *op. cit.*).

22. Different sources give different figures on the number of zamindaris.

23. Place argued a kind of double land ownership of the state and mirasidar. Faced with the mirasidars' strong property position in Chingleput, Place could not assert the exclusive land ownership of the state. His stand was to assure the mirasidars' ownership as long as they fulfilled their obligation to perform their 'duty', i.e., to engage in cultivation and to pay the land tax. See *Place's Final Report to the Board of Revenue*, 1 July 1799, *Board's Miscellaneous Records, Vol. 45* (Tamil Nadu Archives), for instance paras 16, 18.

24. *The Chingleput, Late Madras District, A Manual* compiled under the orders of the Madras Government, by Charles Stewart Crole, Madras, 1879, p. 287.

25. The colonial government consistently tried to persuade the mirasidars to extend cultivation in order to increase its revenue. The pre-empted privilege of the mirasidars over the entire village area, however, hardly allowed the non-mirasidars (i.e. payikaris) to occupy any uncultivated lands against the mirasidars' will. Before 1869, when the durkhast rules specially designed for Chingleput were enforced, the government had made several attempts to subsume their privileges but had faced consistent resistance from the mirasidars. (*The Chingleput, Late Madras District, A Manual*, *op. cit.*, pp. 288–91.)

26. The jajmani system was an institution newly constituted under the colonial rule to fill the vacuum occurring in the service relationship. It was new in the sense the service relation ends between the two households concerned. Under the mirasi system, on the other hand, it was the entire local society that supported basically all the service relationship in the locality.

27. The *Settlement Registers* for the raiyatwari villages are kept either in the Tamil Nadu State Archives or in the Taluk office. The registers utilized

here are from the Archives. It is to be noted that digitizing process of the registers and other related records was not completed when the draft of this paper was submitted. Even so, those already processed offer sufficient empirical basis for the following arguments.

28. As there are a considerable number of unidentified cases, these figures indicate only the main trend.

29. The *Barnard Report* does not have the mirasidars' personal names, so the equivalent figures cannot be produced here.

30. See my village study conducted in a Tiruchirapalli village where the dominant caste as well as its mirasidars gradually lost landownership since the 1860s (T. Mizushima, 1983, *Changes, Chances and Choices—The Perspective of Indian Villagers, Socio-Cultural Change in Villages in Tiruchirapalli District, Tamil Nadu, India*, Part 2, Modern Period-1, Tokyo: ILCAA, Tokyo University of Foreign Studies, pp. 27–221).

31. See note 11.

32. Patta land signifies the land held by a pattadar.

CHAPTER 7

Early Modernity and Colonial Transformation

Rethinking the Role of the King in Eighteenth and Nineteenth Century Orissa, India

Akio Tanabe

INTRODUCTION

This paper considers aspects of the characteristics of early modernity in eighteenth-century Orissa in terms of the characteristic development of the spheres of the kingdom, local community, and market in their interrelationships as well as in terms of the transformation of the nature of people's subjectivity in relation to the development of the *bhakti* cult. It also considers the nature of colonial transformation in the nineteenth century, paying attention to the role of the Khurda king and his relationship to the people through the age, which may, in one manner, represent the aspects of the change and continuity between the eighteenth and nineteenth centuries or early modernity and colonial modernity in Orissa, India.

This paper attempts to apply a totalizing perspective to the history of kingship without reducing the religious–ritual aspect to its political implications, or imposing a dichotomy of ritual kingship and pragmatic society. Recent anthropological (ethnohistorical) works on Indian kingship in the eighteenth century have greatly enhanced our understanding of the rich cultural meanings of kingship,[1] while historical works have expanded our knowledge on the aspect of the pursuit of power and wealth of political actors.[2] The divinization or ritualization of kingship in relation to regional or local cults, and the development of administration technology and intensified relationship of kingship with the market both seem to be true for the little and regional kingdoms of the eighteenth century, while the great kingdoms, like the Maratha, may have concentrated more on politico-economic affairs of trans-regional importance.

In the kingdom of eighteenth-century Khurda, we notice that there was an increase in the administration technology of surveillance permeating into the locality as well as an intensification of the king's relationship with the Jagannath cult resulting in ritualization and divinization of kingship. At the same time, we see the development of the bhakti cult, especially among the non-Brahmin population. It is my contention that these factors should be considered as significant concomitant developments of early modernity in India, rather than mere historical coincidence.

The aspect of ritualization and divinization of the Khurda kingship from the seventeenth to the nineteenth centuries was first pointed out by Kulke. He argued that they were related to the weakening of the political power of Khurda kingship when the king attempted to utilize ritual resources for compensation.[3] In Marglin's interpretation of the same phenomena, by contrast, the continuity of divine kingship throughout history is emphasized.[4] Here, we see that while Kulke attempts to explain the religious–ritual feature of Khurda kingship in terms of changes in political context, Marglin tries to essentialize the nature of 'Indian kingship' in a rather ahistorical manner.

What we must do, however, is to explain the nature of Khurda kingship in its totality, taking account of the cultural paradigm through which the power and sovereignty of the king were expressed and constituted, and at the same time paying attention to the particular historical context by which the expression of the cultural paradigm was conditioned. In considering the role of kingship in the eighteenth century, our task would be to consider how to connect the role of the king in the dynamics of the vibrant political economy as well as in the particular development in the religious–ritual sphere. My approach here is to see the overall development in terms of the characteristics of early modernity, in which the particular and local came to acquire more universal and trans-local importance.

In eighteenth-century Orissa, the Khurda king, while standing outside the spheres of local community and market, can be said to have supported the development of the local administrative and commercial activities as the sacrificer-protector. The working of the state and kingship was instrumental in the development of administration technology in the local community and commercialization of agrarian economy. The flow and distribution of resources in the local community came to be minutely surveyed, and entitlements of different office- and service-holders were defined in monetary numbers and recorded. Importantly, while the local community maintained its autonomous character at the level of division of labour for everyday reproduction, the communal rights and duties of each entitlement-holder came to be considered to have been directly granted and legitimized by the king in the development of interaction between the local community and the kingdom. The connection of local entitlements with the royal authority along with their numeration can be said to have assisted in giving them a more general character, rather than just a particular local one. This universalization of the value of entitlement further led to alienation of some of the office entitlements in certain areas.

This kind of administrative development was concomitant with the development of commerce and manufacturing industry. As I have argued elsewhere, the 'introduction of more advanced and universal administrative technology in the local communities in the process of state formation, such as accounting, measuring, and use of money, meant not only that these communities in the jungles of the hilly tracts of Khurda were more closely incorporated into the royal redistributive system, but also that they came to be connected to the wider network of the flow of money and goods, specifically the trade and commerce articulated with the growth of the world economy'.[5]

In this paper, I would like to focus in terms of early modernity on not only the development of administration technology and commerce, but also the characteristic development of people's subjectivity in relation to the transformation of the nature of their relationship with the divine king. The royal authorization of the communal entitlements enabled each community member to connect himself to the realm of the kingdom and beyond through the king, who by this time represented himself as the *thākur rājā* (divine king) and *ādya sevāyat* (first servant) of Jagannath. The sacrificial community provided the ground in which each entitlement holder sacrificed himself through his duty to the greater divine whole, while remaining in the 'here and now'. In this context, the entitlement holders, while being embedded in the particular, could be linked to the universal through the king as the central sacrificer.

This kind of development in people's positioning and subjectivity is related, I would suggest, to the popularization of the bhakti cult in which the aspect of *Bhakti yoga* and *Karma yoga* were combined to give a religious foundation to the performance of everyday activity as sacrificial duty for the divine. It was the way to connect oneself having a 'secular' duty in the 'here and now', with the 'divine' without the need for ritual involving a Brahmin priest.

It is this concomitant development of the rational and the religious in the eighteenth century through the systematization of the sacrificial community and the divine sacrificer king that characterizes one aspect of early modernity in India. The working of the sphere of the market and the great kingdom complemented this early modern development of subjectivity.

The concomitant development of the rational and the religious, however, came to a halt during the colonial period, as interrelationships between the state, market, local community, and religion were transformed. From this point of view, it is necessary to reconsider previous historical scholarship on India, which focuses on the significant continuities between the pre-colonial and colonial periods in terms of the vibrant and dynamic politico-economic activities beginning from the eighteenth century.

'Revisionist' historians, such as Bayly[6] and Washbrook,[7] note the internal dynamism of pre-colonial India that is connected to the development of colonial domination, and the resilience of Indian agents in pre-colonial and colonial history. They, however, tend to emphasize only the aspects of political economy, and to reduce the dynamism of history from the pre-colonial to colonial period to the process of indigenous development of capitalism. In effect, they reduce the agency of the Indian people to the struggle for power and wealth, and point out the role of Indians as active agents for *creation* of colonialism. By extension of this kind of argument, Washbrook says, 'colonialism was the logical outcome of South Asia's own history of capitalist development'.[8]

In this way, these scholars in effect make the hands of colonizers in colonial history invisible, and trivialize the asymmetrical power relationship between the colonizers and the colonized. Not surprisingly, their formulations have recently met severe criticism especially from Indian scholars such as Chatterjee and Prakash.[9]

It would be fair to say, however, the arguments made by each side both have their points. Indeed, it can be said that colonial rule in Khurda contained both aspects of continuity and disjunction from the previous developments of the early modern state.

If we restrict our point of view to the politico-economic aspect, Bayly and others (Washbrook, Stein, Perlin, and Ludden) seem to be correct in arguing for continuity of Indian social structure from the eighteenth century well into the first half of the nineteenth century. The colonial rule depended upon and extended the early modern development of politico-economic infrastructure. The augmentation of surveillance and control under colonialism was possible due to the transformative momentum of the processes of rationalization and numeration of the administrative machinery already in progress under the pre-colonial kingdom. Moreover, the growth and broadening of commercial activities during the colonial period may also be seen in terms of a continuation of the pre-colonial developments in monetization, market economy, and trade networks, and hence part of the ongoing changes in the region. Even the ritualization of kingship under colonialism can be seen as an extension of the similar tendency among kings in the eighteenth century.

However, if we pay attention to the relationship between politics and religion or that between state and society, we see that major changes were brought about at the onset of colonial rule. Whereas there had been concomitant development of religion and rationality through complementary roles of various levels, including local community, little kingdom, great kingdom, and the market guaranteeing a totality of life, colonial domination brought about a dislocation between secular rationality and religious belief. This was done according to the 'rule of colonial difference'[10] which distinguished between the rational state of the British and religious society of the Indians. The colonial state was supposed to represent the principle of Western modern rationality, and its policy was not to interfere with matters of indigenous society and religion, which were to be entrusted to the colonized.

With the development of this policy, the Khurda king was consigned to the restricted sphere of the socio-cultural and religious, having been stripped of politico-economic power. The system of entitlements at the local level was broken down and replaced by individual land proprietorship, while apparently maintaining the local power structure intact. The landholders came to be directly under the control of the colonial state, which can be seen again as an aspect of continuity of the development of state surveillance over the local at one level. But it is important to note that this also brought about a disjunction of the people's possession of land from their socio-religious identity. That is, their connection with the king became confined to the socio-cultural sphere, and no longer provided a channel linking their everyday productive activity in the 'here and now' with the divine.

Such dichotomous disjunction between state politics and social religion brought about by colonialism seems to be the most important aspect of change from early modernity to colonial modernity in India.

HISTORICAL AND GEOGRAPHICAL BACKGROUND OF THE KHURDA KINGDOM

Although the Khurda kingdom was indeed a 'little kingdom' in its characteristics of being subject to 'fickle and changeable relations'[11] with the paramount power and other kings, it was special among them. Khurda kings were special, if not politically predominant, since they were regarded, despite the comparatively small territory, as the Gajapati (*gajapati*: lord of the elephants)[12] or the paramount ruler of Orissa, at least in name and authority. In a popular verse often cited even today, the Khurda king is described as follows:

> The jewel crown among a hundred thousand kings, he is the king of Khurda. Building his palace under Barunei, he protected his happy subjects.[13]

The Khurda kingdom was established after the collapse of the medieval Orissan empire due to the Afghan invasion of 1568. Ramachandra Deva, the first king of the Khurda Bhoi dynasty, managed to build up a small-scale kingdom with Khurda as its fort capital. He was able to present himself as the successor to the tradition of the great Orissan empire by reinstating the idol of Lord Jagannath in the temple in Puri. His position was further strengthened when, in 1592, the Mughal emperor, Akbar, acknowledged him as the Gajapati. Ramachandra was also given the rank of 'commander of 3500' and was granted authority over the Khurda kingdom and thirty-one small kingdoms under his command in the surrounding area.

The Khurda kingdom can be geographically divided into two parts, the hilly tracts of dryland in the north and west, and the fertile alluvial land of the coastal plains in the south-east. These two can be said roughly to correspond to the ritual and military functions respectively.

The most important domain in the plains area was Puri, the seat of the state deity Jagannath. The Khurda king established his ritual authority by protecting the temple and its various rites as the 'first servant' of Lord Jagannath. The king's ritual relationship with Jagannath is said to have intensified during the Khurda kings' time. The plains area around Puri was relatively fertile. Apart from the *kot* land belonging to the king's palace and set aside 'for furnishing the immediate wants and expenses of the sovereign in payment of his principal servants and ministers',[14] there were *jāgīrs* held by the king's ministers and principal officers, such as the counsellor (*rājaguru*), the minister of the state (*diwān*) and the general (*baksi*), besides the *brāhmaṇ śāsana* villages. At the village level, village heads (*pradhān*) were appointed to supervise cultivation and collect rents, and village accountants (*bhoi*) to keep revenue accounts.[15]

The hilly tract area, which constituted the main territory of the Khurda kingdom, was mostly covered by jungle and wasteland, which accounted for 70 per cent of the area. Most of the land was made up of infertile laterite, and in parts of comparatively fertile land, there was rice cultivation depending mostly on rain (average annual rainfall 1500 mm). There was also slash-and-burn agriculture, hunting and gathering in jungles, and cattle grazing in the waste/pastoral lands.

The fort area, consisting of a fort or central village called 'fort itself' (*niji gada*) and several surrounding villages, made up the local community centred around an area where rice cultivation was possible. The number of surrounding villages was typically twelve, and thus these subordinate villages, in many places, were referred to as 'the twelve villages' (*bārapalli*). But there were also variations in the size of a fort area and the number of the surrounding villages sometimes differed from a few to several tens. This fort area seemed to have constituted 'the enduring and basic unit'[16] of local community in at least the hilly dry lands of Orissa from the medieval to early modern period, and some of them retain their ritual importance to the present day. This unit also had important military and administrative functions for the reproduction of the kingdom. This unit was known simply as 'fort' (*gaḍa, kilā*) or 'county' (*bisi*).[17] There are said to have been 108 forts in the Khurda kingdom, out of which seventy-two were said to be the main ones.

RELATIONSHIP BETWEEN THE STATE AND THE LOCAL COMMUNITY IN THE SEVENTEENTH AND EIGHTEENTH CENTURIES

At the onset of the establishment of the kingdom in the late sixteenth century, it seems that the existing chieftaincies and small kingdoms were allowed some degree of autonomy under the supra-authority of the Khurda king. The Saora (tribal) chiefs (*sauri khaṇḍāyata*) and the 'purified' (ex-tribal) chiefs (*śuddha khaṇḍāyata*) who were presiding over the hilly tract areas were not driven away but were left to rule fairly independently. The distribution of resources within a community was in the hands of the chief, and he was considered to be the distributor of the land to different entitlement-holders. The chief did not have to depend on the state for his authority, except that he sent an annual prestation (*nazarānā*) to the greater king as a token of submission.

This kind of semi-autonomous situation for the local communities began to change in the course of the seventeenth and eighteenth centuries, as there developed a more immediate and penetrating influence of the state. The semi-autonomous chiefs were gradually replaced by another kind of chiefs, called *bisoi* and/or *da!abeherā*, who mediated between the kingship and the community. These chiefs were the military and administrative heads of the locality as well as the servants of the king. They had no independent authority and derived their legitimacy directly from the king.

It was not just the relationship between the state and local leadership that changed. There was also a transformation in the relationship between the entitlement-holders in the community and the state, as they too came to derive their legitimacy directly from the king. Evidence of this is presented by oral family histories that record how each and every entitlement-holder was called and given entitlements by the king. The entitlement-holders in communities, by accepting the king's sovereignty, were thus granted royal authority to their power and rights. As a token of their hierarchical relationships, each entitlement-holder was to pay *taṅki* (a quit rent) to the king.

However, the process by which the state increased its control and surveillance over the local polity-society was not a process of centralization in the same way as in the case of the modern state, where bureaucrats and army are dispatched from the central government and the structure of command is unified. Rather, it involved a kind of decentralization and sharing of sovereignty with the localities.[18] Administrative and military power as well as ritual capacity was guaranteed by the king to the warriors and scribes who resided in the local polity-society. Also, rather than the king extending direct control over the local resources, the existing structure of the communal system of entitlements was legitimized and authorized by the king.

I have argued elsewhere that the particular development of the early modern state in Khurda may be understood in terms of a 'sacrificial community and sacrificer state'.[19] This involved a kind of state formation in which local communities, as the site of the basic social reproductive activities, were incorporated into the state's redistributive structure while retaining their system of entitlements at the local level.

Sacrifice here refers to the actions that were performed as the duty of a part dedicated to the whole. Such sacrificial activities should be thought to have included not only rituals but also politico-economic activities in the cultural paradigm. The duties and shares of each part were defined in the system of assignments and entitlements in the community. The sacrificial communities were the actual sites where productive activities took place according to the system of entitlements. The king, while remaining outside the communities, acted as the centre and source of authority of the sacrificial organizations in the communities as sacrificer through various exchanges, and was thus able to extend his surveillance over the military, administrative, and economic resources in the localities. By the 'sacrificer state', then, I refer to the redistributive role of the king, who granted authority for the assignments and power of each entitlement-holder through various prestations and acted as the central organizer of sacrificial activities, while remaining outside the sacrificial communities themselves and allowing them virtual autonomy.

Thus there was an aspect of integration of the community with kingship through the idiom of sacrifice, as well as an aspect of division and autonomy of the community from kingship. It is this cultural paradigm of balancing integration and separation between the level of the kingdom and local community that I wish to express through the phrase 'sacrificer state and sacrificial community', which came to take shape in Orissa of the seventeenth and eighteenth centuries.

CALCULATION AND RECORDING OF THE FLOW OF RESOURCES

Another important aspect of the development of the early modern state in Orissa, which was closely related to the penetration of king's authority in the region, was the introduction of numeration, accounting, and recording of entitlements: that is, the technology of the state's surveillance over the local resources.

All of the relevant resources produced in the locality came to be calculated and recorded in cowrie units, thus establishing the basis for more efficient administration. The amount of shares of each entitlement-holder was defined in cowrie units and taxes were taken from them by a proportion also defined by cowrie units. Scribes recorded these entitlements and taxes on palm leaf scripts. The minute accounting and recording of entitlements suggest that there was highly developed administrative technology at the local level, by which there was a close surveillance of the distribution of the local resources from which state tax was collected.

The introduction of administrative technology of state surveillance into the locality, however, did not mean that the state extended direct control over local affairs. Notably, the communal system of entitlements remained intact, while the king extended his authority over individual entitlement-holders as the sacrificer. This can be seen from the fact that the state had a direct share of a mere 2.24 per cent of total products, and the remaining 97.76 per cent of resources were distributed among the communal entitlement-holders. The system of entitlements of the local community here did not allow the intervention of the state in defining the right and duty of each community member. After the resources were distributed to the entitlement-holders, however, the state took tax from each of them. This corresponds to the king's authority as the one who legitimized and granted each entitlement.

The administrative records of late eighteenth-century Khurda show how the state handed out specific privileges in the form of tax exemption and reduction to some entitlement-holders in the region. The state also made various gifts on ritual occasions, apart from providing salary and payment, and these constituted a part of various exchanges that reproduced socio-political relationships in the locality. On ritual occasions, moreover, the king and ministers were provided with gifts of goods collected from the region, and these were also one kind of exchange linking them to the region in a hierarchical relationship.

The state accepted products from the region in the form of taxes, but immediately redistributed one-third of this to the expenditure in the locality, which was devoted to reproducing the redistributive structure of royal authority connecting the state and various entitlement-holders in the local community. The redistributed products that local officers received were no longer mere goods but acted as emblems imbued with royal privileges, honour, and dominance, once they had come as gifts from the king. The local officers were thus important members of the region and, at the same time, by accepting these gifts they were imparted with the king's authority and power. Thus each community member, while remaining in the local community, was also connected to the king through various prestations. This kind of arrangement had an important connotation for understanding people's subjectivity, which I will expand on below.

TRADE, MARKET, AND MONETIZATION

The rationalization and numeration of the system of entitlements in terms of cowrie currency enabled the value of products to be translated into monetary terms. This, in turn, led to the different products in the locality being linked to trade and the wider market economy.

The wide usage of money and the increase in importance of the market and trade for the extensive population in the hinterland of Orissa did not, however, entail a breakdown of the community-based system of entitlements. The expansion of cowrie usage was indeed linked to the developing market exchange of food and goods for everyday living by the regional population in local markets (*hāṭa*). It also suited the process of the periphery regions producing and supplying cotton textiles to the coastal centre.

However, in spite of the popular view that the 'caste-based relations of subsistence' which involved 'non-market exchange' were incompatible with the 'money and market',[20] the local community and market may be seen to have developed in a complementary manner. The fact that the surplus of resources for the market was guaranteed by the unequal allotment of shares supported by the system of entitlements, and that the definition and recording of community entitlements were done in monetary terms in the seventeenth and eighteenth centuries, support the notion that 'there was no contradiction but rather compatibility and even interdependence between the community-based system of social reproduction and the monetised market economy'.[21]

Those resources that were allotted by the system of entitlements but were not consumed by the family included, most importantly, raw cotton produced in slash-and-burn fields and surplus rice. These resources (most significantly cotton textiles and rice, but also fish and oil), found their way into the market exchange. This would not have been possible without the opening up of communities and the introduction of monetary institutions through the process of state formation in the seventeenth and eighteenth centuries that significantly transformed the locality. The development of trade and market exchange also nurtured and supported the reproduction of non-entitlement-holder caste people who engaged in the production of market commodities, such as weavers, cotton-carders, fishermen, oil-pressers, sweet-makers, and goldsmiths.

While the Khurda king supported trade and commerce and also received considerable revenue through trade tax, we must also take into account the development of the network of marketing and banking that extended far beyond the confined spheres of the kingdom. It was the great kingdoms, like the Maratha, that maintained close relationships with the wider market and contributed to the development of trans-regional commercial and banking networks and further rationalization of administration.

THE TRANSFORMATION OF SUBJECTIVITY AND RELIGIOUS BELIEF IN THE EARLY MODERN PERIOD

While the politico-economic development in the eighteenth century is indeed important, my concern here in terms of early modernity is not limited to these aspects. In this preliminary attempt to bring a totalizing perspective to the study of early modernity in India, I would like to include the characteristic development of people's subjectivity in relation to the divinization and ritualization of Khurda kingship and the popularization of the Vaishnav bhakti cult.

Seventeenth- and eighteenth-century Orissa saw the widespread rise of the Vaishnav bhakti cult. According to Mukherjee, 'Viṣṇuism became the dominant religion in Orissa' in the seventeenth and eighteenth centuries.[22] There was 'blending of the typical Oriya school of Viṣṇuism and the Jagannatha cult with the Caitanya faith'[23] in the development of this early modern Vaishnav bhakti cult. The Khaṇḍāyatas, the dominant caste in coastal Orissa, mostly accepted Vaishnav monks as their family gurus instead of the householder Brahmins. Monasteries for the Vaishnav monks were built even in remote villages and land was donated for their support.

The teachings of the Vaishnavs towards householders often stressed the necessity of performing all actions in the service of god. Through these teachings, there might have been a blending of Karma yoga (the path of action) with Bhakti yoga (the path of devotion), where people should perform their duty as sacrifice to the divine. The idea of sacrifice, of course, was not a new invention of the early modern period, but can be found in the Hindu classics, such as the Bhagavad Gita. It might be said, however, that the particular manner in which this idea of sacrifice was articulated through the definition of communal entitlements in the seventeenth and eighteenth centuries was concomitant with the penetration of the king's authority into the local communities, which legitimized these entitlements, as well as with the intensification of the king's relationship with the Jagannath cult in terms of his increasing divinization and ritualization.

According to Kulke, the Khurda kings built a palace in Puri, the seat of Jagannath, in the early seventeenth century and also introduced several reforms to the rituals that would enhance the close relationships between the king and Jagannath. The Khurda king, as the 'first servant'[24] of Lord Jagannath, also appeared to have gained divine attributes as 'the Gajapatis became known as *thākur-rājā*s (*Deva-rājā*s) only under the... Khurdā-Rājās'.[25]

This divinization and ritualization of the Khurda kings were significant in the light of the king's role as a sacrificer who legitimized and authorized the entitlements in the sacrificial local community in the development of interaction between the kingdom and the locality in seventeenth and eighteenth centuries. Prior to this development, the communal entitlement-holders were only embedded within the local and particular of the small community.

However, by having the divine king representing Jagannath-Krishna on earth as the sacrificer, the members of the sacrificial community were able to connect themselves to the level of the kingdom and beyond towards the universal divine, by carrying out their prescribed roles and duties in the sacrificial community. Thus each entitlement-holder, while remaining in the limited space and time of the 'here and now', could make the everyday activities of communal duty into acts of service for the divine and link oneself with the universal god. This enabled the entitlement-holder embedded in particular circumstances to have personal and direct contact with the universal being. The entitlement-holders in the community were thus able to conceive of an existential shift from the embedded particular to the generalized universal. Here, the divine king as sacrificer acted as the mediator between community members and God.

While the popularization of the Vaishnav bhakti cult, together with the idea of direct service for the divine, may have compromised the position of the Brahmin priest as the ritual mediator for the divine, it also had the effect of consolidating and legitimizing the positions and roles of different caste members in the system of communal entitlements, which entailed within itself the aspect of socio-economic hierarchy. Thus, the bhakti cult in seventeenth- and eighteenth-century Orissa can be said to have contributed in supporting the system of entitlements based on caste, rather than working to criticize caste inequality.

The development of the viewpoint of placing oneself in relation to the universal divine entails a self-reflexivity in which one's position is objectified from a more abstract referential point of cognition than just being embedded in the local structure through embodied practice. The development of this kind of objectification and universalization of self-positionality may be seen to have been related to the process of numeration and alienation of the communal entitlements. Certain kinds of communal entitlements, like the office of village head or village scribe, were alienated from particular persons in the process of gaining more universal value and acquired marketability in some areas. Here we can see the development of a sense of self that could recognize relativity and detachability of social position and role from itself.

However, the development of Karma-Bhakti yoga along with such self-reflexive objectification meant that one committed oneself to engage in the particular given duty in the service of the divine while recognizing the relativity of one's social role and position. Thus one was able to make an objectified commitment by which one connected the relative position of the 'here and now' with the universal divine. Therefore, the early modern subject, who had acquired the viewpoint of rational objectification, continued with the religious commitment of connecting himself to the universal divine through the service prescribed by the system of entitlements. It is this co-existence of and fine balance between rationality and religiosity that characterize the early modern subjectivity embedded in the sacrificial community under the sacrificer state of the divine kingship of eighteenth century.

THE DISLOCATION BETWEEN RATIONALITY AND RELIGIOUS BELIEF DUE TO THE COLONIAL POLICY OF DIVISION OF STATE AND SOCIETY

By 1751, the Khurda kingdom had already begun to decline under the Marathas, who had taken over large parts of the fertile coastal areas. The British East India Company was granted Diwani (revenue authority) of Bengal in 1765, and the Company tried to win Orissa through diplomacy before it resorted to force. The British conquered the Marathas in Orissa in 1803, and when the Khurda king revolted in 1804 they conquered and annexed his territory, after much calculated diplomacy and negotiation by a series of alliances of various configurations between the British, the Khurda king, and different feudatory kings.

The major disjunction brought about by colonial rule was the dichotomic separation between secularized rationality and religious belief. Colonial rationality, which governed the sphere of institutional politics and the market economy, was opposed to Indian religion, which governed the society and culture of the colonized. By this separation, the organic, interactive relationships between the rationalization of the state machinery, the growth of market economy, divinization, and ritualization of the king, and the development of bhakti through karma of social duty became fragmented and placed in dichotomic framework.

The British colonial policy drew a distinction between the domain of state politics, which came under direct management of the colonial government, and the realm of society with its religion and culture, which was left to the 'natives'. There were several reasons behind this kind of attitude, one being the pressures imposed on the government by the evangelicalists in Britain, who called for the government representing the British people to disassociate itself from the barbarous 'idol worship' of the Hindus. Another factor was the British commitment to liberalism, which led to the separation of the public and the private spheres of life. The logic of this separation was that whereas the public sphere should be governed by universal principles of rationality, people should be left to pursue their own interests in private. There were also other more pragmatic and utilitarian reasons for leaving 'social' matters in the hands of the colonized peoples, as the colonial government was intent on preserving existing socio-political structure and thus maintaining law and order in the country to promote commerce and facilitate tax collection.

The division between the political and religious spheres was based on the colonialist idea that the Indian population were not only 'different' but also 'inferior' and 'backward', and hence the British were justified in colonizing India. Indians were seen as being bound by 'idolatry' in their religion and 'pre-individualistic' caste in their social organization, and were thus considered not fit to participate in state politics, which was supposed to be based on the universal principle of modern rationality. Under the colonial regime, Indians were made subjects to be objectified, classified, and enumerated for rule by the colonial rulers for the purposes of 'good government', but were never themselves active agents in the domain of state politics. They were allowed to act as agents only in the colonially redefined domain of 'traditional society'. Here, the personhood and identity of Indian people were seen to be defined in terms of religion, caste, and kingship, which were reformulated and transformed into non-political 'social' or 'cultural' phenomena.

This colonial policy of division between the political and the religious played an important part in the dislocation between rationality and religious belief in colonial modernity. In the development of early modernity, we saw that the rationalization of administrative machinery, the growth of market economy, divinization, and ritualization of the king and the maturity of bhakti through action were closely articulated and there were no contradictions between rationality and religious belief. This kind of close articulation was no longer possible under colonialism, since what the colonial distinction between the political and the religious effectively meant was that only politics was based on universal rationality, whereas the religion of the colonized was relegated to the irrational. In this sense, the pursuit of rationality was no longer congruent with the pursuit of religious faith, as the British took over the state administration and major commercial activities, and the colonized were seen to be unable to practise rationalization and development in the politico-economic field.

THE RITUALIZATION OF COLONIAL KINGSHIP

After the defeat of 1804, the Khurda king was stripped of all his political rights and lost his estates to the colonial government. The former territory of the Khurda kingdom became *khas mahal*, or government estate under the direct management of the colonial administration. The tradition of Gajapati kingship of Orissa seemed to have ended here, but the king's fate was changed by the British policy toward the Jagannath temple, which was based on the separation of the political and the religious.

In the early years of the colonial rule following the conquest of Orissa in 1803, the British tried to manipulate the Jagannath cult in order to consolidate their position in Orissa, and initially followed the system of administration that had existed under the Marathas. The only exception was the pilgrim tax, which was abolished in 1803, only to be reintroduced in 1806. The temple lands were brought under the direct management of the local officials of the Board of Revenue at Cuttack.[26]

However, when the British tried to control the administration of the temple, they found that they could not look into its administration adequately, since they were forbidden entry into the temple as non-Hindus. As a result, they decided to bring the Gajapati king of Khurda back onto the scene. They released Mukunda Deva II from imprisonment at Midnapur in 1807[27] and vested him with 'the superintendence of the temple of Jagannath and its interior economy, the conduct and management of its affairs, and the entire control over the priests, officers, and servants attached to the idol and to the temple'[28] by the Regulation IV of 1809.

Under increasing pressure from the activities of missionaries and evangelical supporters, the government then decided to sever all connections with the Jagannath temple 'in deference to very strongly expressed views in England that the Government should divest itself of all connections with religious endowments in this country'.[29] The government granted endowments of Ekharajat Mahal to the temple, and it was declared in the deed of 1863 that 'from the time of transfer of the said lands the Government have no further connection, direct or indirect, with the officers of the Temple of Jagannath, its management, revenue or otherwise and that the Rajah of Khurda in his capacity of Superintendent is solely responsible for the due application of its revenues and the due administration of its affairs'.[30] Thus, all financial and administrative links between the colonial government and the Jagannath temple were severed, and the Puri king as the Superintendent of the Jagannath temple was to enjoy enhanced independence, financial as well as administrative, as regards the temple and its endowments.

What is important to note here, however, is that this relative independence granted to the king was without sovereignty. The temple endowments functioned not only to support the economics of kingship under colonialism, but also as the 'territorial' basis for the continuity of royal ritual authority. Hence, paradoxically, the king's position was strengthened as he was granted rights over certain territories, but at the same time his rule came to be restricted to the newly created 'religious' domain constructed in the course of the colonial process. Kingship, in this way, was made to continue in its ritualized form and, although the strengthening of the Puri king's ties with Jagannath appeared to secure his position as the Gajapati of Orissa, it was stripped of sovereignty.

Divinization and ritualization of the king under colonialism, then, cannot just be seen as a continuous development from the early modern period. In the early modern period, the sacrificer state not only numerated and recorded people's entitlements in a rational manner but also connected people's everyday life based on that entitlement to the divine through royal mediation. The disjunction between the rational state and religious society in the colonial modern period, however, meant that the ritualized domain allocated to the king under the colonial regime became a disengaged fragment that was dislocated from the action of the everyday life and which came under minute surveillance by the rational state.

THE BREAKDOWN OF THE SYSTEM OF ENTITLEMENTS AND THE FRAGMENTATION OF THE SACRIFICER STATE AND SACRIFICIAL COMMUNITY

The dislocation between rationality and religious belief, and the colonial domination of state administration and commerce meant the breakdown of the system of entitlements, which had been the basis of the totality of life and under which administrative rationalization, commercial activities, and devotional faith had been developing simultaneously in the early modernity of the pre-colonial state.

The breakdown of the system of entitlements was part of the transformation that accompanied colonial land reforms, which were based in the British policy of taking away politico-economic power from the colonized but leaving their society, culture, and religion intact. By getting rid of 'the sacrificer king', which the British saw as the 'political', and also by destroying the redistributive mechanism of the communal entitlement system through the introduction of individual proprietorship, the land reforms had the effect of superficially retaining the pre-colonial power structure in the locality in terms of the pattern of distribution of wealth, but changed its context and meaning drastically under the colonial regime. Also, the penetration of state surveillance and control into the locality and the establishment of a connection between individuals and the higher state apparatus may be seen on one hand as a continuation of the development of early modernity, while on the other hand, the meaning of landholding drastically changed with its dislocation from the sacrificial, religious, and community values.[31]

The first survey and settlement, which measured the actual land, clarified the various owners and fixed taxes, began in 1827 in the Khurda region and was completed in 1836. According to the colonial administration, the land used for 'religious' purposes was allowed to be retained in the hands of previous occupants either rent-free (*lakhirajdar*) or with light rent (*tankidar*). These privileged landholdings included land donated to the gods and goddesses (*debattār*) and land donated to the Brahmins (*brāhmattār*). Many Brahmins were thus given *de facto* exclusive landownership and tax reduction privileges on the donated lands by the colonial government and came to form a part of the large landlord class by the latter half of the nineteenth century.

In this way, the colonial government's policy of non-intervention in religion led to the preferential protection of people with religious standing, and it might seem at first sight that the Brahmins simply maintained and extended their position as privileged classes. However, it is important to note that the context in which their position was set was greatly transformed under colonial rule. That is to say, in the pre-colonial state, their entitlements were granted by the king, through whom the entitlement-holders took part in the reproduction of the whole in which religion, politics, and the economy were inseparable. By contrast, under the colonial regime, ownership of privileged land-holdings was categorized as part of the restricted sphere of society and religion, which was distinct from the wider context of the political economy that functioned according to the logic of secular rationality.

Similarly, apparent preservation by the colonial administration of the status of local leadership at the community level also involved a dramatic transformation in meaning. The chief and other entitlement-holders such as accountants and village heads came to be employed as tax collectors (*sarbarākāra*) or assistant tax collectors (*tandakār*), and their entitlement land was granted in lieu of that office free of tax. In this way, the entitlement land was transformed into payment of low-class bureaucrats in the colonial government, instead of being an endowment from the king.

The entitlement lands of the community servants, such as carpenters, blacksmiths, and washermen, also enjoyed tax-free status as long as the holder continued to serve the community. Here again, there was apparent preservation of the socio-cultural forms, which in fact underwent considerable change in meaning. The unit of reproduction of social relations supporting the exchange of service and grain had changed from the local community based on the system of entitlements to the household based on the possession of land. Here, the service caste no longer performed service for the community as a whole, but provided individual service to those households that paid their salary. Even though they did the same work, the exchange of service and grain was no longer embedded in the holistic social relations based on the system of entitlements. It was instead transformed into an individualized relationship between the employer (*jajman*) household and the service caste household. The '*jajmani* system', that is, the customary exchange between households, observed by the anthropologists was thus a product of reconstruction of the system of exchange under colonialism.

In this way, the land system, which was intimately linked to the system of entitlements in the pre-colonial state, came to be disconnected from the holistic reproductive process of the community and the socio-political relations embedded within it. Relationships based on traditional status and roles were partly retained, as tax-free lands were given for the land parts of the 'offices' that were seen by the colonial government as 'religious' (for instance, lands donated to deities or Brahmins) or 'based on social customs' (community servants) or 'useful for the colonial administration' (traditional authorities appointed as tax collectors of the colonial government). The majority of the other lands, however, were transformed into 'property' divorced from people's social personhood. Along with this, the unit of reproduction of social relations shifted from the local community to the household, and class relations according to households and caste were formed in the local society based on the amount of land owned.

DERIVATIVE RESISTANCE TO THE HEGEMONIC: COLONIAL DICHOTOMY OF SECULAR RATIONALITY AND RELIGIOUS BELIEF

Resistance by the colonized to the colonial dominance and hegemony had the effect of shifting the boundaries and inverting the semantics of the dichotomy of politics/religion, state/society, and British/Indian, and also resulted in the further dislocation and the fragmentation of the totality of life, as the hegemonic dichotomy between secular rationality and religious belief was retained and made the underlying assumption for the cultural politics of identity by the colonized.

This can be seen in the way that religion, caste, and kingship, which the British had assigned to the social domain outside of state politics, were precisely what the Indian nationalists claimed as the domain for their cultural-political struggles in establishing their identity in an independent nation. The 'rule of colonial difference'[32] that we mentioned above as an underlying assumption held by the British, and which was articulated in colonial policies, was taken up and reinterpreted by Indian nationalists in their search for politically and culturally independent India.[33]

According to the 'rule of colonial difference', the British colonialists regarded the domain of state politics that they introduced into India as 'modern' and 'rational', and Indian society as 'traditional' and 'superstitious'. Colonial rule was legitimized according to this value judgement, and the colonial rhetoric was that India was benefiting from the 'superiority' of the British government. Social affairs were left outside the concern of the state and dealt with as 'customs' among the 'natives'.

In response to this situation, the nationalist elites attempted to get a grip on both the domain of institutional politics as their sovereign right and the domain of 'traditional' society as the basis of their national culture. Their endeavour, however, was very much defined by the hegemonic colonial dichotomy that dislocated secular rationality from religious belief. On the one hand, the nationalist elites saw that the domain of institutional politics was based on the principles of democracy and individual rights, and hence engaged in the strategy of employing the discourses of liberal politics imported from Britain in their struggles for autonomy and independence, insisting on the illegitimacy of British colonial rule.[34] On the other hand, they constructed the 'spiritual' identity of India or Orissa as being grounded on the basis of 'particularity' and 'difference' of the indigenous values represented by such phenomena as religion, caste, and kingship.

In this way, the nationalists' appeal to the greatness of 'Indian spiritual tradition' in the social religious field involved a twist in meaning on their part, but it was simply an attempt to reverse the negative picture of the 'Indian tradition'. It depended on and was heavily bound by the colonial hegemonic framework. 'Tradition' advocated by the nationalists consisted of what was reformulated and objectified in the course of the colonial process and disembedded from the totality of life.

A similar mechanism of application of the hegemonic dichotomy and the disembedding of religion and culture from the totality of life can be seen in the case of subaltern resistance, which inverted the semantic structure defined by colonialism. For the subalterns, the domain of institutional politics had been usurped by the British in an 'unrighteous' (*adharma*) manner, and since then that domain constituted 'unjust' and 'cunning' administration of the 'foreign (*phiringi*)' colonizers. They thus left the domain of state politics in the hands of the spiritually 'inferior', though politically 'cleverer' (*chalāk*), British colonizers. State politics was, from their point of view, unworthy of their participation. The religious spiritual domain of their 'traditional' society, on the other hand, was the only space where they could pursue their 'righteous' (dharma) values, represented by religion, caste, and kingship and untainted by the advent of immoral modernity. While thus denying the value of institutional politics in the colonial regime, the subalterns in fact had no choice but to pursue values represented by religion, caste, and kingship, which came under the domain of the 'native society' and hence fell outside direct state intervention. Within this religious domain, people aspired to acquire honours and privileges in the reformulated 'tradition' under colonialism.

In the case of Orissa, the Gajapati kingship and Jagannath were taken up as the symbols of Oriya nationalism.[35] These symbols were indeed powerful political resources, which could be employed to assert Oriya identity by projecting their cultural differences with the British. By their application in the nationalist cause, however, Gajapati kingship and Jagannath were in effect disembedded from their pre-colonial significance in the context of their particular and specific relationships with the people. In the sections dealing with early modernity in the pre-colonial state, I tried to describe how the king and Jagannath embodied the focal point with which the man-in-the-world with a specific status and a particular role gauged his relationship with and distance from the more universal and the divine. In the process of fragmentation of this totality, however, the sacrificial organization centred around kingship with its relation to the Jagannath cult was disembedded. It was continued only to provide ontological guarantee to the people in the 'traditional' ritualized contexts born under colonialism, and its fragmented idioms came to be used as mere 'metaphors, synecdochic emblems',[36] which were utilized in forming political communities in the struggle for power in the new political context.

CONCLUSION

In this paper, I have tried to sketch out and formulate some preliminary ideas regarding the characteristics of early modernity in India, and the questions of continuity and disjunction in their transformative momentum in the shaping of colonial modernity. I have tried to show that in the development of the sacrificer state and sacrificial community in seventeenth- and eighteenth-century Orissa, there was growth of the administrative technologies of surveillance, numeration, calculation, and recording, which also connected the locality to the wider sphere of the market. This was concomitant with the ritualization and divinization of the king in the kingdom, and the connecting of each entitlement-holder with the divine through the king. The entitlement-holder was thus able to transform the performance of duty according to his place under the system of entitlements into service of the divine. In this way, the developments of the religious and the rational were inseparable.

Colonial rule brought about a fragmentation of the totality of life in which there was a significant disjunction between the rational and the religious, the former being represented by the colonial state and the latter by the colonized society. In this process, the system of entitlements in the community was apparently preserved according to the colonial government's policy of non-interference in the society, culture, and religion of India, but it in fact underwent a profound transformation as it was cut off from the dynamics of state politics and commerce. In this context, the performance of duty according to the system of entitlements as service of the divine was limited to the dichotomized and restricted sphere of ritual and religion, which was set in opposition to the rational sphere of the political economy.

The transition from the early modern of the eighteenth century to the colonial modern of the nineteenth century involved peculiar aspects of continuity and change. From the point of view of continuity from the pre-colonial period, the development of colonial administration can be seen as the logical extension of existing developments in the administrative technologies of numeration, calculation, and recording of entitlements that had become firmly established in locality. It can also be said that the British were able to establish their imperial economy by basing it on and transforming the pre-existing banking and trade networks.

From the point of view of disjunction, however, a dichotomic separation was instituted between the rational state and religious–ritual society. The village, caste, and kingship all came to be placed under the latter category, being denied their relationship with the rational workings of the state. In the domain of the state, the apparatus of the modern regime of power was introduced in the form of state politics and administration. Introduction of a centralized government, army, and court was intended by the colonial government to guide India towards rationalization and civilization according to the universal principle of modernity. In the social domain, there was what can be seen to be a reorganized continuation and even strengthening of fragmented, decontextualized, and substantialized elements of indigenous cultural designs or social structures such as religion, caste, and kingship in their non-political, decapitated 'cultural' forms, which acquired different functions and meanings in the new context.

NOTES

1. N. Dirks, 1987, *The Hollow Crown: Ethnohistory of an Indian Little Kingdom*, Cambridge: Cambridge University Press; N. Peabody, 1991, '*Koṭā Mahājagat*, or the Great Universe of Kota: Sovereignty and Territory in 18th Century Rajasthan', *Contributions to Indian Sociology* (N.S.), Vol. 25, No. 1, pp. 29–56. N. Peabody, 2003, *Hindu Kingship and Polity in Pre-colonial India*, New York and Cambridge: Cambridge University Press.

2. Chris. A. Bayly, 1993, 'Pre-colonial Indian Merchants and Rationality', in M. Hasan and N. Gupta (eds), *India's Colonial Encounter: Essays in Memory of Eric Stokes*, Delhi: Manohar, pp. 3–24; D. Washbrook, 1990, 'South Asia, the World System and World Capitalism', *The Journal of Asian Studies*, Vol. 29, No. 3, pp. 479–508; A. Wink, 1986, *Land and Sovereignty in India: Agrarian Society and Politics under the Eighteenth Maratha Swarajya*, Cambridge: Cambridge University Press.

3. Hermann Kulke, 1978, 'The Struggle between the Rājās of Khurda and the Muslim Subahdārs of Cuttack for Dominance of the Jagannāth Cult', in A. Eschmann, H. Kulke, and G.C. Tripathy (eds), *The Cult of Jagannath and the Regional Tradition of Orissa*, Delhi: Manohar, pp. 321–42.

4. Frederique A. Marglin, 1985, *Wives of the God-King: The Rituals of the Devadasis of Puri*, New Delhi: Oxford University Press.

5. Akio Tanabe, 1999, 'Kingship, Community and Commerce in Late Pre-colonial Khurda', in N. Karashima (ed.), *Kingship in Indian History*, Japanese Studies on South Asia No. 2, Delhi: Manohar, pp. 195–236.

6. Chris A. Bayly, 1988, *Indian Society and the Making of the British Empire,* Cambridge and New York: Cambridge University Press; *idem*, 1992 (1983), *Rulers, Townsmen and Bazaars: North Indian Society in the Age of British Expansion, 1770–1870*, New Delhi: Oxford University Press; Chris A. Bayly, 1993, 'Pre-colonial Indian Merchants and Rationality', in M. Hasan and N. Gupta (eds), *India's Colonial Encounter: Essays in Memory of Eric Stokes*, Delhi: Manohar, pp. 3–24.

7. D. Washbrook, 1981, 'Law, State and Agrarian Society in Colonial India', *Modern Asian Studies*, Vol. 15, No. 3, pp. 649–721 and *idem*, 1988, 'Progress and Problems: South Asian Economic and Social History c. 1720–1860', *Modern Asian Studies*, Vol. 22, No. 1, pp. 57–96.

8. D. Washbrook, 1988, ibid., p. 76. Similarly, Mizushima, based on his detailed study of changes in land utilization pattern, says 'colonization in the 18th century South India was the product of choices of local leaders'. (T. Mizushima, 1990, *18–20 Seiki Minami Indo Zaichishakai no Kenkyu* [A Study on South Indian Local Society in 18th–20th Centuries, in Japanese], Tokyo: Institute for the Study of Languages and Cultures of Asia and Africa, Tokyo University of Foreign Studies, p. 396. The quotation is a translation by Tanabe.) However, his interpretation seems more nuanced than the theory of indigenous development of capitalism. In explaining that local leaders sought

the support of the stronger centralizing force of colonial powers because of the devastating effects of wars on society, Mizushima seems to combine the imperialist–nationalist interpretation of the calamitous effects of continuous exhausting wars in pre-colonial India and the 'revisionist' interpretation that stresses the positive agency on the part of the Indians in construction of colonialism.

9. P. Chatterjee, 1993, *The Nation and its Fragments: Colonial and Postcolonial Histories*, Princeton: Princeton University Press, pp. 27–34; G. Prakash, 1990, 'Writing Post-Orientalist Histories of the Third World: Perspectives from Indian Historiography', *Comparative Studies in Society and History*, Vol. 32, No. 2, pp. 383–408 and *idem*, 1992, 'Can the 'Subaltern' Ride? A Reply to O'Hanlon and Washbrook', *Comparative Studies in Society and History*, Vol. 34, No. 1, pp. 168–84. Also see the rejoinder to G. Prakash by O'Hanlon and Washbrook. (R. O'Hanlon and D. Washbrook, 1992, 'After Orientalism: Culture, Criticism and Politics in the Third World', *Comparative Studies in Society and History*, Vol. 34, No. 1, pp. 141–67.)

10. P. Chatterjee, 1986, *Nationalist Thought and the Colonial World: A Derivative Discourse?*, London: Zed Books.

11. B. Schnepel, 1995, 'Durga and the King: Ethnohistorical Aspects of Politico-ritual Life in a South Orissan Jungle Kingdom', *The Journal of the Royal Anthropological Institute*, Vol. 1, No. 1, p. 145.

12. According to the traditional account in Orissa, there were four main thrones in India, namely: *Narapati* (Lord of Man) in the Deccan, *Aśwapati* (Lord of Horse) in the Maratha, *Chatrapati* (Lord of Umbrella) in Rajasthan and *Gajapati* (Lord of Elephant) in Orissa (Sterling, 1904 [1822], *An Account [Geographical, Statistical, and Historical] of Orissa proper or Cuttack with Appendices*, Calcutta: Bengal Secretariat Press, p. 62).

13. In original Oriya, it is as follows: *Lakshe rājāra mauḍamaṇi, se khordha rāija rājā. aruṇāi taḷe tolāi naara, sukhe pāḷuthile prajā.*

14. *Selections from the Correspondence on the Settlement of Khoordah Estate in the District of Pooree*, Vol. I, Calcutta, 1879, pp. 85–6.

15. Ibid., p. 129.

16. Stein says that the most significant units of social structure and agrarian organization under the Colas in early medieval south India were not villages, but 'peasant micro regions' or *nāṭus* which were 'the enduring and basic units of south Indian peasant society' (B. Stein, 1980, *Peasant, State and Society in Medieval South India*, New Delhi: Oxford University Press, p. 13).

17. According to the gazetteer of Puri by L. O'Malley, *bisi* was an administrative unit of ancient Hindu kingdoms. However, unfortunately, we do not know where he obtained this information (L. O'Malley, 1984 [1908], *Puri: A Gazetteer*, Bengal District Gazetteers, New Delhi: Usha Jain).

18. Cf. F. Perlin, 1985, 'State Formation Reconsidered. Part Two', *Modern Asian Studies*, Vol. 19, No. 3, p. 475.

19. Tanabe, 1999, *op. cit.*, pp. 195–236.

20. Burton Stein, 1989, 'Eighteenth Century India: Another View', *Studies in History*, Vol. 5, No. 1, p. 10.

21. Tanabe, 1999, *op. cit.*, p. 222. Much work has focused on the relationships between the state and trade and between the state and community in pre-colonial India. However, the place of the community in relation to trade has not received enough attention, and it would be worthwhile to investigate the development of the interrelationship between these two. Menon points out, 'There is a tendency to conceive of the economies of town and countryside in opposed terms in which commerce and the market are seen as independent of peasant sociology. The rural sphere is seen as characterized by a moral redistributive economy.' However, he argues, in reference to the pre-colonial situation in Malabar, that 'what we have here is a situation in which both the independence offered by the market and *jajmani* style patronage coexisted largely on account of the volatile nature of the economy.' Menon, 2000, 'Houses by the Sea: State Experimentation on the South-West Coast of India, 1760–1800', in N. Chandoke (ed.), *Mapping Histories: Essays Presented to Ravinder Kumar*, New Delhi: Tulika. His line of thought represents a totalizing perspective which sees the relationship between the community and the market as not necessarily opposed but interdependent. The kind of *jajmani* relationships that developed around the households that Menon describes seem quite different from the communal structure in Khurda, though. His *jajmani* relations may represent the stage when communal structure was inflected by commercialization and reorganized around individual households. In Khurda, the communal 'redistributive economy' in the countryside seems to have been compatible with the co-existence of the trade. There is a need to investigate the conditions and contents of transformation of community in the late pre-colonial period in different areas more closely.

22. P. Mukherjee, 1978, 'Caitanya in Orissa', in A. Eschmann, H. Kulke, and G.C. Tripathy (eds), *The Cult of Jagannath and the Regional Tradition of Orissa*, Delhi: Manohar, p. 319.

23. Ibid.

24. According to Kulke, it was Kapilendra (1435–67) who first called himself a 'servant' of Jagannath.

25. H. Kulke, 1978, 'The Jagannath Cult and Gajapati Kingship: A Contribution to the History of Legitimation', mimeo, p. 23, quoted in Marglin, 1985, *op. cit.*, p. 125.

26. B. Das, 1978, *Studies in the Economic History of Orissa from Ancient Times to 1833*, Calcutta: Firma KLM Limited, p. 143.

27. P.K. Pattanaik, 1979, *A Forgotten Chapter of Orissan History (with special reference to the Rajas of Khurda and Puri) 1568–1828*, Calcutta: Punthi Pustak, pp. 145, 161.

28. Section 2, Regulation IV 1809 quoted in W.F.B. Laurie, 2000, *Orissa: The Garden of Superstition & Idolatry: Including an Account of British Connexion with the Temple of Jagannath*, Calcutta: R.N. Bhattacharya, p. 76.

29. S.L. Maddox, *Final Report on the Survey and Settlement of the Province of Orissa (Temporary Settled Areas) 1890 to 1900 AD, Vol. 1* (Reprinted under the authority of Board of Revenue, Orissa), n.d., p. 435.

30. N.R. Hota, 1972, *Final Report on Ekharajat Mahal 1953 to 1965*, Cuttack: Government Press, p. 102.

31. See Akio Tanabe, 1998, 'Ethnohistory of Land and Identity in Khurda, Orissa: From Pre-colonial Past to Post-colonial Present', *Journal of Asian and African Studies*, No. 56, Institute for the Study of Languages and Cultures of Asia and Africa, Tokyo University of Foreign Studies, pp. 75–112.

32. P. Chatterjee, 1993, *op. cit.*

33. The process in which this was accomplished in the discourse of anti-colonial nationalism has been dealt with extensively by P. Chatterjee, 1989, 'Colonialism, Nationalism and Colonised Women: The Contest in India', *American Ethnologist*, No. 16, pp. 622–33; Chatterjee, 1993, *op. cit.*

34. D. Haynes, 1992, *Rhetoric and Ritual in Colonial India: The Shaping of Public Culture in Surat City, 1852–1928*, New Delhi: Oxford University Press.

35. G.N. Dash, 1978, 'Jagannatha and Oriya Nationalism', in A. Eschmann, H. Kulke, and G.C. Tripathi (eds), *The Cult of Jagannath and the Regional Tradition of Orissa*, New Delhi: Manohar, pp. 359–74.

36. B. Stein, 1998, *A History of India*, Oxford: Blackwell, p. 18.

CHAPTER 8

The Ethnographic State[1]

Nicholas B. Dirks

By the second half of the nineteenth century, the colonial state in India was about to undergo several major transformations. Land, and the revenue and authority that accrued from the relationship between it and the state, had been fundamental to the formation of the early colonial state, eclipsing the formation of Company rule in that ineluctable combination of formal and private trade that itself masked the formidable state-like functions of the Company. But the fact that the rebellion of 1857 so quickly led to general agrarian revolt, and the steadily increasing economic investment in imperial power (propelled both by strategic and economic ones—as for example in the joint stock funding of railway and telegraph infrastructural expansion) made it clear that things had to change. Land tax was still an important source of revenue through the century, as was much of the trade that had been fundamental to the mercantile origins of empire. However, the extractive colonial state increasingly faced other kinds of challenges requiring a new basis for imperium; accordingly, imperial ambition, and anxiety, moved to new levels and concerns. The steady absorption of new lands through the aggressive policies of Lord Dalhousie, that in the taking of Oudh in 1856 had led directly to the Great Rebellion, were brought abruptly to a halt, and policies of indirect rule were mobilized to accommodate, and ultimately appropriate, the incomplete project of colonial conquest. At the same time, the rebellion made it clear that some communities in India could be counted as loyal, as others became doomed to perpetual suspicion. These latter groups were to be substituted by the 'martial' races, as Macaulay's hyperbolic denunciations of effeminate Bengalis were transmuted into state policy. In the new rhetorical economy of colonial rule, political loyalty replaced landed status. And the form of knowledge and argument that seemed most appropriate to assess matters of loyalty rather than revenue was of course knowledge of peoples and cultures. To put the matter in bold relief, after 1857 anthropology supplanted history as the principal colonial modality of knowledge and rule. In even bolder terms, I would label the late nineteenth- and early twentieth-century colonial state in India as the ethnographic state.

☆ ☆ ☆

When V.S. Savarkar wrote his grand history of 1857, he glossed the bloody events following the Meerut mutiny as the first Indian war of independence. The national awakening that grew out of military refusal was an expression for Savarkar of the fundamental injustice of British rule in India. Savarkar wrote of the need for India to attain historical consciousness of itself as a nation, and of the importance of the rebellion for constituting a foundational moment in the emergence of a national history. Savarkar's narrative emphasized the heroic refusal of Indian heroes, ordinary soldiers as well as brave leaders, to accept British domination. He was especially critical of the commonly accepted view that the revolt had little political significance, that it was carried forward merely by the personal vendettas and interests of a few vestiges of an old regime, that indeed it was primarily about Indian concerns over caste and religion voiced in connection with the originary moment of mutiny, concerns that had clearly inflamed the passions of mutineers and rebels alike. He was referring of course to the question of the cartridge.

The mutiny—and for that matter the rebellion—began in the haze of alarm occasioned by the introduction of a new Enfield rifle, the cartridges for which were packed in a combination of beef and pork fat and were to be loaded by the use of the mouth as well as the hands. Fears of pollution were heightened by the growing reach and influence of Christian missionaries, for it was widely assumed that pollution would be used as a technique to usher new converts into the fold. In the years before the mutiny, missionaries had been given increasingly free reign, including within the military where, for example, Colonel Wheler, Commander of the 34th Native Infantry at Barrackpore, openly preached the gospel to his soldiers. Missionaries had already made clear their frustration that caste was their single-most significant obstacle, and spoke of the need to break potential converts of their caste in order to free their souls for possible conversion. Despite the fact that the fat-laden cartridges were speedily withdrawn and sepoys instructed to pack their own cartridges in grease of their choice, their use became the occasion for the first outbreak of resistance in Meerut on 10 May 1857. Eighty-five sepoys who refused the cartridges were placed in irons and sentenced to ten-year imprisonment. Their fellow soldiers rose up in protest, released them, and travelled to Delhi, where they fashioned the dazed and elderly Mughal emperor, Bahadur Shah, as the leader of the revolt. The fall of Delhi was followed by uprisings at many major military stations in the North-west Provinces and in Oudh, and rebellion steadily grew, continuing through the summer of 1858 before it was finally brutally suppressed and contained by British forces.

Historians have debated the causes and ramifications of the rebellion ever since, in what has ultimately become a referendum on the beneficence of British colonial rule during its first century, as well as an explanation for major transformations in the nature of that rule thereafter. Sir Sayyid Ahmad Khan wrote an account of the revolt just months after it was over, making a number of points with extreme care.[2] While he offered no real sympathy to the rebels, he maintained that there were legitimate issues of grievance that the British needed to understand, despite the absence of any manifest conspiracy. At the same time, he wrote to counter the charge that Indian Muslims were responsible, clearly shown by the events of the revolt to be disloyal. Significantly, Sir Sayyid blamed the revolt on ignorance and insensitivity rather than on more fundamental causes. He wrote that, 'Government has not succeeded in acquainting itself with the daily habits, the modes of thought and of life, and likes, and dislikes, and prejudices of the people'.[3] As a result, the government was ignorant not only of local modes of thought and of life, but 'of the grievances through which their hearts were becoming estranged'.[4] Sir Sayyid was further concerned about the 'passing of such laws and regulations and forms of procedure as jarred with the established custom and practice of Hindustan'. He seemed particularly alarmed about the role of missionization, suggesting that recent events had made 'all men whether ignorant, or well-informed, whether high or low, fe[el] a firm conviction that the English Government was bent on interfering with their religion and with their old established customs'.[5] Sir Sayyid noted that missionaries not only began to preach with the sanction of the government, but attacked in 'violent and unmeasured language...the followers and the holy places of other creeds: annoying, and insulting beyond expression the feelings of those who listened to them'.[6] He encouraged greater communication between rulers and ruled, and enjoined the British to pay greater attention to issues of cultural respect. For example, he suggested the institution of state durbars, and the distribution of honours to worthy subjects, as well as far more scrupulous attention to questions of prestige and status among the historically disfranchised Muslim community.

Sir Sayyid, who went on to found the first Muslim University (the Muhammedan Anglo-Oriental College) in Aligarh in 1875, and bore in his title the success of at least one of his recommendations to the British, downplayed the significance of the greater rebellion because of his own greater concern for reconciliation and reform under British rule. Despite his symptomatic critique of the causes of discontent, he focused in particular on the outbreak of the mutiny around the refusal to bite the greased cartridges, which 'did violence to the superstition of the sepoys'.[7] In this, he reassured those British commentators who preferred to attribute the revolt solely to reaction and superstition, at the same time that his conservatism was apparent in early years after the rebellion even to many British, particularly those who had been participants in the events of 1857–8, who were aware of the monumentality of Indian disaffection. Nevertheless, his gentle admonishments did not fall on entirely deaf ears. Sir Bartle Frere wrote that Sir Sayyid's essay clearly showed how 'acts of our Government, well meant and well planned, sometimes do more harm than good, simply owing to our disregard for native opinion and our neglect of the maxim that our measures in India should not only be good in themselves but that they should commend themselves to the approval of the natives. We, as a rule, neither take care enough to know what the natives think of our measures, nor to explain the true grounds and objects of our measures to those affected by them'.[8]

It was in fact widely accepted, even by the colonial historians Malleson and Kaye,[9] that there had been serious reasons for Indian discontent. In the years leading up to revolt, British policy under Dalhousie had favoured annexation wherever possible. As Savarkar pointed out with particular bitterness, adoption even within royal families was frequently disallowed in order to justify annexation through the 'doctrine of lapse', in which princely states without proper heirs would be ripe for colonial plucking. There were manifold political as well as economic reasons that the revolt became such a monumental marker in India's colonial history, a moment when Hindus and Muslims, Marathas and Mughals, legendary heros and yeoman farmers united with countless other unlikely 'conspirators' to challenge British rule and uphold the legitimate claim of the Delhi emperor. Nevertheless, the

British characterized the revolt for the most part as an expression of Indian fanaticism and superstition, as colonial narratives explained the 'heinous massacre of Cawnpore' and the 'barbaric siege of Lucknow' through stories having to do with chapattis, pig fat, and other signs of alien alterity. And even as Savarkar, Sir Sayyid, and other Indian commentators provided alternative narratives for an event glossed variably as the first war of independence and a serious warning against colonial complacency, the revolt ended up by justifying new forms of colonial power and policy, leading in the end to greater complacency, and contempt, than had been in evidence before. The revolt was ruthlessly suppressed, while leaders of the revolt such as Nana Sahib were turned into fiends and monsters. The year 1857 became the pretext for the conversion of religious difference into an argument about political indifference, even as it served to warn against religious interference and cultural ignorance. The revolt served to justify the assumption of direct Crown rule over Company-controlled country, and the inauguration of new forms of indirect rule where full military conquest had left off so abruptly in 1856.

On 2 August 1858, Britain announced that India would henceforth be governed 'by and in the name of Her Majesty, and all rights in relation to any territories which might have been exercised by the said Company...shall and may be exercised...as rights incidental to the Government of India.' Queen Victoria followed her assumption of authority over India with a proclamation, dated 1 November 1858, in which she sought to allay the concerns of her Indian subjects in matters deemed to have been of relevance to the revolt. She announced 'to the native Princes of India that all treaties and engagements made with them by or under the authority of the Honourable East India Company are by us accepted, and will be scrupulously maintained....' She noted that the doctrine of lapse would no longer be used as a pretext for annexation by stating outright that Britain desired 'no extension of our present territorial possessions; and, while we will permit no aggression upon our dominions or our rights to be attempted with impunity, we shall sanction no encroachment on those of others.' Further, she declared an end to aggressive missionization: 'Firmly relying ourselves on the truth of Christianity [this opening phrase was inserted by Victoria herself, into the text prepared by her Prime Minister], and acknowledging with gratitude the solace of religion, we disclaim alike the right and the desire to impose our convictions on any of our subjects. We declare it to be our royal will and pleasure that none be in anywise favoured, none molested or disquieted, by reason of their religious faith or observances, but that all shall alike enjoy the equal and impartial protection of the law; and we do strictly charge and enjoin all those who may be in authority under us that they abstain from all interference with the religious belief or worship of any of our subjects on pain of our highest displeasure.'[10]

Thus Victoria put a halt to the evangelical enthusiasm that had mounted since Charles Grant had reversed Company policy earlier in the century, even as she gave voice to the growing sense among many Britains that 'Christianity was...increasingly a mark of their own difference from, and superiority to, their Indian subjects.'[11] Thomas Metcalf writes: 'Despite the presence of dedicated missionaries throughout India, Christianity had become, as the Secretary of State Lord Stanley put it in 1858, to the consternation of his evangelical countrymen, "the religion of Europe"'.[12] Liberalism did not evaporate overnight. Indeed, many liberals celebrated Britain's new-found commitment to religious toleration in the colonies, and the importance of education remained unquestioned after the rebellion. But for the most part reform foundered against the suddenly hardened shoals of cultural difference.

The most common general explanation for the great revolt was the caste system, a marker of difference even as it seemed to contain the ideologies of pollution and exclusion that had ignited fears around the introduction of the new cartridge. In an essay written in April 1858 in which the renowned Indologist Max Muller took up the question of the true meaning of caste in India, he observed that, 'Among the causes assigned for the Sepoy mutiny, caste has been made the most prominent. By one party it is said that too much, by another that too little, regard was paid to caste.'[13] Muller noted remarks by British officers of the total incompatibility of caste with military discipline. He also reported the remarks of many civilians to the effect that 'the Sepoys were driven mad by the greased cartridges; that they believed they were asked to touch what was unclean in order to lose their caste, and that, rather than lose their caste, they would risk everything.' The revolt occasioned an extraordinary proliferation of writing on the subject of caste, much of it by missionaries who felt that the time had come for an intensified assault on caste by the government. Missionaries had been complaining that caste was the largest single impediment to conversion, that the fear of loss of caste dissuaded potential converts from abandoning Hindu practice more than any other doctrinal consideration. Some missionaries had argued that caste should be broken to make conversion possible, an argument that seemed to many in the government as one of the principal causes of the rebellion, in that it provided evidence behind the assertion that the cartridge had been part of a deliberate strategy. But many missionaries sought to seize the moment, suggesting that Christianity should be imposed on India as a treatment, if not a punishment, for the revolt. The Church Missionary Society's Memorial to the Queen put it like this: 'The Government of India has professed to occupy a position of neutrality between the Christian and false religions. Such profession, your Memorialists believe, dishonours the truth of God, discourages the progress of Christianity, and is inimical to the social welfare of the Natives... [the] evils which have been fearfully exhibited amidst the revolting cruelties of the present rebellion... can only be effectually counteracted by recognizing the Christian religion as the basis of law and social order.'[14]

Alexander Duff, the chief architect and theorist of missionary education in India, was a critic of caste from the time he first came to India with the Church of Scotland Mission in 1829. Like many other missionaries he was concerned that his pupils were overwhelmingly from lower castes, although his opposition to caste segregation in schools clearly discouraged some upper caste families from sending their children to him. In his early writings he held that caste was a sacred institution: 'Idolatry and superstition are like the stones and brick of a huge fabric, and caste is the cement which pervades and closely binds the whole.'[15] Duff gave voice to what became missionary orthodoxy by 1850, when the Madras Missionary Conference put forward a minute in which it was held that, 'Caste... is one of the greatest obstacles to the progress of the Gospel in India... whatever it may have been in its origin, it is now adopted as an essential part of the Hindu religion.'[16] The Madras Missionary Conference had in fact argued further that, 'Caste, which is a distinction among the Hindus, founded upon supposed Birth-Purity or Impurity, is in its nature, essentially a religious institution and not a mere civil distinction.'[17] When Duff published two volumes in the wake of the rebellion, one entitled *What is Caste: How is a Christian Government to deal with it?*,[18] he continued to hold that caste was chiefly religious. However, Duff also held that caste was also civil, simultaneously a social institution and a religious doctrine. Although Duff, more moderate than many of his missionary colleagues, stopped well short of advocating 'an exterminating crusade', he resolved that a Christian government should 'solemnly resolve to have nothing whatever to do with caste.' In the end, Duff was aware both of the limits confronting the government and the reality that caste could only be exterminated by 'the mighty power of the Spirit of God', though he advocated considerably greater support for missions than Victoria finally would concede.

Despite dominant missionary convictions, there were occasional suggestions that the religious and civil components of caste could be separated, and that caste was in large part a social convention as well as a marker of the Hindu faith. Many thought that Indians would hold onto caste distinction far more assertively than they would to their religion. To quote Lord Stanley again: 'The difference between the religion and the caste of the Hindoos was like that between the religious creed of an English gentleman and his code of honour; and that just as an English gentleman would resent any attack on his honour, and yet leave persons perfectly at liberty to attack his religion, so did the Hindoo feel with respect to his caste and religion.... The natives would strongly deprecate any interference with their caste, but were open to instruction and persuasion in religion, provided everything was done openly.'[19] Max Muller developed the notion that caste occupied dual domains with rather more sophistication than Stanley, and directly dispensed with the missionary position. He was concerned that in the aftermath of the revolt and its extraordinary repercussions—including the blaming of all Indians for the extreme actions of a tiny minority—most explanations of the nature and meaning of caste misconstrued both the relationship between religious and social domains, and the extent to which modern manifestations of popular religion deviated from classical Hinduism. On the basis of his examination of the ancient Vedas—the source of greatest authority for all Hindus—he held that none of the objectionable traces of caste could be found in the original constitution of Hindu thought. Indeed, Muller announced that, 'The Government would be perfectly justified in declaring that it will no longer consider caste as part of the religious system of the Hindus. Caste, in the modern sense of the word, is no religious institution; it has no authority in the sacred writings of the Brahmans, and by whatever promise the Government may have bound itself to respect the religion of the natives, that promise will not be violated, even though penalties were inflicted for the observation of the rules of caste.'[20]

However, Muller was also aware that caste as a social formation was little different than the racial, ethnic, religious, and class differences and prejudices that were accepted as natural in most arenas of European social life. He believed that Brahmin priests had grafted religious principle onto social prejudice, thus sanctifying forms of caste exclusion in ways that made questions of intervention sensitive at best. Fulminating against sacerdotal self-interest, Muller nevertheless proposed that caste in many of its aspects be viewed as a social etiquette that circumscribed marriage, dining, and other forms of sociality in ways that could easily be recognized, through appropriate social translation, in Europe. He was convinced that as a religious institution, caste would die away in time, though he was convinced that 'as a social institution it will live and improve.' Indeed, he suggested that caste, 'which has hitherto proved an impediment to the conversion of the Hindus, may in future become one of the most powerful engines for the conversion not merely of individuals, but of whole classes of Indian society.'[21] In any event, Muller argued that caste could not be abolished in India, and that any effort to do so would 'be one of the most hazardous operations that was ever performed on a living social body.'[22] He argued that the government should not actively sanction caste in three fundamental respects: first, the government should not countenance the treatment of any of its subjects with indignity on account of caste; second, the government should pay no attention to caste in any contract or employment, whether in civil or military service; and third, caste should be ignored in all public institutions. But he strongly averred that India must be allowed to mature in its own time. Like earlier generations of Orientalists, his defensive understanding of India was made at the cost of simultaneously belittling the status of modern institutions in India and cautioning against the introduction of rapid change.

Thus the dilemma of liberalism in 1858. Muller was one of the few Orientalists still defending Indian civilization, while the old breed of Anglicists and Macaulayan liberals—who had at any rate condemned caste outright—was also giving way to an unholy alliance of parliamentary pragmatists and imperial crusaders. In assuming Crown rule, Victoria might have announced a new policy of non-interference, but she did so only because of the widespread perception that imperial and missionary interference had just about led to British defeat in India. If caste could not be broken, this was no reason to allow imperial ambitions to fail too. Indeed, by the late nineteenth century, Christian triumphalism was folded into a new kind of imperial nationalism, in which the rule of the world by Britain was sanctioned both by history and faith. The British government shrunk back from its interest in reform as well, ploughing money and concern instead into new technological projects of control and mastery ranging from railways to agricultural canals. The containment of Christian ambition within Europe and the displacement of missionary evangelicalism onto projects of capitalist technological expansion were of course accompanied by the growing sense of irrevocable racial difference. The universal family of Sir William Jones and the racial unity of Aryans posited by Muller became the basis for race theory that cast Britons and Indians in a relationship of absolute difference.[23] Missionary rhetoric was used to celebrate the accomplishments of empire rather than the message of Christ. Even as the empire took on the ideological trappings of a new crusade, missionaries were consigned to the margins of the imperial theatre. Ironically, liberal sentiment took refuge in the margins of missionary frustration both with Indian society and colonial governmental autonomy. Or at least some liberal sentiment was reborn in the unlikely encounters of a few missionaries with subaltern groups in various parts of the subcontinent. While discourses of empire were still largely shared among imperialists and missionaries alike, the internal differences and debates that at certain moments animated the consolidation of imperial authority, at other moments became the fault lines of other kinds of histories.

Victoria's proclamation had unambiguously announced that the British would no longer seek to impose their 'convictions on any of our subjects', and that she would 'strictly charge and enjoin all those who may be in authority under us that they abstain from all interference with the religious belief or worship of any of our subjects on pain of our highest displeasure.' She had further declared that in the 'framing and administration of law, due regard would henceforth be paid to the ancient rights, usages and customs of India.' But while it was clear that the British intended by this never to repeat the provocations—explicit government support for missionization, regular usurpation, and annexation of ancestral and princely lands, and the introduction of military requirements entailing choices between discipline and pollution—that were seen to have led to the revolt, it was equally clear that the British had little idea what non-interference would really mean. If colonial rule retreated from its active phase of colonizing properties and souls, it could hardly stop interfering with India during the years after the rebellion when Britain sought to consolidate its control and make permanent the assumptions and institutions of imperialism. The notion that 'religion' and 'custom' could be genuinely exempted from any interference fell apart in the face of two fundamental flaws in colonial reason: the first that the British did not know how to define either religion or custom; the second that the phase of high imperial rule required the state to appropriate the civilizing mission from the church, both to justify itself at home and in the colonies.

The policy of non-interference thus necessitated a new commitment to colonial knowledge about the subjects of its rule. If the rebellion had put paid to debates over history that had been seen earlier as sufficient justification for the state's claim over revenue and land control, it made the anthropologization of colonial knowledge necessary for several reasons. Ethnographic knowledge could help explain why the rebellion took place, how to avoid such disaffection in the future, new ways to claim the loyalty of subjects on the basis of custom and culture, and how to delineate the autonomous and proper domains of religion and custom. With such knowledge the British could not only avoid interference but, in time, become the primary protectors of India's tradition. Even as the history of colonial conquest could now be conveniently erased, the primacy of history in the rhetorical debates of imperial policy could yield increasingly to other logics and imperatives. It is in this sense that I have argued that colonial rule took on an anthropological cast of mind in the late nineteenth century.

The anthropologization of colonial knowledge proceeded slowly, and in the context of myriad other interests and processes in this period. However, it can hardly be accidental that the decade of the 1860s saw a veritable explosion in the production and circulation of gazetteers and manuals that now included, as a matter of course, extensive reports on the manners and customs of the castes, tribes, and religions of the specific regions being studied. Colonial authors continued to write history, even as they sought with increased concern to adumbrate the moral and material progress of its imperial domains through these and other writings. However, for the first time they began to systematically compile ethnographic facts as if they were administrative necessities rather than antiquarian curiosities. Indeed, much of the new ethnography emerged as part of primary administrative business rather than independent, leave alone antiquarian, research. Most official ethnography, later reported in manuals and then in ethnological catalogues, when it did not come from early missionary accounts, was born in the administrative and policing concerns of late nineteenth-century imperial rule, as the British struggled time after time with the problem of non-interference. Missionaries continued to play an important role off stage, generating sufficient publicity for successive crises to develop around the question of what the colonial state could countenance. Was colonialism on the side of barbarism or civilization, and were there occasions when the colonial power had to take a stand? Did the policy of non-interference hold up under the demands of late nineteenth century high imperialism, when monumental greed and grandeur had to be clothed in the trappings of a civilizing mission, when the moral charter of Christian prosyletization had to be secularized and nationalized as the ground of and justification for imperium? Could an autonomous and sacrosanct sphere of religious belief be separated from a wide range of customs and practices that periodically leaked into public view and made imperial disinterest appear shocking, even barbaric? And what happened when Indian tradition itself became the subject of colonial discipline? But it was the colonial state, not the church, that became the primary actor; and it was the state that was the authoritative adjudicator of Indian tradition.

Colonial ethnography appropriated barbarism from the missionaries in the late nineteenth century. Barbarism was now of interest to science, its scandal as much a justificatory basis for empire as it was something that had to be controlled and periodically contained in order to celebrate the civilizing mission of empire. But by the end of the nineteenth century, the civilizing mission was less urgent, and yielded increasingly to the imperatives of a colonial science that would contain barbarism both through the policing of tradition and the recording of tradition that so frequently emerged out of policing activities. The Victorian policy of non-intervention thus became the charter for a colonial anthropology: involving the delineation of religion, custom, and tradition on the one hand, and the firm maintenance of public order in an imperial regime that held the colonized in place through the knowledge and enlightened protection of tradition on the other. Barbarism was a sign of colonial difference, producing an ever-widening chasm between the subjects and objects of colonial knowledge. And even the benign aspects of tradition, such as the caste system itself, worked both to explain how Indian society could be orderly in the absence of either political authority or tradition, and why it was that Indian society would never become mobilized around the political aims of national self-determination.

After the great rebellion, historical knowledge thus yielded to anthropological knowledge. Caste recapitulated the legacies of tradition, and history was perceived as absent from Indian sensibilities. The Imperial Census represented the apotheosis of this transformation. It also undertook the final conversion of barbarism into civilized data, the transformation of moral condemnation into the moral basis of both science and state. The Census exemplifies ways in which the documentation project of the colonial state attained unprecedented scope, even as the disturbing character of colonial difference became a problem only at the level of documentation. It is perhaps the greatest irony of colonial rule that the very evidence that could finally be accumulated and contained by the extraordinary apparatus of the decennial Census became the basis for the colonial state's ultimate failure to contain both caste and custom. Indeed, it was in relation to the Census that caste resisted the colonial idea of civil society.

H.H. RISLEY, THE CENSUS, AND THE ETHNOLOGICAL SURVEY OF INDIA

Herbert Hope Risley entered the Indian Civil Service in 1873 with a posting in Bengal,[24] where he soon displayed an active interest in W.W. Hunter's statistical survey. In 1875, he was appointed the Assistant Director of Statistics, whereupon he compiled the volume on the hill districts of Hazaribagh and Lohardaga. Although he soon returned to regular service, he was recruited once again several years later to collect detailed information on the castes, tribes, and sociology of Bengal. It was at this time that Risley became convinced that caste endogamy had worked to preserve physical differences among castes in particularly sharp ways. Risley decided to explore whether he could apply to the leading castes and tribes of Bengal, 'the methods of recording and comparing typical physical characteristics which have yielded valuable results in other parts of the world.'[25] Although he was also committed to collecting material about the customs and manners of each group, he felt that there had been far more cultural borrowing and exchange than there had been racial mixing. Using the methods of the French anthropologists Broca and Topinard, Risley began to record the anthropometric details that became the basis for his four-volume work, *The Tribes and Castes of Bengal*.[26] Risley's book was in fact an expanded edition of the Report on the 1891 Census for Bengal, of which he was the supervisor.

As Risley took over the reins of the Census and the ethnological establishment in the wake of his commanding work on Bengal, he found himself relying once again on varna, and more generally on Brahmanical measures and opinions concerning caste rank. Risley seemed unabashed about the scientific status of varna, given his own views on the subject of race. He opened his Bengal book with an account of a stone panel at Sanchi, in which the leader of a procession of monkeys is depicted in an act of reverence and devotion to four stately figures 'of tall stature and regular features'. Whereas most Orientalists had interpreted this scene as a simple act of devotion to the life of the Buddha, Risley found a deeper meaning, 'if it is regarded as the sculptured expression of the race sentiment of the Aryans towards the Dravidians, which runs through the whole course of Indian tradition and survives in scarcely abated strength at the present day.'[27] Risley saw this as another expression of the true moral of the great epic, the Ramayana, in which the army of apes who assisted Rama in the invasion of Ceylon were clearly Dravidians: 'It shows us the higher race on friendly terms with the lower, but keenly conscious of the essential difference of type and not taking part in the ceremony at which they appear as patronising spectators.' Risley went on: 'An attempt is made in the following pages to show that the race sentiment, which this curious sculpture represents, so far from being a figment of the intolerant pride of the Brahman, rests upon a foundation of fact which scientific methods confirm, that it has shaped the intricate groupings of the caste system, and has preserved the Aryan type in comparative purity throughout Northern India.' So for Risley the judgement of science confirmed the attitude of the Brahmin; also race history, and perhaps as importantly race sentiment, was the key to understanding caste.

These inquiries became the basis for much of the material that Risley assembled in his *The Castes and Tribes of Bengal* as well as for the 1891 Census. In retrospect, Risley's reliance on a Brahmanical sociology of knowledge is astounding. He relied almost entirely on Brahmins and other higher castes. He deferred wherever possible to the *Manu Dharma Sastra*s and other Puranic sources that served in part as later commentaries for Manu. And he organized his entire understanding of caste structure and rank according to Brahmanical indices such as the acceptance of food and water, the use of priests, origin stories concerning duties and obligations towards Brahmins as well as about degradation in relation to those duties and obligations, and ritual proximity to and functions relating to Brahmins. Because of his single-minded obsession with the racial origins of caste, he married his own late nineteenth-century version of scientific empiricism with the powerful combination of early nineteenth-century Orientalist knowledge and the clerical Brahmanical opinion that permeated the middle echelons of colonial administration in the localities. Caste might have been justified as a subject of study because it was seen as organizing many administrative matters from famine relief to criminality, but in the same breath it was constituted once again as a Brahmanical ritual system in which the most esoteric forms of social distinction became the basis for administrative knowledge. And despite the efforts of the 1891 Census to downplay matters of social rank and to privilege functional explanations of caste, nowhere did the question of precedence take on greater force than in relation to the Census of 1901.

In 1901, Risley was also appointed the Director of Ethnography for India, both because of his acknowledged pre-eminence as an ethnographer and because the ethnographic survey was designed to be conducted in connection with the Census. In 1899, when the preliminary arrangements for the Census of 1901 were under consideration, the British Association for the Advancement of Science had recommended to the Secretary of State that certain ethnographic investigations should be undertaken in connection with the Census operations. These included an ethnographic survey—'or the systematic description of the history, structure, traditions, and religious and social usages of the various races, tribes and castes in India'—and an anthropometric survey, which would entail the measurements of castes directed to determining the physical types characteristic of particular groups. The Association placed its full faith in Risley: 'The results of the Census itself constitute, of course, by their very nature, an ethnographical document of great value; and my Council feel that, without overburdening the officers of the Census or incurring any very large expense, that value might be increased to a very remarkable degree, if to the enumeration were added the collection of some easily ascertained ethnographical data. They are encouraged to make this suggestion by the reflection that the Census Commissioner is an accomplished ethnographist, well known by his publication on *The Tribes and Castes of Bengal*, the valuable results of which would be supplemented by the inquiries now proposed.'[28] Risley's acclaim can be seen in the attention paid to anthropometry in the proposed survey. The Secretary of State noted, 'It has often been observed that anthropometry yields peculiarly good results in India by reason of the caste system which prevails among Hindus, and of the divisions, often closely resembling castes, which are recognised by Muhammadans. Marriage takes place only within a limited circle; the disturbing element of crossing is to a great extent excluded; and the differences of physical type, which measurement is intended to establish, are more marked and more persistent than anywhere else in the world.' And so Risley's racial theory and anthropometric preoccupations were endorsed by the British government, as they appointed Edgar Thurston to assist him in Madras and empowered Risley to oversee the survey across the rest of British India.

In authorizing funds both for the Director of Ethnography and for the various surveys contemplated over and above the Census operations, the Secretary of State commented on the importance of these investigations. 'It has come to be recognized of late years that India is a vast storehouse of social and physical data which only need to be recorded in order to contribute to the solution of the problems which are being approached in Europe with the aid of material much of which is inferior in quality.... It is unnecessary to dwell at length upon the obvious advantages to many branches of the administration in this country of an accurate and well arranged record of the customs and the domestic and social relations of the various castes and tribes. The entire framework of native life in India is made up of groups of this kind, and the status and conduct of individuals are largely determined by the rules of the group to which they belong. For the purposes of legislation, of judicial procedure, of famine relief, of sanitation and dealings with epidemic disease, and of almost every form of executive action, an ethnographic survey of India and a record of the customs of the people is as necessary an incident of good administration as a cadastral survey of the land and a record of the rights of its tenants.' Using language that was a direct quotation from Risley, the Secretary of State wrote, 'The Census provides the necessary statistics: it remains to bring out and interpret the facts which lie behind the statistics.'[29] No clearer statement could be made of the colonial uses of anthropology, of how by the late nineteenth century the British in India recognized that the task of colonial rule was essentially ethnographic. Virtually no area of governmental policy or activity could be conducted without benefit of extensive anthropological knowledge. The late colonial state was genuinely an ethnographic state.

Risley did not rigidly separate the ethnographic survey, which in the end was never formally completed, from the Census, which stands to this day as a monument to Risley's general influence on colonial anthropology and administration. And while Risley scripted much of the above justification for the conduct of ethnography, his interests were relentlessly 'scientific' rather than attuned to the needs of practical administration. With Risley ethnography escaped the province of statecraft, in the end unleashing a political revolution that the British could neither control nor understand. As we would predict, his commentary on Caste in the 1901 Census is dominated by his interest in race.[30]

Risley began his chapter on caste by repeating his anecdote about Sanchi and racial consciousness, moving quickly into an impassioned defence of the importance of anthropometry. Demonstrating the terrific strides made over craniology by developments within anthropometry, Risley noted that he had introduced scientific anthropometry to India seventeen years before in the ethnographic survey of Bengal. He explained the significance of this scientific revolution in part to counter Mr Nesfield's 'uncompromising denial of the truth of the modern doctrine which divides the population of India into Aryan and aboriginal.'[31] He then turned to a criticism of the 1891 Census, for not altogether unrelated reasons. He averred that the functional grouping of the Census accorded 'neither with native tradition and practice, nor with any theory of caste that has ever been propounded by students of the subject.'[32] He was particularly exercised at the classificatory patchwork that led to such strange affiliations as the grouping within single categories of 'Brahman priests, Mirasi musicians and Bahurupia buffoons', or of the Dravidian Khandaits of Orissa with Rajputs, Jats, and Marathas.

Risley insisted upon the principle of 'social precedence as recognised by native public opinion'. He was convinced that distinctions predicated on the centrality of Brahmins and involving matters of rank on the basis of ritual distinctions would be far more helpful in understanding the nature of the caste system as a whole. He prepared criteria for understanding caste distinction that could have served as research guidelines for the latter-day students of cultural anthropology: 'that Brahmans will take water from certain castes; that Brahmans of high standing will serve particular castes; that certain castes, though not served by the best Brahmans, have nevertheless got Brahmans of their own, whose rank varies according to circumstances; that certain castes are not served by Brahmans at all but have priests of their own; that the status of certain castes has been raised by their taking to infant-marriage or abandoning the remarriage of widows; that the status of some castes has been lowered by their living in a particular locality; that the status of others has been modified by their pursuing some occupation in a special or peculiar way; that some can claim the services of the village barber, the village palanquin-bearer, the village midwife, etc., while others cannot; that some castes may not enter the courtyards of certain temples; that some castes are subject to special taboos, such as that they must not use the village well, or may draw water only with their own vessels, that they must live outside the village or in a separate quarter, that they must leave the road on the approach of a high-caste man or must call out to give warning of their approach. In the case of the Animistic tribes it was mentioned that the prevalence of totemism and the degree of adoption of Hindu usage would serve as ready tests.'[33] That Risley was so invested in the minutiae of caste status, to the point of certifying practices such as infant marriage or the prohibition of widow remarriage at a time of active social reform movements across India, and that Risley's investment was in the context of the administrative enumeration of the population of India, suggests both the extent to which caste had been naturalized as the colonized form of civil society, and the way in which an anthropological imaginary dominated colonial knowledge at this time. Anthropology was no longer merely an administrative tool, but an administrative episteme.

Risley returned to the use of varna as the basis for enumeration and classification, as befitted both his resort to Brahmanical opinion and his interest in social rank. He clearly believed that present-day castes were the 'modern representatives of one or other of the castes of the theoretical Hindu system'. Accordingly, 'In every scheme of grouping the Brahman heads the list. Then come the castes whom popular opinion accepts as the modern representatives of the Kshatriyas, and these are followed by the mercantile groups supposed to be akin to the Vaisyas.' As always, Risley was on less sure ground when he left 'the higher circles of the twice-born', for it was here that the difficulty of classification by rank was legion. Thus his seventh category, after the three twice born castes and the castes 'allied' to them, was 'castes of good social position distinctly superior to that of the remaining groups'. The degree to which Aryan blood was retained by a group was marked by the direction in which women were exchanged hypergamously or endogamously, and by exchanges of food, water, and services between castes, and thus the eighth category was made up of castes from whom some of the twice-born would take some kinds of food and water. For these 'Sudras' and other mixed castes, Risley was aware that the criteria for social precedence varied considerably by region. Not only did the Sudra category vary greatly in social status, it made up the dominant groups in most parts of western and southern India, where in any case Brahmins would only take food and water from their own caste or sub-caste. In many parts of north and north-west India, exchanges with Brahmins among other castes were possible and determined ritual status among high castes, but strangely it was in these very areas that the status of Brahmins seemed less secure than where no exchanges were countenanced. Varna also seemed of little value for non-Hindu populations, but Risley—once again using his extensive research and correspondence of earlier years—noted, 'In India, however, caste is in the air; its contagion has spread even to the Muhammedans; and we find its evolution proceeding on characteristically Hindu lines.'[34] Risley also contemplated the extent to which caste might be breaking down as a consequence of new ideas and institutions, and determined that technological change such as the introduction and extension of the railways was having a paradoxical effect. Railways worked to diffuse Brahmanical influence, education to expand the reach of Hindu scriptures. While greater 'laxity' in matters of food and drink might be observed in some cases, Risley noted that he observed 'a more rigid observance of the essential incidents of caste'.[35] And Risley repeated his critiques of other theorists of caste (most especially Nesfield), reiterating his own view that the dominant factor in the formation of caste was the conquest of one race by another. Marriage restrictions developed around the two races, and then were further elaborated around the groups that were born of mixed unions. The principle of the caste system rests on the distinctions of race.[36] 'Once started in India the principle was strengthened, perpetuated, and extended to all ranks of society by the fiction that people who speak a different language, dwell in a different district, worship different gods, eat different food, observe different social customs, follow a different profession, or practise the same profession in a slightly different way must be so unmistakeably aliens by blood that intermarriage with them is a thing not to be thought of.'[37] And for Risley, the principle was enshrined in the person of the Brahmin and the doctrine of karma.

The ultimate proof for Risley of the wisdom of his system was the great number of petitions and memorials to which it gave rise. Census officers had received similar petitions and representations since the first Census, but the announcement by Risley that the Census would be reorganized on the basis of social precedence made the Census into a political instrument in a way it had never been before. Risley noted several major struggles, including an attempt by Khatris of the Punjab and United Provinces to be classified as Rajputs which was ultimately successful, asserting that these efforts vindicated his belief that 'the sole test of social precedence ... was native public opinion.'[38] For the most part, of course, Risley used the opinion of just a small group of 'natives', overwhelmingly the class of official Brahmins and higher castes with whom he had such a regular ethnographic correspondence over the years, to develop the textual and ethnographic parameters for the assignment of social status and the determination of categories. And yet he had no real conception that the list of social precedence could become a political document rather than a detached scientific survey. He was unable to respond to the politics his system unleashed.

Risley's ethnological report on the 1901 Census of India was republished, with some additions and revisions, as *The People of India* in 1908.[39] The most significant revision was the addition of a single concluding chapter, entitled, 'Caste and Nationality'. Risley wished to address in this chapter the effects of recent social and economic change on caste, as well as to speculate about whether caste would be 'favourable or adverse to the growth of a consciousness of common nationality among the people of India,'[40] perhaps in response to the clear indications of a developing nationalist movement that had erupted after the partition of Bengal in 1905. Risley obviously believed in the importance of caste; he wrote that it was the cement that held Indian society together. And he had little but scorn for those 'philanthropic' Englishmen who, on the basis of their experience of Presidency towns, predict the immediate demise of caste. He wrote that 'anarchy is the peculiar peril of a society that is organized on the basis of caste,' noting that ancient Indian monarchy had functioned well precisely because it could control caste antipathies, at the same time that it could take advantage of the exclusion of most castes from politics. But for the same reason, caste hardly contributed to the formation of an idea of common nationality. 'So long as a regime of caste persists, it is difficult to see how the sentiment of unity and solidarity can penetrate and inspire all classes of the community, from the highest to the lowest, in the manner that it has done in Japan where, if true caste ever existed, restrictions on intermarriage have long ago disappeared.'[41] British influence, both through the common study among Indian elites of English history and literature, and through the 'consciousness of being united and drawn together by living under a single government,'[42] had begun to suggest the possibility of change. However, for Risley, change would have to occur through traditional means, both because the vast majority of Indians were yet untouched by the idea of nationality, and because the construction of an idea of nationality would best be built on the foundation of traditional institutions, such as the village community and the village council, 'the common property of the Aryan people both in Europe and in India'. Thus Risley's racial theory predicated his hope for India's national future, even politics served as his retreat, even as he cautioned Indian nationalists against the temptation of sudden change. In the most paternalist of ways, he concluded his chapter by advocating the 'orderly development of the indigenous germs of such institutions', warning at the same time that progress would in any case be slow.[43]

Risley's final ethnographic contribution to colonial knowledge thus reiterated the divisiveness of caste, as well as its fundamentally compatibility with politics only in the two registers of ancient Indian monarchy or modern Britain's 'benevolent despotism'.[44] He warned Indian nationalists and European liberals not to give in either to 'impatient idealism' or a belief in the force of modern change in India. And he did so by invoking the full authority of an anthropological view of India which reckoned India as fundamentally unpolitical and caste as essentially divisive. Indeed, caste was the basic obstacle. As he wrote: 'Were its cohesive power withdrawn or its essential ties relaxed, it is difficult to form an idea of the probable consequences. Such a change would be like a revolution; it would resemble the withdrawal of some elemental force like gravitation or molecular attraction. Order would vanish and chaos would supervene'.[45] He did not mention that this revolution would be pitted against British rule in India, rather suggesting that the kind of revolution envisioned perhaps by Indian nationalists would be in the order of a natural disaster. Change could only be gradual, the introduction of something akin to representative politics only the eventual outcome of the cultivation of village forms of political representation and activity. Risley's own antipathy to change, whether expressed in relationship to his implicit advocacy of Brahmanic customs in the face of pressures for social reform, or in his consternation that the enumeration of caste by rank would unleash a politics that his own social theory could not explain, was of course profoundly mired in his commitment to race science. It is hard to think of another 'impartial' observer of society in the Indian context who had so profound an impact on the very society he observed. It is also hard to imagine another figure who so admired India's ancient constitution precisely because of the ways it enshrined a late nineteenth-century European conception of race.

If Risley's views on caste so clearly mark his imperial conceit, they also reflect a curious conjuncture in the history of empire. Risley, whose advocacy of race science was akin to that of Galton and other late nineteenth-century eugenicists, fashioned a peculiar exchange between the racial anxieties of imperial Britain and the ritual anxieties of Brahmins and other higher castes at the turn of the century. While Risley was so obsessively committed to the measuring of skulls and bodies and the appropriation of the enumerative project of the Census by his zeal to prove a racial theory of origins, he found a strange kinship with his interlocutors in the imperial theatre of India. Brahmans used their late imperial access to political privilege to deny the political character of their influence. Meanwhile, the British relied on Brahmin knowledge; at the same time they denied Brahmins any real relation to the racial privilege they sought, despite all the claims about Aryan affinity, to preserve for themselves. All this was accomplished with the authority of ancient Brahmanic knowledge, both textual traditions that had been authorized by Orientalist knowledge, and ethnographic assumptions that were confirmed by 'native' informants. And so the British enumerators kept returning, despite all the manifold difficulties, to a reliance on the old varna scale for their all-India enumerations, even as they maintained a keen interest in caste as fundamentally about rank and social precedence.

At a time of resounding efforts to engage in social reform against Brahmanic privilege, Risley directed the full apparatus of colonial power to the task of using India to prove the truth of racial difference. In his enterprise, he accepted Brahmin claims about the superiority of such customs as the prohibition of widow remarriage or the importance of infant marriage, even as he rejected the claims of manifestly non-Aryan racial groups to twice-born status. One imagines that Risley would have set himself up as an ancient Indian monarch if only he could, adjudicating competing claims over status with callipers in one hand and statistical tables about nasal indices in the other. And in his last work on caste he effectively denied the capacity of Indians for the formation of an idea of nationality, let alone self-rule. At a time when India was beginning to mobilize the momentous struggle of nationalism in such early theatres as the struggles of Savarkar and Tilak in western India and the Swadeshi movement in Bengal, Risley used his racial theory of caste to vindicate his views that nationality would be unable to explode the tenacious grip of caste feeling. Race could simultaneously explain Britain's imperial role in India and India's inability to contest it. And while race justified Risley's imperial project, it also became the unfortunate wedge by which Risley's not inconsiderable influence, on the subsequent careers of imperialism and nationalism both, would be felt in the years to come.

If Risley's racial vision gave the Census an especially significant role in the production of modern caste identities in India, it also provided the ideological basis for an even more dramatic contribution to the modern rise of communalism. As Home Secretary to the Indian government, a position he assumed after his stint as Director of Ethnography, Risley played a key role in the 1903 proposal that Bengal be partitioned into two provinces, in large part because of the political benefits thought to attend the separation of the politically threatening Hindu minority from the majority Muslim population.[46] A few years later, Risley argued strongly against the view of John Morley, Secretary of State for India, that serious political reforms were necessary in the wake of the agitation over the 1905 partition, in particular the Swadeshi movement of 1905–7. Risley was against territorial representation and parliamentary government for India, and used the demand of the newly-formed Muslim League for separate electorates to make his case. In the end, the award of separate electorates for Muslims in the Morley– Minto reforms of 1909 was in large part the result of the energetic role played by Risley, who used his ethnological view of India to make one of the most influential, and deadly, decisions of Britain's colonial era.[47] It was this award of separate electorates in 1909 that set the stage for the demand for Pakistan and the eventual partition of the subcontinent.[48] Risley's anthropology worked not so much to retard nationalism as to render it communal. In so doing, it also left a bloody legacy for South Asia that continues to exact a mounting toll.

☆ ☆ ☆

Thus the anthropological transformation of colonial state interest played out the larger story of empire. In this story, power became an end in itself and never felt checked by the need for legitimation or accountability. As Hannah Arendt has noted, 'It is characteristic of imperialism that national institutions remain separate from the colonial administration although they are allowed to exercise control. The actual motivation for this separation was a curious mixture of arrogance and respect: the new arrogance of the administrators abroad who faced "backward populations" or "lower breeds" found its correlative in the respect of old fashioned statesmen at home who felt that no nation had the right to impose its law upon a foreign people. It was in the very nature of things that the arrogance turned out to be a device for rule, while the respect, which remained entirely negative, did not produce a new way for peoples to live together, but managed only to keep the ruthless imperialist rule by decree within bounds.'[49] But Arendt did not understand the extent to which these bounds only worked to serve imperial power, substituting culture for civil society, tradition for politics, and total domination for any expectation of a democratic relationship to the exercise of power. This symbiosis was expressed in the development of colonial anthropology, in which ethnographic accounts of the social became quite literally the history of the colonized. Knowledge about India was largely produced by or in terms of the logic of colonial rule, the imperatives and institutions of the colonial state.

It was unfortunate enough that the colonial state began its career in India as an extractive state, disrupting the circuits of political and economic vitality that have been by now so well demonstrated by generations of historians during the long eighteenth century. But in retrospect one might argue that things became worse, in the short and long runs, when the colonial state converted itself from an extractive state to an ethnographic state in the late nineteenth century. Not only did the ethnographic state continue to rule long after its contradictions unleashed the historical inevitability of partition, it also worked to legitimate not just the nationalism of a figure like Savarkar, but also the extreme nationalist ethnographic imaginaries that have converted parody into tragedy time after time in contemporary South Asia. Arrogance and respect combined in the colonial embrace to leave lasting legacies of communal discord and national struggle.

NOTES

1. This essay is a revised version of a paper first delivered at the International Conference on the State in India, held in Kyoto in December 1999. It is based on and summarizes the argument of a longer work, *Castes of Mind: Colonialism and the Making of Modern India* (Princeton: Princeton University Press, 2001).

2. Sir Sayyid Ahmad Khan's *History of the Bijnor Rebellion*, translated with notes and introduction by Hafeez Mallik and Morris Dembo, published by Asian Studies Center, Michigan State University, East Lansing, Michigan.

3. Ibid., p. 122.

4. Ibid., p. 124.

5. Ibid.

6. Ibid., p. 126.

7. Letter of 1869 to Sir John Kaye, from Sir Syed Ahmed, dated 14 December 1869, enclosed in ibid.

8. Notes by Frere and Outram of 28 March 1860 in Canning Papers Miscellaneous, No. 558, quoted in T.R. Metcalf, 1964, *Aftermath of Revolt*, Princeton: Princeton University Press, p. 91.

9. See John W. Kaye, 1875, *A History of the Sepoy War in India 1857–1858*, 3 Vols, London, 7th edn; G.B. Malleson, 1896, *History of the Indian Mutiny*, 3 Vols, London.

10. C.H. Philips *et al.* (eds), 1962, *The Evolution of India and Pakistan, 1857–1947: Select Documents*, London: Oxford University Press, pp. 10–11.

11. T. Metcalf, 1964, *Ideologies of the Raj*, Cambridge: Cambridge University Press, p. 48.

12. Ibid.

13. F. Max Muller, 1867, 'Caste, 1858', in Muller, *Chips from a German Workshop*, London: Longmans, Green, and Co.

14. Duncan Forrester, 1980, *Caste and Christianity*, London: Curzon Press, p. 57.

15. Quoted in Forrester, p. 33.

16. Minutes of the Madras Missionary Conference on the Subject of Caste, printed for the Conference at the American Mission Press, 1850, p. 1.

17. Ibid., p. 4.

18. Calcutta, 1858.

19. Forrester, pp. 55–6.

20. Muller, pp. 318–19.

21. Ibid., p. 355.

22. Ibid.

23. See Thomas Trautmann, 1998, *Aryans and British India*, Berkeley: University of California Press.

24. H.H. Risley, only son of Rev. John Holford Risley, Rector of Akeley, was born on 4 January 1851. He went to Winchester and Oxford, where he was selected for an appointment in the Indian Civil Service before his graduation in 1872. He stayed in India until 1910, when he was appointed as Permanent Secretary in the India Office, a post he only held for a short time, as he died in September 1911.

25. H.H. Risley, 1891, *The Tribes and Castes of Bengal*, Calcutta: Secretariat Press, Preface, p. xix.

26. *Man*, 1901, Nos 112–13, p. 137.

27. Risley, *op. cit.*, 1891, p. i.

28. Letter from Michael Foster to the Secretary of State for India, December 1899, in Extract No. 3219–32 from the Proceedings of the Government of India in the Home Department (Public), under date Simla, 23 May 1901.

29. Resolution of the Government of India, Home Department (Public) No. 3919, 23 May 1901, Simla.

30. *Census of India, 1901*, Vol. I., Part I, Report, by H.H. Risley, with the assistance of E.A. Gait, Chapter XI, pp. 489–557.

31. Report on the Census, 1901, p. 493.

32. Report on the Census, 1901, p. 538.

33. Report on the Census, 1901, p. 538.

34. Report, p. 543.

35. Report, p. 544.

36. Risley did not believe that caste was confined to India. 'It occurs in a pronounced form in the southern States of the American Commonwealth, where Negroes intermarry with Negroes, and the various mixed races mulattos, quadrrons, and octoroons each have a sharply restricted *jus connubii* of their own and are absolutely cut off from legal unions with the white races (555).'

37. Report, p. 556.

38. Report, p. 539.

39. H.H. Risley, 1915, *The People of India*, second edn, London: W. Thacker.

40. Ibid., p. 287.

41. Ibid., p. 293.

42. Ibid., p. 294.

43. Ibid., p. 301.

44. Ibid., p. 281.

45. Ibid., p. 278.

46. See, for example, Sumit Sarkar's thorough discussion of this in his *The Swadeshi Movement in Bengal, 1903–1908*, New Delhi: People's Publishing House (1973).

47. See Hermann Kulke and Dietmar Rothermund, 1986, *A History of India*, New York: Routledge Press, pp. 271–2.

48. See Ayesha Jalal, 1985, *The Sole Spokesman: Jinnah, the Muslim League and the Demand for Pakistan*, Cambridge: Cambridge University Press.

49. Hannah Arendt, 1979, *The Origins of Totalitarianism*, New York: Harcourt Brace.

SECTION III

Ideas and Problematics of the State

CHAPTER 9

The Secularity of the State

Peter van der Veer

INTRODUCTION

In recent years much doubt has been thrown on the secularity of the Indian state, colonial and post-colonial, and about the ultimate triumph of secularism. The anthropologist T.N. Madan has, for instance, argued that 'secularism as a widely shared worldview has failed to make headway in India'.[1] Indians comprise followers of a number of religions such as Hinduism, Islam, Buddhism, Sikhism etc., they are not Protestant Christians in majority. They cannot and will not privatize their religion.[2] Madan points out that in sociological theory, especially that of Max Weber, there is an essential linkage between Protestantism, individualism, and secularization. He argues, accordingly, that secularism is a 'gift of Christianity to mankind' and that it is part of the unique history of Europe.[3] The secularity of the Indian state has been the subject of much scepticism at least since the publication of Donald Smith's work in the early 1960s.[4] Madan expresses what appears to be a general consensus among both social scientists and the general public that the modern West is uniquely secular and the East uniquely religious. The problem with this consensus is that it reduces complex and diverse histories to the binary opposition of secularity and religiosity. The history of religiosity and secularity in Western societies is varied and complex; the same can be said about Indian society and, as I have argued elsewhere, these histories are not separate, but interact within the imperial framework.[5] Nevertheless, the appeal of these essentializations cannot be dismissed by providing ever more complicated narratives of social change. It is in fact hard to go beyond theories of modernization and secularization, however much one tries to get away from them. One is compelled to address the conceptual complexities and contradictions involved in them. This is required more because of the moral and political judgements which pertain to the question of the secularity of the state and its implications for liberty and tolerance.

Historically, it is important to understand the secular and the religious as mutually interdependent. Their definition cannot be separately reached, but depends on this structural relationship. This interdependence is crucial in the formation of the nation state, but that formation follows different historical trajectories in different societies. Here I want to limit the discussion to what I see as the central feature of the idea of secular modernity—the separation of church and state. I will examine this feature in the context of the imperial encounter of India and Britain.

THE SEPARATION OF CHURCH AND STATE

According to historian Owen Chadwick, Britain developed a 'secular' atmosphere of public life between 1860 and 1890.[6] The question is what a 'secular' atmosphere entails in this period of high nationalism and high imperialism. Perhaps the most significant historical development in this regard is the building of a 'wall of separation' between Church and State, to use Thomas Jefferson's language.[7] The European wars of religion of the sixteenth and seventeenth centuries had been concerned precisely with the question of the relation between political and ecclesiastical authority. They were fought around the central issue of political loyalty: can one be loyal to the state when one is not following the religion of the state?[8] As Hobbes and other political thinkers realized, it was the nature of the state which was at issue here. The outcome of the political revolutions of the late eighteenth century was that political loyalty could rest on citizenship instead of membership of the state-church. The relationship between these two, however, was differently decided in different societies depending on their historical trajectories. Both the American and the French revolutions put an end to the association between royal absolutism and the established church. The French revolution developed into something decidedly anti-clerical in its secularism (*laicite*) and carried a direct attack on religious institutions. The American revolution carried the spirit of religious dissent from Britain to American shores and was aimed at gaining religious freedom from oppressive state interference. In Britain itself, disestablishment has even today not been carried out fully, although the early nineteenth century saw the gradual enfranchisement of Catholics and Dissenters.

The location of religion is therefore different in these societies and the expression 'secular society' does not do justice to these differences.

Secularism as a set of arguments in favour of a separation of Church and State has a genealogy in the Enlightenment, but these arguments work out very differently in a variety of historical formations. If it does so already in the interconnected spheres of philosophical and political radicalism of France, Britain, and America, one should not be at all surprised that it also does in the interconnected spheres of Britain and India. The separation of Church and State is often conceptualized in relation to liberty and a way to approach the secular is thus through the question of freedom as posed in the liberal tradition by John Stuart Mill (1806–73).

In his celebrated essay *On Liberty* (1859), Mill argues for complete liberty of opinion and the expression thereof and thus advocates a free exchange of ideas, close to what Jurgen Habermas has called '*burgerliche Öffentlichkeit*' or 'bourgeois public sphere'. Critics of this view have generally objected that the liberal public sphere does exclude certain groups of people. It is in that connection interesting to read the motto of Mill's famous essay, taken from Wilhelm von Humboldt's *Sphere and Duties of Government* (1792): 'The grand, leading principle, towards which every argument unfolded in these pages directly converges, is the absolute and essential importance of human development in its richest diversity'.[9] This in fact contains the principle of exclusion in Mill's views on liberty:

> It is perhaps unnecessary to say that this doctrine is meant to apply only to human beings in the maturity of their faculties. We are not speaking of children, or of young persons below that age which the law may fix as that of manhood or womanhood. Those who are still in a state to require being taken care of by others, must be protected against their own actions as well as against external injury. For the same reason, we may leave out of consideration those backward states of society in which the race itself may be considered in its nonage. The early difficulties in the way of spontaneous progress are so great, that there is seldom any choice of means for overcoming them; and a ruler full of spirit of improvement is warranted in the use of any expedients that will attain an end, perhaps otherwise unattainable. Despotism is a legitimate mode of government in dealing with barbarians, provided the end be their improvement, and the means justified by actually effecting that end. Liberty, as a principle, has no application to any state of things anterior to the time when mankind have become capable of being improved by free and equal discussion. Until then, there is nothing for them but implicit obedience to an Akbar or Charlemagne, if they are so fortunate as to find one. But as soon as mankind

have attained the capacity of being guided to their own improvement by conviction or persuasion (a period long reached in all nations with whom we need here concern ourselves), compulsion, either in the direct form or in that of pains of penalties for non-compliance, is no longer admissible as a means to their own good, and justifiable only for the security of others.[10]

I have reproduced this long quotation from Mill's essay, because it lays out so clearly that his concern is with liberty in the service of progress. It depends on the notion that some societies are at a lower stage of evolution. Such a notion of evolutionary stages had already been developed in the Scottish Enlightenment and is the basis of all historical thought in the nineteenth century. Societies at lower stages of evolution have to be educated like children to make them capable of enjoying freedom. Mill is not in any simple way prejudiced in racial or religious terms, as his position in the controversy over the behaviour of Governor Eyre in Jamaica and in his response to the Indian Mutiny shows. For instance, in a long footnote on the British response to the Mutiny later in the essay he accuses both Evangelicals and the state of persecution of Muslims and Hindus. His position allows for the toleration of diverse religious opinions, but only if they already belong to modern civilization and thus contribute to the moral principle of progress. One has to be free to be able to express oneself freely; that is the idea. Mill's view allows him to be at the same time a radical advocate of freedom and a supporter of enlightened (progressive) imperialism. It is not insignificant to remember here that it is not only evolutionary theory which leads him to claim freedom at home and support despotism in the colony, but also his lifelong employment in the service of the East India Company where, at the end of his career, he held the highest administrative position, a post earlier held by his father, James Mill. Evolutionary theory is therefore not just a grand narrative of progress and modernity, but belongs to the mutual predicament of nationalism and imperialism.

The evolutionary difference between metropole and colony is simply asserted by Mill, not argued. His argument is about progress and liberty and it uses religion as its foil. Both the Roman Catholic church ('the most intolerant of churches') and Calvinist churches are depicted by Mill as intolerant institutions which only when they cannot convert others to their opinion by force or persuasion reluctantly accept difference of opinion.[11] It is of great concern to Mill to defend the right of atheists and blasphemers to express their opinion and he defends that right by arguing that Christ was put to death as a blasphemer.[12] The persecution of Christians as heretics is his main historical example in his argument for liberty. He rejects firmly the idea that Christian doctrine provides a complete morality, while at the same time arguing that the recorded teachings of Christ contain nothing that contradicts what a comprehensive morality requires.[13]

As remarkable as his defence of unbelief and blasphemy and his attacks on Calvinism are Mill's examples from comparative religion. He cites the Muslim prohibition of the eating of pork and the tendency that in a society in which the majority is Muslim, the eating of pork is prohibited. He compares that to the Puritanical prohibition of dancing and music in regions where they have the majority and to sabbatarian regulations. Mill's conclusion is unequivocal. Individuals and minorities have to be protected against the religious sentiments of the majority. Again, this line of argument has a history in the persecution of dissenters by the state and the established church in the seventeenth and eighteenth centuries and the response to that in America by Jefferson (as well as Madison and other 'founding fathers') with the separation of Church and State.

The idea that it is especially religion which is a threat to freedom of thought and expression and thus to an open public sphere as the basis of a democratic nation-state has thus a history in the Enlightenment, is firmly established in the liberal tradition, and indeed is expressed till the present day. An example is a recent argument by the philosopher Charles Taylor. According to Taylor, 'secularism in some form is a necessity for the democratic life of religiously diverse societies'.[14] In his view democracy needs 'what used to be called patriotism, a strong identification with the polity, and a willingness to give of oneself for its sake'.[15] The legitimacy of modern nation-states depends on participation and a relatively strong commitment on the part of citizens. When groups are systematically excluded from the process of decision-making, the legitimacy of rule is under challenge. That is why the nation, according to Taylor, should not be defined in religious terms, since that definition would exclude groups with religious allegiances that are different from the majority population. He suggests that exclusion by religious majorities often goes from barely tolerating the presence of a minority to its expulsion.

The 'secular atmosphere' in the second part of the nineteenth century, which Owen Chadwick refers to, may indicate the fact that the question of political loyalty does not immediately emerge when citizens follow different religions in the modern nation-state. The loyalty to one's king and state does not follow from one's religious affiliation, but from one's national identity, of which religion can be one ingredient among others. It is nationalism which replaces religion in this regard and one can come to nationalism via a variety of religious affiliations. Another way of expressing this is that in the modern era religions are nationalized. There is not much reason to fear a religious majority more than a secular majority as far as the treatment of minorities in a modern, democratic polity is concerned, but an understanding of European history, based upon a particular Enlightenment tradition, as highlighted for instance in Peter Gay's work, leads Eurocentric thinkers to assume a connection between secularity, tolerance, and freedom.[16] The assumption that religious views are absolute and allow no tolerance for difference may be true in theory, but historical record shows that people with different religious opinions have lived in a variety of polities without immediately coming to violent conflict with each other.[17] Historical record also shows that in Britain the nineteenth century was a century of considerable religious expansion in a number of spheres of life without open, violent conflict. Although anti-Catholicism continued to be a strong element in forging a Protestant national identity during the nineteenth century, the Gordon Riots of 1780 were the last seriously violent outburst of that antagonism. The kind of violent religious conflict Britain was involved in the nineteenth century was increasingly directed outward and, of course, related to the colonial project. Separation of Church and State did not lead to the decline of the social and political importance of religion. With the rise of the nation-state, there was an enormous shift in what religion meant. Religion produced the secular as much as vice versa, but this interaction can only be understood in the context of the emergence of nationalism in the nineteenth century. And, in the case of Britain, when we deal with the national, we deal simultaneously with the imperial.

POLITICAL LOYALTY AND THE PUBLIC SPHERE

The question of political loyalty in the colony is different from that in the metropole. The culturally diverse plural states, which preceded British imperial control over India, depended on the collaboration of Muslim and Hindu elites of a variety of sectarian affiliations. That the people would have religions different from that of the rulers and that these rulers would extend royal patronage to these other religions had been a historical fact in most of these states for a long time. The British

East India Company initially just conformed to this established pattern of rule. From 1817 onwards, the Government of Madras took over direct responsibility for the administration and upkeep of Hindu temples and rituals. This looks like the establishment of a direct relation between British rule and Hindu religion which makes Robert Frykenberg speak of a de facto 'Hindu Raj'.[18] This led in Britain to strong protests from Evangelicals who formed an Anti-Idolatry Connexion League. These Christian protesters demanded from the government that the British would at least be 'neutral' towards native (Hindu or Muslim) institutions and at best support Christian missionization in India.

The anti-Hindu rhetoric of the opponents of the government's policy aroused public consciousness among Hindus that their religion was under attack.[19] This consciousness was further strengthened by the facts of missionization and conversion. A great number of organizations emerged in south India in the 1820s and 1830s to resist the missionary onslaught. We find thus an extraordinary situation in which the colonial officials desire to infiltrate into the native, religious institutions and to rule by patronage in the Indian tradition, but in which also movements outside the state challenge these policies, demand a secular state, and transform the nature of religion in significant ways. According to Frykenberg, this dialectic of aggressive missionization and Hindu resistance created a public sphere in south India in the nineteenth century which does not at all evoke the image of a 'secular atmosphere'. Secularity and religion receive particular historical meanings in this atmosphere of debate, however. The Government of Madras was forced by the anti-idolatry activists to retreat from its policies and accept a new policy of 'non-interference', made into law in 1863. This left the administration and upkeep of Hindu temples and rituals to new, emergent elites which used the British legal apparatus to create a new, 'corporate Hinduism' which was fully modern.[20] These elites were not only interested in controlling Hindu institutions which (especially in south India) were quite powerful and immediately connected to political control, but also had a reformist agenda concerning religious education, ritual action, and customs which is crucial even today.[21]

The question of political loyalty in India led the British first to follow the established pattern of religious patronage, but religious activism in Britain made them change this policy into 'non-interference', that is secularity. The shift of their policy towards religious institutions is similar to the shift from Orientalism to Anglicism in educational policy in colonial India. It is remarkable to see that both in the American colony and in the Indian colony it is the Christian dissenters who try to erect 'a wall of separation' between Church and State. The hostility of religious people towards liberty that Mill assumes is belied by the great push towards freedom of religious opinion made by dissenters. Obviously, their aim is not to create a 'secular atmosphere' or a secularization of society. On the contrary, their aim is minimally not to be hindered by the state in their efforts to convert people in a free market of opinion, and maximally to have that aim supported by the state. Certainly, white settler society in America had a very different relation with the British state than the Indian colony and therefore the reasons for secularization of the state were quite different. The effects in both cases, however, were not that dissimilar in allowing an expansion of religious activity in civil society.

The separation of Church and State in Britain took place gradually and partially in the nineteenth century. A major step was the enfranchisement of religious minorities, such as the Catholics and Dissenters, which resulted in the shift of the site of political loyalty from religious identity to national identity. Religious institutions and practices were crucial in the formation of national identities, but gradually in the second half of the nineteenth century the opposition between Britain as a Protestant nation and France as a Catholic nation became less relevant than the opposition between a Christian, civilized nation and colonized peoples without civilized religions. Race took over the place of religion as the most important marker of difference, but there religion and race were often combined. Enlightened Christianity belonged to a stage in the process of civilization to which the British had proceeded. The conclusion is that, *pace* Taylor, it is not so much that religion cannot be allowed to enter the public sphere in order to let the modern nation-state exist, but that religion creates the public sphere and in doing so is transformed and moulded into a national form.

In India, obviously, political loyalty could not be transferred from the religious to the national. When the period of religious patronage of native institutions had come to a close under evangelical pressure, the British did not only attempt not to interfere with native religions, but also did much to disavow any connection to the missionary project and to Christianity as such. One can indeed speak of a definite secularity of the British state in India which was much stronger than in Britain itself. The British considered a sharp separation of Church and State essential to their ability to govern India. Their attempts to develop a neutral religious policy in a society in which religious institutions played an important political role could not be anything but ambivalent. Both in the management of south Indian Hindu temples and north Indian Sikh and Muslim shrines, the colonial government remained involved, despite all efforts to the contrary.[22] Nevertheless, externality and neutrality became the tropes of a state which tried to project itself as playing the role of a transcendent arbiter in a country divided along religious lines. Again, however, this did not contribute to a secular atmosphere in society. Indian religions were transformed in opposition to the state and religion became more important in the emergent public sphere. As in Britain, religion was transformed and moulded in a national form, but that form defined itself in opposition to the colonizing state. The denial of participation in the political institutions of the colony led Indians to develop an alternative set of institutions of a jointly political and religious nature. Indians did not conceive the colonial state as neutral and secular, but rather as fundamentally Christian. As Nita Kumar puts it, 'The Sanskritists of Banaras today have a collective memory of a threat in mid-nineteenth century when government wanted to anglicize and Christianize them'.[23] Similarly, popular conceptions of British rule, as evident in the Cow Protection Movement of the 1880s, portrayed it as of an alien, Christian nature. When in 1888 the North-Western Provincial High Court decreed that the cow was not a sacred object and thus did not have to be protected by the state, the decision galvanized the movement not only against Muslims, but also against the Christian rule of 'cow-eaters'.[24] When the state started to use religion among its Census categories, it came itself to be understood in religious categories. A distinct feeling that the modernizing project of the colonial state was based on Western values and thus Christian in nature remained important. This feeling was further enhanced by the fact that many high-ranking officials were self-conscious Christians who felt it their duty to support the missionizing effort. Perhaps one of the best examples of this kind of official was John Muir (1810–88) who served in the North-Western Provinces as an administrator and was a qualified Sanskritist who reorganized the Sanskrit College at Benares in the mid-1840s. Muir wrote a critical examination of Hinduism in Sanskrit, the *Mataparīksha* (1839) and was responded to by three Hindu pandits.[25] While these were intellectual challenges and responses, one cannot ignore the fact that John Muir was not simply a philosopher posing some intellectual questions, but a high-ranking colonial official whose views had a considerable impact on issues of education. At the same time it is important to see how

Muir's theological position vis-à-vis Christianity developed in the course of his dialogue with Hindus from a negative evangelical stance to a more conciliatory and intellectual one.

Although the legitimizing rituals and discourses of the colonial state were those of development, progress, and evolution and meant to be secular, they could indeed easily be understood as essentially Christian. The response both the state and the missionary societies provoked was also decidedly religious. Hindu and Islamic forms of modernism led to the establishment of modern Hindu and Muslim schools, universities, and hospitals, superseding or marginalizing pre-colonial forms of education in Muslim *madrasas* and Hindu *pathshalas*. Far from having a secularizing influence on Indian society, the modernizing project of the secular, colonial state, in fact, gave religion a strong new impulse.

The separation of Church and State as the sign of secularity did not result in a secular society in Britain or in India, but indicated a shift in the location of religion in society from being part of the state to being part of a newly emerging public sphere. This was a historical development that took place between 1750 and 1850 and one that was perhaps best exemplified by the emergence of voluntary, missionary societies in the 1790s and the emergence of Hindu voluntary, revivalist societies in the 1820s. The crucial term here is 'voluntary', that is fully independent of the state, financing its activities with its own means. It is also important to observe here that while there was an element of 'response' to missionary activities in Hindu revivalism, it is also true that the missionary societies themselves responded to the imperial project and received their significance within that project. This is a shared, historical space of interaction.

Religion is crucial for the creation of the public sphere, both in Britain and in India. This may come as a surprise to those who accept Jürgen Habermas's understanding of the rise of 'the public sphere'. In his *Strukturwandlung der Oeffentlichkeit*, Habermas argued that private individuals assembled into a public body in the eighteenth century to discuss openly and critically the exercise of political power by the state.[26] These citizens had free access to information and expressed their opinion in a rational and domination-free (*herrschaftsfreie*) manner. Crucial to this development was the emergence and expansion of a market for newspapers and other printed materials. Another crucial element was the rise of the bourgeoisie, the reason why Habermas speaks of the bourgeois public sphere. These bourgeois turn out to be secular liberals rather than religious radicals. In my view, Habermas's analysis of the Enlightenment tradition belongs, at the theoretical level, very much to a discourse of modern, European self-representation. A striking element in this self-representation is the neglect of religious, public opinion since it cannot be regarded as 'rational' and 'critical'.

In Habermas's model, we have a picture of European development in which 'secularity' is one of the distinguishing features of 'modernity'. This picture is simply false. Enlightenment did not do away with religion in Europe. On the contrary, in the eighteenth century, there continued to be a direct connection between natural science and natural religion as well as between political debate and religion. As Margaret Jacobs has argued, 'Habermas's individuals are far too secularized'.[27] Jacobs focuses on the new religiosity of the enlightened few, such as the deists in England.[28] The productive side of Habermas's argument, however, is his focus on the sociology of the public sphere: both the discursive possibilities of critical debate and the tendency of the public sphere to expand and allow a growing number of participants. In that connection I would like to draw attention to the organizational activities which developed out of eighteenth-century evangelism. While early evangelism (for example, methodism) was already developing new communication networks, this development received a very strong impetus at the turn of the century. I am thinking here of anti-slavery societies, Bible societies, and missionary societies around 1800 which, at least in Britain (the prime subject of Habermas's analysis), were instrumental in creating a modern public sphere on which the nation-state could be built. I would therefore suggest that the notions of 'publicity', 'the public', and 'public opinion', captured by Habermas's concept of 'the public sphere' are important and can be used for comparative purposes if we are not going to be constrained by Habermas's secularist perspective.

CONCLUSION

Let me briefly summarize what I have tried to do in this contribution. First, I have argued that the location of religion and secularity has to be related to the emergence of a public sphere that is relatively independent of the state. In the creation of the public sphere in Britain, the role of evangelical movements is crucial. In India, these missionary movements are mirrored by a whole range of religious movements which are instrumental in creating a public sphere in India. In Britain, a modern sense of the Christian self is created which connects theological notions with progress and a sense of a 'mission in the world'. The Christian self in nineteenth-century Britain is formed in connection with the 'white man's burden in India', missionary and colonial. In India, the Christian missionary activities demand a secularity of the state and this leads to a public sphere in which religious movements produce an anti-colonial Hinduism which is fully modern.

Second, I have argued that the opposition between religious intolerance and secular liberty is mistaken. The rise of the nation-state and the related emergence of a public sphere made new, modern forms of freedom and unfreedom, tolerance and intolerance possible. Nonconformist Christians demanded freedom of religious opinion and evangelical movements were crucial in the formation of the public sphere in the beginning of the century, but embraced notions of evolutionary progress which underpinned the colonial project. Hindu movements resisted the colonial project, while adopting some of its most important features, but created a Hinduism that is becoming more and more anti-Muslim.

NOTES

1. T.N. Madan, 1997, 'Secularism in Its Place', *Journal of Asian Studies*, Vol. 46, No. 4, pp. 747–59. See also his *Modern Myths, Locked Minds*, New Delhi: Oxford University Press.
2. Ibid., p. 747.
3. Ibid., pp. 753–4.
4. Donald Smith, 1963, *India as a Secular State*, Princeton: Princeton University Press. See also Marc Galanter, 1965, 'Secularism East and West', *Comparative Studies in Society and History*, Vol. 7, No. 2, pp. 133–59.
5. Peter van der Veer, 2001, *Imperial Encounters: Religion and Modernity in India and Britain*, Princeton: Princeton University Press.
6. Owen Chadwick, 1975, *The Secularization of the European Mind in the 19th Century*, Cambridge: Cambridge University Press, p. 27.
7. Thomas Jefferson in a letter to the Baptists of Danbury, Connecticut, January 1802 in Merrill D. Peterson (ed.), 1984, *Jefferson's Writings*, New York: Library of America, p. 510.
8. See Keith Luria, 1996, 'The Politics of Protestant Conversion to Catholicism in Seventeenth-Century France', in Peter van der Veer (ed.), *Conversion to Modernities: The Globalization of Christianity*, New York: Routledge, pp. 33–8.
9. John Stuart Mill, 1993, *Utilitarianism, On Liberty, Considerations on Representative Government*, edited by Geraint Williams, London: J.M. Dent, p. 69.

10. Ibid., pp. 78–9.

11. Ibid., p. 76.

12. Ibid., p. 93.

13. Ibid., p. 118.

14. Charles Taylor, 1998, 'Modes of Secularism', in Rajeev Bhargava (ed.), *Secularism and its Critics*, New Delhi: Oxford University Press, p. 46.

15. Ibid., p. 44.

16. Peter Gay, 1966 and 1969, *The Enlightenment: An Interpretation* (two volumes), New York: Knopff.

17. To take only two examples: the Dutch Republic in the sixteenth and seventeenth centuries and the Kingdom of Awadh in the eighteenth century.

18. Robert E. Frykenberg, 1997, 'The Emergence of "Modern Hinduism"', in Gunther Sontheimer and Hermann Kulke (eds), *Hinduism Reconsidered*, Delhi: Manohar, p. 90.

19. Ibid., p. 94.

20. Ibid., p. 94.

21. C.J. Fuller, 1984, *Servants of the Goddess: The Priests of a South Indian Temple*, Cambridge: Cambridge University Press.

22. Arjun Appadurai, 1981, *Worship and Conflict under Colonial Rule: A South Indian Case*, Cambridge: Cambridge University Press; David Gilmartin, 1988, *Empire and Islam: Punjab and the Making of Pakistan*, Berkeley: University of California Press.

23. Nita Kumar, 1998, 'Sanskrit Pandits and the Modernisation of Sanskrit Education in the Nineteenth to Twentieth Centuries', in William Radice (ed.), *Swami Vivekananda and the Modernization of Hinduism*, New Delhi: Oxford University Press, p. 54.

24. Sandria Freitag, 1989, *Collective Action and Community: Public Arenas and the Emergence of Communalism in North India*, Berkeley: University of California Press, p. 150.

25. Richard Fox Young, 1981, *Resistant Hinduism: Sanskrit Sources on Anti-Christian Apologetics in Early Nineteenth-Century India*, Vienna: De Nobili Research Library.

26. Jürgen Habermas, 1979, *Strukturwandlung der Offentlichkeit*, Darmstadt: Luchterhand.

27. Margaret C. Jacobs, 1992, *Living the Enlightenment: Freemasonry and Politics in Eighteenth-Century Europe*, Oxford: Oxford University Press.

28. See also David Zaret, 1992, 'Religion, Science, and Printing in the Public Sphere in Seventeenth-Century England', in Craig Calhoun (ed.), *Habermas and the Public Sphere*, Cambridge: MIT Press, pp. 212–36.

CHAPTER 10

Hindu Priests under Secular Government

A Case Study of the Nataraja Temple at Chidambaram, South India

Masakazu Tanaka

INTRODUCTION

This article considers the reaction of a temple side to the establishment of laws concerning the property (land) and administration of Hindu temples in the twentieth century, and how the temple was caught in the web of the state's judicial system. I will first examine the changes in government policies regarding Hindu temples of south India. Then I will take up the case of the Nataraja Temple, giving an outline account of the temple before investigating a series of lawsuits between the temple and the local government. I also discuss major related disputes that arose after Indian Independence and finally make some general observations on the relationship between religion (represented by a Hindu temple) and secular authority (represented by the state government) before and after Independence.

HINDU RELIGIOUS ENDOWMENT LAW[1]

In south India, especially in the state of Tamil Nadu, many huge temples have been constructed since the tenth century and have received generous support from successive kings. As devout Hindus, kings donated vast amounts of land and supported the temples financially. Moreover, the temple priests prayed for the prosperity of its patrons and authorities headed by the king. The temple not only legitimated the position of the king as the paramount authority of the land, but also played an important role in the economy and the development of the arts.[2]

From 1639, when the East India Company acquired the area which later became known as St George, Madras, the British engaged increasingly in trade and commerce in south India. Later, as colonial rule became more firmly established, they also started taking on the traditional role of the king mentioned above. Namely, the colonial government began to deal with the reported appeals from many places that the trusts based on land and other donations to temples were used personally by the managers against the donors' will, and that temple management was neglected. The colonial government also understood and accepted that the temples were economically and politically important, and in 1817 enacted the first law that regulated the temple property management (Regulation VII of 1817) with the broad agreement of the general populace.

From around 1833, however, the policy of the colonial government in Madras was criticized in mainland Britain, and by the 1840s it was forced to cease its intervention. This policy of non-intervention was established through the new law of 1863 (Act XX of 1863). The extent to which this law was actually effective, however, should be carefully considered. Moreover, the policy of non-intervention was overturned again after World War I.

Under the reforms implemented in 1919 in line with the recommendations of the Montague–Chelmsford Report, jurisdiction over each region was vested in a regional council, of which over half of the members were regionally elected. The rights of temple management were also placed under the regional council's control. With this, the Justice Party, which came into power in Madras district in 1920, promoted the centralization of temple policies and in 1926 established the Board of Hindu Religious Endowments (abbreviated now as the HRE Board) (Act I of 1926). After some amendments, a new law was established in 1927 (Act I of 1927).

At this point, however, centralization was not complete. One of the main reasons for this was the presence of a temple committee in each district; another reason was the presence of temples that were not subject to the legal regulations. In the beginning, problems concerning management were dealt with by the temple committee, consisting of an elected body of distinguished local persons. At that time, the opinions of the HRE Board were executed only through the temple committee. However, in 1935 this was amended so that the temple was notified of the Board's decision and an executive officer was dispatched to take action instead of the temple managers (Act XII of 1935). In this way, the temple committees became practically powerless, and in 1944 they were abolished. In their place, an assistant commissioner was appointed in each district.

Furthermore, up till then it had been the principle that if a temple manager's post was hereditary or the manager was appointed by the person who established the temple, then the temple was considered as a private establishment and there was no government intervention. This principle, however, was also ignored. On the other hand, the HRE Board was not able to be completely neutral politically, since it was influenced by the government policies of the time. The majority of the staff also consisted of government supporters, and the Board tended to appoint party supporters as the managers of district temples.

After Independence, according to a law established in 1951 (Act XIX of 1951), the HRE Board came under the control of a government minister as a department known as the Department of Hindu and Religious Charitable Endowment (abbreviated henceforth as HRCE Department). As a result, it became increasingly difficult for it to function independently of government opinion. An area committee was established. However, the HRCE Department appointed its members. In this way, the area committee was not given independent and autonomous rights, but became an extension or a mere tool of the central government. In addition, the members were given the right, if it were deemed necessary, to enter the inner sanctum hitherto reserved for the priests. In this way, the centralization of the temple management was strengthened. However, this law, as we will see later, was judged to be unconstitutional in the disputes concerning the Nataraja Temple of Chidambaram.

NATARAJA TEMPLE

Chidambaram is situated 245 km south of Madras, the capital state of Tamil Nadu. According to the 1981 Census, the population is approximately 5600. The present main buildings of the Nataraja Temple were constructed between the tenth and thirteenth centuries, since when countless renovations have been performed and new buildings have been added.

The priests of the Nataraja Temple are called Dikshitars. In 1988, the Dikshitars constituted a small community of 196 households with a total population of 686. What is to be noted here is that as well as being priests, the Dikshitars are also the joint administrators of the temple as their collective property.

The temple is administered by an executive organ called the '*potu* Dikshitar', which is composed of all the married male Dikshitars. Once every ten days they hold regular meetings and discuss matters of concern. It may happen that several married men from the same household participate in the meeting. The potu Dikshitar has a supervisory organ in the form of a committee of nine members, whose term of office is from 1 April to 31 March of the following year. The committee chairman assumes in particular the role of representative of the Dikshitars when dealing with the outside world, but he is neither leader nor head of the Dikshitars community, for the Dikshitars maintain that their leader is Śiva himself. This committee is directly concerned with the administration and maintenance of the temple. If, for example, a priest on duty has not been discharging his duties properly, the committee will hold a hearing and impose a fine on him in accordance with the code of laws compiled in the late nineteenth century.

In 1988, there were 265 married male Dikshitars, whose names were listed in a roster in the order in which they had married. Teams of twenty Dikshitars are formed following the order in the roster. The members of these teams are called *muṟaikkārar*, and they serve as priests for twenty days, or one *vaṭṭam*, at the five main temples. To this end, each team of twenty is further subdivided into five groups of four members each. Each group is in charge of one temple for four days. The four members of each group take turns in acting as the officiating priest (*pūjakkārar*), and the other three act as his assistants. After four days, when each has taken his turn as the officiating priest, they move on to another temple. By moving as a group through all five temples in this manner, one vattam is concluded.

From the tenth century, the Nataraja Temple grew under the patronage of successive kings, and it is to be assumed that, as in the case of other temples, lands donated by kings formed the basis of the temple's economy. But with the passage of time, this supposedly donated land lost its economic significance. Details of this process are unclear, but it does appear that at least by the second half of the nineteenth century, the Nataraja Temple was looked upon as having no land, and in its place contracts with specific patrons (*kaṭṭaḷaitār* or *upayatār*) came to play important roles.

The practice whereby a patron (kattalaitar) would financially support a certain ritual through the agency of a particular Dikshitar (kattalai Dikshitar) had taken root at the Nataraja Temple by the nineteenth century at the latest. These patrons sponsor only specific rituals; they do not administer the temple itself. The administration of the temple remains in the hands of the Dikshitars.

Patrons are divided into three types. First, there are those who provide financial support for the daily worship that takes place six times a day. They are called 'potu kattalaitar' (common patrons) or '*kōyil kattalaitar*' (temple patrons), and they meet the expenses for worship with the interest accruing from their savings.

Second, there are the patrons of particular ceremonies. In the case of Nataraja Temple, these include not only major festivals lasting several days, but also the monthly new moon ceremony and the ceremonies celebrating the birth dates of saints, of which there is one held almost every week. The performance of these ceremonies is made possible through the patrons' support. Because these patrons of particular ceremonies have become fixed over successive generations, it is difficult for a newcomer to become a patron of this type. To each patron is attached a particular Dikshitar. Each year an *ācarya* is appointed among the Dikshitars to conduct basic rituals of major festivals, but the minor rites incorporated within these festivals and ceremonies in which the ārcarya has no involvement whatsoever are performed by this kattalai Dikshitar in his capacity as priest. This does not follow the roster system, but is a right that is inherited by particular Dikshitar families.

Because the number of services and rituals is limited, not all Dikshitars can become the kattalai Dikshitar for a particular ritual, and since this position is an inherited one, some sort of adjustment becomes necessary when the kattalai Dikshitar has two or more sons. If the father should be in charge of several rituals, then they will be shared equally among the sons; but if he is responsible for only one ritual, the sons will serve as kattalai Dikshitar in turn.

Third, there are people referred to as patrons who are not associated with any particular ritual. They will ask a Dikshitar (occasionally several Dikshitars) to become their kattalai Dikshitar and then have him perform private ritual acts such as *arcanā* (offerings of coconuts and bananas). In some cases this relationship will continue from one generation to the next. Insofar as this relationship is unconnected with ceremonies, services, and similar public activities of the temple, it is a private affair. In such a relationship the kattalai Dikshitar undertakes to make arcana offerings to Nataraja on behalf of the patron every month on the day corresponding to his birth star (*naksatara*) and to then send him some sacred ashes and vermilion powder as the *prasāda*. Some Dikshitars have as many as 1000 patrons of this type. If this type of patron should wish to have a *rudra-abhiṣeka* (similar, but large-scale ritual) performed, he will again approach the same kattalai Dikshitar. The rudra-abhiseka differs from the arcana in that the kattalai Dikshitar only makes the arrangements for the rite, and the rite itself is performed by the priest on duty for that particular day. Coliya Brahmins and more than ten Dikshitars who chant mantras also participate in this rite.

A person may be introduced by an acquaintance to a particular Dikshitar, but it is more common for a patron to make the acquaintance of a Dikshitar at the temple and to pay him a sum of approximately 100 rupees to cover the expenses for one year. A Dikshitar may acquire as many as 100 new patrons of this type in a single month, but the relationship with patrons gained in this manner does not usually last very long. Pilgrims from afar, in particular, tend not to send the fees for the following year, and so the relationship dissolves after the first year. These private patrons do not belong to individual Dikshitars, but are rather the common property of the household. Therefore, if the household should split up, they are shared equally among the sons as in the case of the festival patrons. In order to keep a large number of patrons, it is necessary for a Dikshitar to go almost daily to the temple to make arcana offerings, and in order to acquire new patrons it is to the Dikshitar's advantage to be placed in charge of arcana at a particular temple, a position he can acquire by auction or some other means, for it is in such a situation that he will find pilgrims who may be prepared to enter into an annual contract.

In some cases the relationship between the patron and kattalai Dikshitar will develop beyond a contractual one into a more personal relationship. For example, when a domestic rite is performed at the kattalai Dikshitar's home, the patron will offer a special gift of money, and the two may also become trusting confidants.

Dikshitar households may be said to be in competition with one another in regard to the acquisition of patrons, for the greater the number of patrons they have, the more stable their level of income becomes. But to the best of my knowledge there have in recent years been no major disputes among the Dikshitars concerning patrons.

THE DISPUTE WITH THE STATE GOVERNMENT DURING THE EARLY TWENTIETH CENTURY (1930–51)

The dispute between Nataraja Temple and the government (Madras district and Tamil Nadu state) goes back to the 1930s. The following is a brief explanation of the development. When a new law was established in 1926, Nataraja Temple sent a written petition to the governor for an exemption from the regional council's control of management. The temple's plea was accepted, but with conditions. In 1930, people who were dissatisfied with the Dikshitars' temple management appealed to the HRE Board. The Board compiled a reformation proposal, but for practical reasons this was not carried out. In 1932 the same Board again brought up the topic and in 1933 compiled a second reformation proposal. The Dikshitars objected to this and brought a lawsuit to the district court. In 1936, the court passed judgement amending the Board's proposal. Dissatisfied with the decision, the priests appealed to the Madras High Court. According to the 1939 ruling, the High Court upheld the district court's decision, but part of the reformation proposal was further re-examined. In the process of this lawsuit, the exemption acquired in 1926 became invalid.

Some of the main points of the reformation proposal are briefly stated as follows. The potu Dikshitar, which is the official executive organ of the priests, has the management rights. The actual administration is executed by a committee of nine members, of whom six are elected and three are appointed through rotation of duties. The proposal stipulates the following duties of the administrative committee with respect to the HRE Board: to obtain the permission of the HRE Board in order to hire managers, to prepare an offertory chest, to declare the offerings and worship fees received by the temple, to keep an account book, to select an honorary manager from among the devotees, to inspect the temple's account book, to make a catalogue of the temple's jewels and submit it to the HRE Board.

A new reformation proposal was compiled in 1946 but abandoned the following year. However, procedures were started by the HRE Board for the 1950 appeal by local people, and on 28 August 1951 the HRE Board appointed an Executive Officer. The temple side was dissatisfied with this and brought a lawsuit. The problem was that the reformation proposal, which was upheld by the district court, was not being followed. However, during this dispute, a new law (Act XX of 1951) was established, and the validity of the earlier law was called into question. According to the ruling passed by the Madras High Court on 13 December 1951, the Dikshitars' livelihood is totally dependent on the income received from religious activities. From this point of view, they cannot be considered as trust managers who uphold the principle of not receiving profits from the property trusts (in this case the temple's). The argument runs as follows.

The Dikshitars, as citizens of the State of India, are guaranteed individual property rights. Henceforth, would not the declaration made by the HRE Board deprive them from these rights? Furthermore would not this sort of declaration restrict their rights to obtain, possess, and dispose of properties?

According to the judgement, the appointment of the Executive Officer would threaten the Dikshitars' property rights, which are guaranteed by the law.

Furthermore the judgement considers the Dikshitars as a closed religious group (denomination) and that the appointment of the executive officer would threaten their rights to execute religious matters. In the first place, an Executive Officer is appointed when some sort of misconduct over the management arises, and the court rejects the position that such misconduct occurred in the Nataraja Temple. From there it questions the reformation proposal of 1939 itself and justifies the fact that the Dikshitars did not observe this.

What is evident from the decision is that it fully considered the uniqueness of the Nataraja Temple. In comparison with other temples of the same scale, the priests are entrusted with the management, financial support is supplied from outside, but patrons do not participate directly in the temple management; and the financial infrastructure of Nataraja Temple includes very little land, so there is no need for strict management in this regard. The administration of the temple, regardless of its situation in the past, is conducted in accordance with a proper collection of rules drawn up over a century before, and the effort to avoid mismanagement of the temple's communal assets and administration was recognized.

In this way, the judgement of 1951 considered that the declaration of the execution officer threatened the individual's property rights and religious freedom which are guaranteed by the law. However, the state government established a new law in 1959, and the related disputes with the Nataraja Temple are continuing to this day, as I shall discuss below.

RECENT MOVEMENTS

Finally, I would like to introduce the related disputes that have arisen since the end of the 1950s.

The first is a lawsuit concerning the confiscation of duty rights. In 1958, money was stolen from the temple, so the priests introduced a duty system of keeping watch. However, one priest did not agree with this. He was ordered to pay a fine but ignored the order. For this reason, his right to carry out his duty as a priest was removed. He objected to this decision and appealed to higher court.

Rulings were passed at the Chidambaram sub-district court in 1959 (OS No. 112 of 1959), at the Kadarol district court in 1961 (AS No. 216, of 1961), and at the Madras High Court in 1967. According to the rulings, the decision to institute the duty system of keeping watch had not followed the proper procedures, and was therefore invalid. Whether the court could intervene in the temple's internal disputes was also a point of discussion, and it was judged that it could intervene. Although this was a case between one priest and a group of priests, and thus an internal problem of the temple, it brought into question the extent to which the law was applicable. This sort of problem regarding legal procedure had already been considered as one of the points of issue during the nineteenth century.

Next I will introduce the conflict between the state government and the temple, and this was again a case of disputes relating to management. Here I will only introduce the process.

On 29 February 1974, the government instructed the Chidambaram Temple to make reforms. However, the temple ignored this. On 14 April 1980, the same problem occurred. On 24 April the temple replied. On 27 October, the same problem occurred again. On 31 October, the temple replied. On 31 January 1981, the appointment of an honorary member of the management committee was notified by the HRCE Department (RC55342/80/H4). The government then ordered an investigation of the temple. The temple objected to this and appealed to the district court (WP No. 616 of 1981), which ruled in favour of the temple on 20 January 1982.

During this period, on 2 April 1981, one priest complained of the deficiency of the temple's management. On 11 May, another priest complained about the reporting of the temple's assets. This was followed by complaints from local residents on 15 June. On receiving these complaints, the HRCE instructed the temple to enumerate and clarify the points of deficiency on 22 June. On 8 October, a devotee made a further complaint. In the following year, on 9 March, complaints were lodged by five priests. The temple answered the complaints for the first time on 8 April, but the HRCE Department rejected this, passing a notice

(RC No. 5275 A/8 B-6) on 20 July, and appointing an Executive Officer. The temple objected to this move and lodged an appeal (WP No. 5638 of 1982). On 8 August 1983, the court ruled that the appointment of the Executive Officer was invalid. The HRCE Department declared its objection to this on 9 January 1984. On 25 July 1987 the HRCE Department sent a notification (P 52754/82/L.1) to the temple and appointed an Executive Officer. On 10 August, the temple again lodged an appeal (WP No. 7843 of 1987). The HRCE Department declared its statement of objection on 7 November.

This dispute is still continuing, but from the case examples above it is clear that the government side will lose.

FROM DHARMA TO MODERN LAW

In spite of the past, the Śiva Temple of Chidambaram has a good reputation. The reason for this, ironically, is that it is the only major temple in Tamil Nadu that has succeeded in resisting the state government's intervention. At present, there are no factional conflicts among the priests or power struggles within the local society taking advantage of such conflicts. A realm of 'pure religion' is realized outside the influence of politics.

The government tries to justify its intervention by saying that the temple's financial situation is in chaos due to the power struggles among the local leaders and trouble between those close by, and that it is necessary to rescue it from corruption by introducing law and order. Here it can be interpreted that the government is comparing itself to the king, who maintains righteous law (dharma). The government presents its argument as follows. The land owned by the temple was donated by the leaders of the time in order to execute rituals, etc., so it is necessary to respect the will of the donors and utilize it according to the original purpose. However, in reality it has not been utilized in this manner and the managers have been filling their own pockets. Moreover, the priests are not sincere and spend their time importuning money from the devotees. Priests who should be religious specialists are completely ignorant about rituals. For these reasons, if the temple's management is corrected, its financial situation will also take a turn for the better. In addition, it is also possible to use part of the increased revenue for the education of the priests in order to enhance their abilities. In this way, the tradition will be restored and this will lead also to the development of Hinduism.

The government's reforms from above have gained little support among the general populace. The politicians and the bureaucrats are not accepted either as the keepers of dharma or as faithful devotees (*bhakta*s), and their actions have brought them into conflict with the temple.

What has actually happened in south India is the nationalization of temples or the centralization of temple management. In spite of the principle of separating politics and religion, the religious sphere has been brought under government control, and the process of politicization of the temple has continued. A situation has arisen in which the government even appointed an untouchable or Harijan as a manager, who would not have been permitted inside a temple half a century ago. This was a government tactic to gain popularity and collect votes from the untouchables. It is not that the politicians themselves are donating to temples or that they are particularly pious. A politician of a ministerial rank might ignore the religious feelings of the common people by not removing his shirt and shoes upon entering a temple. Furthermore, even if donations were utilized for the management and renovation of other temples, and for educating the priests, this would still go against the management law that emphasizes the original purpose of the donations.

In reality, the government faced resistance to its policies in the form of lawsuits brought by temples, and things have not been proceeding according to its will. As can be seen from the case of the Nataraja Temple, since Independence the judiciary has put emphasis on past traditions and criticized the temple policy of the state government for violating the rights over private property and freedom of religion guaranteed by the law. The original significance of the HRCE Department (and the HRE Board that preceded it) was to mediate conflicts concerning temple management among the local men. However, a situation arose in which the judiciary arbitrated between the HRCE Department and the temple. In this situation, the temple has to depend on another state organization, namely, the judicial system, in order to protect itself. The judiciary has the tendency to support the temple's opinions in principle, but this is a modern interpretation of the result of the law and does not come from dharma. Here dharma is subordinated to modern secular law and restated in the language of the latter. The fact that the temple also requires the law may be interpreted as indicating increasing secularization of the temple. In this way, today's Hindu temples are forced to fight for their existence in the world of modern law that has nothing to do with either righteous law (dharma) or devotion (bhakti).

CONCLUSION

In the twentieth century, the conflict between the priests and the state government became more apparent. But even here it is not a straightforward case of the temple boldly resisting government intervention. There were also internal indictments among the priests and also indictments from local residents. Above all, there is the growing independence of the judiciary from government administration. Despite various problems, the Indian judiciary has been consistent in supporting the temple's views since Independence, at least as far as the lawsuits concerning the Nataraja Temple are concerned. However, from a broader perspective, this is also a process in which the temple is getting caught up in the web of the judiciary system.

NOTES

1. The descriptions below are taken from Arjun Appadurai, 1981, *Worship and Conflict under Colonial Rule: A South Indian Case,* London: Cambridge University Press; C.J. Baker, 1975, 'Temples and Political Development', in C.J. Baker and D.A. Washbrook (eds), *South India: Political Institutions and Political Change 1880–1940*, Delhi: Macmillan Company of India; J. Duncan and M. Derrett, 1966, 'The Reform of Hindu Religious Endowments', in Donald Eugene Smith (ed.), *South Asian Politics and Religion*, New Jersey: Princeton University Press; Christopher J. Fuller, 1984, *Servants of the Goddess: The Priests of a South Indian Temple*, London: Cambridge University Press; Anthony Good, 1989, 'Law, Legitimacy, and the Hereditary Rights of Tamil Temple Priests', *Modern Asian Studies*, Vol. 23, No. 2, pp. 233–57; Chandra Mudaliar, 1974, *The Secular State and Religious Institutions in India: A Study of the Administration of Hindu Religious Trusts in Madras*, Wiesbaden: Franz Steiner; Franklin A. Presler, 1987, *Religion under Bureaucracy: Policy and Administration for Hindu Temples in South India*, Cambridge: Cambridge University Press.

2. See Stella Kramish, 1946, *The Hindu Temple*, Calcutta: University of Calcutta Press; and Bryan Pfaffenberger, 1992, 'The Hindu Temple as a Machine, or the Western Machine as a Temple', *Techniques et Culture*, Vol. 16, pp. 183–202 for the general characteristics of Hindu temples. See David West Rudner, 1987, 'Religious Gifting and Inland Commerce in Seventeenth-Century South India', *The Journal of Asian Studies*, Vol. 46, No. 2, pp. 361–79; Cynthia Talbot, 1991, 'Temples, Donors, and Gifts: Patterns of Patronage in Thirteenth-Century South India', *The Journal of Asian Studies*, Vol. 50, No. 2, pp. 308–40 for specific case studies dealing with economic aspects.

CHAPTER 11

Democratic Culture and Images of the State

India's Unending Ambivalence

Ashis Nandy

Of the various instruments of democracy that the non-Western world borrowed from the West, one of the most problematic has been the modern nation-state. I sometimes suspect that many Afro-Asian and South American activist-scholars just do not know what to make of the state. Some think that the absence in their context of a proper state, modelled after the European nation-state, was *the* reason for the humiliation of non-Western societies in colonial times. Others think that without radical changes in the concept of the state they cannot negotiate contemporary social problems. Still others believed that the state itself has become the root of all problems in third world societies, unless these societies learn to disengage themselves from the state, no creative initiative can be taken in public life that would make sense, culturally, to citizens. Simultaneously, a deep chasm has grown between those who think that the state should have priority over culture in society as well as the right to retool the culture for the state's purposes, and those who think that culture should have priority over the state, for after all, the state is supposed to protect a lifestyle and not empty territory.[1] In societies like India, these diverse opinions have little to do with the contemporary debate on economic globalization and the state's role in it. Indeed, the opinions frame the debate and make Indian attitudes to globalization more ambiguous and incomprehensible to many outsiders.

A few societies in Asia have apparently bypassed these problems, perhaps because they were never directly colonized. I have occasionally met Japanese scholars who find it difficult to think of the state as dissociated from society and politics. The Japanese state, too, sometimes seems to be part of a single seamless cultural and socio-political process. However, even if this is true—and it does always seem so—Japan is one among very few exceptions. Usually, in the non-Western world, there is a constant ambivalent affair with the modern state, even among those who hate everything Western. During the last hundred years we have seen the odd spectacle of virtually every major revivalist movement seeking to capture the state—by which I mean capture the standard nation-state—and use it for ethno-chauvinist or fundamentalist projects. Few of these movements have seriously tried to return to the traditional ideas of the state in Asia or Africa. Fundamentalists and revivalists seem equally comfortable with the conventional nation-state as they seem with modern technology when it comes to jihad, holy war or *dharmayuddha*. They usually only want to capture the nation-state, not alter it. In the process, they end up legitimizing the nation-state—even within societies that are the least comfortable with it.

The culture of the state, therefore, is often the crucial clue to the way democracy functions or does not function in an Afro-Asian context. No study or analysis of long-term cultures of politics in this part of the world is complete unless expectations and anxieties over the state within the political leadership and among ordinary citizens are systematically explored. I try in this essay to use the example of India, where this ambivalence towards the state has reached a particularly high level during the last thirty years. This is a country where the intellectual culture and traditions of political analysis can be divided into two parts. One comprises those who think that the state is a major instrument of social and political change and must be given primacy in social life; the other comprises those who think that, for civil society to thrive, the state must be contained and redefined.[2] I have come to suspect that many of the pathetic, often violent attempts to introduce hard-boiled, mechano-morphic, ultra-positivist, socialist ideologies into the third world were actually half-hearted attempts to redefine and make more acceptable the nineteenth-century European nation-state. After all, that was the only kind of European state which the first generation post-colonial Asian and African leaders had really known, first-hand, during the colonial period. The attempts can be read as counterparts of the tacit, unwitting project of the revivalists that I have already mentioned.

I

Let me now turn to the story of the Indian state. During the last 150 years, the popular culture of Indian politics has been dominated by three images of the Indian state. These images have sometimes supplemented each other; sometimes they have acted as competing stereotypes; sometimes they have encroached on each other. The interplay of these images has linked the Indian state to the culture of Indian politics, and even shaped most analyses of the linkage. There is some evidence that the images also dominate the political cultures of most non-Western societies with a colonial past. For there is something vaguely inescapable about the emergence of these images in societies where the traditional idea of the state has a hoary career but the idea of a modern nation-state is often a new acquisition.

The first of the three images is that of *the state as a protector*. The Indian state is expected by many Indians to protect society against arbitrary oppressors and marauding outsiders. As in most societies in the Southern world, large sections of Indian society, too, have lived for ages with experiences of domination and victimization that seem *prima facie* inescapable. These sections have often seemed more comfortable with predictable, rule-bound injustice; they have preferred predictable oppression to less but more arbitrary governance. This is understandable: non-arbitrary governance gives its victims more room. It gives more scope for finding loopholes and devising means of survival. Arbitrary or random oppression is more difficult to contain. Parts of Indian society, those which have been at the receiving end of the Indian and global political economy, primarily expect the Indian state to eliminate, control, make rule-bound, or manageable the second kind of oppression.

As a corollary, the state is expected to protect native life-styles. Indian ultra-nationalists bemoan the frequency with which Indians have collaborated with foreign political authorities throughout history, and ultra-Hindus lament the fact that Hindus have often sung, at the slightest provocation, paeans to their non-Hindu rulers. Neither seems fully sensitive to the widespread expectation in ordinary Indian citizens that state authority, in exchange for demonstrative political loyalty, should try to leave its subjects culturally alone and protect their everyday life. Indians seem willing to tolerate a certain amount of low-level, predictable violence of which they have—or think they have—learnt to take out the edge to avoid a total onslaught on their lifestyle.

During the colonial period, rulers recognized this expectation from the state as part of its 'mandate' and reaped the benefits.[3] Even an ardent nationalist like Bankimchandra Chattopadhyay (1838–94) suggested, in his novel *Anandamath,* that British rule protected Indians from the country's erstwhile Muslim rulers who, during the last days of Mughal rule, were unable to provide even minimal cultural and personal security.[4] Attempts have been made to explain this attitude either as sectarianism or as a cover for the novel's anti-British tone. Attempts have also been made to debate whether the last days of Mughal empire were really as bad, and to argue that apologists of the Raj promoted the stereotype. The fact remains that the expectation of state protection was widespread throughout the colonial period and has survived the demise of colonialism.

The colonial administration tried to live up to this expectation the hard way. In the case of virtually every major social or religious reform, the British-Indian government supported reform, through administrative or legislative action, only after decades of pressure from Indian leaders. Instances of this are the movements against sati, infanticide, human sacrifices, and child marriage. Likewise, missionary activities in India were banned for the first sixty-five years of the Raj, English laws were not introduced until the mid-1820s, English education until about the same time, and the Western medical system was not introduced until the 1830s. These policy choices, justified or otherwise, do give an idea of the extent of state protection of culture in the first phase of colonialism. There *were* specific political considerations behind each British refusal to interfere in Indian culture. Nonetheless, there was a general belief in the rulers that large parts of Indian society expected rulers to ensure, against some protection payment, that Indian lifestyles were not going to be unduly disturbed. That this strategy did not in the end protect lifestyles, and managed only to increase the protection payment to unacceptable levels, is beside the point.

In our times, many of the arguments for a hard state in India, given by both liberal democrats and neo-Bismarckians, derive their appeal from this image of a state that will first ensure security to its citizens. First, there must be a proper state authority, they argue, before secondary needs such as democratic freedom and cultural authenticity are met. Weak and gullible Indians require a strong state and the kind of governance that such a state can supply before being granted the luxury of full-fledged participatory democracy.[5] Also, the Indian state must provide security to Indians first, before providing it to others. Therefore, if such security can be ensured by turning a blind eye to violence abroad, or even to the export of violence, exploitation, and authoritarianism into the neighbourhood—as done by 'advanced' and powerful democratic societies elsewhere—the Indian citizen should be so protected. The same argument is applied to sub-national groupings. Today, statists in India feel fully justified in being ruthless with ethnic groups and peripheral cultures to protect the 'mainstream', in the event that such groups or cultures stand in the way of the authority of the state.[6] The official concern with the fate of oppressed cultures and races elsewhere in the world is now matched by a deep fear of, and readiness to suppress, the self-assertion of ethnic minorities within India.

The second image of the Indian state dominates the politics of India's modern elite, though it is also now becoming a feature of the urban middle class as whole. It is the image of the *state as a modernizer or liberator*. Traditional Indian culture and modernity are seen here as antonyms, and it is presumed that the state's main function is to introduce Indian society to the modern world. Though some elements of Indian culture are seen as compatible with modernity, it is assumed that much of the culture is not. The expectation is that traditions incompatible with modernity will be eliminated by enlightened statecraft and the modern Indian state will thus gradually create a modern Indian culture in order to sustain a modern polity. Even during the non-interventionist phase of the Raj there were thinkers and political leaders who attacked the regime for not interfering, as opposed to those who saw the British as good rulers because they did not interfere with religion and society. In the early years of the Raj, Rammohun Roy (1772–1833) entered into virulent theological disputes with Christian missionaries but also forged a coalition with them to fight official non-interference in culture. In the last days of the Raj, Jawaharlal Nehru (1890–1964), while attacking the destructive role of the colonial state, also held it against the Raj that it had left the country mired in unchanging, oppressive traditions.

Today, all along the ideological spectrum are Indians to whom the main function of the Indian state is to change Indian culture and personality to liberate underprivileged, underdeveloped Indians. Capturing and using the state to direct social change, and for that reason seeing the state as the nerve centre of the Indian polity, are important parts of this image. As a result, transferring control to the state, be it in the matter of industrial units or of the performing arts, was for a long time an end in itself, for the nation-state was seen as the ultimate principle of social creativity in India. (In the case of industries, nationalization may no longer be fashionable; in education, sports and culture, it continues to be so.) Predictably, Indian society has thrown up an entire sector that lives off its control over the state, often in the name of distributive justice. This sector sees itself not as a privileged class thrown up by the new role of the state in society, but as a declassed vanguard working for the future liberation of the Indian people.

Like the first image of the state, this image too is wedded to a dualist vision of politics. If the state is the phalanx or tool of progress and culture an object waiting to be retooled, rebuilt, renovated or repaired, the latter is bound to become psychologically associated with retrogression and obscurantism. And it becomes justifiable then to retain, somehow or the other, some access to state power, even if that means ideological or moral compromises. Many who change loyalties overnight after the fall or rise of a regime, notably within the bureaucracy and the intelligentsia, and many radicals who are willing to adorn the smallest offices of power under regimes they themselves attack as reactionary, justify themselves through this widely shared image of state and culture. They may look like seedy opportunists and turncoats, but they believe they follow what was once a grand and romantic strategy for altering the civilizational face of India. They feel that, by somehow being close to power, they contribute to good governance and radical social transformation.

Not surprisingly, in recent years this image of the state has become a major means of justifying state violence and bureaucratic centralism in India. During the colonial period many Indian leaders saw the Indian steeped in his culture as a child weighed down by childish superstition, yet they did not see it as the bounden duty of the political or social leadership to drive citizens like cattle towards a better future. It is only after the introduction of participatory democracy in free India, and only when facing more determined resistance to the modern elite as the ultimate social pacesetters, that a touch of 'repressive developmentalism' and some patriarchal versions of 'conscientization' begin to look like unavoidable minor hazards on the way to a new Indian society.

Finally, there is the image of the Indian state as a small but significant and well-defined part of Indian society and politics. This image sees the Indian *state as an arbiter* and the sphere of the state as an area where social relationships can be renegotiated. The state in this image is theoretically delimited—the image has obviously something to do with the frequently observed marginality of organized politics in traditional Indian lifestyle—and is seen to provide a bargaining table or marketplace where new power relationships among social aggregates can be worked out.

Such an image can be both creative and otherwise. For instance, when the politics of mass mobilization first entered Indian society in the 1920s, it did in three or four decades, things which one-and-a-half centuries of social reform had not done. Within the Hindu social order, mass politics consummated changes initiated in the early nineteenth century, unleashing forces comparable in strength to the *Bhakti* movement. Social mobility patterns changed dramatically. The traditional unit of social mobility in India was caste, not the individual. But such mobility generally took decades, sometimes even centuries. Participatory politics speeded up the process. It is true that the image of a static, backward-looking Indian society was a caricature produced for middle-class consumption by colonial progressivist discourse, but it is also true that mass politics established a more creative and open relationship between citizenship, ethnicity, and vocation. Overtly, this underscored traditional caste divisions, because the unit of mobility still remained caste. Covertly, it opened up the social order. After all, what is so traditional about a competition for power between, say, the Brahmins and the Sudras, when they compete on the basis of numbers, without reference to their centuries-old unequal ritual or cultural status?

On the negative side, the image of the state as a delimited marketplace for the renegotiation of traditional social relationships has made the Indian state exactly that: a marketplace. Those who have entered politics for the first time, usually the less privileged and less exposed, have a weaker commitment to the rules and conventions which define the limits of statecraft in society. They thus contribute to the classical picture of political decay in which political participation outstrips the institutionalization of politics and the growth of system legitimacy. The decay has pushed the Indian polity towards a situation of limitless politics or *matsyanyay*—the ancient term for the condition in which big fish eat the little fish. Such politics does not allow one to build even a new basis for alternatives because both support to and dissent from the system are seen from a cynical, Machiavellian vantage ground. The strengthening of the image of the state as a marketplace has also generated in recent years a deep hostility towards the growing self-assertion of social aggregates seeking to express their politics through an adversarial relationship with the state. Such self-assertion, even when it takes place within the bounds of the culture of Indian politics, is seen as something that requires ruthless repression by the state.[7]

In post-colonial societies, living with self-doubts about their own ability to run a proper nation-state, the two processes cannot but constitute a vicious circle. The more the participation, the more the hostility towards new participants as threats to the system. More the threat perception, more the hostility towards those who take on the state in areas such as civil rights and cultural survival.

II

The balance among the three images once gave the culture of Indian politics its distinct flavour. The imbalance among them explains much of the fluidity in the political culture of the country now. A crucial aspect of this imbalance is the inadequate legitimacy for the last image of the Indian state—of the state as an area within the public realm where terms for new transactions among old social grouping are settled—as compared to the first two images. This has distorted and split the third image. The pathology of the state as a marketplace in India has overshadowed the creative use of the state as a means of cultural self-renewal through the open renegotiation of social relationships. It is possible that the demands of the first two images have brought the worst out of the third image.

This is not a convoluted denial of the creative role of the first two images. During the last 150 years, these images have often been justifiably salient at the expense of the third. The idea of the post-colonial state as a defender of culture and society had to be re-emphasized during the colonial period, when the state had become, for most Indians, an alien entity. Likewise, the idea of the state as a liberating force powered social reform movements during the last century and social changes brought about through legislative and judicial actions in this century. However, politics in India has reached a stage when the state's role as a protective agency and as a catalyst of social change confronts the scepticism of those fighting for survival through a basic transformation of power relations in society. To these sceptics, all emphasis on the protective and emancipatory roles of the Indian state has now become an overemphasis, if not a ploy to subvert dissent and underwrite a national consensus tilted in favour of the dominant ideology of the Indian state. Strangely, scepticism towards the Indian state within its critics often does not translate into scepticism towards the ideas of the modern nation-state. One peculiarity of the culture of Indian politics is that the most strident critics of the state are the ones who protest most vociferously when one suggests any limit on the role of the state in Indian society.

The reasons for this scepticism are obvious. First, the image of the state as a protector of Indian civilization has consistently justified the right of the state to reorder that civilization for purposes of the state. This has gradually removed all cultural and normative restraints on the state and allowed it to set the standards for judging all aspects of Indianness. The demands of the state are no longer conditional in India; they have become absolute. This has taken away the primacy of cultural life, in which the moral order of Indian society is encoded, creating in turn large-scale normlessness in the public realm.

On the other hand, evaluations of the state from the point of view of culture or lifestyle—when such evaluations are admitted into public discourse in modern India—are mostly conditional. They are supposed to accept the primacy of the state and strengthen it further through 'informed criticism'. Thus, even an entirely corrupt, totally inefficient, ruthlessly exploitative, and authoritarian state is supposed to deserve the allegiance of all Indians, because even such a state supposedly protects Indian civilization from destruction by dedicated enemies outside. If in the process, the civilization itself is altered beyond recognition or annihilated, that is not the concern of the state or of the statists. Echoing the feelings of that clever American army officer who saved a Vietnamese village from the enemy by destroying it, many Indian politicians, bureaucrats, intellectuals, and journalists are willing to say that to protect Indian culture and society, and for that matter Indians, it may be necessary to abolish them altogether.

The reach of the protective image of the Indian state is best exemplified by India's foreign policy which, to protect Indian interests, now lives with a vague fear of anything which smacks of Indian culture. For that matter, any invocation of culture looks like empty moralism to India's politically articulate middle classes. The culture of the Indian state no longer has a built-in critique of the dominant style of international politics; Indian foreign policy is now squarely a part of what the Indian elite sees as the only possible style of handling international relations. India's ruling elite now looks back on the earlier idealism of the nationalist movement and that of the immediate post-Independence period as a Gandhian or Nehruvian voodoo that has fortunately been lifted. Consequently, the 'play' that Indian foreign policy once had, by being less than predictable in conventional terms, has diminished. The principles of foreign policy are now seen as universal and fixed. India's hard-eyed foreign policy is less and less a reflection of India's political traditions; rather, it increasingly shapes the culture of the country's national elite.[8] The nuclear tests of 1998 can be seen as a direct product of this retooled culture of politics.

Simultaneously, the dominant global culture of international politics is being hawked within India as the 'state of the art' in politics and as an indicator of mature statecraft. For the modern Indian, there is no longer any Indian foreign policy. There is only a foreign policy of the nation-state called India, which has taken upon itself the full responsibility of protecting gullible Indians not merely from a devious, scheming external world but from their own soft, effeminate, ill-defined self, and from the threats to their survival that this self poses. This is of course very different from the days of Jawaharlal Nehru who, ignoring all accusations of faint-hearted sanctimony and woolliness, and despite his own Eurocentric worldview and Edwardian whimsies, did attempt to bring into international politics something of the civilizational perspective of Indian society. Large parts of the Indian elite that have ritually sworn by Nehru, in order to be close to the dynasty he founded, have shown little sensitivity to the nature of the enterprise. They have made it possible to analyse the vicissitudes of India's foreign policy—trying to shed its earlier cultural sensitivity as a liability in the world of *realpolitik*—as the vicissitudes of the foreign policy of a national security state.[9]

Likewise, many aspects of India's bureaucratic socialism or state capitalism can be directly traced to the overuse of the image of the Indian state as a protector and liberator. Legitimized as a form of socialism, such state-ownership left the content of an industry or an institution intact; it merely brought the unit under the control of the state and within easy reach of the tertiary sector. Whatever the original vision, socializing the means of production in practice meant nationalizing red-tapism, gigantism, inefficiency, and corruption—mainly to cater to the small but vociferous urban middle class, to neutralize a noisy and middle-class-based public opinion. It meant sustaining and pampering the middle-class belief that the choice was one between state and private ownership, and could never be one among different forms of decentralized public ownership or between them and socially responsible forms of private ownership.

The system merely took advantage of the idea that had gradually gained ground in the middle-class culture of Indian politics that nationalized corruption, gigantism, and bureaucracy were better than their privatized versions. In retrospect, one can hypothesize that the ills of state capitalism in India were actually its goals, and the egalitarian ideology that went with it was paradoxically a successful legitimation of an unequal order. Institutions were designed so that they would not perform their stated function but meet other needs. The images of the state as a protector and a liberator merely used the ideologies of liberal and Leninist democratic centralism in India to contain full-scale political participation—and what sociologist Edward Shils used to call the dispersal of charisma. If the masses are definitionally ignorant, or devoid of revolutionary consciousness, and the state has the responsibility of bringing them into the modern world, then there has to be some limit to the politics of those without historical sensitivities. Such a state has to have a special dispensation for the willing teachers of the masses—the secular rationalists, the scientifically-minded, the 'declassed' intellectuals with their superior cognition of history, and the myriad experts on national security with their deeper understanding of India's external and internal enemies. In each case, the attempt is to curtail the legitimacy of the collective political choices of those who refuse to grant centrality to the nation-state in Indian life. Indians as a politically underdeveloped, ahistorical, less-than-rational collectivity—which for that reason is particularly vulnerable in international politics—is a stereotype that constitutes the underside of the images of the Indian state as the liberator, modernizer, and protector of the Indian people. The stereotype has successfully dissociated large parts of the analysis of Indian politics from the categories used by a majority of the citizens to understand that politics.

III

The obverse of this disjunction is the tension between the image of the state as marketplace and the protective and emancipatory images of the state among the middle classes.

During the last decades, in public discourse the Indian state has retained and strengthened its image as a protector and a pacesetter. Yet, in terms of its functions and accessibility, it has less resemblance to the moderate, liberal nation-state to which many in the articulate, urban middle classes give their allegiance.[10] The legitimacy granted to the Indian state by large parts of the bureaucracy, the media, the professions, and academia is now mostly an allegiance to a shadowy, idealized state. Like the smile of the Cheshire cat, what lingers in the air is the legitimacy of the Indian nation-state built by the nationalist movement and the first generation of India's post-Independence leaders. That legitimacy survives mainly in the media, textbooks, and middle-class consciousness. The present instruments and institutions of the state, rightly or wrongly, do not have the capacity to elicit or hold the allegiance of Indians outside this charmed circle. What looks like allegiance to the state is really an allegiance to democracy. As a result, many of those who live with the older culture of modern politics in India, though they perceive themselves as tough-minded realists, are in effect what the sociologist Bharat Wariavwalla, echoing Iris Murdoch, calls 'romantic realists'. Their realism derives from the existing literature on the modern nation-state, not from the existent Indian state.

The Indian state may have outwardly grown stronger, thanks to its growing coercive might and its technological and industrial support base. But it has become, over the years, less legitimate among the ruled as a reasonably just arbiter among different religious, ethnic, and regional entities, as a protector of the weak and the poor, and as a reasonably—only reasonably—incorruptible pacesetter of desirable social changes. This is a dramatic change from the days when the modern Indian nation-state, though legitimized in terms of keywords such as security, development, and science, derived power from its role as a new moral arbiter in society.

The overemphasis on the state's role as a protector and liberator of society has unleashed three processes that have become increasingly salient over the last decade: (1) It has endorsed the dominance of the tertiary sector—from which political analysts and political theorists mostly come—creating a vested interest in perpetuating the split between the *principles of legitimation* used by Westernized Indians and the rest of society. (2) It has made successive regimes more dependent on theatrical science and spectacular organizational feats as the new opiates of the middle classes; it has made them more inclined to use the rhetoric of national security and development to mobilize political support; and more inclined to exploit, for electoral and other secular political purposes, religious, and ethnic conflicts.[11] It has contributed handsomely to the criminalization of the apparatus of the Indian state during recent years. To use an imperfect indicator, allegedly one-fifth of India's state legislators have criminal police records; in some states, the proportion goes up to about half.[12]

The last process needs more detailed comment. It is not as if the Indian state was a perfectly moral entity that has suddenly turned criminal. However, the nature of the link between crime and politics has changed. Earlier, a few criminals supported politicians and sought protection in exchange. Now, in many cases, large numbers of criminals operating outside or at the borderlines of law have entered public life. They protect themselves and sell protection to others.

To give a few lovable examples, some years ago the queen of illicit distillation in Bihar became a respected member of the ruling party in the Bihar state assembly, and in 1978 the hijacker of an Indian Airlines plane was elected a member of the Uttar Pradesh state assembly on the ticket of the Indian National Congress. Both were naturally protected by the privileges of the legislatures. Likewise, a gun-running guru was for a decade the person closest to the family of Prime Minister Indira Gandhi. At least three members of the 1998 central cabinet of the Bharatiya Janata Party are facing charges of directly fomenting communal riots. And if this looks just natural to a Hindu nationalist government, the main opposition, the Indian National Congress, also included in its cabinet two ministers who had taken leading parts in a communal riot. Some state governors and party presidents have in recent years been involved in nepotism and theft; others in direct attacks on the press. The police, in many states, have been involved in major criminal enterprises—from drug trafficking to smuggling, from rape to robbery. For a while, the boss of a coal mines mafia was the closest friend of a prime minister; and, as if to prove that ideology was no barrier in 'real' politics, a now-deceased minister of the West Bengal's Leftist government who had an illustrious criminal record publicly threatened to shoot political opponents even while he was a minister. A few years ago, the police burnt two newspaper presses in Ahmedabad and killed well-known civil rights activists in Andhra, and the number of deaths from officially justified fake encounters staged by the police in Uttar Pradesh, Punjab, Andhra, Maharashtra, and Kerala runs into thousands. If these look like the misadventures of lower-level functionaries, two prime ministers of India have been accused of theft.[13]

One suspects that middle-class political culture, so protective about the Indian state, is pegged to a state already more accessible to criminals than to the state's ideologues within the middle classes. Of this Indian state, which for a number of years now has been run as the private business venture of a new class, the romantic realists have no clue. They neither understand the nature of the business nor exercise any influence over its fate, except as *post facto* legitimizers, minor beneficiaries, and ineffective critics.

Two features identify these romantic ideologues of the state. First, when they talk of strengthening the state, they never speak of strengthening all the institutions of the state equally. They never speak, for instance, of strengthening the judiciary or parliament; they mostly speak of strengthening the military or the police, intelligence and counter-intelligence, the prime minister or the prime minister's secretariat. Second, when they admit the criminalization of the Indian state, they absolve of responsibility those who have presided over the state during the period—as if the present state of Indian politics were *sui generis,* or perhaps an accidental by-product of social change.

It is thus fair to argue that more realistic analysts of the Indian state today are the criminalized elements in the policy. They are in close touch with the state and can get the best out of it. This political counter-community includes a proportion of the displaced traditional elite, but it primarily includes uprooted, anomic sections that have found access to the state through their socio-economic and political mobility.

There is a reason why the term 'counter-community' is particularly apt. During the last twenty-five years, the concept of counter-culture has been often used to describe the fringe of Western society which has been forced out—or which has itself opted out—of mainstream politics. Such counter-cultures have in the West often been moved by utopian visions of the state, which, for the counter-cultures, are not so much realizable goals but intellectual and moral critiques of the existing state.

That relationship has been reversed in India. Unlike the West, in India mainstream middle-class culture and a majority of the intellectuals brought up within its confines are loyal to a shadow state—an imagined state, a state as it ought to be rather than as it is—while the counter-community owes allegiance to and understands the workings of the present Indian state better than the ordinary, law-abiding citizen, and the establishment intellectual. This counter-community has not merely greater access to and control over the state, it is also more realistic and hard-headed about Indian politics.

Here, too, the images of the state as protector and liberator play a role. They allow many Indian intellectuals, especially political analysts, to maintain double ledgers. Many of them have rather clear-cut ideas about the nature of the present Indian state. But the more they see the state deviating from the norms of democratic governance and 'managing' dissent at the peripheries of the society through force, and the more the state uses the languages of national security, science, and development to cover up its criminalization, the more desperately they cling to the state as a protector and redeemer. The more destruction and violence the state produces, the more they point to all-round destruction and violence as the reason why the Indian state deserves the unqualified support of all Indians.

Underlying these paradoxes is a deeper problem: the images of the state as a protector and liberator encourage most urban middle-class Indians to see the Indian state as the key to the fate of Indian civilization. The Indians are neither capable of redefining the Indian nation-state from the point of view of Indian civilization, nor able to escape the existing grid of rationality which prompts them to see their own form of statism as scientific, rational and, therefore, sagacious and practical. The main concepts of the statist ideology—national security, strong centre, national mainstream, national interest, military preparedness, constant vigilance against foreign conspiracy, nuclear weaponry, hard state and hard choices, central authority—all these have now acquired sanctity and become ends in themselves. Instead of being an instrument of the larger goals of Indian society and a temporary compromise with the demands of 'normal' statecraft in an imperfect world, this cluster of concepts has now become the *raison d'etre* of Indian civilization.

To some this is a matter of sorrow, to others of pride. Many Indians are happy that an unwieldy Indic civilization is now being squeezed into a proper modern nation-state. For such people, those who do not accept the absolute primacy of the Indian nation-state are woolly-headed idealists or the stooges of foreign powers.

All this is a long-winded way of saying that the first two images of the state have been taken over by that part of the Indian public consciousness which has accepted the absolute primacy of the state and which sees salvation in India becoming a true copy of the 'advanced' nations of the world. The ideologues of the system justify their politics mainly by referring to that core assumption. To an increasingly vocal minority of Indians, in turn, these statists look like vandals in league with the counter-community, trying hard to turn the country into a second-class imitation of the modern West, sacrificing Indians who culturally and politically resist their project.

IV

Let me now sum up my arguments by teasing out some of their implications. One, the images of the state-as-a-protector and the state-as-a-liberator have cornered the image of the state-as-an-arbiter in India. (The last is a somewhat misleading description of the third image but I must request the reader to bear with it for the moment.) As a result, the third image has fractured, and that part of it which finds expression in unlimited pure politics has freer play than the part which finds expression in the use of the state to politically renegotiate relationships among various social aggregates.

Two, the pursuit of social justice, human rights, and cultural survival, which could have been facilitated through the open political process in India, have become, for participants in the mainstream culture of politics, the prerogative of the state—the state seen as the protector and liberator of the Indian people. Yet, given the nature of the state, actualization of these values through the state has become more, not less, difficult. On the other hand, pursuing these values outside the domain of the state remains illegitimate or looks utopian to the high culture of Indian politics.

Three, the fragmentation and decline of the third image have paradoxically set the context to a state that neither protects nor liberates. It legitimizes a state that endorses the new hierarchies defined by modern institutions such as the bureaucracy, the development community, the technocracy, and the security establishment. All of these institutions articulate on behalf of the citizen state-oriented millennial ideologies of the left and the right, and help vest all hope in the emancipatory role of the state. In the meanwhile, the citizen's access to the Indian state and its major institutions diminishes further.

Four, despite the unrestrained, pure politics it has endorsed, some aspects of the third image have retained the capacity to underwrite an open polity and, perhaps, the capacity to underwrite a new equation between open politics and Indian traditions. At the moment, while India has a surfeit of politics, that politics is of a special kind. There is ample scope for politics organized around the state and for dissent that accepts the absolute primacy of the state, but the space for politics that challenges the existing definition of the state has shrunk over the last forty years. Those who find their politics thus restricted are, therefore, increasingly forced to seek alternative means of political self-expression.[14]

Five, the emphasis on its protective and emancipatory roles is pushing the Indian state to become more and more independent of the political process in the country. The legitimacy of the political order now partly depends on the performance of sectors outside the political system, but related to the state. Thus, the state has to often find legitimacy through the spectacular feats of scientists, technocrats, or sportsmen; through the successful organization of international cultural and art events, even through the performance of individual expatriates.

This analysis has a lesson even for the avowed statist. If such a statist does not happen to be allergic to all criticisms of the idea of the modern state and does not view the idea as a space-and-time-defying entity, he or she may have to seriously consider if the survival of the Indian state itself does not now demand: (1) a less absolute idea of the state and a more attenuated role for it in society, (2) more institutional and political efforts to avoid overloading the state, and (3) a greater play for the politics of cultures to provide the basis for new forms of political imagination and political intervention. A generation ago, most political analysts would have considered such formulations a sure prescription for national suicide or a plea for old-style conservatism. Gradually and painfully many of them have come to realize that both modern India and the Indian state have 'made it'; neither needs unqualified support from the citizen, and the social violence associated with the modern sector in India has gradually overtaken the violence organized around traditions. There is also the realization that India needs a new social critique of the idea of the nation-state, for the idea now provides an institutional and ideological axis for the growing violence in the modern sector.

Such an attenuated role for the state is not unknown to Indians. Throughout the colonial period, they lived with the image of a 'distant' state. True, that distance was imposed, and Indians had the right, on attaining political freedom, to give a more central place to the state in public life. But they have over-corrected the distance, and by over-extending the state, have narrowed the scope and the concept of politics. Only that which centres on the state and its formal structures is considered politics now. As a result, the struggles of child labourers, women's movements, and environmentalism, even the politics of trade unions and landless agricultural labourers, look less political these days than defections and factional realignments in parties.

Perhaps the definition of politics in India is becoming more open-ended, even in the Indian middle classes. The foibles of politicians who cannot survive without access, or promise of access, to the state has already begun to pall. However, it is unlikely that the pathologies of the Indian state will immediately induce a fundamental rethinking of the role of the state. It is more likely that, as in other post-colonial societies, in the coming decades the state will be forced to exercise some restraint on itself. Presumably, that process will be quickened by the withdrawal of the absolute legitimacy previously given to the state by large sections of citizens.

To express that hope is also to recognize that many of the baroque theories of political praxis, imported through the university system and the global media, have already become disjunctive with Indian life. Given this, it may be useful to remember the *Yoga Vashishtha,* which claims that while knowledge with action is superior to knowledge without action, knowledge without action is superior to action without knowledge.

I can put it differently—and more conservatively—for those who may find my argument as reification it criticizes. A political analysis could be for fellow analysts; it could be for those trying to express their vague, disorganized experiences of Indian politics in communicable terms but failing. This failure in turn can be for many reasons, but if it is because the experiences which the victims of the system are trying to express are not communicable within the existing conceptual frames, it becomes our responsibility to create a new language or borrow it from the victims. The victims are under no obligation to fit their experiences within our models.

NOTES

1. I have discussed these issues at length elsewhere. Ashis Nandy, 1995, 'Culture, State, and the Rediscovery of Indian Politics', in Patrick C. Hogan and Lalita Pandit (eds), *Literary India: Comparative Studies in Aesthetics, Colonialism, and Culture*, New York: The State University of New York, pp. 255–74 and 'The Political Culture of the Indian State', *Daedalus*, Fall 1989, Vol. 118, No. 4, pp. 1–26.

2. For instance, Pranab Bardhan, 1998, 'The State Against Society: The Great Divide in Indian Social Science Discourse', in Sugata Bose and Ayesha Jalal (eds), *Nationalism, Democracy and Development*, New Delhi: Oxford University Press. This paper, however, uses the slightly different political-cultural distinction that Ali Mazrui draws between those deliberately or unwittingly caught in the intrinsic logic of one of the most dangerous and seductive political innovations of our times, the sovereign state, and those self-consciously resisting the projects of the state. Mazrui's analysis recognizes that many who begin by fighting the oppressive presence of the Frankenstein state end up by internalizing that logic; those who capture the state invariably end up by being captured by the state. No wonder, in the Southern hemisphere at least, states have successfully crushed most social movements. Ali Mazrui, 1996, 'The Frankenstein State and Unequal Sovereignty', in D.L. Sheth and

Ashis Nandy (eds), *The Multiverse of Democracy: Essays in Honour of Rajni Kothari*, New Delhi: Sage Publications, pp. 50–77.

3. Queen Victoria's proclamation, while taking over as the ruler of India from the East India Company in 1857, is ample evidence of this. In that proclamation, the British were trying, belatedly, to go back to the first phase of colonialism, when the culture of the ruled was respected and even feared.

4. One can give similar examples from the writings of religious and social reformers like Dayanand Saraswati (1825–83) and Keshab Chandra Sen (1838–84).

5. This ideology has been blatantly proclaimed in the writings of many Asian leaders, especially by the late Ferdinand Marcos of Philippines, Mahathir Mohammad of Malaysia, and Lee Kuan Yew of Singapore. For a while Prime Minister Indira Gandhi picked up the same rhetoric, but then left it to her hangers-on to articulate. For instance, B.K. Nehru, 1980, *Western Democracy and the Third World*, London: Third World Foundation, monograph 8.

6. Three important publications that came out at the same time in mid-1980s illustrate this point neatly. Sunanda K. Datta Ray, 1984, *Smash and Grab: Annexation of Sikkim*, New Delhi: Vikas; Luingam Luthui and Nandita Haksar, 1984, *The Nagaland File: A Question of Human Rights*, New Delhi: Lancer International; and Amiya Rao, Aurobindo Ghose, Sunil Bhattacharya, Tejinder Singh Ahuja, and N.D. Pancholi, 1985, *Report to the Nation: Oppression in Punjab*, Delhi: Citizens for Democracy. In recent years, the argument has been articulated by the likes of K.P.S. Gill, the police officer who helped crush the Punjab militancy, with accusations of human rights ringing in his ears, and Arun Shourie, journalist-politician.

7. Ashis Nandy, 1980, 'Indira Gandhi and the Culture of Indian Politics', in *At the Edge of Psychology: Essays in Politics and Culture*, New Delhi: Oxford University Press, pp. 112–30 and Nandy, 1995, 'Culture, State and the Rediscovery of Indian Politics'.

8. Cf. Giri Deshingkar, 1980, 'Civilisational Concerns', *Seminar* (257).

9. For instance, Bharat Wariavwallah, 1983, 'Indira's India: A National Security State', *Round Table*, Vol. 72, No. 287, July, pp. 274–85.

10. Rajni Kothari, 1988, 'The Decline of the Moderate State', in *The State Against Democracy: In Search of Humane Governance*, Delhi: Ajanta, pp. 13–36.

11. If this seems too harsh a judgement, there is a series of reports by civil rights groups and other independent bodies on issues involving development, science, national security, and ethnic relations. These studies show that issues such as development, science, national security, and secularism have now entered the political lexicon as new justifications of large-scale violence, corruption, and environmental vandalism. These slogans are now gradually displacing older justifications of violence and domination, such as religion, language, caste, and kinship. For instance, People's Union of Democratic Rights and People's Union of Civil Liberties, 1985, *Who are the Guilty? Report of a Joint Inquiry into the Causes and Impact of the Riots in Delhi from*

31 October to 10 November, Delhi: PUDR and PUCL; S.M. Sikri, Badrud-din Tyabji, Rajeshwar Dayal, Govind Narain, and T.C.A. Srinivasvardan, 1985, *Delhi, 31 October to 4 November: Report of the Citizens' Commission*, Delhi: Citizens' Commission; Justice Srikrishna Commission, 1998, *Report on Bombay Riots, 1992–93*, Bombay: Srikrishna Commission. For a discussion of the clear break between the old and new forms of ethnic violence, see Ashis Nandy, 1995, 'An Anti-Secularist Manifesto', *India International Centre Quarterly*, Vol. 22, No. 1.

12. A large mass of data and insights has accumulated on the subject, thanks often to those who reject the thrust of their own writings. For example, Amnesty International, 1986, 'India: Some Reports Concerning Deaths in Police Custody Allegedly as a Result of Torture or Shooting During 1985', London: Amnesty International, ASA, 20 March, mimeo; A comprehensive work is A.R. Desai (ed.), 1986, *Violation of Democratic Rights in India*, Bombay: Popular Prakashan, Vol. I. The experience, however, is not unique to India. It is shared, in different degrees by a number of democratic polities—notably, Italy, Nigeria, Columbia, Pakistan, Bangladesh, the USA, and Japan.

13. Nothing is more revealing than an insider's report to the government on the nexus between criminals and politicians, written by a home secretary as the head of an official committee that included the Directors of the Intelligence Bureau and the Central Bureau of Investigation. The report was submitted in 1993. See N.N. Vora, 1997, *Vora Committee Report and Right to Information*, New Delhi: Lok Shakti Abhiyan.

15. Perhaps for the first time in India, the slogans of the ruling party have become predominantly non-political and non-economic: computers, modern management, and 'futuribles'. A large proportion of ultra-elites in the system has begun to come from the worlds of showbiz, advertising, and public relations. Even membership of the Indian Planning Commission, the major instrument of development in the country, has begun to reflect the same shift away from economists and politicians—scientists and managers are now often in a majority in the Commission.

CHAPTER 12

The Indian State in the Evolving International Order

Matin Zuberi

The contemporary international order embodies the existing inequalities of power—scientific, technological, economic, and military. This anarchic order seeks to build a durable structure of inequality and peace enforced by the powerful. Conflict is built into it because the entrenched powers resist accommodation of the new aspirants to equality. Victory in war has traditionally facilitated acceptance of a new aspirant as an acknowledged great power. Once Japan defeated China in the Sino-Japanese War of 1894–5, it was invited to attend the first Hague Peace Conference of 1899. Articulating his worries about the moral character of his new companions, the Japanese delegate could not resist the observation: 'We show ourselves at least your equal in scientific butchery, and at once we are admitted to your council table as civilized men!'[1]

The main currency of power in the contemporary world has been nuclear weapons. Possession of these weapons sets a state apart from all other members of the international community. The nuclear club is an exclusive one. Entry into the club is even more difficult than gaining recognition as a great power had been in the past. An international regime of treaties and informal agreements, inspections, technology controls, and economic sanctions blocks entry into the club. With the nuclear tests of May 1998, the Indian state has crossed the nuclear threshold. The early nuclear weapon powers may be reluctant to acknowledge its new status. But in the face of its resoluteness, their reluctance may erode over a period. Externally, the Indian state has staked its claim on the basis of its newly acquired capabilities, but domestically much needs to be done to buttress this claim.

II

The colonial Indian state was fundamentally pre-modern; it did not have the capacity to reorganize Indian society or to develop its productive resources and generate power. Indian nationalists realized very early that only a modern state could protect independence and undertake social, economic, and political development—and overcome backwardness and social divisiveness that were the legacy of colonial rule. The formation of a modern democratic state based on adult franchise, deriving its authority and legitimacy from the Indian Constitution, represents a major, perhaps *the* major, Indian achievement.

Modern states require successful economies and coherent societies to generate power so that they can function effectively in the international system. If they fail on either count, they face instability at home and dependency in their foreign relations. At independence, India was economically weak and socially fragmented. The modern sector of its economy was very small; it lacked skilled manpower; it was deficient in capital; its population was largely illiterate; its agriculture traditional and food supply insufficient to feed its rapidly growing population; its burden of poverty was heavy. Indian society was deeply divided between communities of religion, caste, language, and tribal ethnicity. These conditions set the agenda for the Indian state's developmental effort.

India, as one scholar has pointed out, 'is actually constituted by politics' and its post-Independence history can be viewed as 'the adventure of a political idea: democracy.'[2] Barring the aberration of the 'Emergency',[3] India has had regular, periodic elections to choose its lawmakers. A significant feature of democratic politics in India has been the mobilization of voters on the basis of distinct group identities. In some cases, such mobilization has snowballed into demands for autonomy and even separation. The democratic process, however, has been flexible enough to absorb these demands. The Indian state adopted the modernist principle of secularism to govern its policies towards religious minorities, and of positive discrimination in education and state employment for the Scheduled Castes and Tribes. The Babri Masjid–Ram Janmabhoomi controversy, however, damaged the secular character of Indian polity. India also has to contend with the anti-secular policies of neighbouring countries. The state has to ensure that the exigencies of 'vote bank' politics are not allowed to transform 'the respect for all religions enshrined in the Constitution' into 'respect for all varieties of fanaticism and obscurantism'.[4]

The very success of democratic politics has, at the same time, resulted in a growing 'crisis of governability'.[5] The cost of elections due to the vastness of parliamentary and assembly constituencies has fostered an unhealthy relationship between corrupt politicians and their financial patrons. This has led to erosion of state authority at a time when it faces serious domestic challenges from diverse elements in the Indian social fabric. It is, therefore, imperative that the state decisively demonstrate its determination and political will to deal with such challenges, and to convince foreign investors that India is a safe, stable, and profitable destination for investments.

The Indian state adopted a policy of economic development that could be characterized as 'undogmatic socialism', giving a central role to the public sector but allowing the private sector in its rather restricted zone. This policy appeared eminently rational in the 1950s, but its drawbacks became evident in the early 1960s when the growth rate got stuck at 3.5 per cent, leaving no surplus either for investment or welfare for the ever-expanding deprived section of the population. Six years of drought in the early 1960s laid the nation low. State-led economic development, however, generated the green revolution. India was transformed in a single decade from an apparent basket case into a country self-sufficient in food grains.[6]

The financial crisis of 1991 prodded Indian leadership into launching structural economic reforms. Their basic objectives were 'to remove structural constraints in the factor and product markets, let competitive forces to improve efficiency and productivity... and provide necessary outward orientation... for bringing about a higher degree of integration of the Indian economy with the rest of the world.'[7] This has led to the delicensing of industry, rationalization of tax structure, freer trade policies, freedom for private capital, both domestic and foreign, to play a larger role in economic development and a greater emphasis on exports. Economic reforms have already begun to push the Indian economy cnto a higher growth trajectory. After growing at 7 per cent during the mid-1990s, the economy has stabilized at a more moderate rate of about 6 per cent a year. While the reforms are being progressively implemented and the economy is growing, the gap between the rich and the poor continues to grow. The Indian state will have to cope with the resulting social tensions generated by such disparities.

The Indian state has enlisted science and technology for its developmental endeavours. Technology denial has only spurred Indian scientists and engineers; when the United States (US) embargoed the sale of

Cray supercomputers, they succeeded in producing the PARAM 10000 supercomputer with a capability of 100 Gigaflops. State support for science and technology has created a wide industrial base, with a large pool of skilled personnel and broad technological capabilities. There are success stories in the development of technology and in pure science as well. These include areas of titanium technology, maraging steel, solar photovoltaics, and proton decay studies. All this has been achieved despite limited financial and human resources. The annual R&D budget in all areas including agriculture, atomic energy, defence, and space is only $1.5 billion—less than the R&D budget of a multinational drug company. The R&D allocations for the space programme during 1998–9, for instance, were only $400 million, 'an amount that some countries spend on their Space Museums!' While India has 150 scientists and engineers per million, South Korea has ten times and Japan thirty times as many. As a result, Indian science and technology remain a 'minor force on the periphery of the "world knowledge system".'[8]

Computer software has emerged as India's forte in the era of globalization. Given its large computer-literate, English-speaking population, India is already being billed as the IT superpower of the twenty-first century. Indian software exports have grown phenomenally in recent years, from $747 million in 1995–6 to $4.015 billion in 1999–2000.[9] An Indian scientist has rightly observed that 'the only areas in which India is internationally competitive are all intellectual' and that this is a reflection of the gap between intellect and artefact.[10] As the world moves into the information age, India could have new opportunities to bridge this gap. The Indian state must concentrate on science and technology that is not only internationally competitive but also caters to the basic needs of the people. Meanwhile, India will continue to live simultaneously in several eras, symbolized by satellites and bullock carts.

III

The Indian state's ability to provide security and to conduct an independent foreign policy is dependent on the degree of self-reliance in defence. 'As a potential regional power', says a former scientific advisor to defence minister, 'India is one of the main targets for various export controls or technology denial regimes.'[11] Reflecting the goal of self-reliance, India's approach to military acquisition and modernization was a mix of direct purchase, licensed local production of foreign technology, and production on the basis of indigenous R&D. Direct purchase, though unacceptable to the political leadership, was the dominant pattern during the initial years after Independence. In later years, purchases from abroad were made whenever the gap between the Indian armed forces and those of the regional adversaries became wide enough to pose an immediate threat. It is, however, licensed production of foreign technology that played a major role in meeting the needs of the armed forces. This was especially so in the case of the highly sophisticated equipment that made up the weapons systems of the Indian Air Force and the Indian Navy. Licensed production, which was initiated in the mid-1950s, became the dominant pattern by the 1970s.

The Defence Research and Development Organization (DRDO) is the vehicle for indigenous R&D. Over the years, its infrastructure has grown and so has its budget. But given the fact that India has been a reluctant spender on defence, most of which in any case goes towards weapons acquisitions and pensions, the share of R&D in the total defence budget has been paltry. Modest inputs over the years have evidently resulted in modest results. But there have also been some success stories, including an array of ballistic missiles and the recent test flight of the Light Combat Aircraft, and the Arjun Main Battle Tank.[12]

Starting with the establishment of an Atomic Energy Commission in 1948, the Indian state embarked on a comprehensive atomic energy programme to acquire the entire spectrum of scientific and technical skills required to build and operate nuclear power stations. Two momentous decisions were taken during the period when Jawaharlal Nehru was at the helm. The first was to acquire a Canadian research reactor before the establishment of an elaborate system of nuclear inspections. The second was the decision to build a plutonium reprocessing plant, which became operational in 1964. These decisions were designed to enable Indian scientists to acquire skills in handling plutonium, needed for what was then called the 'plutonium economy' of the future. Though unintended at that time, the decision to build a reprocessing plant without any foreign assistance later gave India the nuclear weapons option.

Nehru laid the basic framework of India's nuclear policy and diplomacy. As early as 1954, he declared that India was prepared '*even to limit, in common with other countries our independence of action... provided we are assured that it is for the common good of the world and not exercised in a partial way, and not dominated over by certain countries, however good their motives.*'[13] At the Conference on the Statute of the International Atomic Energy Agency (IAEA) in 1957, Homi Bhabha, the first chairman of the Atomic Energy Commission, articulated the Indian stand with respect to the imposition of international safeguards on nuclear facilities. While India would accept international safeguards on nuclear power stations established with foreign collaboration, it would not allow any foreign inspections and controls over its indigenously produced nuclear installations. It is this insistence on insulation from foreign intrusions that has provided room for the indigenous development of Indian nuclear power stations, research reactors, reprocessing plants, and now the weapons option. These criteria continue to determine India's responses to global nuclear issues, including the Nuclear Non-Proliferation Treaty (NPT), the Comprehensive Test Ban Treaty (CTBT), and the proposed Fissile Material Cut-off Treaty (FMCT).

A central element of Indian nuclear policy has been consistent advocacy of global nuclear disarmament. As early as 1954, Nehru had made an appeal for a nuclear test moratorium. At that time, there were only three nuclear weapon powers—the US and the Soviet Union both of which had recently conducted their first thermonuclear tests, and Britain that had exploded its first fission device. If this appeal had been heeded, most of the subsequent nuclear follies, like the deployment of multiple independently targetable vehicles (MIRVs), could have been avoided. In 1988, Rajiv Gandhi proposed a detailed plan for a phased elimination of nuclear weapons, which again proved to be a cry in the wilderness. Year after year, India tabled resolutions at the United Nations to declare the threat or use of nuclear weapons a crime against humanity and actively participated in disarmament negotiations in the belief that a world without these terrible weapons would be a safer place.

The nuclear weapon powers, however, believed that their weapons provided stability and made conventional wars redundant. They sought to use arms control as a mechanism to *preserve* and *perpetuate* their nuclear monopoly. The NPT, which was thrust upon a beguiled world in 1968, is the crown jewel of arms control. Its goal was not only to *limit* but also *legitimize* the possession of nuclear weapons by a handful of countries. Two original targets were Germany and Japan. Japanese nuclear power reactor operators had unpleasant experiences of early IAEA inspections.[14] India refused to become a party to this discriminatory treaty.

When China went nuclear in October 1964, India faced a grave predicament. As a first step, the Indian state sought a nuclear umbrella from the superpowers. When this did not materialize, it began to consider the weapons option. Bhabha assured the public that Indian scientists could explode an atomic device within eighteen months of a decision. In the event, Indira Gandhi sanctioned a limited demonstration of the Indian capability in May 1974, but in the form of a peaceful nuclear explosion. The US and the former Soviet Union then had ambitious programmes to exploit such explosions for peaceful purposes.[15]

The US, as the conductor of the global nuclear non-proliferation orchestra, viewed the Indian peaceful nuclear explosions (PNE) as a challenge to the established nuclear order. It began concerted efforts to reshape the non-proliferation regime and tighten technology controls and assembled a new cabal of supplier countries in order to stem the flow of nuclear technology to developing countries. Furthermore, it unilaterally changed the definition of proliferation, and consequently the objectives of nuclear safeguards. This sudden shift in American nuclear policy was resented by West European countries as well as by Japan.[16] Not only nuclear weapons but even enrichment and reprocessing capabilities (not prohibited by the NPT) became a forbidden fruit. And the objective of safeguards was no longer to detect the diversion of nuclear material from peaceful to military pursuits, but to prevent 'nuclear explosive capability'. While the industrialized countries could continue to develop enrichment and reprocessing plants, the developing countries could not have these facilities even under IAEA safeguards. A new layer of discrimination was thus added to the non-proliferation regime—nuclear fuel cycle states vis-à-vis countries with only fragmented fuel cycle capabilities. Apart from these, the US took several domestic measures, like the passing of the 1978 US Nuclear Non-Proliferation Act, to close any loopholes left in the NPT regime. The non-proliferation regime has now expanded to include not only technology denials and inspections, but also the Missile Technology Control Regime (MTCR) and the Wassenaar Arrangement. India insisted on retaining its nuclear weapons option without *exercising* it. It could not afford the luxury of *renouncing* its nuclear weapon option when other nuclear weapon powers were determined to maintain their 'enduring' nuclear stockpiles.

Even as the cold war was drawing to a close, the regional security situation took a turn for the worse. Pakistan attained nuclear weapons capability with considerable Chinese assistance. China supplied highly-enriched uranium, tritium for boosting the yield of nuclear weapons, ring magnets for producing weapons-grade uranium, a special furnace to melt plutonium or enriched uranium into the shape of a bomb core, and an unsafeguarded plutonium reprocessing facility. The most significant of all Chinese nuclear supplies was the complete design of the nuclear warhead, which it had tested in 1966.[17] Though the Central Intelligence Agency (CIA) is reported to have discovered this transaction in 1983, the US refused to invoke its domestic legislation till after the Soviet withdrawal from Afghanistan. China also supplied M-11 missiles and launchers to Pakistan and even built a factory to produce these.[18] In the face of Pakistan's acquisition of nuclear weapon and missile capabilities and China's assistance to this effort, outflanked India had no choice but to move towards exercising its nuclear option.[19] Rajiv Gandhi gave the go-ahead for nuclear weaponization after the failure of the nuclear weapon powers to respond to his plan for a nuclear weapon-free world.[20]

In May 1995, the discriminatory NPT was extended indefinitely and unconditionally. Many influential Japanese politicians, including the Mayors of Hiroshima and Nagasaki and non-governmental experts, strongly opposed the indefinite extension of the treaty because they were afraid that it would perpetuate the special status of the five permanent members of the Security Council.[21] The Entry-into-Force clause of the draft CTBT was designed to coerce India into acceding to it.[22] This pushed India into exercising the nuclear option; five nuclear tests, including that of a thermonuclear weapon, were conducted in May 1998.[23]

Sanctions were imposed in the wake of the 1998 nuclear tests. There were, however, some experts who understood India's predicament as well as its security concerns. They pointed out the hypocrisy of some countries keeping their nuclear arsenals but denying these to others.[24] Even the UN Security Council finally woke up to the dangers of nuclear testing by passing a critical resolution. This was in total contrast to its utter neglect of the dangers of global pollution and the threat of a nuclear catastrophe during the cold war. For instance, the Security Council was silent in 1958, when the US conducted sixty-two atmospheric tests and the former Soviet Union thirty-four. The total number, including underground tests, in that single year was 116. Again, it remained passive in 1962 in the face of the mind-boggling number of 178 tests in a single year.[25]

India voluntarily declared a moratorium on testing immediately after the nuclear tests of 1998. The response of the industrialized world to the tests was not uniform; though general anxieties about the tests' effect on the non-proliferation regime were articulated by most of them, primarily the US and Japan imposed punitive economic measures against India. Two nuclear weapon powers, Russia and France, however, showed a measure of understanding of the reasons that forced India to exercise the nuclear option. Given the size of its economy coupled with the reforms that have begun to integrate it with the world economy, the Indian state easily absorbed the effects of punitive measures. The growing clout of the Indian-American community in the US, symbolized by the India caucus consisting of 115 members of the US Congress, also helped to modify American perceptions of Indian security concerns.[26] The high-level visits of dignitaries from Britain, China, France, Germany, Japan, Russia, and the US and the strategic dialogue that has been initiated with these countries indicate that the Indian state has weathered the storm of protests following the 1998 tests. Recognizing the growth potential of East Asian countries, India has joined the Association of South-East Asian Nations (ASEAN) as a dialogue partner and is keen to join the Asia-Pacific Economic Cooperation (APEC) forum. Bilateral contacts with individual countries of the region have been strengthened by high-level reciprocal visits.

Meanwhile a draft nuclear doctrine, proposed by the National Security Advisory Board, was released in August 1999 for informed public debate. It is anchored in India's continued commitment to a global, verifiable, and non-discriminatory nuclear disarmament. This is its unique feature distinguishing it from the nuclear doctrines of other nuclear weapon powers. Rejection of nuclear war fighting strategies and a categorical commitment to a no first use of nuclear weapons in case of failure of deterrence would determine the contours of the Indian state's credible, minimum nuclear retaliatory capability. This will be reflected in the 'structure, deployment and state of readiness of Indian nuclear forces'.[27]

India faces a Sino-Pakistan nuclear-missile axis. For the first time in the nuclear age, three nuclear weapon powers have contiguous borders. Pakistan and China are in military occupation of portions of the Indian state of Jammu and Kashmir. India and China have yet to agree on where exactly their border lies. These disputes have led to military conflicts between these countries. The triangular nuclear relationship can only be stabilized through arms control negotiations and confidence-building measures. The commitment of the new Republican administration in Washington to build National and Theatre Missile Defence systems would indirectly affect the development of nuclear and missile forces in these three countries.

The lesson of the last fifty-five years of the nuclear age is that nuclear adversaries have a common interest in avoiding military conflict. Nuclear restraint necessitates maintenance of the territorial status quo. Pakistan's rulers do not appear to have grasped the implications of this lesson. As they go through the nuclear learning process, a non-official dialogue on reducing nuclear risks between the two countries has already been initiated. This writer has participated in the Indo-Pakistani dialogue on reducing nuclear risks.[28] It is hoped that continuation of this dialogue will eventually lead to a measure of transparency and arms control agreements.

The Indian space programme was conceived as an important component of the quest for self-reliance. Vikram Sarabhai, the architect of this programme, believed that it would enable the country to leapfrog some of the stages of industrial/technological development and achieve within a few decades 'a change which has historically taken centuries in other lands'.[29] The programme envisaged the application of space technology in areas of telecommunications, weather forecasting, and remote sensing. It was oriented from the beginning towards the acquisition of competence in the design and development of both satellites and launch vehicles.[30] The Indian Space Research Organization (ISRO) has achieved considerable success in operationalizing dedicated satellites for telecommunications, weather forecasting, and remote sensing. The INSAT series of satellites with their seventy transponders have revolutionized telecommunications in India, as well as providing valuable data about the weather. Data generated by the IRS series of remote sensing satellites are now marketed worldwide by an American company, with expected revenue earnings in the region of $10 million a year.[31] The most significant achievement in the area of launch vehicles is the operationalization of the Polar Satellite Launch Vehicle (PSLV), whose first stage is the third biggest booster in the world after the US Space Shuttle and the Titan rocket.[32] Indian satellites are rated some of the best in the world. Another aspect of the space programme is its contribution to Indian industry; 227 technologies developed by ISRO have been transferred for commercial application.[33]

The space programme, like its nuclear counterpart, was originally designed only for peaceful purposes. After ISRO demonstrated its ability to place a satellite in orbit in July 1980, India set about translating this technology for military purposes. Missile capability had also become important in the wake of the decision to retain the nuclear weapons option. In July 1983, an Integrated Guided Missiles Development Programme (IGMDP) under the leadership of A.P.J. Abdul Kalam was inaugurated. He had earlier led ISRO's project in developing the Satellite Launch Vehicle, SLV-3, which was India's first rocket booster. The mandate of the missile programme was to develop four tactical missile systems and one intermediate range ballistic missile (IRBM) 'technology demonstrator'. All these missiles are in various stages of development or deployment. The short-range Prithvi missile has been inducted but in a conventional mode. The intermediate-range Agni ballistic missile has gone through two stages of development and is now fully solid-fuelled with a range of more than 2000 km and a payload of 1000 kg. The latest test on 17 January 2001 was conducted in its 'final operational configuration' as the missile took off from a mobile rail launcher. This is a major landmark in making Indian nuclear deterrence operational.[34]

Regional peace is a prerequisite if the Indian state has to play an appropriate role on the international stage. This requires that it take into consideration the economic and security concerns of the smaller neighbours. During the 1990s, New Delhi fashioned a regional policy based on the principle of non-reciprocity vis-à-vis its South Asian neighbours. This has helped improve relations with Bangladesh, Bhutan, Nepal, and Sri Lanka. A regional policy based on non-reciprocity legitimizes the Indian state's pre-eminent status in the region 'by demonstrating its willingness and capacity to act as the benevolent provider of public goods in South Asia'.[35] This has also given a boost to regional economic cooperation.

The India–Pakistan equation is the most important bilateral relationship in the region. Viewing Jammu and Kashmir as the unfinished business of Partition, Pakistan has continued to hold its relationship with India hostage to the resolution of this issue but on its terms, namely the state's merger with itself. Since its creation, Pakistan has repeatedly resorted to military and quasi-military methods to acquire Kashmir. The impact of the Cold War on the subcontinent took the form of American-assisted enhancement of Pakistan's military capabilities, imposing a corresponding burden on India. It has also meant that India's larger possibilities remained unrealized; it was effectively contained within the South Asian jacket. The Sino-Pakistani axis is also designed with the same objective. In February 1999, Indian Prime Minister Atal Behari Vajpayee undertook a historic bus journey to Lahore in the hope of removing old animosities, especially in the aftermath of the nuclear tests conducted by the two countries. The visit produced the Lahore Declaration, which included confidence-building measures in the nuclear arena. Even as Pakistani Prime Minister Nawaz Sharif was hosting his Indian counterpart, his government was covertly preparing an assault on the Kargil heights of Kashmir. In the face of this provocation, India exercised considerable restraint by not crossing the Line of Control and confining its military response within its own territory. The Indian Army, at the loss of more than 700 officers and soldiers, took back the heights. The international community responded positively to India's restraint and advised Pakistan not to redraw territorial boundaries with blood and to observe the sanctity of the Line of Control.

New Delhi has insisted on Pakistan dissociating itself from the activities of terrorist outfits operating from its territory as a precondition for the resumption of bilateral talks. In response to the Indian government's unilateral cessation of counter-insurgency operations in Jammu and Kashmir, the military government of Pakistan has announced that it would exercise maximum restraint along the Line of Control. However, the fact remains that General Pervez Musharraf is the first Pakistani ruler to make *jihad* an instrument of foreign policy. Militant religious groups operating from Pakistani territory openly collect funds in mosques and *madarasas*. During the last decade or more, the Indian state has borne the brunt of attacks by these trans-border terrorists operating from Pakistani territory. Islamic militant groups like the Lashkar-e-Taiba, the Harkat-ul-Mujahideen, and the Jaish-e-Mohammad have the financial and military support of the Pakistani ruling establishment. Without the logistics support of Pakistan's armed forces and intelligence agencies, these terrorist outfits would not have been able to sustain their operations in Indian territory over such a long period.[36] In the aftermath of the US-inspired jihad against the 'Evil Empire' in Afghanistan, the Pakistan-Afghanistan region has emerged as the centre of international terrorism and narcotics trafficking. The region, according to one influential observer, has been transformed into a 'lawless frontier'.[37]

IV

Even as market forces swept the world and barriers to the movement of goods and capital across national boundaries were reduced, rapid advances in communications, information flows, and travel resulted in 'intrusive and intense economic interaction...between a large and growing number of entities outside government control'.[38] Known as 'globalization', this phenomenon promises tremendous economic opportunities, even as it challenges national sovereignty, erodes local culture and tradition, and threatens economic and social instability. Interdependence enthusiasts have revived the idea that consequent to global interdependence, the state has lost its 'monopoly over internal sovereignty', and will soon 'become a thing of the past' as an external sovereign actor as well.[39]

It has been argued that since the state's functions—from waging war to providing internal security and welfare services—are on the wane, the state itself is inevitably declining, with its functions being increasingly taken over by new non-territorial and non-sovereign actors and networks.[40] The fact remains, however, that the only economic sector to have become truly global is the money market, with finance capital able to move freely across frontiers. Even here, the successive financial crises of the 1990s have begun to raise doubts about the desirability of unhampered financial flows.[41] Most economies remain largely national, and almost all multinational corporations are firmly anchored in their home bases.[42]

The world economy is, in fact, deeply rooted in the American-led cold war economic order, underpinned by the US dollar and Washington's security networks with Western Europe and East Asia.[43] It is a bifurcated world. The triumphalist tripe peddled by some globalizers notwithstanding, the combined wealth of 475 billionaires of the world exceeds the income of the poorest half of mankind.[44] Robert Kaplan has depicted this bifurcated world in lurid colours: 'Part of the world is inhabited by Hegel's and Fukuyama's Last Man, healthy, well-fed, and pampered by technology. The other, larger part is inhabited by Hobbes' First Man, and condemned to a life that is "poor, brutish and short".'[45]

As for the state's domestic functions, while West European governments spent about 25 per cent of their national products after World War II, they now spend about 50 per cent. Kenneth Waltz asserts that 'the range of governmental functions and the extent of state control over societies and economies has seldom been fuller than it is now.'[46] The fact that the state performs essential political, social, and economic functions, and ensures internal peace and prosperity, is ignored in analyses about its decline. The state provides the steel frame binding communities together, as well as the legal framework within which individuals and corporations act. In the absence of these public goods, there will only be chaos and anarchy. Contemporary examples of the consequences of the state fading away abound, as can be seen in Somalia, the Republic of Congo, and Afghanistan.

Though the US emerged as the sole superpower at the end of the cold war, the resulting international order was not characterized by unipolarity. Instead, it passed through a 'unipolar moment' (marked by the 1991 Gulf War) into what Samuel Huntington calls a 'uni-multipolar' system. It is a hybrid system with one superpower and several major powers; the former can settle key international issues but only with the support of 'some combination of other major states'. The 'lonely' superpower can, however, 'veto action on key issues by combinations of other states', because of its pre-eminence in economic, military, diplomatic, ideological, technological, and cultural domains. Because the superpower would naturally prefer a unipolar system and the major states a multipolar system, many principal players are not happy with the status quo. Consequently, the system is unlikely to be stable, and is bound to eventually move towards multipolarity. Huntington identifies the major regional powers as: the German-French condominium in Europe, Russia in Eurasia, China and potentially Japan in East Asia, India in South Asia, Iran in South-west Asia, Brazil in Latin America, and South Africa and Nigeria in Africa.[47]

The increasing ability of major regional powers to assert themselves is essentially a factor of their growing military muscle. This is especially evident in Asia, which contains five of the nine major powers mentioned above. Including Russia as a Eurasian power, Asia already has five nuclear weapon countries. To this must be added the American military presence, especially in East Asia. This trend heralds the birth of a 'second nuclear age', when 500 years of Western domination of the world will be increasingly challenged by the rising powers of Asia.[48]

Asian countries are emerging as major players in world affairs. And for the first time in recent history, a distinct regional state system, comprising a cluster of states that intensively engage one another in economic, diplomatic, and security matters, has developed. Intensive economic and political interactions are, however, more evident in East Asia, comprising China, Japan, South Korea, and the members of ASEAN. This has occasioned a tendency to look upon East Asia *as* Asia, for example in the debate centring on Asian values and exceptionalism.

The tendency to look at 'East Asia as Asia' is indeed flawed.[49] While analysing the special values prevalent in East Asia, it should be noted that Buddhism and other Indian cultural influences, as well as Islamic traditions, permeate the region's culture. The copious energy demands of Asian countries are forging new linkages. It has been estimated that about seventy tankers will be constantly engaged in loading and unloading oil and oil products from the Gulf region destined for China. The volatile region of West Asia will get more closely integrated with the dynamic East Asia. With the opening up of the vast energy resources of Central Asia and of the Russian Far East, oil and gas pipelines are expected to link different regions of Asia into a vast network of energy transactions. These changes will transform the global energy scene and will have a great impact on the Asian balance of power.[50] Moreover, long-range missile delivery systems of Asian countries are creating a new geography of strategic interactions.

Closely connected with the articulation about Asian values is the idea that Asian countries would not be so foolish as to pursue European-style security policies, but will be guided more by what has been termed as 'the Pacific Impulse'. A 'tidal wave of common sense and confidence' is supposed to have swept East Asia, which would be guided by its own unique 'corporate culture'. The basic principles of this culture include non-interference in the internal affairs of neighbours, importance attached to ensuring that the adversary does not lose 'face', acceptance of hierarchy, and build-up of 'networks' through the initiative of middle or small powers.[51] This articulation has found support among interdependency enthusiasts and even some realists. Samuel Huntington, for example, has argued that international relations in East Asia have been characterized by regional states either co-operating with, or subordinate to, imperial China. Given their history and culture, they are more likely to 'bandwagon' with rising China rather than attempting to balance it. Huntington concludes that instead of replicating Europe's past, Asia is much more likely to repeat its own historical pattern; 'Asia's past will be Asia's future.'[52]

The so-called Asian acceptance of hierarchy was not much in evidence when Vietnam took on China in 1979. It is also unlikely that Japan would willingly assume a subordinate position vis-à-vis China. ASEAN countries have succeeded in promoting cooperation among themselves and in persuading other states to participate in the ASEAN Regional Forum. Its success in containing conflicts among its members can, however, be explained by convergent interests and the roughly equal strengths of member states.[53] While the advent of nuclear weapons has to a great extent bottled up warfare among major powers, the preservation of peace also depends on creating a stable strategic equilibrium with clear lines drawn on the sand.

The main determinant of the emerging balance of power in Asia is China.[54] Its long economic tentacles extend into South-east Asia, Central Asia and the Russian Far East. Though China seemingly remained immune to the crisis that shook East Asia in 1997, its economy has indeed slowed down. It seems unlikely that China would repeat its earlier double-digit growth performance.[55] After much exaggeration about China soon emerging as the leading economy in the world as well as a global military power, a measure of balance is being restored now in analyses about its actual place in the international system.[56] Its military capabilities are bound to become greater in tune with economic progress. It is also seen as the most likely challenger of the status quo—whether it pertains to the status of Taiwan or that of the disputed islands in the East and South China Seas, or the projection of political–military influence as a counter to that of the US.

Continued American engagement in the region could potentially lead to conflict between the two countries. It would also depend on how the US balances its relations with China and Japan. Unlike the challenge from the former Soviet Union, the US is likely to face an economically and technologically dynamic China that is deeply engaged in the world economy. Moreover, China has so far successfully avoided any arms control restraints on its nuclear-missile arsenal. The Bush Administration's commitment to build Theatre and National Missile Defence systems is likely to provide a justification for China's already ambitious nuclear and missile modernization programmes. This would have a direct bearing on the larger security of Asian countries, and could well trigger a new arms race.[57]

American military presence in the region, however, could come under pressure if ongoing contacts between the two Koreas eventually lead to unification. China, along with the US, would be involved in any negotiated unification of the Koreas, and is likely to insist upon the phased withdrawal of American troops from the peninsula.[58] The departure of US troops from the Korean peninsula would, in turn, generate pressures for their withdrawal from Japan as well. While Germany and South Korea annually pay for maintaining American forces on their soil only $60 million and $290 million respectively, the American military presence costs Japan more than $4 billion annually. This burden, according to a former Japanese Prime Minister, 'hangs like a darkening cloud' over the future of the US–Japanese alliance. He had advocated the removal of American forces from Japan by the end of the twentieth century.[59]

Two recent developments have shaped Japanese thinking on security issues—the Gulf War, for which Japan's financial contribution of $13 billion was the third largest after Saudi Arabia and the US, and the North Korean nuclear crisis of 1994 followed by the launching of Taepodong missile across Japanese airspace in April 1998.[60] Despite voluntarily limiting its defence spending to about 1 per cent of national income, Japan already has the third largest defence budget in the world. Its 'Self-Defence Forces' constitute a 'state-of-the-art military machine'. Japan is also capable of manufacturing nuclear weapons and long-range missile delivery systems.[61] Collaboration with the US in the development of Theatre Missile Defence system in East Asia that encompassed Taiwan would exacerbate Sino-Japanese tensions.[62]

Referring to a lingering distrust, Kenzaburo Oe has pointed out that 'the distance between Japan and China, and between Japan and Korea is perhaps greater than that between Japan and England'.[63] Global economic vulnerability is the price Japan paid for 'achieving global economic pre-eminence, and that vulnerability is, if anything, increasing.'[64] Japan's policy towards Asian countries 'has really been its policy with respect to the United States.'[65] Indo-Japanese relations have been traditionally friendly, except for the recent Japanese criticism of the Indian nuclear tests. The emerging balance of forces in Asia, however, may necessitate closer relations, especially to balance an assertive China as well as to bolster the security of Japan's energy lifelines that run through the Indian Ocean.[66] A reappraisal of Tokyo's policy in the next decades cannot be ruled out.

Russia's economic performance continues to be poor, and its problems are many.[67] Even if economic recovery were to proceed at an average annual rate of 5 per cent, Russia would still account for only 2 per cent of the world's gross domestic product (GDP) by 2015. Population figures have dropped from 151 million in 1990 to about 146 million in 1999, and it has been projected that they would dip below 135 million by 2025. In addition, many Russians are moving out of the northern and eastern peripheries to the central region west of the Urals, leading to the emptying of these already sparsely populated regions.[68] Russia would find its own way out of its present difficulties so that it could shape the balance of power in Asia.[69]

V

The history of the last 200 years may be said to consist of two major alternating themes—international order and balance of power. While the purpose of international order was to maintain peace, that of balance of power had been to preserve stability. But history suggests that a peaceful world is not necessarily stable and a stable world may not be peaceful. Diplomats, therefore, have blundered repeatedly through a failed international order to emergence of a new balance of power; from a balance of power to competitive alliances and wars; and from the horrors of war to a renewed effort at establishment of international order. War, especially hegemonic war, has been the basic determinant of the international system of states and of the global economy. The emergent hegemonic power has set the rules of international politics and the terms and conditions for the operation of the global economy. The nuclear revolution, however, has created a stalemate and arrested the cycle of hegemonic wars.

Balance of power can be viewed as a political counterpart of Newtonian physics. The sovereign states of Europe followed their course poised in harmony of mutual attraction and repulsion. Rousseau described it as more the work of nature than of art. States were, in the words of Gibbon, spectators and judges of each other's merit. The wholesome jealousy of rival powers contributed to maintaining the balance. As the distribution of power was never even, the balance could never be rigid or static: it was subject to the effects of the law of uneven development. During the eighteenth century war became a major instrument for maintaining the balance, while diplomacy played such a role in the nineteenth and the early twentieth centuries.

The contemporary international order is a sum total of several specific regimes or orders. Some of these are *negotiated orders,* like the regimes for the Oceans, Antarctica, or Outer Space. There are also a number of *imposed orders* consisting of regimes fostered by major industrialized states through a combination of coercion, co-optation, and manipulation of incentives. One such order is the Nuclear Non-Proliferation Regime, which has raised the factual domination of the original five nuclear weapon powers to a rule of law. Designed by the US, it consists of a vast complex of national, bilateral, and multilateral regulations, trade embargoes, and sanctions. Based on a 'managed system of deterrence' and a manipulated system of non-proliferation, this order is ironically now being challenged by the US itself.[70] Then there is the technological order of which the world military order and the international economic order are major components. International order is based on a delicate adjustment of power to power; it is an order that may not be fully satisfactory but is just tolerable to all the members of the system of states. The international order of the first decades of the twenty-first century is likely to be marked by American attempts to maintain a preponderance of power at the global level while establishing balances of power in various regions of the world.

The Indian state's aspirations for autonomy will continue to govern its future choices. It has demonstrated an ability to cope with diverse international and domestic pressures in a democratic framework. Successive general elections, a free press, and an independent judiciary have injected dynamism into the polity. Indian economy has shown its resilience in the face of sanctions and technology controls. The reconstitution of society, however, on which the state is currently engaged will be a long- drawn-out process. It will generate its own tensions entailing continuous adjustments and even periods of turbulence and instability. The primary instrument for managing this process will be the state and its resources will be heavily stretched. Although history has generally not been kind to optimists, one can venture to suggest that economic prosperity and diplomatic leverage are propelling India towards the role of an 'actor' rather than that of a 'subject' in the evolving international order.

* This paper, originally presented at the International Workshop in Kyoto, was revised in 2002.

NOTES

1. Cited in B.V.A. Rolling, 1960, *International Law in an Expanded World*, Amsterdam: Djambatan, p. 27.
2. Sunil Khilnani, 1997, *The Idea of India*, London: Penguin, pp. 4, 9.
3. P.N. Dhar, who was head of the Prime Minister's Secretariat during the Emergency, has argued that it was a systemic failure and that its causes lie in the way the Indian political system had evolved. See his 2000, *Indira Gandhi, the 'Emergency', and Indian Democracy*, New Delhi: Oxford University Press, pp. 223–68.
4. Ibid., pp. 388–9.
5. For a detailed study on the roots of this crisis, see Atul Kohli, 1991, *Democracy and Discontent: India's Growing Crisis of Governability*, Cambridge: Cambridge University Press.

6. S.R. Rudolph and L.H. Rudolph, 1987, *In Pursuit of Lakshmi: The Political Economy of the Indian State*, Chicago: University of Chicago Press.

7. C. Rangarajan, 2000, *Perspectives on Indian Economy: A Collection of Essays*, New Delhi: UBS Publishers' Distributors, pp. 65–6.

8. L.K. Sharma, 'Opening Lines', R.A. Mashelkar, 'India as a Global Research Platform', and R. Narasimha, 'Scientists Shaping the Future of India', in L.K. Sharma and Sima Sharma (eds), 2000, *Innovative India*, London: Medialand Limited, pp. 14–19, 29–32, and 71–3.

9. Reserve Bank of India *Annual Report* 1999–2000, New Delhi: RBI Publications, p. 106.

10. R. Narasimha, in Sharma and Sharma (eds), *Innovative India, op. cit.*, p. 72.

11. A.P.J. Abdul Kalam, 'Defence R&D: Key to Self-reliance,' in Sharma and Sharma (eds), *Innovative India, op. cit.*, pp. 169–72.

12. Ravi Sharma, 2001, 'Airborne, at last,' *Frontline*, 2 February, pp. 42–5.

13. Jawaharlal Nehru, 1962, *India's Foreign Policy*, New Delhi, p. 193 (emphasis added).

14. '...inspection takes place on all sorts of time; sometimes, at two o'clock in the morning while everybody is sleeping, or five-thirty in the afternoon when the main control room is full of maintenance men working on reactor instrument cables. Only those with experiences of power reactor operations can appreciate how much bother these all are.' Cited in 'Experience in International Inspection—Information to Fellow Reactor Operators', *Atoms in Japan*, October 1970, p. 8; see also John E. Endicott, 1977, 'The 1975–76 Debate over Ratification of the NPT in Japan', *Asian Survey*, March, pp. 275–92.

15. Matin Zuberi, 1999, 'Building the Bomb: Collaboration for Self-Reliance and the Counter-Example of India', *Journal of the United Service Institution*, Vol. CXXIX, No. 535, January–March, pp. 29–49.

16. An influential Japanese nuclear expert criticized the American posture of 'God-granted guardian of this dangerous technology.' Ryukichi Imai, 1980, in Ryukichi Imai and Henry S. Rowen, *Nuclear Energy and Nuclear Proliferation: Japanese and American Views*, Boulder, Colorado: Westview Press, p. 7.

17. Mohan Malik, 1999, 'Nuclear Proliferation in Asia: The China Factor', *Australian Journal of International Affairs*, Vol. 53, No. 1, April, pp. 31– 41; Ming Zhang, 1999, *China's Changing Nuclear Posture*, Washington DC: Carnegie Endowment for International Policy, p. 7.

18. Stockholm International Peace Research Institute, *Yearbook 1993: World Armaments and Disarmament*, Oxford: Oxford University Press, p. 588; Tom Weiner, 1998, 'US and Chinese Aid was Essential as Pakistan Built Bomb', *International Herald Tribune*, 2 June, p. 4.

19. William Walker, 1998, 'International Nuclear Relations after the Indian and Pakistani Explosions,' *International Affairs*, Vol. 74, No. 3, July, p. 518.

20. K. Subrahmanyam, 1998, 'Indian Nuclear Policy—1964–98 (A Personal

Recollection)', in Jasjit Singh (ed.), *Nuclear India*, New Delhi: Knowledge World with Institute for Defence Studies & Analyses, p. 44.

21. Kumao Kaneko, 1996, 'Japan Needs no Umbrella,' *Bulletin of the Atomic Scientists*, March–April, p. 47.

22. For an account of the Indian participation and position in the CTBT negotiations, see Arundhati Ghose, 1997, 'Negotiating the CTBT: India's Security Concerns and Nuclear Disarmament', *Journal of International Affairs*, Vol. 51, No. 1, Summer, pp. 239–61.

23. Jaswant Singh, 1998, 'Against Nuclear Apartheid', *Foreign Affairs*, Vol. 77, No. 5, September–October, pp. 41–52.

24. For instance, a former Director of Nuclear Energy Division of the Japanese Ministry of External Affairs has pointed out that as a non-aligned country without any other power's nuclear umbrella, India is exposed to potential attack from China. Kumao Kaneko, *op. cit.*, p. 49. Seiroku Kajiyama, a former Chief Cabinet Secretary, said after the Indian tests, 'I cannot bring myself to accuse India and loudly call for sanctions against it in chorus with the United States without showing a sliver of sympathy for India's political posture of having to counter the logic of the superpowers.' Cited in *Asahi Shimbun*, 1999, 'The Road to the Abolition of Nuclear Weapons', Tokyo, p. 37.

25. 'NRDC Nuclear Notebook: Known Nuclear Tests Worldwide, 1945–98', *Bulletin of the Atomic Scientists*, November–December 1998, p. 66.

26. Robert M. Hathaway, 2000, 'Confrontation and Retreat: The US Congress and the South Asian Nuclear Tests', *Arms Control Today*, January–February, pp. 7–14.

27. Matin Zuberi, 2002, 'The Proposed Indian Nuclear Doctorine', *Contemporary India*, Vol. 1, No. 1, January–March, pp. 53–64.

28. Matin Zuberi, 2001, 'Use and Nonuse of Nuclear Weapons', unpublished paper presented at a conference in Islamabad, 13–15 January, pp. 13–15.

29. Cited in Kamla Chowdhry (ed.), 1974, *Vikram Sarabhai: Science Policy and National Development*, New Delhi: Macmillan, p. 3.

30. M. Zuberi and S. Kalyanaraman, 1995, 'Science and Technology for Development: India's Space Programme', *Strategic Analysis*, Vol. 18, No. 11, February, pp. 1431–47.

31. R. Ramachandran, 1998, 'India's Space Programme Lauded', *The Hindu* (New Delhi), 3 August, p. 7.

32. T.S. Subramanian, 1994, 'The Launch and After', *Frontline* (Madras), 3 June, p. 84.

33. K. Kasturirangan, 'India Soars Higher as Space Club Member', in Sharma and Sharma (eds), *Innovative India*, *op. cit.*, pp. 185–7.

34. A.P.J. Abdul Kalam, 'Defence R&D: Key to Self-reliance', in Sharma and Sharma (eds), *Innovative India*, *op. cit.*, p. 170; John Cherian, 'The Agni test and after,' and T.S. Subramanian, 'Behind the Success', *Frontline*, 16 February 2001, pp. 41–4.

35. Mohammad Ayoob, 2000, 'India Matters', *The Washington Quarterly*, Vol. 23, No. 1, Winter, p. 30.

36. Jessica Stern, 2000, 'Pakistan's Jihad Culture', *Foreign Affairs*, Vol. 79, No. 6, November–December, pp. 115–26. Also see Joel E. Starr, 2001, 'Can the US and India be "Steadfast Friends"?' *Orbis*, Vol. 45, No. 1, Winter, pp. 113–14.

37. Robert Kaplan, 2000, 'The Lawless Frontier', *The Atlantic Monthly*, September, pp. 66–80.

38. Richard N. Haass and Robert E. Litan, 1998, 'Globalization and Its Discontents: Navigating the Dangers of a Tangled World', *Foreign Affairs*, Vol. 77, No. 3, May–June, p. 2.

39. Wolfgang H. Reinecke, 1997, 'Global Public Policy', *Foreign Affairs*, Vol. 77, No. 6, p. 137.

40. See for example, Martin van Creveld, 1999, *The Rise and Decline of the State*, Cambridge: Cambridge University Press; for a contrast, see Peter Evans, Dietrich Rueschemeger, and Theda Skopol (eds), 1986, *Bringing the State Back In*, Cambridge: Cambridge University Press.

41. For example, see Jagdish Bhagwati, 1998, 'The Capital Myth: The Differences between Trade in Widgets and Dollars', *Foreign Affairs*, Vol. 77, No. 3, May–June, pp. 7–12.

42. Kenneth Waltz, 2000, 'Globalization and American Power', *The National Interest*, No. 59, Spring, p. 50.

43. Robert Gilpin, 2000, *The Challenge of Global Capitalism: The World Economy in the 21st Century*, Princeton: Princeton University Press.

44. Robin Broad and John Cavanagh, 1999, 'The Death of the Washington Consensus', *World Policy Journal*, Vol. 16, No. 3, Fall, p. 81.

45. Cited in David Rieff, 2000, 'The Ruthless Luxuries of Peace', *World Policy Journal*, Vol. 17, No. 1, Spring, p. 110. This is a review of Robert Kaplan, 2000, *The Coming Anarchy: Shattering the Dreams of the Post-Cold War*, New York: Random House; see also John Gray, 1998, 'Global Utopia and Clashing Civilizations: Misunderstanding the Present', *International Affairs*, Vol. 74, No. 1, January, pp. 149–63.

46. Kenneth Waltz, *op. cit.*, p. 51; see also Dani Rodrik, 1997, 'Sense and Nonsense in the Globalisation Debate', *Foreign Policy*, No. 107, Summer, pp. 19–36.

47. Samuel P. Huntington, 1999, 'The Lonely Superpower', *Foreign Affairs*, Vol. 78, No. 2, March–April, pp. 36–7.

48. Paul Bracken, 1999, *Fire in the East: The Rise of Asian Military Power and the Second Nuclear Age*, New York: Harper Collins, p. 95.

49. There is a historical precedent to this, but in Europe. When the distinct identity of Europe came to be articulated consequent to the 'European Miracle', it drew upon the progress attained in western Europe to the exclusion of the lands of middle and eastern Europe. On how 'Europe' came into existence, see Robert Bartlett, 1993, *The Making of Europe: Conquest, Colonization and Cultural Change*, London: Allen Lane.

50. Matin Zuberi, 2000, 'Energy Anxieties in East Asia and the Security of the Sea Lanes', in S.Z. Qasim (ed.), *Indian Ocean in the 21st Century*, New Delhi: Sai Publishers, pp. 70–8.

51. Kishore Mahbubani, 1995, 'The Pacific Impulse', *Survival*, Vol. 37, No. 1, Spring, pp. 105–20.

52. Samuel P. Huntington, 1996, *The Clash of Civilizations and the Remaking of World Order*, New York: Simon & Schuster, p. 234. Huntington's thesis shifts the responsibility for wars from the realm of political decision to civilizational imperatives beyond human volition. Civilizations compete, coalesce, and engage in long-term conflict—all at the same time. Historically, clashes of civilizations have been at the edges of zones of leading civilizations; but more often people at these edges also created fruitful exchanges between civilizations. Such clashes cannot be made the basis of relations between states. International relations focus on rather more urgent, and somewhat less grand, matters of specific interests. The outcome of conflicts between states undoubtedly have consequences for the fortunes of civilizations represented by the states involved; but it does not help understanding the nature and causes of conflicts between states to subsume them under the grandiose formula of 'clash of civilizations'.

53. Aaron L. Friedberg, 2000, 'Will Europe's Past be Asia's Future?', *Survival*, Vol. 42, No. 3, Autumn, p. 153.

54. For a comprehensive analysis of Chinese policies, see Michael D. Swaine and Ashley Tellis, 2000, *Interpreting China's Grand Strategy: Past, Present, and Future*, Santa Monica: Rand.

55. Avery Goldstein, 1999, 'China's New Economic Scenario: Political Implications of a Slowdown' *Orbis*, Vol. 43, Spring, No. 2, pp. 203–21.

56. See, for example, Gerald Segal, 1999, 'Does China Matter?', *Foreign Affairs*, Vol. 78, No. 5, September–October, pp. 24–36.

57. Brad Roberts, Robert A. Manning, and Ronald N. Montaperto, 2000, 'China: The Forgotten Nuclear Power', *Foreign Affairs*, Vol. 79, No. 4, pp. 53–63; and Aaron L. Friedberg, 2000, 'The Struggle for the Mastery of Asia', *Commentary*, No. 4, November, pp. 17–26.

58. Rajan Menon and S. Enders Wimbush, 2000, 'Asia in the 21st Century: Power Politics Alive and Well', *The National Interest*, No. 59, p. 80.

59. Morihiro Hosokawa, 1998, 'Are US Troops in Japan Needed?', *Foreign Affairs*, Vol. 77, No. 4, July–August, pp. 2–5.

60. Yoshio Okawara, 1999, 'US-Japan Relations: A Reminiscence', IIPS Policy Paper 239E, Tokyo.

61. Selig S. Harrison (ed.), 1996, *Japan's Nuclear Future*, Washington DC: Carnegie Endowment for International Peace. Three Japanese Prime Ministers—Nobusuke Kishi, Masayoshi Ohira, and Yasuhiro Nakasone—have argued between 1957 and 1984 that Japan's peace constitution did not prohibit the acquisition of nuclear weapons for defensive purposes. In June 1994, Prime Minister Tsutomu Hata asserted that his country already had 'the capability to

produce nuclear weapons'. Andrew Mack, 1997, 'Potential, not Proliferation', *Bulletin of the Atomic Scientists*, July–August, pp. 48–53.

62. Ryukichi Imai, 2000, 'Ballistic Missile Defence, the Nuclear Non-Proliferation Treaty Review and a Nuclear Free World', IIPS Policy Paper, 254E, Tokyo.

63. Kenzaburo Oe, 1996, 'The Dangers of Neo-nationalism: Can Literature Bridge the Gap among the Countries of Asia?', *Times Literary Supplement*, 25 October, p. 15.

64. Paul Kennedy, 1993, *Preparing for the Twenty-first Century*, London: Harper Collins, p. 159.

65. Kazuo Ogura, 1996, 'Japan's Asia Policy: Past and Future', *Japan Review of International Affairs*, Vol. 10, No. 1, Winter, p. 8.

66. The Indian Navy's blue-water force is the fourth largest in Asia, after Russia, China, and Japan. Rahul Roy-Chaudhury, 2000, *India's Maritime Security*, New Delhi: Knowledge World in association with Institute for Defence Studies and Analyses, p. 125.

67. See Lee S. Wolosky, 2000, 'Putin's Plutocrat Problem', and Sam Nunn and Adam N. Stulberg, 'The Many Faces of Modern Russia', *Foreign Affairs*, Vol. 79, No. 2, March–April, pp. 18–31 and 45–62.

68. Zbigniew Brzezinski, 2000, 'Living With Russia', *The National Interest*, No. 61, Fall, p. 7.

69. John Erickson, 1999, 'Russia will not be Trifled with: Geopolitical Facts and Fantasies', *The Journal of Strategic Studies*, Vol. 22, nos 2–3, June–September, pp. 262–8.

70. William Walker, 2000, 'Nuclear Order and Disorder', *International Affairs*, Vol. 76, No. 4, October, pp. 703–24.